DOING ENVIRONMENTAL ETHICS

DOING ENVIRONMENTAL ETHICS

Robert Traer
Dominican University of California

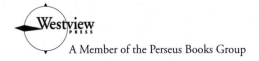

Westview
PRESS

A Member of the Perseus Books Group

Set in 10.5-point Adobe Garamond by the Perseus Books Group

Library of Congress Cataloging-in-Publication Data
Traer, Robert.
Doing environmental ethics / Robert Traer.
    p.   cm.
  Includes bibliographical references and index.
  ISBN 978-0-8133-4397-6 (pbk. : alk. paper) 1. Environmental ethics. 2. Environmentalism—Moral and ethical aspects. I. Title.
GE42.T73 2009
179'.1—dc22   2008039522

10   9   8   7   6   5   4   3   2   1

Contents

v

III LEARNING FROM NATURE

Preface

What you do matters, and the person you are matters. In ethics we look for reasons to explain why this is so. Ethics is about what we do, and who we are, and why it matters.

Ethics is always a conversation. Ethical reasoning takes place in a community and not simply inside our heads. What follows is my part of our conversation, and I have tried to write and think as clearly as I can. Only you, however, can make sense of what you read, as we are each responsible for ourselves and for what we think and do.

When I say "we" I am either referring to the discussion we are having as you read, or am stating a conclusion that is strongly supported by reasons and facts. I only say "I" to let you know that I am speaking for myself. Moral philosophers disagree about many ethical issues, and my responsibility to you is to explain this diversity of thought. At times, however, I will affirm my own convictions.

The topic of environmental ethics has, like a coin, two sides. One side is the *discipline of ethics*, and parts 1 and 2 offer ways of understanding what this discipline involves. The other side is *our environmental crisis*, which we consider primarily in part 3.

The noun *crisis* comes from the Greek *krisis*, meaning decision. To say that we are facing an environmental crisis is to assert that we are at a decisive moment in human history and in the natural history of our planet, and that our decisions now are crucial. Also, by identifying the environmental crisis as *our* crisis, I am affirming that *we are the crisis*, not the environment.[1]

Part 1 presents reasons for this conclusion. The first chapter locates our conversation about environmental ethics within the traditions of moral philosophy. The second and third chapters consider how scientific and economic reasoning affect ethical reasoning, especially arguments about our responsibility for the environment. Chapters in part 3 address particular aspects of our environmental crisis.

Most scientists agree that the impact of human civilization on the earth now constitutes an environmental crisis. Yet, public awareness and support for this conclusion in the United States is much lower than in Europe and Japan. Americans should wonder why.

Our challenge is to see how we are involved in the environmental crisis and how, individually and together, we can live more ecologically. To address this challenge we consider:

- Our place in nature as well as our use of natural resources.
- Four ways of reasoning about doing what is right and being good persons.
- Predicting likely consequences as a way of testing ethical presumptions.
- Environmental laws, philosophical arguments, and religious teachings.

As ethical beings, we are responsible for understanding the ecology of the earth and for evolving a sustainable way of life. This may be the greatest moral and social challenge of our time.

To address our environmental crisis, we must see more clearly our place in nature. We are ethical primates.[2] We are creatures of the earth and depend on its natural cycles, habitats, and other species. It is also our human nature to create a world of culture that sets us apart from the natural world.

Therefore, to make ethical decisions about the environment, we must understand the lessons of nature. We look to the scientific theory of evolution and the discipline of ecology to learn what being fit for survival means, and how human life relies on the ecosystems of the earth. Then, we consider what these facts and insights mean for doing ethics.

Our knowledge is limited, yet we know that the environmental crisis is of our own making. We know that our use of natural resources has disrupted the natural cycles of nitrogen, phosphorus, and carbon, with consequences that include the loss of forests and topsoil, as well as global warming. We know that our industrial way of life has also disturbed the earth's water cycle, resulting in acid rain, falling water levels in underground aquifers, a loss of fertile land due to salts deposited by irrigation, more intense storms, and devastating drought, as well as a scarcity of water for many. We know that economists have ignored the environmental costs of extracting and using natural resources, and leaving waste products in the air, water, and soil.

Resolving these environmental problems will require a new awareness of our place in nature, as well as careful actions (acting with care) based on our moral convictions.

We bring to this crisis from the history of our cultures *four patterns of reasoning* about *doing what is right* and *being good persons*. These ethical arguments concern duty, character, relationships, and rights. We find these ways of reasoning about what is intrinsically right and good mainly in environmental laws, philosophical arguments, and religious teachings, but also in children's stories, human history, and our own experience. We will draw on these diverse sources to help us construct ethical presumptions as to how we may live with greater ecological awareness and responsibility.

Also, humans have evolved the capacity to estimate outcomes, and modern culture requires that ethical decisions concerning public policy consider the projections of science and economics. Therefore, we *predict the likely consequences of acting on our ethical presumptions as a way of testing our reasoning*. When the predicted consequences are more beneficial than adverse, our presumptions are confirmed. If this is not the case, we should review our options.[3]

Some moral philosophers assert that all ethical issues should be resolved simply by predicting the foreseeable consequences of taking an action. I argue, instead, that this way of reasoning is necessary but not sufficient for ethics. Not long ago, few foresaw our present environmental crisis. It seems unwise, therefore, to rely solely on our ability to predict the likely consequences of actions we might now take.

What can we learn from the mistakes of the past? From the history of the last century we need to learn that our way of life is unsustainable. From evolution we can see that natural history is "heading" toward greater complexity and diversity, and that empathy is natural as well as crucial for moral reasoning. From ecology we should learn that our well-being depends on restoring and maintaining the integrity of the natural habitats we share with other species.

Doing Environmental Ethics offers an inclusive and practical way of addressing our ecological crisis. It builds on our commonsense understanding of doing what is right and being good persons, suggests how we might live more sustainably, and explores how governments, corporations, and citizens can work together to address environmental problems. To protect the natural cycles of the earth's biosphere, *Doing Environmental Ethics* supports public policies that would reduce air and water pollution, transform industrial agriculture, preserve endangered species, promote urban ecology, and end global warming. Questions after each chapter and a worksheet aid readers in deciding how to live more responsibly as consumers and as citizens.

Our way of living—our dependence on fossil fuels, our polluted cities, our global economy, our industrial agriculture, our consumer society—is the environmental crisis. At issue, therefore, is not only *what we must do* to reverse our devastating impact on the environment, but *who we may become* as members of the only ethical species to evolve on earth.

Acknowledgments

This book relies on the insightful arguments of many environmental advocates, moral philosophers, and contemporary scientists. I am especially grateful to Mary Midgley and Holmes Rolston III for guiding me along the tangled trails of environmental philosophy, and to scientists Menas Kafatos, Lynn Margulis, Robert Nadeau, and Henry P. Stapp for helping me sort out what we know and cannot know about the natural world. I also want to recognize economists Herman E. Daly and Joshua Farley and designers William McDonough and Michael Braungart for providing creative and practical alternatives to our unsustainable growth economy.

Among those who offered helpful comments on the first draft of this book are readers for Westview Press, my nephew Kenneth Edelman (Associate Director, Proctor & Gamble), V. James Lamphear (friend and retired school teacher), Erik Peterson (friend and forestry expert), and my brother James F. Traer (retired president of Westminster College). Although I take full responsibility for what follows, I hope each of you will see in the book the contribution that you made.

Finally, a word of thanks to my grandson Noah Traer, who at age five accompanied me on many walks while I was working on this book. "I'm always wondering about things," he once said to me. Then, wanting to be more precise, he qualified this statement. "Well, I'm not always wondering about things. But mostly I'm wondering." Together we wondered about intricate flowers, brightly colored fallen leaves, sprouting mushrooms, spiders spinning fantastic webs, butterfly acrobatics, birds pulling up worms, tumbling clouds in the sky, and rain plunking on our umbrellas. We also wondered about constructing things out of Legos, and after we built a solar-powered car we watched with wonder as it sped across the playground in the sunlight and then immediately stopped after it moved into the shade.

My wife, Nancy, my five children, and my six grandchildren keep me wondering about the ethical choices we all need to make for the sake of those who are young today and for future generations as well. For that, and much more, I am especially grateful.

PART I
Ethics and Science

Environmental ethics is not science, but involves science in at least three respects. First, the reasoning process used in science is helpful for doing ethics. Scientists rely on knowledge and intuition to construct a tentative explanation (hypothesis) about what has happened or will happen. Then they test this hypothesis, using other evidence including empirical measurements and thought experiments, to see how well the hypothesis holds up.

Chapter 1 explains how we may rely on diverse patterns of reasoning to consider our experience, and then construct moral presumptions about what is intrinsically right and good. We test these ethical hypotheses by predicting the likely consequences of acting on them.

Second, science gives us insight into nature, and reminds us that our observations shape what we know. Also, the theory of evolution and the discipline of ecology enable us to see how human life depends on and impacts nature. Chapter 2 considers the relevance of these scientific insights for ascribing moral consideration to nature, and for constructing ethical presumptions about living more responsibly in the natural world.

Third, the public debate about environmental policy relies on the social science of economics to weigh the likely costs of preserving natural resources against the impact on economic growth. In order to assess this reasoning, we need to understand why economic theory and practice has failed to protect the earth's biosphere. Chapter 3 considers this concern.

1

Moral Philosophy

AN ADVENTURE IN REASONING

The word *ethics* comes from the Greek *ethos*, for custom, but ethics has long meant prescribing, and not simply describing, what our customs ought to be. Ethics answers the question, how should we live?[1] Some philosophers distinguish *morality* from ethics by claiming that ethics necessarily involves critical reflection, whereas morality may simply refer to the moral rules and customs of a culture.[2] In everyday usage, however, the adjectives *ethical* and *moral* are interchangeable. Ethics is moral philosophy.[3]

Studying ethics, I suggest, is like hiking on a (conceptual) mountain, where the wider paths reflect the main traditions of ethical thought, and the narrower trails branching off these paths represent the arguments of individuals. As we have little time to explore this mountain (ethics), I will generally guide us along the paths (theories), but endnotes offer observations about some of the trails (philosophers/issues).

To illustrate what *doing ethics* means, consider how we might describe an actual mountain in diverse ways. We could emphasize its unusual rock formations, or point out a striking waterfall, or recall the sweep of the forest below the summit, or identify wildlife in the meadows. Each of these four descriptions would tell us about the mountain, but all four would be necessary to convey our impression of the whole mountain.

Thus, to gain an overview of moral philosophy, I will lead us along paths that reflect four patterns of thought, which I identify by the keywords *duty*, *character*, *relationships*, and *rights*, and a fifth path identified by the keyword *consequences*. Each keyword represents the crux of the debate within the pattern

3

of thought it identifies. The first four patterns of ethical thought (concerning our duty, character, relationships, and rights) assert that some actions or ways of being have *intrinsic worth*. The fifth pattern of thought (involving predicted consequences) rejects the notion of intrinsic worth, and argues that actions and goods only have *extrinsic value* (derivative or *use value*) based on their *utility* (usefulness) for us.[4]

To prepare for our trek, we "stretch" our minds a bit by considering four questions. How are the words *right* and *good* used in moral philosophy? What is the role of reason in ethics? How is environmental ethics different from traditional ethics? Why rely on diverse patterns of moral reasoning instead of deciding which ethical theory is best?

RIGHT AND GOOD

Traditional ethics is about human life in societies. The natural world, which is center stage in environmental ethics, has for centuries been merely the backdrop for the drama of moral philosophy. Because ethics developed without any direct concern for the environment,[5] the main patterns of thought were constructed without considering many of the issues that we now face.

Our challenge, therefore, involves drawing on the traditions of moral philosophy to construct arguments that address our environmental crisis. We begin our trek on the mountain (of ethics) below the (environmental) slope, along the main paths that have been worn smooth by seeking to know what is "right" and "good."

What do we mean by taking the *right action*? That we are acting "in accord with what is just, good, or proper."[6] We take a right action by correctly applying a principle (norm, premise, presupposition, rule, standard, or law).[7] We offer reasons to justify the principle and its application. We do our duty, or act to protect a person's rights. For instance, we might assert that not littering in a public park is right, because we have a duty to respect the rights of others who use the park.

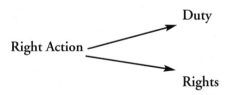

By *being a good person*, we mean that a person is "virtuous."[8] Being good involves having the character and personal qualities that we justify by reason as having moral worth. The traditional word for such character traits is *virtues*, and chapter 5 gives reasons for the virtues of gratitude, integrity, and frugality. Would a person who is grateful for the beauty of the flowers in a park throw a candy wrapper in the flowerbed? Not if he has integrity.

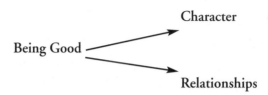

The adjectives *good* and *right* are related in meaning, but are not synonyms. It makes no sense to speak of a "right person" when we mean a "good person." *Good* has a broader range of meanings than *right*, and both words have meanings that do not concern ethics.

For instance, we speak of the "good looks" of a person, or of a "good joke." Saying someone is the right person for a job means that we think the person will do a good job, but in this statement the adjectives *right* and *good* have nothing to do with moral philosophy. The phrase "good science," which appears in debates about climate change, does not refer to an ethical presumption, but to relying on proper procedures in scientific research.

As ethics concerns how we ought to live together, our goal is "a good society." No one argues that our goal is "a right society" or "the right society." Also, we speak of "the common good" and "good relationships," rather than "right relationships," to identify the ethical goals of ensuring freedom, equality, and social justice for everyone.

Both the adjectives *right* and *good* have opposites that help to define their meanings. If an action is morally wrong, it is not right, and a good person is not a bad person. (Yet, a good person may act badly.)[9] Good has comparative and superlative forms (better and best), but right does not. Also, we speak of "goodness" meaning "the quality or state of being good," but not of "rightness" although we talk of being "right." Right takes the form of a verb, for we may try "to right a wrong," but good does not have a verb form.

These differences in our everyday language are reflected in diverse patterns of thought in moral philosophy. *"Right" involves taking an action*, whereas *"good" refers to a state of being*. I suggest that the keywords *duty* and *rights* are largely concerned with right action and that the keywords *character* and *relationships* are primarily about being good persons. Right action and being good identify different paths on the mountain, and ethical theories emphasizing duty or rights branch off the "right action" path, whereas ethical theories concerning character or relationships diverge from the "being good" path.

The words *right* and *good* are also nouns with distinctive meanings. *A right* refers to a moral claim that a person has against other persons. If backed by law, this moral right is a legal right. *A good* is a way of being (an end, a goal) that has moral worth in itself, not because it is a means to realizing some other moral value. Having respect for other persons, most moral philosophers argue, is a good not because we are likely to receive better treatment from those we respect (although we may hope that this happens), but because each person is autonomous and rational and thus should have respect for every other person.

When I use the plural noun *rights* I am referring to *legal rights*, some of which are *human rights* under international law. *Moral rights* are not necessarily legal rights, and ethics has a larger concern than the law. Yet, making and enforcing law is an ethical challenge. The plural noun *goods* is sometimes used by moral philosophers to speak of moral values, interests, or ends. In economic theory, however, "goods" are simply commodities.

REASONING ABOUT OUR FEELINGS

Broadly stated, ethics is "concerned with making sense of intuitions"[10] about what is right and good. We do this by reasoning about our feelings. Biologists verify that: "Emotion is never truly divorced from decision making, even when it is channeled aside by an effort of will."[11] Physicists now confirm that seeing the world with complete objectivity is not possible, as our observations affect what we perceive.[12]

Moral philosopher Mary Midgley writes: "Sensitivity requires rationality to complete it, and vice versa. There is no siding onto which emotions can be shunted so as not to impinge on thought."[13] We rely on our reason to guard against feelings that may reflect a bias, or a sense of inadequacy, or a desire simply to win an argument, and also to refine and explain a felt conviction that passes the test of critical reflection and discussion. We rely on feelings to move us to act morally and to ensure that our reasoning is not only logical but also humane.[14]

Empathy and Reason

Scientific evidence supports this approach to ethics. As children, we manifest empathy before developing our rational abilities, and there is evidence for the same order of development in the evolution of the human brain.[15] "Empathy is a unique form of intentionality in which we are directed toward the other's experience."[16] This involves feeling, at least to some extent, what another person is feeling. "[I]n empathy we experience another human being directly as a person—that is, as an intentional being whose bodily gestures and actions are expressive of his or her experiences or states of mind."[17]

Empathy enables us to identify with others and may generate a "perception of the other as a being who deserves concern and respect."[18] This does not guarantee ethical conduct, but encourages it. "Aid to others in need would never be internalized as a duty without the fellow-feeling that drives people to take an interest in one another. Moral sentiments came first; moral principles second."[19]

Conscience reflects our integration of moral sentiments and principles. We should test our conscience, however, by explaining to others the reasons for our moral presumptions, and we should listen carefully to concerns they may have. Peter Singer probably speaks for all moral philosophers when he says that an ethical argument should only appeal to "emotions where they can be supported by reason."[20]

Both our feelings and our reason reflect our participation in a *moral community*, or more likely several moral communities. As children, our moral community is our family, which soon broadens to include our friends and then is defined largely by the rules of our school. As adults, our moral community extends from our family to our friends (at work, in our neighborhood or a support group, and perhaps in our religious community), to our city, our country, the people of the world whose moral and legal rights are defined by international law, and even to a moral community that includes nonhuman organisms and ecosystems.

Critical Reasoning

A reason is "a statement offered in explanation or justification" that expresses "a rational ground or motive" and "supports a conclusion or explains a fact."[21] As a verb, *reason* means "to use the faculty of reason so as to arrive at conclusions."[22] Reasoning is thinking. Being rational refers to having a reason, being reasonable means "being in accord with reason."[23] In moral philosophy *arguing* involves giving reasons for a conclusion. An argument, therefore, is not about opinions or beliefs, but about the reasons for our opinions or beliefs. In ethics, the goal of arguing is (or should be) not to win, but to clarify our reasoning.

This means *unmasking rationalizations.* In some disciplines of thought *rationalize* means "to bring into accord with reason," but in ethics it means "to attribute (one's actions) to rational and creditable motives without analysis of true and especially unconscious motives."[24] A reason is not a rationalization, in moral philosophy, because reasoning involves analyzing our motives. It is often difficult, however, to distinguish reasons from rationalizations.

For example, if I own land that I want to log to make a profit, but argue at a public hearing that logging should be allowed because it will bring jobs into the community, my public statement is a rationalization. If, however, I state publicly that I support logging because I will benefit from it *and* think that the community will also benefit, I am giving two reasons for my position. Self-interest is rational and is not a rationalization, unless self-interest is concealed or is the unconscious motivation for making an argument.

Reasoning *by analogy* explains one thing by comparing it to something else that is similar, although also different. In a good analogy, the similarity outweighs the dissimilarity and is clarifying. For instance, animals are like and unlike humans, as humans are also animals. Is the similarity sufficiently strong to support the argument that we should ascribe rights to nonhuman animals as we do to humans? Chapter 7 reflects critically on this analogy.

Deductive reasoning applies a principle to a situation. For instance, if every person has human rights, and you are a person, then you have human rights like every person. Drawing an *inference* means much the same, for it involves "passing from one proposition, statement, or judgment considered as true to another whose truth is believed to follow from the former."[25]

Inductive reasoning involves providing evidence to support a hypothesis. The greater the evidence for a hypothesis, the more we may rely on it. Chapter 15 notes that there is growing scientific evidence for the hypothesis that the burning of fossil fuels in power plants, factories, motor vehicles, and airplanes is contributing to global warming. This evidence substantiates the ethical argument that human communities have a duty to reduce carbon emissions in order to prevent the further degradation of the earth's biosphere.

The words *therefore* or *thus*, or *because* or *it follows*, or *given that* imply a conclusion is about to be drawn in an argument. Critical reasoning involves raising questions when we hear these words or phrases. What principle is being asserted, and is it rational? Have the motives behind the argument been clarified? Does the conclusion being drawn follow from the facts and reasons given?

Faith and Reason

For many people, morality and religious faith go hand in hand. Moral philosophers, however, warn against relying on religious arguments in ethics. Some turn to Plato (ca. 428–327) for support, as his dialogue *Euthyphro* considers whether "right" can be understood as "that which the gods command."

Socrates challenges this view by asking if conduct is right because it is commanded by a god, or if a divine command makes conduct right.

The second view implies that a god can make unethical conduct right by commanding it. The inference that may be drawn from the first view is that if a god only commands what is right, we are able to know (and do) what is right without relying on any divine commandments.[26] Therefore, god and religion are unnecessary for ethics.

The argument is logically sound, but not necessarily convincing. Plato's reasoning does not take into account the limits on human knowledge (as to what is right), or how the moral teachings of a religious tradition may help to persuade the public to embrace a higher moral standard. We do not need divine commands to tell us that human actions have created an environmental crisis requiring significant changes in our way of life. Yet, we may need persons motivated by religious faith to help bring about the social and personal changes required to reduce the human threat to the biosphere.

Moral philosophers are right to insist that ethical principles and decisions be justified by rational arguments, and this is why the study of ethics requires critical thinking. Relying on reason, however, does not mean that we should ignore all religious arguments, especially those that emphasize reasoning (as many do). Therefore, I include religious arguments among the reasons given for moral presumptions concerning our care of the environment.

ENVIRONMENTAL ETHICS

The discipline of environmental ethics took off in the 1970s, in response to the environmental movement protesting air and water pollution. Moral arguments for laws to protect the environment initially emphasized the government's duty (moral and legal) to protect the public welfare. Scientific evidence that environmental pollution is a threat to human health was used to argue that taking action to clean up the environment is rationally justified (right).

A few activists, however, argued that reducing pollution and taking other actions to preserve the environment are justified simply because nature has moral worth, and not because humans will benefit. Blazing this trail meant diverging from the main path of moral philosophy, which these activists now identified as anthropocentric (centered on humans). They proposed various adjectives (*biocentric*, *ecocentric*, and *holistic*) to distinguish their new non-anthropocentric ethics from traditional ethics.[27]

Those who defend anthropocentric ethics hold that only humans have value, so ethical decisions about nature only involve assessing human welfare.[28] Our

actions may adversely impact other organisms, but we have no duty to these organisms to mitigate these consequences. Proponents of nonanthropocentric
ethics assert that nature has value for itself, which humans should recognize. In
using natural resources for our own ends, we have a duty to preserve the natural
habitats of other organisms.[29]

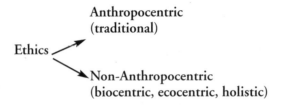

In traditional ethics our *moral community* consists only of persons. The argument for a duty of mutual respect, and the argument for the goal of personal
and social happiness, each presume a moral community that includes all humans. Also, the moral community for international human rights law includes
every person. In environmental ethics, however, nonanthropocentric advocates
assert that our moral community also includes other organisms, endangered
species, ecosystems, and even the entire biosphere. Chapter 2 considers this debate about what aspects of nature should be given *moral consideration.*

Environmental ethics is a hike you don't want to miss! Learning more about
the paths (theories) of traditional ethics will help you appreciate this. So, we do
that next, to give you a sense of the terrain that lies ahead and an overview (of
the world) that each path offers.

LEARNING FROM DIVERSE THEORIES

Conceiving of ethics as a mountain with many paths raises the question of
which path to follow. In moral philosophy this is identified as the problem
of *pluralism.* How are we to choose among different ethical theories when each
is supported by reasoning that makes sense to at least some moral philosophers?
Three answers seem possible. First, one theory is right and the others are wrong.
Second, we can gain insights from every theory that has stood the test of time.
Third, we have no way to know whether any of these ethical theories are right.

Continuing support for more than one theory is evidence that there is no
way to prove only one ethical theory is right. As long as reasonable people disagree, we should resist the temptation to defend one way of thinking against all

the others. Therefore, I opt for the second answer and take a pluralist approach to ethics. I have learned from the varied traditions of moral philosophy, and in part 2 will explain how we might draw on five patterns of moral reasoning to construct and test ethical presumptions. Before doing this, however, I offer a brief explanation of why moral philosophers reject the third answer, which is known as ethical relativism.

Ethical Relativism

If we are unable to know whether or not any view of ethics is right or wrong, it is hard to avoid the conclusion that ethics is nothing but "different strokes for different folks."[30] This would mean that what individuals think is right *is* right for them, and that this is true for every culture. Philosophers refer to these notions as *individual* and *cultural relativism*.

Many of us are relativists to some extent, because we think people should be free to make their own moral choices as long as no one else is harmed. In law, this is reflected in property laws and the right of privacy. We may also argue, however, that some land use choices—such as watering your lawn when there is a drought, or clear-cutting forests on private land—should be restrained by governments to protect the environment and promote the public good. If you agree that personal freedom should be limited in some way, even when there is no direct harm to others, you are not completely a moral relativist.

Cultural relativism poses a more difficult question, as history and anthropology reveal that human cultures have evolved diverse ethical standards. Does this mean that ethical reasoning simply rationalizes the customs and values of a culture? To assess this claim, I suggest we assume that the answer is yes, and then consider the implications of this position.

If values are merely the customs of various cultures, this would mean that values are whatever the majority in a society believes is right. But if this were so, how could values change, as they obviously do? A change in cultural values begins with a minority arguing that some values are better than others, which would be unpersuasive if we really believed that all values are relative.

Changes in cultural values are evidence that experience and ideas have led many people to change their mind about what is right and good, or better. Cultures are not simply different games played by different rules, but instead reflect diverse patterns of reasoning that people modify as they experience alternative ways of living.

This argument against cultural relativism does not imply that it is reasonable to believe there is a single version of ethics, which every culture should accept.

Nor does it prove the existence of universal or absolute values. As a discipline of thought, "Ethics has universal intent."[31] But as long as moral philosophers argue rationally for different ethical theories, we should expect that cultures will continue to have diverse values.

Nonetheless, the nature of ethical reasoning presumes that some actions and ways of being are better than others. Moreover, the presumptions of international human rights law affirm that some actions, such as torture, are absolutely wrong, and other human rights, such as the presumption of innocence, are absolutely right—and that these rights should be universally enforced. The reasoning behind these claims is Western in origin, but has now been affirmed within many cultures, which is evidence that our moral community is becoming global.[32]

Ethical Traditions

We begin our overview of the main traditions of thought in moral philosophy by noting an early fork in the path between *teleological* and *deontological* ethics.[33] The following paragraphs are limited to the Western tradition of moral philosophy, but chapters in part 2 refer to ethical reasoning in indigenous traditions and in East and South Asian thought.

The word *teleological* comes from the Greek word *telos*, meaning purpose or goal, and *logos*, referring to science or study. Moral philosophers identify the ethical thinking of Aristotle (384–322 BCE) as teleological, because he argued that we discover our human nature and what it means to be good persons by discerning in nature that our purpose is to seek happiness and the civic virtues it requires. Thomas Aquinas (1225–1274 CE) adapted this view to a Christian perspective, and today this theory of ethics is known as the *natural law* tradition.[34]

Five hundred years later, after Isaac Newton (1642–1727) proposed mathematical laws to explain nature (and thereby displaced its "purpose" with physics), philosophers such as Jeremy Bentham (1748–1832) and John Stuart Mill (1806–1873) argued that ethics is simply doing what yields the greatest benefits. This form of reasoning (concerning utility, so it is called *utilitarian*) is also teleological, but in a different sense.

Philosophers in the natural law tradition hold that doing what is intrinsically right leads to happiness, whereas utilitarian philosophers (in what is now often called the *consequential* tradition of ethics) argue that actions resulting in greater happiness are "right" because they achieve the best possible results. These different forms of teleological reasoning identify two of the main theories in moral philosophy.

A third way of reasoning is characterized as *deontological*, an adjective derived from the Greek word *deon*, meaning duty.[35] Immanuel Kant (1724–1804) argued persuasively for this tradition of moral philosophy. He asserted that human beings have the rational capacity to discern and do their duty, and rejected consequential arguments that we should rely on the likely results of taking an action to determine what is right. Kant believed that we could act rationally with a good will, but accepted the view of Newtonian mechanics that overturned the science of Aristotle and thus made it irrational to look for any purpose in the laws of nature.

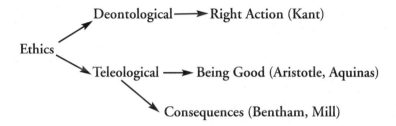

These three main traditions of thought are the context for doing environmental ethics.[36] Chapters 4 and 7 follow the deontological path to consider ethical arguments for duty and human rights. Chapters 5 and 6 pursue the teleological trek of being a good person, looking at issues of individual character and virtues, and then at a concern for relationships and an ethics of care. Chapter 8 explores the teleological terrain along the well-traveled path of consequential ethics.

DOING ETHICS TOGETHER

Our goal in doing ethics is to learn from diverse ethical theories in order to bring our understanding closer to the truth that we cannot fully comprehend, as "*all* our reasoning extrapolates from limited experience."[37] To address environmental issues we construct moral presumptions to act on, unless the likely consequences of doing so seem sufficiently adverse to justify revising a presumption or setting it aside.

Rule of Law

This approach to ethics involves reasoning by analogy to the rule of law. The rule of law is how we agree, as a society, to both disagree and aspire for greater agreement. The rule of law defines our society as a *moral community* by affirming ethical presumptions that should apply in creating and enforcing laws. Stated as two moral principles, the rule of law affirms that *no one is above the law* and *everyone is equal before the law.*

Ethical rules derived from these two principles are now asserted as *human rights* by international law, which affirms human rights as necessary social conditions for human dignity. This means every person is included in the moral community defined by international human rights law. The conduct of governments and individuals often falls short of this high moral standard, but this fact does not make striving to enforce the rule of law any less important.

The rule of law provides an ethical framework for making public policy. It asserts ethical standards as legal presumptions, but also affirms that changing circumstances and new insights may lead to modifying some of these presumptions. The word *presumption* may only be familiar to most readers in phrases such as "the presumption of innocence" in criminal law, but this same meaning applies to doing ethics. *What we take to be right or good is a presumption.*

Reasoning by analogy, in doing ethics we rely on the same kinds of moral arguments that sustain the rule of law. We affirm that our moral community is defined by our moral presumptions and that those who challenge these presumptions bear the burden of explaining why some other action would be better. We affirm that: "Ethics underpins law, criticizes it," and "becomes a guide to what law ought to be."[38] We resist rationalizations and strive to give reasons for doing our duty, acting with exemplary character, respecting and strengthening our relationships, and protecting rights.

Constructing Ethical Presumptions

Each of the five chapters of part 2 explores how a pattern of ethical reasoning derived from the traditions of philosophy may help us define our moral community. Chapters 4–7 focus on actions and ways of being that philosophers affirm have intrinsic worth, and argue for revised presumptions that express these insights. Chapter 8 considers arguments that moral action involves doing whatever will result in the best consequences. In doing ethics, we rely on consequential reasoning to test presumptions affirming right actions and being good persons.

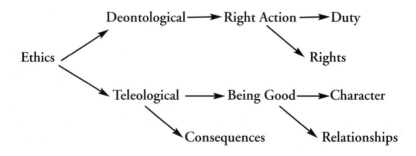

Chapter 4 assesses our *duty* to act on the basis of reason. Traditional deontological reasoning distinguishes between direct duties to persons and indirect duties that are implied by our moral duties to others. This means any duty we may have for the environment is, by definition, an indirect duty reflecting our actual duty to other persons. In environmental ethics, however, reasons have been given for affirming direct duties to nature. Now that science has confirmed the self-organizing character of every organism and ecosystem, might this analogy to human autonomy justify ascribing moral consideration to both?

Chapter 5 considers how individual *character* is relevant for ethics. Most moral philosophers rely on duty and consequential arguments to draw conclusions about human responsibility for nature. Yet, there is a tradition of thought affirming that personal happiness, as well as a good and just society, can only be realized by good persons. Should environmental ethics encourage virtues such as integrity, gratitude, and frugality?

Chapter 6 argues that *caring relationships* should be at least as much the focus of moral philosophy as individual virtues generally have been. This concern is especially relevant for doing environmental ethics, because our cultural traditions have long relied on rationalizations to excuse the abuse of women and nature. Might we now learn from nature, and also from the experience of women, how to live more ecologically?

Chapter 7 addresses deontological arguments about our duty to respect *rights.* In law rights are supported by the secular argument that individuals have natural rights as autonomous and rational beings, and by the religious affirmation that rights come from God. International human rights law affirms the right of every people to social and economic development, and the right to a healthy environment of every person. Recent laws offer some protection for animals, but generally do not grant them rights. How are we to resolve the moral and legal conflicts between protecting human rights and preserving endangered species and the earth's ecosystems?

In doing environmental ethics we explore these four patterns of reasoning to construct ethical presumptions as to what we should do and the kind of persons we should be. These presumptions assert what we understand to be intrinsically right and good. We test these ethical hypotheses by predicting the likely consequences of acting on them, to see if the possible or probable outcomes confirm or challenge our reasoning.

Most of us already think much like this, although we probably describe ethical presumptions as feelings or intuitions. We have a sense of what we believe to be right that is based on our experience, which we explain to others by referring to our feelings and the reasons that support these feelings. Also, we usually consider the likely consequences of acting on our sense of what is right, before we make a decision and carry it out. Doing ethics is a way of trying to clarify our moral reasoning.

Testing Ethical Presumptions

We test an ethical hypothesis (presumption) by predicting the likely consequences of acting on it. If we find evidence that seems to "falsify" our hypothesis,[39] we should take this into account. Evidence that seems to verify our presumption should be taken as supporting it.

As with the rule of law, some ethical presumptions may be stronger than others. For example, consider the presumption of innocence. To overturn this moral and legal presumption and find a person guilty of a crime, the law requires the state to present evidence that is beyond all reasonable doubt. In a civil lawsuit, however, where one party has accused the other of breaking an agreement, the burden of proof on the party bringing the action requires showing only that the claim is supported by a preponderance of the evidence.

Reasoning by analogy, in doing ethics we may distinguish moral presumptions that require *compelling* adverse evidence to be set aside, from those that may be set aside when the showing of adverse likely consequences is merely *convincing*. For example, an elected official should tell the truth about the threat of global warming, unless there is compelling evidence that the consequences of doing so are likely to be dire. Convincing evidence, however, that the consequences of telling the truth will likely be detrimental is all that is needed for an adult to justify setting aside the moral presumption to be completely truthful when a child asks, for instance, if global warming will kill all the polar bears.

As human rights are the social conditions necessary for human dignity, I will argue that setting aside the moral presumptions affirmed by international human rights law requires compelling evidence. Also, as the ecosystems of nature are necessary for sustaining all life on earth, I will argue that compelling evidence should be required to set aside our duty to protect the integrity of the earth's ecosystems.

Chapter 8 examines issues involved in predicting the likely consequences of acting on a moral presumption. The tradition of ethics that relies on utilitarian reasoning and consequential arguments is a modern response to the use of deontological and teleological arguments by entrenched social elites to justify and maintain their power. Affirming that we should do whatever brings about the greatest good for the greatest number of persons has been an effective way of promoting political and economic freedom, and today this seems to be the dominant reasoning in environmental ethics.

Both natural science and social science utilize consequential methods of reasoning, and scientists and economists claim that their knowledge of the natural world is reliable. As these two disciplines of thought evolved from philosophy and now have an enormous impact on environmental decisions, the next two chapters consider what lessons we should learn from each.

Chapter 3 argues that current economic theory and practice must be changed if economics is to fulfill its purpose of allocating resources for the common good. Chapter 2 explains recent scientific arguments for the limits of our knowledge, and also the theory of evolution and the discipline of ecology, and considers the implications of current scientific research for ascribing moral consideration to nature.

QUESTIONS—MORAL PHILOSOPHY: AN ADVENTURE IN REASONING

1. Write a sentence using the words *right* and *good* that states an ethical principle. Would you describe your sentence as teleological or deontological? Explain your reasoning.

2. Give an example of empathy, and explain why empathy is significant for ethics.

3. Explain the difference between teleological and deontological ethics. How is consequential ethics different from deontological ethics? Give examples.

4. Explain the difference in deontological ethics between direct and indirect duties. Why is this distinction relevant for environmental ethics?

5. What reasons might you give for not littering? Are any of your reasons religious? How would you argue that your reasons are justified and are not rationalizations?

6. Give an example of a religious argument that is supported by reason. Explain how this is different from a divine command.

7. Give a reason for rejecting the idea of cultural relativism.

8. Reason by analogy to support a moral presumption concerning the environment.

9. Why do some moral philosophers argue that environmental ethics should not be anthropocentric?

10.   Explain why the rule of law may be helpful for doing ethics and give an example.

11.   Identify a conflict of duties concerning use of the environment, and give a reason for supporting the action you think is best. Who should be involved in resolving this conflict?

12.   What are the likely consequences of acting on the presumption that you constructed in the previous question? Explain why your predictions weigh against taking the action or confirm it.

2

Ethics and Science

MORAL CONSIDERATION

In 1972 an essay titled "Should Trees Have Standing?—Towards Legal Rights for Natural Objects" triggered a fierce debate among lawyers and moral philosophers about ascribing moral consideration to nature.[1]

It has long been accepted in ethics and law that standing[2] (and thus moral consideration) is given only to persons and their institutions.[3] In the reasoning of deontological ethics, humans have direct duties only to one another. Thus, a duty to care for a forest is really a duty to care for private property or for public land including the trees on it.[4] Similarly, the natural law tradition of teleological ethics restricts our moral community to humans by reasoning that the natural world exists for human happiness.[5]

The consequential approach to ethics known as utilitarianism allows an alternative view. In his *Introduction to the Principles of Morals and Legislation* (1789), Jeremy Bentham defines happiness as pleasure and the absence of pain and argues that animal suffering should be considered in predicting what actions will yield the most pleasure.[6] A leading contemporary utilitarian, Peter Singer, also includes sentient animals in our moral community.[7]

Chapter 1 argued that reasoning evolved from the social experience of primates, and in this chapter we learn that the self-organizing nature of organisms and ecosystems has parallels with human autonomy. As rationality and autonomy are grounds in traditional ethics for limiting moral consideration to humans, might these new scientific insights prompt us to revise our ethical presumptions and embrace duties directly to (or for) nonhuman animals and ecosystems? Might current science also give us reason to redefine the consequential standard of happiness, so that it extends our moral community to include animals that suffer as well as the integrity of forests and other ecosystems?

To address these questions, we assess first how current science limits as well as expands our knowledge. Then we consider how our understanding of evolution and ecology is relevant for doing environmental ethics.

WHAT WE KNOW AND CAN'T KNOW

"It is often claimed that science stands mute on questions of values: that science can help us to achieve what we value once our priorities are fixed, but can play no role in fixing these weightings. That claim is certainly incorrect. Science plays a key role in these matters. For what we value depends on what we believe, and what we believe is strong influenced by science."[8]

This is as true for us today, as it was for Aristotle and Kant. What we believe about the world depends on what we know, and the most recent studies in science reveal not only how our brains work, but also the limits of our ability to know the world as it is.

Sense-Making

Biologists now verify that *our brains construct our perceptions.* Our neurological system does not simply record data. "Perception is not a process of passive absorption, but of active construction."[9] The human brain has complex feedback systems that filter and interpret sensory experience, and these systems are affected by our experience.[10] "Your understanding of reality is constructed in large part according to your expectations and beliefs, which are based on all your past experiences, which are held in the cortex as predictive memory."[11]

This means that no matter how objective we may try to be, our knowledge is also subjective.[12] "No observations can be made at all, without some initial predispositions to notice some things rather than others."[13] Our *worldview* is always *our* worldview.

Physicists now confirm that *our perceptions affect what we experience.* The theory of quantum mechanics holds that we create what we experience by selecting among the many possibilities that may be made actual. "The observer does not create what is not potentially there, but does participate in the extraction from the mass of existing potentialities individual items that have interest and meaning to the perceiving self."[14]

Furthermore, quantum mechanics has verified experimentally that we live in a *nonlocal universe.* We are unable to understand the total reality of a particular event, because the entire universe is entangled.[15] Whatever we know, we know only from within the entangled relationships that constitute our sense of reality.[16] Yet, these entangled relationships also transcend our "local" knowing.[17] Thus, our observations cannot fully disclose reality, for perceiving one aspect of what is happening hides complementary aspects that we might otherwise see.[18]

This scientific view of the limitations of our understanding "in no way denies the existence of a real physical world, but rather rejects an objectivist conception of our relation to it. The world is never given to us as a brute fact detachable from our conceptual frameworks. Rather, it shows up in all the describable ways it does thanks to the structure of our subjectivity and our intentional activities."[19]

Our minds emerge from the natural world, so we are unable to stand apart from the world to observe it.[20] As conscious beings living in a world that is affected by our observations, we shape ourselves and our world as we seek to understand both.[21] *Our knowledge only approximates reality.*

These scientific insights have three critical implications for ethics. First, we must take into account the effect of our consciousness on what we observe and describe.[22] The "transition from the 'possible' to the 'actual' takes place during the act of observation."[23] In actuality, "the world comes into being through our knowledge of it."[24] If we address environmental issues from within the environment, which is our habitat, we will see that *we are the environmental crisis.*

Second, because we shape what we know, our responsibility in making ethical decisions is crucial. "Living is a process of sense-making, of bringing forth significance and value."[25] Our knowledge may be limited, but acting on our knowledge makes sense both of the world and our own lives. Therefore, *we are the only solution to the environmental crisis.*

Third, current science reveals that every conceptualization is a human construction and not simply reality.[26] This means that the dichotomy in traditional ethics between humans (as rational and autonomous beings) and other living organisms is a way of seeing the world, and not simply the way life is. Each ethical pattern of thought actualizes some of the potentialities of life, but obscures other possible ways of understanding the world.[27]

Science confirms that moral consideration is a human decision. Traditional ethics has limited the moral community to humans and their institutions. On the basis of current science, however, we may decide that it is rational to ascribe moral consideration to organisms, species, and ecosystems. *We are responsible for realizing the moral potentiality of nature.*

In the next section we see that these implications are supported by recent proposals for modifying the theory of evolution and by some of the work done in the discipline of ecology.[28] Like every form of human knowledge, scientific reasoning is dynamic.[29] We are responsible now for discerning how to apply scientific conclusions to our environmental crisis.[30]

AN EVOLVING THEORY OF EVOLUTION

When Charles Darwin described evolution as the result of "natural selection," he was drawing an analogy to the breeding of animals, which involves artificial selection. It was well known that animal breeders could make changes in a species by breeding stock with certain traits. Darwin's hypothesis was that changes also occur spontaneously in nature, and that changes contributing to the survival of an organism in its environment are more likely to be passed on to the next generation.

Darwin proposed that natural selection might account not only for changes within a species, but also for the evolution of diverse species. Thus, the word *selection* had a different meaning for Darwin than for animal breeders, as they select animals for breeding with the purpose of improving a trait. Darwin conceived of natural selection as a *natural process* resulting in the greater survival of organisms that are fit for their environment.[31]

Fit for an Environment

Many organisms in an environment are predatory. Herbivores eat plants, and carnivores eat herbivores and smaller carnivores. This obvious fact and Darwin's theory about why the more fit survive in nature were used as evidence to support a political and economic theory known as social Darwinism. A moral philosopher was the first to characterize natural selection as "the survival of the fittest."[32] The phrase was applied uncritically to rationalize the success of the rich and the suffering of the poor, without challenging the economic and political injustice that at least partly explains this disparity.[33]

Some scientists now see predation as primarily a process of *coevolution*.[34] "Predator and prey or parasite and host require a coevolution where both flourish, since the health of the predator or parasite is locked into the continuing existence, even the welfare, of prey and host."[35] Such relationships involve complex patterns of fitness for an environment.[36] Seeing evolution in this way changes our view of nature.

Social Darwinism, nonetheless, continues to cast a shadow over environmental ethics. We find this thinking, for example, in the "lifeboat ethics" that makes an ecological argument "against helping the poor."[37] Clearly, there are dangers in drawing ethical inferences from scientific theories. We should keep this in mind as we consider how genetics has led to a revision of the Darwinian theory of evolution that is known as the neo-Darwinian synthesis.

Genetic Environment

Darwin proposed the theory of natural selection before scientists were able to confirm the presence and role of genes. Now the scientific discipline of genetics explains how the traits of an organism are transmitted to subsequent genera-tions and also how changes may occur among genes that will affect the traits of an organism.[38] It is important to emphasize that *genes function in their environ-ment* as parts of chromosomes in a cell within an organism.

"How, when and to what extent any gene is expressed—that is, how its se-quence is translated into a functioning protein—depends on signals from the cell in which it is embedded. As this cell is itself at any one time in receipt of and responding to signals, not just from a single gene, but from many others which are simultaneously switched on or off, the expression of any single gene is influenced by what is happening in the whole of the rest of the genome."[39]

That is, a gene does not simply produce a trait. Genes are part of a process that constructs proteins, which depend not only on the amino-acid sequence dictated by a gene, but also "on their environment, on the presence of water, ions and sometimes other small molecules, and on acidity or alkalinity."[40] Genes contain information about development, but the *expression of genetic in-formation depends on the environment.*

"For individual gene-sized sequences of DNA, the environment is consti-tuted by the rest of the genome and the cellular machinery in which it is embed-ded; for the cell, it is the buffered milieu in which it floats; for the organism, it is the external physical, living and social worlds. Which features of the external world constitute 'the environment' differ from species to species; every organism thus has an environment tailored to its needs."[41]

The active *engagement of organisms and genes with their environments* makes a summary like "the survival of the fittest" too simple. Also, it is misleading to assert, as Richard Dawkins does, that: "We [humans] are survival machines— robot vehicles blindly programmed to preserve the selfish molecules known as genes."[42] The word *selfish*, expressing an analogy to caring only for oneself, does not reflect the process by which genes are expressed through interactions in the environment of a cell, which occur within the environment of the organism as the organism interacts with it.

Learning

The claim that humans are "blindly programmed" is also overreaching, for there is ample evidence that all kinds of organisms, as well as humans, learn to change themselves and their environment. Animals have the ability to learn because the same genes that respond to signals from within also respond to experience in the environment that impacts the organism. "The reason that animals can learn is that they can alter their nervous systems on the basis of external experience. And the reason that they can do that is that *experience itself can modify the expression of genes.*"[43]

Most "animals are born not just with the ability to perceive and act but also with the ability to learn and to use past experience to improve subsequent behavior."[44] For instance, sea slugs "can learn to ignore the irritating prods of curious experimenters."[45] Honey bees are "prewired" to orient by the sun's position on the horizon, but have to learn "the sun's trajectory at the bee's particular latitude at a particular time of the year."[46]

Complex systems of communication are also present among animals. Bees "dance" in the hive to indicate to other bees where pollen is to be found and, after locating new sites suitable for nesting, refrain from communicating in the hive the direction of a new nesting site until the bees "agree" as to which potential site is best.[47]

Among some chimpanzees, older chimps teach youngsters how to forage for food by using a stick to draw termites out of their nest. In other communities, adult chimps use stones to crack open nuts while younger chimps watch. As not all chimps do these things, we know that these traits are not caused by genes.[48] Diverse *phenotypes* (chimps using sticks, chimps using stones, and chimps using neither) are expressed by one *genotype* (chimpanzee). These various behaviors are taught and learned, which is what we mean by *culture*.[49]

Brain Plasticity

In humans and other mammals changes in the brain take place as an organism responds to changing environments. This making, pruning, and rewiring of neural circuits is called *neuroplasticity*. "[F]rom the earliest stages of development, laying down brain circuits is an active rather than a passive process, directed by the interaction between experience and the environment."[50] Until recently scientists thought that aging brought an end to neuroplasticity. "In the past two decades, however, an enormous amount of research has revealed that the brain never stops changing and adjusting."[51]

Our experience changes our brains. "Without question the brains of adult mammals in general, and humans in particular, are endowed with a plasticity that enables them to continually adjust their behavior with experience. The development process does not tie down every conceivable synapse in a rigid and unalterable form, but leaves considerable scope for ongoing readjustment in the adult."[52]

As a biological process, neuroplasticity is constrained by an organism's genetic expression and natural development,[53] but humans have an extraordinary capacity to recover from some brain injuries.[54] Changes in our brains are largely the result "of what we do and what we experience of the outside world. In this sense, the very structure of our brain—the relative size of different regions, the strength of connections between one area and another—reflects the lives we have led."[55] Exercise enhances brain function.[56] *Doing changes our thinking.*

We can also change our brains in significant ways by *focusing our attention* on the changes we want to make. "Paying attention matters. It matters not only for the size of the brain's representation of this or that part of the body's surface, of this or that muscle. It matters for the dynamic structure of the very circuits of the brain and for the brain's ability to remake itself."[57] *Our minds can change our brains!* This fact is crucial for doing ethics.

How we understand evolution affects our thinking about ethics, so we need to be clear about what we now know from recent science:

- Organisms evolve and change the environment that "selects" them.
- Organisms coevolve as well as eat one another and compete.
- Humans (and many other organisms) learn, communicate, and choose.
- Mammals change their brains and humans change their minds.

"In natural selection as we now understand it, cooperation appears to exist in complementary relation to competition."[58] Social Darwinism is wrong. We are not "survival machines" for our genes. Mind matters.[59]

ECOSYSTEMS AND EMERGENT PROPERTIES

To consider how we should change our minds, we look to *ecology*: "The study of the relationships between and among organisms and their environment," which "consists of both non-living factors and other organisms."[60] Like every scientific discipline, ecology is a tradition of thought that includes diverse explanations. Throughout the twentieth century, ecologists have debated whether the environment is best represented by organic models that emphasize a dynamic community or economic models that analyze the whole in terms of its parts.[61]

The present environmental crisis as well as recent research has shifted the focus to ecosystems. Analyzing the environment as a living system involves assessing the relationships within the system as well as its emergent properties, which are not reducible to the functions of the parts of an ecosystem. Ecology now seeks to describe the *integrity* of an ecosystem.[62]

Relationships

Many relationships within the environment are mutually beneficial, or *symbiotic*. Fungi in the soil attach to the roots of trees to form structures called mycorrhizae, a relationship that benefits both the trees and the fungi. The trees supply carbohydrates to the fungi, and the fungi increase the ability of the root system to absorb water and minerals.[63] It is estimated that 95 percent of all plants on earth participate in this symbiotic relationship, and some species of trees would not survive without the assistance of fungi.[64]

We find in the environment of cells another important example of symbiosis, which is the result of *coevolution*.[65] The mitochondria, which are specialized structures that convert carbohydrates, fats, and proteins into a usable form of energy,[66] evolved from bacteria that were incorporated into the cells of organisms early in the evolution of life.[67] The fact that a typical cell in every animal, plant, or fungus has about two thousand mitochondria "powering" it,[68] suggests that this evolved symbiotic relationship is important for being fit to survive.

The ecological relationships of tree roots and fungi, and also mitochondria within every plant, fungi, and animal cell, illustrate mutually beneficial coevolution that is not accurately characterized using notions such as the "survival of the fittest" or "selfish genes." So, we should not be surprised by the definition of an *ecosystem* as: "An ecological community together with its environment, functioning as a unit."[69]

Ecosystems

Ecosystems are everywhere. Many consist of "a community of plants and animals in an environment that supplies them with raw materials for life, i.e., chemical elements and water. The ecosystem is delimited by the climate, altitude, water and soil characteristics, and other physical conditions of the environment."[70] Within an ecosystem, "Every species is bound to its community in the unique manner by which it variously consumes, is consumed, competes, and cooperates with other species. It also indirectly affects the community in the way it alters the soil, water, and air."[71]

An ecosystem, however, may also be defined as "the collection of biotic and abiotic components and processes that comprise and govern the behavior of some defined subset of the biosphere."[72] And the biosphere may be understood as "a global ecosystem composed of living organisms (biota) and the abiotic (nonliving) factors from which they derive energy and nutrients."[73] This description emphasizes the contribution of the parts to the whole.

Bacteria, for instance, which are the most abundant form of life on earth, play a crucial role in the *complex processes* of ecosystems. Without bacteria, we would not have nitrogen in our soil, and the ground would not sustain the trees that produce much of the oxygen we need to breathe and the crops we grow for food.[74] Hundreds of millions of bacteria live in our intestines, stomach, and mouth and assist with our digestion.[75]

In fact, "The vast majority of the cells in your body are not your own; they belong to bacterial and other microorganismic species."[76] Every person is a community of life and not simply an individual.[77] Even the crook of your elbow is "a special ecosystem, a bountiful home to no fewer than six tribes of bacteria" that help "to moisturize the skin by processing the raw fats it produces."[78]

If "all organisms larger than bacteria are intrinsically communities,"[79] then we need to *understand evolution more ecologically.*[80] In every multicellular organism, there are bacteria participating in the life of the organism rather than "competing" with it for survival. Thus, evolution is more accurately described as a process of natural selection in which communities that are fit for changing environments are more likely to survive.

Emergent Properties

Ecologists also verify that ecosystems have emergent properties "such as energy transfer, nutrient cycling, gas regulation, climate regulation, and the water cycle. As is typical of emergent properties, ecosystem functions cannot be readily explained by even the most extensive knowledge of system components of ecosystem structure."[81] Because emergent processes are not adequately understood, *the consequences of damaging ecosystems are unpredictable.*[82]

"While emergent cooperative behaviors within parts (organisms) that maintain conditions of survival in the whole (environment or ecosystem) appear to be everywhere present in nature, the conditions of observation are such that we distort results when we view any of these systems as isolated."[83] No one view of the whole explains the whole.

The *emergent processes of ecosystems are irreplaceable.* "There are no plausible technological substitutes for soil fertility, clean fresh water, unspoiled landscapes, climatic stability, biological diversity, biological nutrient recycling and environmental waste assimilative capacity. The irreversible loss of species and ecosystems, and the buildup of greenhouse gases in the atmosphere, and of toxic metals and chemicals in the topsoil, ground water and in the silt of lake-bottoms and estuaries, are not reversible by any plausible technology that could appear in the next few decades."[84]

Yet, these *emergent processes have resiliency.*[85] "Ecosystems remain resilient in the face of change through high biodiversity of species, organized in complex webs of relationships. The many relationships are maintained through *self-organizing processes,* not top-down control."[86] In an ecosystem, "each individual in a species acts independently, yet its activity patterns cooperatively mesh with the patterns of other species. Cooperation and competition are interlinked and held in balance."[87] Also, *diversity* matters: "the more species that inhabit an ecosystem, such as a forest or lake, the more productive and stable is the ecosystem."[88]

Ecosystems are relevant for doing environmental ethics because:

- Ecosystems sustain symbiotic and predatory relationships among organisms.
- Ecosystem processes are complex, self-organizing, diverse, and resilient.
- The emergent properties of an ecosystem are irreplaceable.
- The consequences of damaging ecosystems are unpredictable.

These lessons do not determine our ethical choices, but are the "environment" of these choices.

Adopting this worldview means considering possibilities or probabilities, rather than simply describing facts, as every environment is always changing due to its dynamic nature and our impact on it.[89] Therefore, our ability to predict the likely consequences of our actions is always limited. In the words of philosopher of science Karl Popper, "The future is open."[90]

Taking an ecosystem approach means shifting our focus from the parts to the whole, from structure to process, from objective claims to contingent descriptions, and from objects to relationships.[91] In environmental ethics, this requires considering *the identity of organisms within their environment* and also *the integrity of natural systems.*

ASCRIBING VALUE TO NATURE

Science cannot verify that nature has a purpose, nor can scientific reasoning determine whether the natural world has intrinsic worth. Yet, scientific knowledge is relevant for addressing these questions by moral reasoning. The next three sections consider the ethical implications of the scientific conclusions that: nature generates diversity, evolution is an emergent process of life, and ecosystems, as well as organisms, are self-organizing. I argue from these considerations that it is reasonable to ascribe objective value to nature.

Nature Generates Diversity

The "biosphere is profoundly generative—somehow fundamentally always creative."[92] Life fills every niche of nature, and as the environment changes, the dynamic process of evolution enables some species to adapt. Random genetic changes and competition play a crucial role, but organisms (including human beings) also coevolve.[93] If the result has value (as humans beings, we certainly think that *we* have value), *and* the process is necessary for the result, it seems reasonable to ascribe value to the natural means that have led to the valued result.

The main argument against attributing value to evolution points to the random genetic changes leading to new traits that are selected due to their fitness. The claim is that random events cannot be purposeful, as purpose gives value to human action. Yet, the lack of evidence for a purpose in nature itself does not prove that nature is merely random or without value.

"It is certainly true that there is randomness in evolutionary nature, but it is not random that there is diversity. Four billion species do not appear by accident. Rather, *randomness is a diversity generator*, mixed as it is with principles of the spontaneous generation of order . . . *randomness is an advancement generator*, supported, as advancement comes to be, by the trophic pyramid[94] in which lower ways of life are also conserved."[95]

When we are unable to solve a problem, we sometimes try whatever we can think of, and this may lead us to a solution. Our own experience confirms that making *random changes need not be without value*. Similarly, in evolution: "Randomness guarantees the trial-and-error exploration of the potentialities of the system. Randomness sifts through new options for both diversity and advancement."[96]

Evolution Is an Emergent Process

Both physics and biology now assert that "the old view of evolution as a linear progression from lower atomized organisms to more complex atomized organisms no longer seems appropriate. The more appropriate view could be that all organisms (parts) are emergent aspects of the self-organizing process of life (whole), and that the proper way to understand the parts is to examine their embedded relations to the whole."[97]

That is, evolution generates not only organisms but diverse and complex ecosystems, and these natural processes have a "heading" toward "species diversification, support, and richness."[98] Moral philosopher Holmes Rolston III writes: "Ecosystems are in some respects more to be admired than any of their component organisms because they are generated, continue to support, and integrate tens of thousands of member organisms. The ecosystem is as wonderful as anything it contains. In nature there may sometimes be clumsy, makeshift solutions. Still, everything is tested for adaptive fitness."[99]

The counterargument is that valuing ecosystems may result in "harmful consequences to human individuals or human projects and institutions."[100] Yet, contrasting the value of humans and ecosystems ignores the scientific facts that humans can only live in ecosystems and are themselves ecosystems. Therefore, it makes sense to value these natural facts as well as our own purposes. This reasoning also supports ascribing value to biodiversity and the survival of other species, as well as the habitats that sustain all life.

"Moral consideration should first be directed toward the natural community or ecosystem as a whole, so that the overall good for the ecosystem is the primary goal of action. But this communal good should be supplemented by a consideration of natural individuals and species, so that in cases where ecosystemic well-being is not an issue, the protection of endangered species or natural individuals can be morally justified."[101] I argue in chapter 4 that this is more reasonable than including only individual organisms in our moral community.[102]

I agree with Mary Midgley that we may have duties to plants and trees, as well as animals and species, because "as beings forming a small part of the fauna of this planet, we also exist in relation to that whole, and its fate cannot be a matter of moral indifference to us."[103] I argue in chapter 7, however, that this need not mean ascribing rights to animals.[104]

Expanding our moral community will likely increase our conflicts of duty. Yet, conflicts are the stuff of ethics and law, so this is no reason to deny moral consideration to organisms and ecosystems. Moreover, the law has already extended our responsibility to include protecting endangered species and the integrity of ecosystems.[105]

Organisms and Ecosystems Are Self-organizing

Life is self-organizing at all levels. "Far more complex than any computer or robot, the common bacterium perceives and swims toward its food."[106] In pursuit of their own survival, bacteria have made the earth's environment viable for us and other life by removing carbon dioxide from the atmosphere, producing oxygen, and "inventing every major kind of metabolic transformation on the planet."[107]

A bacterium maintains its identity "by making sense of the world so as to remain viable."[108] Also, to maintain its identity, a bacterium (like every organism) must constantly change its material composition by metabolizing nutrients from the environment.[109] Not even a bacterium is a survival machine. "If the organism must change its matter in order to maintain its identity, then the organism must aim beyond itself."[110]

Having such an *identity* is certainly not the same as having autonomy or rationality, which are the human attributes that philosophers have argued justify limiting moral consideration to persons. Yet, such an identity distinguishes organisms from nonliving natural resources, and is the evolutionary root of autonomy and reason.[111] "Every organism has a *good-of-its-kind;* it defends its own kind [its own way of life] as a *good kind.*"[112]

Every organism is oriented toward the future. "Thus life is facing forward as well as outward and extends 'beyond' its own immediacy in both directions at once."[113] There are no conscious intentions in the actions of bacteria or most animals. Yet, the emergent properties of self-organization and sense-making, and the forward trajectory of every organism in seeking its own good, are evidence that *all life has value for itself.* This is true of plants as well as animals, for plants "sense all sorts of things about the plants around them and use that information to interact with them."[114]

We can distinguish, as two forms of intrinsic worth, this intrinsic value *for itself* and the intrinsic value *in itself,* which we ascribe to rationality and autonomy: "The former is common to human and nonhuman nature (at least its biotic components) and is connected with their capacity to strive to maintain their functioning integrity. The latter is confined only to humans and is connected . . . with their unique type of consciousness, reason, and capacity for language."[115]

This distinction allows us to affirm both the good of nature and the good of human culture. We recognize that a self-organizing natural system has intrinsic worth (for itself), but we also acknowledge the intrinsic worth (in itself) of the science that identifies this natural fact, and the ethics that ascribes value to it.

Rolston writes: "Ecology discovers simultaneously (1) what is taking place in ecosystems and (2) what biotic community means as an organizational mode enveloping organisms. Crossing over from science to ethics, we can discover (3) the values in such a community-system and (4) our duties toward it."[116]

Why do we have a duty to care for ecosystems? "The ecologist finds that ecosystems *objectively* are *satisfactory communities* in the sense that, though not all organismic needs are gratified, enough are for species long to survive, and the critical ethicist finds (in a *subjective* judgment matching the *objective* process) that such ecosystems are imposing and *satisfactory communities* to which to attach duty."[117]

Nature Has Objective Value

Is nature without value until there are humans to value it? Not if we understand the act of ascribing value as recognizing value, rather than creating value. We attribute value to our lives because we *reason* that human life has worth. *Valuing is the subjective recognition of objective value.*[118] If our (subjective) valuing of nature is reasonable, then nature has (objective) value.

Understanding that human beings have evolved and rely on the earth's ecosystems makes it clear that human life is only part of the generative process we call nature. Furthermore, if there are good reasons for ascribing intrinsic worth to nature, then we have a duty toward nature, as it is, to act with care.[119] The evolutionary and ecological processes that led to human life—and thus to consciousness, knowledge, and ethics—have objective value not only after humans exist, but in the millennia of natural history that generated a profusion of organisms and ecosystems.

We may draw two inferences for ethics from this conclusion. First, *we cannot limit our ethical reasoning to predicting likely consequences*, as the consequentialist approach does not take into account the intrinsic worth of nature, but only values natural resources for their utility. Many moral philosophers assert that some form of consequential ethics is the best we can do. Nonetheless, if there are reasonable arguments for attributing intrinsic value to nature, then ethics requires considering what is best for the habitats we share with other species and not simply calculating our best use of natural resources.

Second, ascribing intrinsic value to nature requires that we distinguish the world of human culture from the world of nature. In the *world of culture,* which is the traditional worldview of moral philosophy, we do not reason from what is to what ought to be. For example, murder in society *is* a fact, but no one suggests that it *ought to be* morally acceptable. Deriving what "ought to be" from what "is," and reducing "the question of values to that of facts," is known in moral philosophy as "the naturalistic fallacy."[120]

Yet, as we contemplate the world of nature, and also ascribe intrinsic value to organisms and ecosystems, it is reasonable to infer that what is (in wild nature) is what ought to be. For example, predation in the natural world involves killing, which "ought to be" in the sense that we "ought to let it be," because this is how life in ecosystems has evolved and survives.

"What is ethically puzzling, and exciting in the marriage and mutual transformation of ecological description and evaluation is that here an *ought* is not so much *derived* from an *is* as discovered simultaneously with it. As we progress from description of fauna and flora . . . of stability and dynamism, and move on to intricacy . . . to unity and harmony with oppositions in counterpoint and synthesis, to organisms evolved within and satisfactorily fitting their communities, arriving at length at beauty and goodness, it is difficult to say where the natural facts leave off and where the natural values appear."[121]

Our environmental crisis is a conflict between the world of human culture and the world of nature. Our way of life is the problem, and thus also the solution. This crisis is due largely to our ethical failure, in the world of human culture, to grant moral consideration to the intrinsic worth of the world of nature.

How are we to resolve this problem? Rather than rejecting anthropocentric thinking for an ecocentric perspective, I argue that we must learn from both. An ecocentric perspective extends our moral community beyond ourselves to the world of nature, and anthropocentric reasoning defends the moral standards of social justice in the world of human culture.

QUESTIONS—ETHICS AND SCIENCE: MORAL CONSIDERATION

1. Why does current science argue that our knowledge of the natural world is limited? Identify two ethical implications of this reasoning.

2. What is our moral community? How is current science relevant in the debate about ascribing moral consideration to the intrinsic worth of nature? Explain your reasoning.

3. What is coevolution? Give an example. What relevance does coevolution have for ethics?

4. Explain what *fit* means in the neo-Darwinian theory of evolution.

5. What is the environment of genes? How are they affected by their environment?

6. How have bacteria contributed to evolution? Why is this relevant for environmental ethics?

7. What is brain plasticity? Why is this natural fact significant for ethics?

8. Identify three characteristics of ecosystems in addition to diversity.

9. Identify an ecosystem "emergent property." How might we "value" this property?

10. What ecological facts would you rely on to argue for our duty to protect ecosystems? Does your argument avoid the naturalistic fallacy? Explain your reasoning.

11. Give two reasons for asserting that nature has intrinsic value. Why is this moral presumption significant for environmental ethics?

12. Explain the distinction between intrinsic value for itself and intrinsic value in itself, and how this distinction supports both ecocentric and anthropocentric views of moral consideration.

3

Ethics and Economics

THE COMMON GOOD

Economics began as a discipline of moral philosophy concerned with the use of natural resources to produce and allocate goods and services *for the common good.* Moral philosophers reasoned that economics "should not be devoted to the most efficient means of producing material goods, but rather to the most efficient means of producing human well-being."[1]

What has gone wrong? The short answer is that our economic system has hidden the real costs of economic growth, including the enormous damage to our natural environment. It has always been true that: "All economic decisions have an environmental consequence, just as all environmental decisions have economic consequences."[2] Yet, economists have ignored the environmental impact of economic growth.

To understand why our environmental crisis is an economic as well as an ethical crisis, we first look at how the real economy differs from the idealized economy of neoclassical economic theory. Then we consider how globalization in trade exacerbates the degradation of the environment and the depletion of natural resources. Finally, we assess revisions to economic theory and practice that may make our global economy environmentally sustainable.[3]

INVISIBLE HAND?

Modern economics began in 1776 with the publication of *The Wealth of Nations* by the Scottish moral philosopher Adam Smith.[4] He argued that free trade would foster civil and political freedom, and that laws encouraging the pursuit of *individual self-interest* would result in the greater good. Smith offered two ethical arguments in support of his economic theory: that human dignity requires political and economic freedom and that the consequences of free markets are generally beneficial.

Every person, Smith wrote, "endeavors as much as he can both to employ his capital in the support of domestic industry, and so to direct that industry that its produce may be of the greatest value; every individual necessarily labors to render the annual value of society as great as he can."[5] In the pursuit of self-interest, Smith believed, each individual is "led by an *invisible hand* to promote an end which was no part of his intention. Nor is it always the worse for the society that it was no part of it. *By pursuing his own interest he frequently promotes that of society more effectually than when he really intends to promote it.*"[6]

Smith's economic philosophy reflects the worldview of eighteenth-century Newtonian mechanics, for Smith "conceived of the economy as a closed system in which interactions between parts (consumers, producers, distributors, etc.) are controlled by forces external to the parts (supply and demand)."[7] His belief that an "invisible hand" ensures the common good is an analogy to Newton's law of gravity, which sustains the universe. "In the real economy," however, "the invisible hand does not exist."[8]

There are relationships between supply, demand, and market prices, but there is no "invisible hand" that prevents economic growth from damaging the environment and causing global warming. "Market fundamentalists claim that human governance is always an impediment to markets, but in fact human governance is what makes markets possible."[9] We now need to regulate markets to ensure that they are environmentally sustainable.

"Here's the problem in a nutshell. Industrialism developed in a different world from the one we live in today: fewer people, less material well-being, plentiful natural resources. What emerged was a highly productive, take-make-waste system that assumed *infinite* resources and *infinite* sinks for industrial wastes. Industry [now] moves, mines, extracts, shovels, burns, wastes, pumps and disposes of four million pounds of material in order to provide one average, middle-class American family their needs for a year. Today, the rate of material throughput is endangering our prosperity, not enhancing it."[10]

Fifteen hundred of the world's leading scientists confirm this conclusion. "The *earth is finite*. Its ability to absorb wastes and destructive effluents is finite. Its ability to provide food and energy is finite. Its ability to provide for growing numbers of people is finite. And we are fast approaching many of the earth's limits."[11] Current economic practices "cannot be continued without the risk that vital global systems will be damaged beyond repair."[12]

Therefore, we must address these economic and ethical issues:

- Many natural resources are nonrenewable and cannot be fully recycled.
- Renewable resources are being harvested beyond their optimal scale.
- The waste absorption capacity of the environment has been exceeded.
- The loss of ecosystem benefits due to economic exploitation is a real cost.

ECONOMIC AND ETHICAL ISSUES

First, *many natural resources are nonrenewable and cannot be fully recycled.* This includes metals and fossil fuels that are extracted from the earth.[13] The supply of these natural resources is finite and in some cases is rapidly diminishing. Yet, in neoclassical economics, those mining these nonrenewable resources are not required to include *in their costs* any calculation of the investment required to find or create replacements, or to make that investment. These issues are simply left to the marketplace.

Both ethics and economics agree that we have a duty to allocate and use resources to ensure the common good. Chapter 4 argues that in using natural resources we have, as well, a duty to give moral consideration to future generations. Therefore, we need to ensure that those who profit from using nonrenewable resources at least fund investment in developing replacements. As markets do not impose this cost on producers, it must be assessed by law.

Second, *renewable resources are being harvested beyond their optimal scale.* Renewable resources (such as fish and forests) will not be used up, as long as these organisms are harvested below an optimal scale that allows their populations to replenish. Yet, nothing in an unregulated market prevents the loss of these renewable resources.[14] In fact, as renewable resources become scarce, those harvesting these natural resources tend to intensify their efforts in order to maximize their short-term profit before a resource is depleted.

Harvesting renewable resources at greater than the optimal scale is wasteful, for this depletes a natural resource that otherwise is self-sustaining. This waste cannot be morally justified when there is scarcity and the loss of resources allocates greater costs to others. Thus, governments need to restrict the harvesting of renewable resources to less than optimal scale.

Third, *the waste absorption capacity of the environment has been exceeded.* In neoclassical economics waste left in the environment is treated as an *externality*—a consequence external to the market economy that does not need to be included as a cost in determining the market value of an economic activity.[15] "When firms compete with each other in the free market, their decisions are not guided by environmental considerations. They can produce more cheaply when they dispose of their wastes in the least expensive way—for example, in the nearest river."[16] So, they do.

Nature has evolved many ways of recycling waste, but the natural processes that purify air and water and reconstitute the soil take time and have limits. To protect these natural processes, we must support laws that require the effective treatment of waste before it is emitted into the environment. This not only makes good economic sense, but reflects our ethical duty to one another and to other species.

Fourth, *the loss of ecosystem benefits due to economic exploitation is a real cost.* Neoclassical economic theory has failed to recognize that renewable resources provide not merely *stock-flow resources*,[17] such as fish to eat and wood to use, but also *fund-service resources*[18] that have significant ecological benefits. For example, in addition to providing lumber that may be harvested, forests are *ecosystems* that absorb carbon dioxide and release oxygen, provide habitats for other organisms, and regulate rainfall and prevent soil erosion.

The loss of these ecological benefits[19] when forests are cut is presently contributing to global warming due to increased carbon dioxide levels in the atmosphere, which has significant economic costs. Yet, neoclassical economic theory ignores the loss of ecosystem benefits (by identifying these costs as externalities) in calculating the costs used to set the price of lumber.

What Went Wrong?

Since World War II the richest and most powerful nations have been "cooperating for the sake of the growth of the global economy" on the assumption that this "massive shift of power from nations to transnational corporations" will yield the greatest good for the world's peoples.[20] Emphasizing economic growth, "while on balance quite useful in a world with empty land, shoals of undisturbed fish, vast forests, and a robust ozone shield, helped create a more crowded and stressed one."[21]

Economic theory "did not adjust to the changed conditions it helped to create; thereby it continued to legitimate, and indeed indirectly to cause, massive and rapid ecological change."[22] Moreover, democratic institutions have "been weakened by three decades of market fundamentalism, privatization ideology and resentment of government."[23]

In the last third of the twentieth century the environmental movement in the United States fought back in Congress and in the courts.[24] Nonetheless, in the first eight years of the twenty-first century the "Bush administration, which favors energy production over energy conservation, has engineered a reversal of a generation of progress on environmentalism that threatens to leave the [hazardous wastes cleanup] Superfund program underfunded, air-quality standards compromised and global warming unchecked. These politics can be traced directly to that proud disdain for the public realm that is common to all market fundamentalists, Republican and Democratic alike."[25]

The ethical measure of an economic policy is its contribution to the common good. This not only requires political decisions that protect the environment, but also economic policies that ensure a fair distribution of the economic benefits that are realized. Adam Smith argued that political freedom requires economic freedom, and this seems to be true. Yet, ethics requires that laws protect political freedom by regulating economic freedom.

Wealth Disparity

Has the common good been realized by our growth economy? Increasing wealth disparity is evidence to the contrary. "According to the United Nations Human Development Report in 1999, the income differential between the fifth of the world's population in the wealthiest countries and the fifth in the poorest was 30 to 1 in 1960, 60 to 1 in 1990, and 74 to 1 in 1995."[26] In 2006 the wealth of the world's 475 billionaires exceeded the income of the poorest three billion people on earth, and this disparity is growing.[27]

Economic inequity is also rising in the United States. "Virtually all of the growth in wealth between 1983 and 1989 in the US went to the top 20 percent. The bottom 80 percent was excluded from this growth and the bottom 40 percent saw their wealth decline in absolute terms."[28] Ten years later, "the richest 1 percent of Americans controlled 95 percent of the country's financial wealth. . . ."[29] In addition, "There is a growing inequity in pay. From 1976 to 2006, the average salary of workers in the bottom 90 percent of the income distribution—nearly everybody—rose by only 2.3 percent, to $38,800, tax data show. Among the top 10 percent, [however,] average salaries rose 57 percent, to $195,000."[30]

Why is this disparity an ethical concern? It favors speculation over rational investment[31] and drives up prices. Investment funds that bet on rising prices for oil[32] and other commodities, and on currency exchange rates, have turned the economy into "a very gigantic version of Las Vegas."[33] Even a fund manager, who benefits from this speculation, warns "that the widening divide among the

richest and everyone else" is a problem: "We are clearly in a period of excess, and we have to swing back to the middle or the center cannot hold."[34]

Economist Robert J. Samuelson agrees that "productivity gains (improvements in efficiency) are going disproportionately to those at the top," and that this growing inequality "threatens America's social compact."[35] By this "social compact" Samuelson means the implicit agreement among Americans to accept the authority of government and its lawfully imposed restrictions on individual freedom—which is expressed by individuals who obey the law, pay taxes, and participate in the political process.[36]

Two centuries ago Thomas Jefferson and Benjamin Franklin were so concerned about economic disparity weakening democratic government that they opposed legislation protecting inheritance rights.[37] Now economic globalization is increasing wealth disparity and threatening democracy, as well as undermining efforts to protect the natural environment.[38]

GLOBALIZATION AND ECONOMIC GROWTH

The neoclassical economic theory of *comparative advantage* holds that trade between two countries should not be restricted by government tariffs (taxes) or other restraints because, in general, "free trade" will benefit both societies.[39] "If our country can produce some set of goods at lower cost than a foreign country, and if the foreign country can produce some other set of goods at a lower cost than we can produce them, then clearly it would be best for us to trade our relatively cheaper goods for their relatively cheaper goods. In this way both countries may gain from trade."[40] This argument asserts that unregulated markets yield the common good.

Absolute Advantage

Today, however, goods are not produced by countries, as the theory of comparative advantage assumes, but by corporations that are often transnational. The theory of comparative advantage also assumes that capital will be invested at home in the country of the investor, but now capital goes wherever there is *absolute advantage* for profit.

"A country has absolute advantage if it can produce the good in question at a lower absolute cost than its trading partners."[41] To maximize profits, financial capital is invested where production costs are lowest. When trade takes place between two countries and one country has an absolute advantage in the goods traded, the other country will likely lose both income and jobs as financial capital is shifted to the country with absolute advantage in order to yield a higher return.[42]

Why is this relevant for environmental ethics? First, achieving absolute advantage usually involves minimizing the costs of extracting or processing natural resources and disposing of waste. Therefore, investors seeking absolute advantage in their pursuit of short-term profits avoid countries with strong environmental protection policies, or use their influence to weaken the enforcement of laws intended to protect the environment. This is why, in the past twenty years, "a large share of the world's polluting industries have migrated to the largest low-wage country of all, China, helping to turn big swaths of its landscape into an environmental disaster zone."[43]

Second, the theory of comparative advantage promises mutual benefits for countries involved in trade, but absolute advantage offers economic gain largely for investors. The pursuit of absolute advantage moves financial capital from one country to another, when there is greater profit to be realized, causing a loss of jobs and income in the first country that makes it even harder to protect or clean up its environment.[44]

Economic globalization is the pursuit of absolute advantage everywhere. "Globalization is the effective erasure of national boundaries for economic purposes.

National boundaries become totally porous with respect to goods and capital, and increasingly porous with respect to people, viewed in this context as cheap labor, or in some cases cheap human capital."[45] The main beneficiaries of economic globalization are multinational corporations, which gain power over economic decision-making as national governments lose control over their economies.

Neoclassical economists, however, defend economic globalization by arguing that it has many benefits, including:

- Greater efficiency in using resources and more rapid economic growth.
- More national specialization on the basis of competitive advantage.
- Global enforcement of "trade-related intellectual property rights."
- Control by international organizations over local and national decisions.[46]

Some of these claims, however, actually contradict the principles of neoclassical economics.

Contradictions

Consider the following three arguments concerning efficiency. First, neoclassical theory holds that economic *efficiency requires market competition* involving a large number of companies. The moral justification offered in support of market competition makes sense, because ensuring competition is fair to all and the overall consequences of competition are likely to be beneficial. Yet, *economic globalization reduces competition*, as only large businesses have the resources to compete in foreign markets. Moreover, these giant firms can lower their prices until small firms are forced into bankruptcy or into accepting a buyout.

"As a rule of thumb, many economists agree that if 40 percent of a given market is controlled by four firms, the market is no longer competitive. Such concentration is not at all unusual in the agricultural sector: in the US Midwest, four firms control well over 40 percent of the trade in most major agricultural commodities, and the top four agrochemical corporations reportedly control over 55 percent of the global market."[47] In 1995, with unusual candor, the chairman of one of these firms admitted: "There is not one grain of anything in the world that is sold in the free market."[48]

Second, neoclassical economists rail against *central planning* by governments as being inefficient. Why then should we assume that an economy dominated by the *corporate planning* of larger multinationals will be more efficient? Nobel laureate economist Ronald Coase argues that "firms are islands of central planning in a sea of market relationships."[49] We should not expect larger corporations due to globalization to increase economic efficiency.

Third, neoclassical theory *opposes regulatory controls over the market*, claiming that government intervention is inefficient. Yet, *globalization relies on regulations by international institutions*, which undercut local and national decision-making. Three of these institutions now wield enormous power over international trade: the International Monetary Fund (IMF), the World Bank, and the World Trade Organization (WTO).

Why are these ethical issues? Efficiency reduces waste, which means less environmental damage. In fact, transnational corporations may not only be less efficient, but may use their vast financial resources to resist environmental regulations imposed by national governments—by threatening to curtail investment in a nation, or by appealing to international institutions, like the WTO, to override a nation's laws. Economic globalization, therefore, is largely unjust as well as unsustainable.

Intergovernmental Institutions

In the last half of the twentieth century international institutions were created by the most powerful national governments to promote human welfare through economic development. The purposes of the IMF include facilitating international trade, promoting high employment and sustainable economic growth, and reducing poverty.[50] The World Bank was charged with the duty "by wise and prudent lending, to promote a policy of expansion of the world's economy."[51] The WTO was created to reduce tariffs and other barriers to multinational trade.[52]

These institutions, however, have uncritically promoted neoclassical economics. In 1991, Lawrence Summers, as chief economist at the World Bank, suggested that "the bank should encourage the world's dirty industries to move to developing countries. The forgone earnings of workers sickened or killed by pollution would be lower in low-wage countries, he noted, while people in poor countries also cared less about a clean environment. 'The economic logic of dumping a load of toxic waste in the lowest-wage country is impeccable,' he wrote."[53]

A 2007 report on the World Bank concludes: "The World Bank, financed by rich nations to reduce poverty in poor ones, has long neglected agriculture in impoverished sub-Saharan Africa, where most people depend on the farm economy for their livelihoods."[54] Imposing neoclassical economics via international intervention and regulation has not, in fact, contributed to the common good of the people in sub-Saharan Africa.[55]

Critics of the IMF and the World Bank argue that these institutions "are no longer serving the national interests of their member countries, according to their charters."[56] Renato Ruggiero, former director general of the WTO, has admitted that the purpose of the WTO is no longer to facilitate multilateral trade, but to create a globalized economy. "We are no longer writing the rules of interaction among separate national economies," he acknowledged in 1996, because the WTO is involved in "writing the constitution of a single global economy."[57]

What are the ethical issues here? Actions of the IMF, the World Bank, and the WTO have undercut the authority of national governments and strengthened transnational corporations, which has made it harder for countries to protect their natural environments. Also, the economic policies of these institutions have not alleviated the chronic poverty of hundreds of millions of people, and have increased the disparity between rich and poor.[58]

The total number of people in the world living on less than a dollar a day has declined between 1990 and 2002, although it remains at about 1.1 billion. But this decline in poverty is largely due to the rapid development of China's economy, which was achieved largely without World Bank assistance and regulation. Poor countries that have relied on World Bank loans—and have accepted conditions promoting free trade and requiring cuts in public spending for health and education—have generally not made progress in alleviating poverty.[59]

The consequences of WTO regulation are also discouraging. WTO rules prohibit national trade policies that promote small businesses, if the effect of such national policies may be interpreted as discriminating against foreign companies, even though such policies are needed for small businesses to compete with transnational corporations. The WTO also requires participating nations to protect intellectual property rights for twenty years, which puts domestic firms at a disadvantage in competing with foreign corporations that own most of these patents.[60]

Environmental Consequences

Neoclassical economic theory affirms the utilitarian goal of producing the greatest good for the greatest number of people. Do the consequences of economic globalization and the decisions of international institutions that support globalization meet this ethical standard?

Continuing poverty has a direct impact on the environment, for the poorest of the poor destroy their environment to survive when they are desperate. In many countries the poor have been pushed to marginal lands, and they have cut trees for wood and planted crops that can only be grown inefficiently. This unsustainable economic activity damages the local environment and reduces the capacity of the earth's ecosystems to replenish and recover.

Also, WTO policies promoting economic growth and trade have required national governments to set aside laws intended to limit environmental damage. "While technically countries are allowed to pass environmental legislation, the WTO frequently declares such laws barriers to trade."[61] For example, "Challenged by Venezuela, the United States was forced to allow the import of gasoline that does not comply with US Clean Air Act regulations."[62]

WTO support for global trade has benefits, but has also made it harder for countries to regulate businesses in order to protect nature.[63] "[T]he need to compete for market share reduces national incentives to legislate against externalities in what is known as standards-lowering competition (a race to the bottom). The country that does the poorest job of internalizing all social and environmental costs of production into its prices gets a competitive [absolute] advantage in international trade. More of world production shifts to countries that do the poor job of counting costs—a sure recipe for reducing the efficiency of global production."[64]

To sum up, support for economic globalization and neoclassical economics by the IMF, the World Bank, and the WTO has exacerbated environmental problems by:

- Stimulating environmentally destructive economic development.
- Decreasing the ability of national governments to protect the environment.
- Undermining local control over the use of natural resources.
- Supporting corporate power and the ideology of economic growth.[65]

To address these environmental issues, we have to change our global economic system.

GREEN ECONOMICS

Economist Duncan K. Foley wrote *A Guide to Economic Theory* "to give people more confidence in their own moral judgments" about economics.[66] He argues that simply promoting self-interest will not lead to the best world for the greatest number of persons, and that globalized trade will not "solve the problems of poverty and inequality."[67] Nor will an economic theory based on an uncritical view of self-interest and open markets resolve the environmental crisis.

Economist Paul Krugman agrees, quoting Franklin D. Roosevelt to make the point: "We have always known that heedless self-interest was bad morals. We know now that it is bad economics."[68] Krugman says, "These words apply perfectly to climate change. It's in the interest of most people (and especially their descendants) that somebody do something to reduce emissions of carbon dioxide and other greenhouse gases, but each individual would like that somebody to be somebody else. Leave it up to the free market, and in a few generations Florida will be underwater."[69]

What are we to do? Our analysis supports four ethical and economic presumptions.

Ethical and Economic Presumptions

First, *our goal should be an environmentally sustainable economy.*[70] We have a duty to protect our habitat, whether we understand this only as a duty to other people or also as a duty to other species. In addition, I argue that we have a duty to give our descendents moral consideration, because we feel our ancestors had a duty to consider our well-being in making decisions about the environment.[71]

Therefore, we must ensure economic policies that value ecosystem functions and biodiversity, as well as efficiency, by supporting laws that effectively regulate our use of finite natural resources. The harvest of renewable resources (such as fish and forests) should be limited to less than the optimal scale, so these populations may replenish. The extraction of nonrenewable natural resources that are being depleted (such as oil) should be taxed to fund the development of alternative ways, utilizing other material, to meet the same needs.

Second, *we should pay as we go for the costs of environmental externalities.* We cannot rely on an "invisible hand" to repair the environmental damage caused by economic development. Moreover, if we accept that our moral community includes future generations as well as the living, we have a duty to limit the adverse impact of our economy on the environment.[72]

Therefore, we should include in our economic accounting the investment needed to develop substitutes for nonrenewable resources being depleted, treat waste that exceeds the environment's absorption capacity, and restore degraded environments.[73] Environmental costs should be assessed by law to the business that generates them or, if this is not feasible, to the country under whose jurisdiction the business is operating.[74]

Third, *environmental policies should affirm the precautionary principle*, "which states that when a practice or product raises potentially significant threats of harm to human health or the environment, precautionary action should be taken to restrict or eliminate it."[75] This ethical principle puts the burden of proof for an action, which may likely harm the environment or human life, on those who propose to take the action, rather than on those who caution against it.

Reasoning on the basis of the precautionary principle involves rejecting the claim that environmental issues should be decided simply by predicting likely consequences. The precautionary principle asserts that we have a duty to do no harm to the environment when consequential predictions are not sufficiently confirmed by scientific evidence to address the risks of taking an action.

Ecosystems are poorly understood and thus unpredictable, so to be on the safe side economic policies should leave a margin for error. For instance, harvesting a renewable resource, such as fish or trees, should be limited to less than the predicted optimal scale, as this estimate is inherently imprecise.

Acting on the precautionary principle also requires *protecting ecosystem processes from market pricing*. The emergent properties of ecosystems (fund-services resources) are of great value for life, and the consequences of damaging these processes are unpredictable. Although market pricing is efficient for manufactured goods, it does not adequately protect ecosystem benefits. (The value of a forest, for example, is not simply the market value of its cut lumber.) Therefore, governments have a duty to protect the integrity of ecosystems.[76]

Fourth, *economic power should be constrained by the rule of law*. Both economic freedom and political freedom require decision-making with checks and balances, so that power is distributed and limited. This basic principle of civics is an ethical imperative as well.

At the global level this will likely require new international treaties that place the activities of international economic institutions, such as the IMF, the World Bank, and the WTO, under the political control of the United Nations. As this change would also strengthen national governments, it might foster a political process with greater checks and balances, which is the only effective way to promote economic trade and also protect the natural environment.

"The primacy of the political over the economic, combined with weakening global economic institutions [such as the World Bank, the IMF, and the WTO], would make possible economic decentralization. It would be possible for nations and even regions within nations to develop relatively self-sufficient economies. They would then trade with one another only as this did not weaken their capacity to meet their own basic needs. They would cooperate in establishing larger markets for goods that cannot be efficiently produced for smaller ones."[77]

In this new political and economic order, environmental problems would be the responsibility of those making decisions on the same scale as the problem. Garbage collection takes place in municipalities and thus should be managed by local authorities. "By contrast, global warming is fundamentally a global problem, because emissions anywhere affect the climate everywhere. Here we really do need global policy."[78]

Growing wealth disparity should be checked at all levels of the economy, and this means replacing the rhetoric of "free trade" with procedures that ensure *fair trade*.[79] Both employees and the environment should be protected by laws that are effective and fair. Workers ought to be guaranteed a living wage and safe working conditions, and producing and trading goods should be subject to regulations that ensure environmental sustainability.[80] This means international as well as national constraints on economic activity.

Our primary focus, however, should be local. Seeing the world as a global economy through the lens of neoclassical economics has hidden for too long an alternative view of the world as a biosphere of diverse political and economic communities. Embracing this new view now matters.

"For example, most of the rapid deforestation of the planet is for the sake of export, either of lumber or of beef that can be raised on formerly forested land. If the focus of attention is on the local economy, the value of the standing forest counts for more. In this and other ways, in regions which were not heavily oriented to export, the people would often be concerned that their region continue to provide a habitable home to their children, and they would be more likely to adopt sustainable relations to the environment."[81]

Steady-State Economy

Unfortunately, "Instead of recognizing that the human economy is a dependent subset of the biosphere, many economists still assume that economic growth and liberalization, with wealth creation, is the key to affording adequate environmental management. Environmental quality is believed to be most effectively achieved through market forces, even as social and environmental costs are 'externalized.'"[82]

To ensure that economic development is ecologically sustainable, perhaps our long-term goal should be a *steady-state economy*—an economic system that would "maintain constant stocks of wealth and people at levels that are suffi-

cient for a long and good life."[83] John Stuart Mill, who supported both political and economic freedom, argued that "a stationary condition of capital and
population implies no stationary state of human improvement. There would
be as much scope as ever for all kinds of mental culture, and moral and social
progress . . . when minds cease to be engrossed by the art of getting on."[84]

What might such an economy be like? "Material well-being would almost
certainly be indexed by the quality of the existing inventory of goods, rather
than by the rate of physical turnover. Planned obsolescence would be elimi-
nated. Excessive consumption and waste would become causes of embarrass-
ment, rather than symbols of prestige."[85]

This would mean discarding the gross national product (GNP) and gross
domestic product (GDP) indices[86] used to measure economic growth, for these
do not measure economic well-being but only the quantity of economic activity. "GNP reflects all expenditures, including many corrective measures such as
policing, prisons, hospital services, homeless shelters, lawsuits, and every form
of pollution and waste. . . . The onwards-and-upwards rise of GNP presumes
that the more people spend, the better their lives must become. But GNP
makes no distinction between desirables and undesirables; it only distinguishes
more from less."[87]

The genuine progress indicator (GPI)[88] and the index of sustainable economic welfare (ISEW)[89] offer alternative ways of measuring economic success.
"Computation of the ISEW begins with personal consumption, but then ad-
justs this in relation to income distribution. (Our assumption is that the well-
being of the society as a whole is affected by the condition of the poorest.) The
index then adds for household services, chiefly the contribution of housewives.
It subtracts for 'defensive costs,' that is, costs that result from economic growth
and the social changes, such as urbanization, that accompany it. (For example,
the cost of commuting to work should not be viewed as an addition to welfare
just because it adds to the GNP.) This applies also to the cost of pollution.
Since it is an index of *sustainable* welfare, it subtracts for the reduction of natural capital, and adds or subtracts for change in the net international position."[90]

Also, we need to construct "economic models that provide a better cost accounting of the short- and long-term impacts of real-world economic activities
and that privilege, through taxation and incentives, the development and implementation of nonpolluting technologies and processes."[91]

Becoming a Green Economy

Given the complexity of the real economy, "the task of developing new economic
models must be an intensely interdisciplinary activity. Any realistic evaluation of

the costs of doing business in this economy will require the use of models in which economic systems, or parts, are treated as open systems that mutually interact within the single system of the whole biosphere."[92]

We must *transform our growth economy into a green economy.* Only a joint effort by business and government leaders, at the prodding of citizens, will lead to the economic and political changes needed to make our industrial society environmentally sustainable. William McDonough and Michael Braungart, who make their living by creating sustainable products, buildings, and communities, are convinced that this is our future.

"We believe that humans can incorporate the best of technology and culture so that our civilized places reflect a new view. Buildings, systems, neighborhoods, and even whole cities can be entwined with surrounding ecosystems in ways that are mutually enriching. We agree that it is important to leave some natural places to thrive on their own, without undue human interference or habitation. But we also believe that industry can be so safe, effective, enriching, and intelligent that it need not be fenced off from other human activity."[93]

McDonough and Braungart affirm that we will have an environmentally sustainable and productive economy when people and industries are committed to creating:

- buildings that, like trees, produce more energy than they consume and purify their own waste water
- factories that produce effluents that are drinking water
- products that, when their useful life is over, do not become useless waste but can be tossed onto the ground to decompose and become food for plants and animals and nutrients for soil; or, alternately, that can return to industrial cycles to supply high-quality raw materials for new products
- billions, even trillions, of dollars' worth of materials accrued for human and natural purposes each year
- transportation that improves the quality of life while delivering goods and services.[94]

Chapter 14 pursues this commitment to building green and recycling waste in an urban ecology.

QUESTIONS—ETHICS AND ECONOMICS: THE COMMON GOOD

1. Should the purpose of the economy be human well-being? Explain your reasoning.

2. Adam Smith believed that an unregulated economic system would yield the common good. How would you argue for or against this belief?

3. Identify a renewable resource and a nonrenewable resource. What "costs" of using natural resources have neoclassical economists generally ignored?

4. Give an example of an ecosystem benefit (fund-service resource). In calculating the consequences of our actions, how might we assess the value of this natural resource?

5. Why has neoclassical economics treated air and water pollution as externalities?

6. Explain the reasoning for the theory of comparative advantage. How has economic globalization undermined this theory?

7. What does absolute advantage mean, and who benefits most from it?

8. What does the ethical presumption that "we should pay as we go" mean with respect to externalities? How should responsibility be assessed?

9. Why is recognizing "environmental uncertainty" important for both economics and ethics?

10. What do poverty and increasing wealth disparity have to do with environmental ethics?

11. How has economic globalization affected the control of investment and trade? Illustrate how WTO policies may clash with national environmental policies.

12. How would a green economy differ from a growth economy?

PART II
Constructing and Testing Ethical Presumptions

In part 2, chapters 4–7 consider arguments for intrinsic values concerning our duty, character, relationships, and rights. Chapter 8 analyzes ethical arguments that rely only on predicting the likely consequences of taking an action.

Chapter 4 concerns *doing our duty.* Traditional moral philosophy holds that we have a direct duty to respect others and only an indirect duty to nature, but Gandhi affirmed a duty of nonviolence to all animals. How are we to understand our duty to ecosystems, species, landscapes, and animals in our care? Jews and Muslims accept a duty to obey the teachings of their scriptures, which include a responsibility for the earth. John Locke and Thomas Jefferson argued that governments have a duty to protect God given rights and to preserve the commons for future generations. Following the Golden Rule seems to mean accepting a duty to future generations and also to people in this generation who are struggling to survive.

Chapter 5 considers *being a good person.* The natural law and Tao traditions affirm what reason and nature reveal about character and virtue. Stories of Antigone and Socrates, as well as children's stories, portray being a good person, but do not directly address the issue of living more ecologically. Christians find in the Bible what loving our neighbor means and now teach that God expects us to be good stewards of the earth. Does it seem reasonable that persons who respect and appreciate nature will live more frugally? Will emphasizing the beauty of nature and the wonder of life persuade others to have greater respect for nature?

Chapter 6 explores why *caring relationships* are crucial for ethics. Native American and traditional Buddhist cultures value relationships with animals in ways that challenge modern culture. Advocates of "deep ecology" assert that Eastern spirituality is more ecological than Western religious thought and claim that all organisms have equal rights. Ecofeminists argue that the domination of nature and women in Eastern and Western cultures must be addressed together, if we are to embrace a more caring approach to ethics that will not only protect the equal rights of women and men, but also transform our relationship with nature. And the law has begun to protect ecosystem integrity.

Chapter 7 concerns *protecting rights*. Deontological ethics justifies recognizing the rights of persons. International human rights law affirms civil and political rights, as well as economic, social, and cultural rights. International covenants and the laws of many nations assert the right of peoples to sustainable development and the right of persons to a healthy environment, but the United States has not recognized these rights. Western jurisprudence requires humane treatment for animals in our care, and has begun to protect endangered species. As we extend moral consideration to some animals, should we also affirm animal rights?

Chapter 8 considers *predicting consequences*. Instead of affirming intrinsic values, many argue that actions resulting in greater happiness are morally right. This means acting on our predictions of the future, even though our knowledge is limited. Cost-benefit analysis is an effective way to value the financial impacts of environmental decisions, but should not be used to assess damage to ecosystem integrity or the denial of human rights. Thus, a consequential approach to environmental ethics is necessary, but not sufficient. Science is crucial for predicting consequences about environmental decisions, but should not replace moral reasoning. Should we include the suffering of animals in consequential predictions? If this seems reasonable in some circumstances, how are we to compare human and nonhuman suffering?

4

Duty

NATURE AND FUTURE GENERATIONS

In this chapter we look first at Immanuel Kant's argument for our duty to act rationally, which is a milestone in moral philosophy, and then at Gandhi's reasoning that doing our duty requires nonviolent action.[1] We consider reasons for asserting a duty not to litter and draw inferences from this argument for the care of nature.

We also review Jewish and Muslim teaching about nature, and note the reasons given in Western thought for a duty to protect public land. Then we consider our duty to future generations and to those who are poor, before assessing what our duty might be for animals, species, ecosystems, and landscapes.

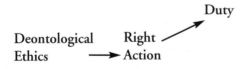

DOING OUR DUTY

How do we know our duty? The answer given by Immanuel Kant (1724–1804) continues to be the foundation of deontological ethics. Kant lived a century after Isaac Newton explained the mechanics of the world without relying on divine intervention (except for the act of creation), which may be why Kant shunned religious reasoning despite being a Christian. Kant claimed to rely on reason alone in asserting that our duty is simply to do what is rational.

More than a century and a half later, when colonized societies in Africa and Asia were struggling for independence, Mahatma Gandhi (1869–1948) transformed the Hindu idea of duty, which is rooted in the caste traditions of Indian culture, into an imperative to seek truth-power (*satyagraha*) through nonviolent action (*ahimsa*). For Gandhi, too, our duty is rational.

Rational Imperative

Kant argued that reason enables us to do our duty because it reflects the moral law within us. Doing our duty means acting on our conscience, which Kant saw as our rational nature. Actions are ethical, he asserted, when we do with a good will what reason reveals to be right. This does not mean acting to achieve the best consequences. Instead, it means acting rationally with good intentions.

For Kant, an ethical principle is rational if we all, as rational beings, agree that it may be applied without any exceptions. Such a *categorical imperative*, he argued, is the opposite of hypothetical thinking, which involves conditional statements, such as "I would take an action, if I thought it would have primarily beneficial consequences."

Kant reasoned that acting in a way which has universal application requires respecting the dignity of every person. Our autonomy is linked to our rationality, which is distinctly human. Therefore, we contradict ourselves and act irrationally, if we treat other persons as less than ends in themselves, by using them as means to gain our own ends.[2]

Moral philosophers rely on Kant's deontological argument on behalf of our rationality and autonomy to justify asserting the rights of individuals. Chapter 7 considers this argument and the development of human rights law.

From Karma to Ahimsa

Traditional Hindu society is divided into castes having different activities, and morality in this tradition involves performing the duties identified for each caste. Hindu teaching affirms that those who do their duty will eventually achieve release from the suffering of this world through the chain of cause and effect (*karma*) that leads to liberation from the cycle of rebirth.[3]

The Bhagavad Gita, a Hindu classic, teaches that doing our duty means renouncing "the fruits" of our actions. In this ancient tale the god Krishna tells Arjuna, who believes that fighting a battle is futile, that he cannot foresee the consequences that will come from his decisions, because he is a mortal, and thus should simply do his duty as a warrior, leaving the future to *karma*.

In the context of the Indian struggle for independence, Gandhi interpreted this story figuratively to mean that everyone has a duty to pursue the truth through nonviolent action, leaving the consequences to God. Gandhi reasoned that taking nonviolent action is the only way to verify that we are not acting to benefit ourselves. In the practice of *satyagraha*, he wrote, we should "always try to overcome evil by good, anger by love, untruth by truth, *himsa* (violence) by *ahimsa*."[4]

Gandhi agreed with Kant that we should not use others for our own gain and should always try to act with a good will and without ulterior motive. His conviction that moral action, truth, and God are one is a Hindu way of affirming that we should always act on rational principles that apply universally.

Duty to Nature?

Kant's categorical imperative does not extend to animals, as he argues we have a duty to respect human autonomy because we are rational beings, and this is not true of other organisms.[5] "So far as animals are concerned, we have no direct duties. Animals are not self-conscious and are there merely as a means to an end. That end is man."[6]

Yet, Kant realized that Newtonian mechanics does not explain the natural world. Half a century before Darwin published *The Origin of Species*, Kant wrote: "Nature organizes itself."[7] Every organism, he argued, is "both an organized and a self-organizing being, which therefore can be called a natural purpose."[8] As things (such as machines) are organized, but not self-organizing, Kant reasoned that organisms are not things. Yet, he held, humans have direct duties only to each other, and only indirect duties with respect to nonhuman organisms and things.[9]

Gandhi's argument for respecting all persons does not rely on their individual autonomy and rationality, but instead affirms the rationality manifested in *karma*. As the cycle of life, death, and rebirth offers an accounting of moral action over time that includes animals as well as humans, Hindus believe that we have a duty to respect all organisms. Therefore, Gandhi was a vegetarian and thought everyone should be.[10] "The greatness of a nation and its moral progress," he wrote, "can be judged by the way its animals are treated."[11]

Gandhi's argument for nonviolence to animals is religious and rational. The Bhagavad Gita is read as a religious text, and Krishna is a Hindu god. Yet, Krishna's injunction to Arjuna is more a rational argument than a divine command. Krishna urges Arjuna to have faith in *karma*, rather than in his limited ability to foresee the future.

RIGHT ACTION

Kant sees that animals have natural purpose, but sees no reason to conclude that humans have any direct duty to creatures that are not autonomous and rational.[12] Gandhi argues that our duty of nonviolence rationally requires respect for all life, but allows that consequential reasoning may justify setting this presumption aside, if there is an irreconcilable conflict between human life and other forms of life.[13] Kant and Gandhi agree and disagree because they have different worldviews. Kant sees nonhuman life as lacking the rationality that defines our moral community, whereas Gandhi sees *karma* as defining a moral community that includes both nonhuman and human life.

Darwin's argument for natural selection emphasizes random change and thus undermines Kant's reasoning that we should think of every organism as having its own "natural purpose." Our current view of evolution, however, supports the ecological argument that *nature has value for itself.* It does not confirm the Hindu belief in *karma*,[14] but it does give us reason to accept a duty for all life. "Insofar as we regard any organism, species population, or life community as an entity having intrinsic worth, we believe that it must never be treated as if it were a mere object or thing whose entire value lies in being instrumental to the good of some other entity."[15]

To clarify how our understanding of duty differs from the reasoning of Kant and Gandhi, it may be helpful to consider how we might argue for a duty not to litter.

Respect for Others

It seems clear that we have a duty not to throw litter in our neighbor's yard, because it is well accepted that *we should respect the rights of our neighbors* to their privacy and property. If asked why we should respect the rights of other persons, we could refer to the arguments of Kant and Gandhi, or we might state a widely accepted moral principle, such as the Golden Rule: "Do to others, as you would have them do to you."

This is, in fact, a text from Christian scripture[16] that has many parallels in other religious traditions,[17] and in the next section we will consider what it means to have a duty because a scripture says that God commands it. Yet, the Golden Rule is usually not invoked as being right because it is in the Bible, but because it makes sense. We do not want neighbors putting litter in our yard, so it is rational to treat our neighbors the way we want them to treat us.

This argument is less useful, however, in considering a law that would impose a penalty for littering along the highway. As the side of the road is not anyone's property, tossing trash from a car window is not the same as throwing it into a neighbor's yard. Littering a public space does not seem to violate the rights of others in the way that putting trash in their yard does.

Suppose, however, that the law against littering is an ordinance passed by a town meeting and, as citizens of the town, we were invited to participate in making this decision. Would these facts strengthen the argument that we have a duty to support the law? Even if only a majority of those voting favored the law, we would probably find it reasonable to conclude that a town has the authority to make such a law and, if it did, that everyone has a duty to obey the law.

Thus, *our commitment to abide by rules made in a fair way for our community* seems to generate a duty. If an issue is within the jurisdiction of the decision-making body, and the procedures used for making a law are fair, and the law itself is reasonable, then we accept that everyone has a duty to obey the law, whether or not they voted for it or took part in making it. This kind of reasoning supports the idea of *citizenship* (the duty of every citizen) and provides a rational basis for the rule of law and representative government.[18]

Respect for Nature

Do we, however, have a duty not to litter because we have a duty to nature? The question here is whether a landscape has intrinsic value. Kant held that we have no duty to the natural world, as it lacks rationality. Gandhi affirmed that we have a duty to animals, because they participate in the moral rationality of *karma*, but this tells us nothing about the intrinsic value of nature. Arguing that we have a duty to care for nature for its own sake means affirming that a landscape has *intrinsic worth* apart from anyone's use and enjoyment of it— that fields, forests, and beaches have *intrinsic value*, which we should respect by accepting a duty not to litter there.

Chapter 2 argues that the intrinsic worth of nature rests on biological facts: that every organism is self-organizing and pursues its own good, and that ecosystems are self-organizing and life-sustaining. Accepting this argument seems to justify a law against littering anywhere, which creates *a duty to protect the environment simply because it has intrinsic value.* Reasoning by analogy would allow us to extend this duty to other ways of respecting the environment, such as recycling, reducing pollution, and protecting biodiversity.

We have other duties, of course, and these may be in conflict with our duty to protect the environment. For example, our duty to care for ecosystems may clash with our duty to help others realize their economic rights through economic development. How are we to resolve such conflicts of duty? We might consider *the kind of person that we think we should be*, or we might *predict the likely consequences* of taking an action. If we are religious, we may turn to the religious teachings of our tradition for ethical guidance.

COMMANDED BY GOD: JEWS AND MUSLIMS

Jews, Christians, and Muslims have faith in one God, who has created nature and given human beings responsibility for it. Jewish and Christian scriptures share the same creation stories in Genesis 1 and 2, and Muslim scripture acknowledges these narratives. The ethical duty that human beings have with respect to the natural world is defined, by each of these religious traditions, in its scripture and in teachings about these scriptures.

Jews and Muslims read the commandments in their scriptures as giving humans a *duty to care for nature*. For Christians, however, the commandments of Jewish scripture are superseded by the commandment to love one another and others, which is embodied in the story of Jesus. Being a loving person is the heart of Christian ethics, rather than doing our duty. So, I take up Christian teaching about nature in chapter 5, where we consider arguments about character.

Jewish Teaching

Jewish scripture begins with the story of creation in Genesis 1. The God who creates the cosmos and all life in six days, and then rests on the seventh day (which becomes the Sabbath in the Jewish tradition), affirms that every aspect of creation is good. In this narrative God creates man and woman, and then gives them responsibility over life on earth.

The fourth of the Ten Commandments recorded in Jewish scripture asserts the duty to: "Remember the Sabbath and keep it holy" (Exodus 20:10, Deuteronomy 5:14). This commandment requires rest for livestock, as well as rest for those who use livestock in their work. Other duties in Jewish scripture concern the welfare of domesticated animals. "There is also the law forbidding the yoking together of animals of unequal strength (Deuteronomy 22:10), for this would cause pain to the weaker animal. And one is not permitted to muzzle an ox during the threshing of the grain (Deuteronomy 25:4),"[19] allowing the ox to eat what falls to the ground.

Genesis 1:29 in Jewish scripture gives only plants to humans for food, but Genesis 9:3 revises this earlier commandment and adds meat to the human diet. Genesis 9:4 requires respect for animals that are slaughtered. "This limitation on the eating of blood, the eating of life itself, became the basis for the laws of kosher slaughtering, laws designed to minimize the pain of animals being killed. Although eating meat was thought essential for human survival, it did not nullify an obligation for compassion for all living animals."[20]

Deuteronomy 20:19–20 also prohibits the "wanton destruction" of nature: "When you besiege a city for a long time . . . you shall not destroy its trees by wielding an ax against them. You may eat of them, but you may not cut them down. . . . Only the trees which you know are not trees for food you may destroy and cut down, that you may build siege-works against the city."[21] Jewish scripture teaches a duty to care for trees, because trees have use value. Jews also refer to this text to condemn vandalism.[22] Clearly, the teaching expresses a concern for the character of Jewish life, rather than a duty to protect the environment because it has intrinsic value.

Finally, the commandments in Jewish scripture that define duties concerning animals and plants apply only to domesticated animals and cultivated plants. The suffering of wild animals was of no concern to those who wrote the Jewish scriptures, as the world "belongs to God" because "it is literally God's world."[23] Psalm 24:1 affirms: "The earth is the LORD's, and the fullness thereof; the world, and they that dwell therein."

Muslim Teaching

The Qur'an teaches: "It is God [*Allah* is the Arabic word for God] who created heaven and earth . . . that you may distinguish yourselves by your better deeds" (Surah 11:7). Muslims affirm "that God owns" the universe and that "nature is a blessed gift of God" given to human beings, who are to use it responsibly.[24] The Qur'an does not include commandments concerning the treatment of domesticated animals and cultivated trees, but Islamic teaching recalls that the first caliph ordered his army "not to cut down trees, not to abuse a river, not to harm animals and [to] be always kind and gentle to God's creation, even to your enemies."[25]

Nature is not sacred for Muslims, but is seen as reflecting God's will. "To attribute sacredness to nature is to associate other beings with God," and this is against the faith of Muslims in "the Oneness of God."[26] This transcendental vision, however, "does not relegate nature to the secular or profane. It is not a duality of separate domains of God the creator as sacred and the creation as profane. It is rather a totality, a dependency where nature reflects the glory of sacredness but is not itself sacred."[27] The Qur'an gives responsibility for nature to humans, who on earth are the *khalifah* (vice-regents or managers) of God's world.

Humans are given this duty because, the Qur'an teaches, they have the capacity to know good and evil (Surah 91:7–8) and also the ability to prevent evil

(Surah 79:40 and Surah 90:8–9). Moreover, the Qur'an records that humans have agreed to accept this responsibility: "God offered his trust to heaven and earth and mountain, but they shied away in fear and rejected it. Humans only carried it" (Surah 33:72).[28] This trust is implied in acknowledging, as all Muslims do, that there is no God but God.

There are no divine commandments in Islam concerning care for the earth, for the Qur'an simply commands that Muslims do good deeds. Yet, there are teachings identifying human life with all life. The Qur'an states that God "made from water every living thing" (Surah 12:30) and "created humans from water" (Surah 24:45). The Qur'an also affirms that life is communal. "There is not an animal on earth, nor a being that flies on its wings, but (forms a part) of a community like you" (Surah 6:38).[29]

There is also concern in the Islamic tradition for animal suffering. The prophet Muhammad reportedly said, "Verily Allah has prescribed equity (*ihsan*) in all things. Thus if you kill, kill well, and if you slaughter, slaughter well. Let each of you sharpen his blade and let him spare suffering to the animal he slaughters."[30]

The Qur'an commands humans to use the earth's resources. "God has subjected to your [use] all things on the heavens and on earth" (Surah 31:20). And, "It is He who made the earth manageable for you, so . . . enjoy of the sustenance which He furnishes" (Surah 67:15). But Muslims are to guard against waste: "Eat and drink but waste not in indulging in excess, surely God does not approve" (Surah 7:31).[31] Muslims must weigh their duty to manage the earth against their duty to use and enjoy its bounty, as both requirements are in the Qur'an.

We see, therefore, that Jews and Muslims do not simply assert divine commandments about caring for nature but also give reasons. Jewish teaching reasons that rest is good for livestock as well as humans, that ritual slaughter avoids unnecessary suffering, that trees are useful and should not be wasted. Muslim teaching affirms that humans are part of nature and have accepted duties to use the bounty of the earth, without squandering it, and to minimize suffering in slaughtering animals.

GOVERNMENT, LAND, AND PROPERTY

The American Declaration of Independence asserts, as self-evident truths, "that all men are created equal" and are "endowed by their Creator with certain unalienable Rights."[32] The claim is that the creator has given rights to all men that cannot be set aside for any reason (cannot be alienated) and thus should be recognized by everyone. The Fourteenth Amendment to the Constitution of the United States has been held by the Supreme Court to extend equal protection of the law to all persons.

Moral Claims

The American Declaration of Independence offers a moral argument to justify rebellion from British rule: "When in the Course of human events, it becomes necessary for one people to dissolve the political bands which have connected them with another, and to assume among the powers of the earth, the separate and equal station to which the Laws of Nature and of Nature's God entitle them, a decent respect to the opinions of mankind requires that they should declare the causes which impel them to the separation."[33]

Jefferson and other founders of the United States were strongly influenced by the writings of the British moral philosopher John Locke (1632–1704), who argued that those who govern have a duty to God to seek the common good. "Their Power," Locke wrote, "*is limited to the public good of the Society* . . . [because] the Law of Nature stands as an Eternal Rule to all Men, *Legislators* as well as others."[34]

Locke also asserted that the labor a person adds to land justifies claiming it as his *private property.* He affirmed, however, that the right to private property is limited in three respects: no harm should result to others from such a claim of private property, enough property that is "as good"[35] must be left in common for others, no one has a right to property beyond the ability to use it.

Locke believed that the Law of Nature has given human beings property to enjoy. "As much as any one can make use of to any advantage of life before it spoils; so much he may by his labor fix a Property in. Whatever is beyond this, is more than his share, and belongs to others. Nothing was made by God for Man to spoil or destroy."[36]

These arguments assert our duty, and the duty of every government, to:

- Respect the inalienable rights of others.
- Accept that individual rights are not absolute but are limited by the public good.
- Protect natural resources and use them productively.
- Ensure sufficient "good" land for common use.

Locke and Jefferson affirmed that the Law of Nature gives the right of property to persons who put it to good use. This right is necessary, in Jefferson's words, for "the pursuit of happiness." Yet, Locke and Jefferson also thought that this right must be limited for the public good.

This tradition of thought is relevant for identifying our duties today with respect to the environment. For instance, this moral heritage opposes any claim that the land we own (in law, our *real property*) is simply ours to do with as we please. If we accept the ethical arguments of Locke and Jefferson, we do not have a right to use our land in a way that undermines public welfare, and we have a duty to protect land held in trust for common use.

Public Trust

The duty to conserve publicly held land includes a duty to ensure that everyone has fair access to the use of this commons. As the federal government owns almost 30 percent of the land in the United States,[37] federal management of public land has a significant impact on the nation's environment and thus should be of concern to every US citizen.

The notion of "public trust" came into American jurisprudence as part of the common law tradition, and now is the foundation for land use regulations imposed by governments to protect natural resources.[38] Land use decisions by the federal government, however, are limited by the final clause of the Fifth Amendment to the US Constitution, which asserts that private property may only be taken for public use and with just compensation.[39] What is known as the "taking" clause of the Constitution has been used to protect private property rights, when these clash with securing the public environment. Thus, preserving public land in the United States for future generations depends on how courts interpret the Fifth Amendment.[40]

In 1970 the Council on Environmental Quality recommended that a national land-use policy be adopted, and President Nixon sent this recommendation to Congress with the following statement. "We have treated our land as if it were a limitless resource. Traditionally Americans have felt that what they do with their own land is their own business. This attitude has been a natural outgrowth of the pioneer spirit. Today, we are coming to realize that our land is finite, while our population is growing. The uses to which our generation puts the land can either expand or severely limit the choices our children will have. The time has come when we must accept the idea that none of us has a right to abuse the land, and that on the contrary society as a whole has a legitimate interest in proper land use."[41]

Because the Nixon administration and Congress did not agree on a federal approach to land use planning, this duty has been left to state, county, and municipal governments.

APPLYING THE GOLDEN RULE

We tend to think of the Golden Rule as concerning only how one person should treat another person. Yet, this ethical principle, which has parallels in many cultural traditions,[42] affirms a moral community that includes not only our neighbors, and even our enemies, but also future generations. "Doing to others as we would have them do to us" involves acting with concern for the welfare of our society, which is always directed toward the future.

Duty to Future Generations

This is why Jefferson strongly supported the right of private property, but also argued against using laws to protect inheritance rights. He reasoned that inheriting wealth would undermine democracy by reinforcing an imbalance of power in the society between the rich and the rest of the population. Benjamin Franklin believed, as did Jefferson, in "restricting property rights only to what we can use ourselves, only to what we are entitled to through labor (not what we inherit), and only to what we can use in ways that serve the common good."[43]

This moral argument asserts a duty for a generation concerning what it passes on to future generations. Jefferson and Franklin thought it was imperative that *economic and political power be distributed* throughout society and not be concentrated in the hands of a wealthy minority. They sought to ensure that the laws of the new republic would fulfill this moral duty. Although Locke did not oppose inheritance rights, he did require that "property rights be subject to the proviso that as much and as good be left for others," and this implies that "the use of land ought to be subject to the proviso that as many and as good opportunities be left for members of future generations as for members of present ones."[44]

Accepting a duty to future generations to reduce our impact on nature seems much like leaving a public park (after having a picnic in it) in as good condition as we found it, so that those coming later to enjoy this common space would find it as we did.[45] Whether or not we think that our ancestors acted responsibly, it seems reasonable that we should act with concern for those who will inhabit the earth after us.[46]

Laws That Are Fair

The public welfare requires not only ensuring *an equitable distribution of resources* over time, but also among those alive at any time. For "what ethical system can justify a concern for the well-being of those yet to be born, while not caring for the well-being of those alive today?"[47] If it is reasonable to conclude that we have a duty of care to future generations, then surely we also have *a duty to those in our generation who are struggling to survive.*

A limited supply of oil, greater demand for oil worldwide, and market speculation have already caused sharp increases in the price of gasoline and food, and there is no reason to think that global markets will produce lower prices in the future. To help those who are struggling financially during the difficult transition to a more sustainable economy, we have a duty to support policies that check wealth disparity. These include ending public subsidies for the exploitation of nature, supporting a more progressive tax system, and providing (in the United States) a universal health care system.[48]

The *public subsidies* for mining, logging, grazing cattle on federal land, irrigating crops, and for maintaining price supports for commodities such as corn, milk, and cotton, benefit the rich far more than those with low incomes.[49] We have a duty, therefore, to support economic and environmental policies that would phase out these unfair government expenditures. Making these changes will also help to attain a more sustainable economy.

A *progressive tax system* recognizes that government expenditures on infrastructure disproportionately benefit those who are wealthy, so taxing them at higher rates is fair. Also, more progressive taxes would reduce wealth disparity. In addition, lower taxes for those who are struggling to survive not only help people in need, but also contribute to the public welfare. For those who are unable to pay their bills create social costs.[50]

Finally, families struggling to make ends meet in the United States spend much of their income on health care.[51] A *universal health care system*, like the Canadian single-payer system, would likely save money (as health care in Canada is more efficient than health care in the United States) and also reduce costs for most of those now without health insurance.[52] Implementing the Golden Rule in this way would also address the social problems created by increasing wealth disparity.

Correcting an Inequity

How are the costs of cleaning up our environmental mess to be fairly distributed? Moral philosopher Henry Shue responds to this question by arguing for the following principle: "When a party has in the past taken an unfair advantage of others by imposing costs upon them without their consent, those who have been unilaterally put at a disadvantage are entitled to demand that in the future the offending party shoulder burdens that are unequal at least to the extent of the unfair advantage previously taken, in order to restore equality."[53]

There is considerable evidence that industrialized societies have unfairly taken advantage of less powerful societies in accumulating wealth through economic development that has degraded the environment. We might rationally conclude, therefore, that industrialized societies have a duty to pay for a larger portion of the costs required to rectify this inequity.[54]

Peter Singer thinks this is clearly true with regard air pollution and increasing greenhouse gases. "To put it in terms a child could understand, as far as the atmosphere is concerned, the developed nations broke it. If we believe that people should contribute to fixing something in proportion to their responsibility for breaking it, then the developed nations owe it to the rest of the world to fix the problem with the atmosphere."[55]

In response to the objection that *our generation* did not cause this unfairness, it is reasonable to argue that our generation has nonetheless greatly benefited from the inequity. "[O]ne generation of a rich industrial society is not unrelated to other generations past and future. All are participants in enduring economic structures. Benefits and costs, and rights and responsibilities, carry across generations."[56] Chapter 9 explains how this argument for equity is now being asserted through international law.

ANIMALS, SPECIES, ECOSYSTEMS, AND LANDSCAPES

How are we to understand our duty with respect to animals? The diverse worldviews of Kant and Gandhi led them to very different conclusions, but adopting either point of view would not lead us to care for ecosystems or landscapes. Current science, however, as we saw in chapter 2, helps us distinguish our duties: for animals in human culture and for animals in the wild.

Human Culture

In human culture we have a duty to provide humane care for sentient animals. This includes our pets as well as animals raised to be eaten.[57] This also means that animals used in research should only be subjected to pain when the research is crucial for human well-being, as in the testing of vaccines, and all research involving animals should minimize their suffering.

Those who embrace the Hindu tradition of *karma* also have a duty to refrain from eating meat and to avoid violence to animals unless they threaten human life. There are other ethical arguments for being a vegetarian, and we consider some of these in chapters 8, 9, and 12.

In the Wild

Protecting animals in the wild means preserving their habitats, not preventing some animals from killing and eating other animals. Thus, our duty with respect to wild nature is to care for ecosystems and species, and not for individual animals, unless our intervention has put an animal at risk. Also, whenever we intervene in wild areas, by creating national parks or building roads, we have a duty to *minimize our impact on the environment.*

If biodiversity is threatened by human activity, we may have a duty to try to *restore an ecosystem.* Wolves are a key predator in Yellowstone National Park, as they keep the deer population from outgrowing its natural food supply. After most of the wolves in and around the park were killed by ranchers trying to protect their cattle, federal policy changes restricted the killing of wolves and reintroduced them into the park.[58]

Do we have a duty of care for *landscapes*? Federal laws and regulations define such a duty for some landscapes, such as the Grand Canyon, Yellowstone, Yosemite, and the Everglades, as a way of protecting the commons of humanity. Chapter 13 considers in greater detail the conservation and preservation of forests, deserts, and wetlands.

Duties and Rights

Having a duty to other persons generally means that they have a right to expect us to do our duty. When we affirm *human rights,* we mean both that every person has certain rights as a human being, and that every person and every government has a duty to respect and protect these rights. Duties and rights are often derived together, as part of a deontological argument.

Yet, *not every duty implies a right.*[59] It does not follow that our duty to refrain from littering requires us to ascribe a right (to be kept free of litter) to a landscape or an ecosystem. Nor does affirming a duty to future generations make it necessary for us to attribute rights to future generations. Also, having a duty to care for animals does not mean that we must assert, on behalf of animals, a right to our care. We return to this issue in chapter 7.

QUESTIONS—DUTY: NATURE AND FUTURE GENERATIONS

1.   Summarize in your own words Kant's argument for duty. How does he distinguish our duty with respect to humans and to (nonhuman) animals?

2.   Why does Gandhi affirm that we have a duty to act with nonviolence? Give a reason for and against his argument that, to act rationally, we should be vegetarians.

3.   Make an argument for the duty not to litter. Is your reasoning about utility or intrinsic worth? Raise a critical question about your argument.

4.   Identify two duties in Jewish scripture for the care of animals. In Jewish scripture, who is responsible for wild nature?

5.   Identify two of the reasons given in the Qur'an for why humans have a duty to care for nature. What does the Qur'an say about using natural resources?

6.   According to Jefferson, where do inalienable rights come from? Identify two of these.

7.   Explain how Locke's arguments concerning property are relevant for environmental ethics.

8.   Make an argument for having a duty to future generations. Why did Jefferson and Franklin believe this duty requires the prohibition of inheritance rights?

9.   Give a reason for asserting that we have a duty to be fair to those struggling to survive. Identify a public policy that seems to reflect this duty, and consider it critically.

10.   Argue that industrial societies should bear a larger proportion of the costs of cleaning up the environment than poorer societies. Give a reason opposing this argument.

11.   How would you distinguish our duty to animals in the wild from our duty to animals in research labs, zoos, and our homes? Explain our duty to animals being raised for food.

12.   Do we have a duty to care for some landscapes? Explain your reasoning.

5

Character

ECOLOGICAL VIRTUES

How does a concern for character differ from doing our duty? In this chapter we shift our attention from taking the right action to being a good person. These two ways of reasoning are related, as we expect good persons to take good actions. A focus on character, however, requires considering an individual's motivation and goals, and recognizing that conduct is shaped by acts that are neither good nor bad. It also means appreciating personal qualities that are intrinsically good.[1]

Most moral philosophers do not make a *character argument* in support of environmental ethics, but instead assert duties and rights or rely on consequential predictions. Their emphasis is on action. Yet, reflecting on the value of character directs our attention to the teleological goal of being a good person, which is thought by many to be the basis for right action.

We begin with the natural law tradition of Europe and the Tao tradition of East Asia.[2] Then we reflect on the stories of Cinderella and Johnny Appleseed to see what light such tales might shed on our character. We also consider Christian teaching that urges us to be stewards of the earth. Finally, we reflect on the virtues of integrity, gratitude, and frugality, and assess philosophical arguments for appreciating nature.

BEING GOOD

In the play *Antigone* by Sophocles (495–406 BCE) a young woman defies the king's edict by burying the body of her brother, who was slain as a rebel. Antigone justifies disobeying the law of the land by proclaiming her allegiance to an eternal law, which she claims has greater authority than the decisions of any human ruler.[3] Tragically, her act of love and faith results in her death.

In ancient Greece the death of Socrates was also tragic, as Plato (424–348 BCE) tells us in his *Apology*. Plato's accounts of Socrates concern living a good life. We learn in these dialogues that "the unexamined life is not worth living"[4] and that we should remain true to our ethical principles. Socrates accepts the judgment of the Athenian senate, for corrupting young people, although he knows his sentence is unjust. He drinks the cup of hemlock that causes his death, as a way of affirming that a good citizen should abide by the rule of law.[5]

Stories of Antigone and Socrates reflect thinking that would later be known as the *natural law* tradition. Both individuals gave their lives for a higher ethical standard, which each expressed in opposition to the laws of the state. Each affirmed that being a good person means striving to know what is right and having the strength of character to live by this truth, no matter what the consequences.

The Natural Law Tradition

The writings of Aristotle (384–322 BCE) offer a philosophical argument for this way of thinking. Plato had looked for the source of virtue in eternal forms, but Aristotle thought we would find our clues in the natural world, which is why his method of inquiry is seen as an early form of science. The phrase "natural law," however, does not refer to what modern science means by the laws of nature, but instead reflects a belief in the rational structure and moral purpose of the natural order.

According to Aristotle, there is a reason for everything, and every living organism has a good of its own. We discover our human nature and what it means to be good persons—and thus our purpose and goal in life—by seeing how to live together rationally in the natural world as it is. This process of reasoning led Aristotle to conclude that the pursuit of happiness is our natural disposition. Because we are social beings, happiness requires cooperating to realize the common good. Aristotle used the Greek word *eudaimonia,* which is usually translated as "flourishing," to express this notion of individual and social happiness.[6]

Many centuries later Thomas Aquinas (1225–1274) reaffirmed Aristotle's argument that being good persons involves understanding human nature through reason. Aquinas also agreed that happiness is a social as well as an individual goal, and thus requires efforts to develop civic as well as personal virtues. Aquinas embraced Aristotle's reasoning, but rejected his belief that the natural world is independent of God.

We see this difference reflected in what they thought about virtue. Aristotle concluded that virtue requires practical wisdom, and so he proposed that moderation was the virtue of all virtues, "the golden mean." Aristotle argued, for instance, that too much courage is foolhardy, and that too much pride is vanity. Following nature, he reasoned, means always acting with moderation. Aquinas had faith in divine law, which he argued was revealed in natural law. He believed that moderation was less important for being a good and happy person than the spiritual and moral virtues of faith, hope, and charity that are verified in Christian scripture.[7]

Both Aristotle and Aquinas reasoned that maintaining good habits would strengthen the virtues necessary for human flourishing. We learn to do what is right by becoming, through discipline, the good people that we are created (naturally or by God) to be. The natural law tradition affirms that we will flourish individually and as a people, if we support the character traits of being a good person—by encouraging and rewarding those who exemplify these virtues.

The Tao Tradition

In ancient Chinese literature, which has shaped East Asian cultures, being a good person means conforming to the way of Tao, which is understood as the order of nature or the natural order of society (or even the divine will). Although Taoist and Confucian perceptions of Tao differ, each school of thought follows this same pattern.

Legend has it that Lao Tzu wrote the *Tao Te Ching* around 500 BCE, as he was leaving China to die in the wilderness. The *Tao Te Ching* says, "The greatest Virtue is to follow *Tao* and *Tao* alone."[8] In this classical text virtue is *not* perceived to be a character trait that a person can achieve through diligence, but is rather the delight that comes with finding and following the Tao. This is why a "man of highest virtue will not display it as his own."[9]

In the *Analects* of Confucius (551–479 BCE) Tao is understood as the ideal way of human existence and thus the best way of governing a people. This means that those who strive for a position of power in order to create the good society are foolish. "Do not worry about holding high position," Confucius taught. "Worry rather about playing your proper role."[10]

Virtue requires "balance," he reasoned. "When substance overbalances refinement, crudeness results. When refinement overbalances substance, there is superficiality. When refinement and substance are balanced, one has Great Man."[11] This differs from Aristotle's virtue of moderation, for Confucius is not talking about avoiding extremes, but about balancing what is done and the way it is done.

In this respect the *Tao Te Ching* and the *Analects* diverge in their understanding of how to follow Tao. To promote the virtue of refinement Confucius teaches the importance of ceremonies, music, and public rituals, whereas the *Tao Te Ching* evokes images from nature to suggest what living a virtuous life involves. As "water overcomes the stone," a person of virtue "is like water, which benefits all things," but "does not contend with them."[12]

The two schools of the Tao tradition agree, however, that refraining from action, rather than trying to make the world right, is the way to harmony, which is the goal of good living. The *Tao Te Ching* teaches:

> *The Way takes no action, but leaves nothing undone.*
> *When you accept this*
> *The world will flourish,*
> *In harmony with nature.*[13]

"Nature is not kind," the *Tao Te Ching* reminds us, but "treats all things impartially." So, virtue also involves treating "all people impartially," rather than having mercy on some and not others.[14] Furthermore, Taoists and Confucians concur that from "mercy comes courage," as the *Tao Te Ching* affirms, and from "humility comes leadership."[15]

Moral Presumptions

The natural law tradition asserts that *we should resist human law that conflicts with higher law*, which Aristotle discerned in the rational order and purpose of the natural world. Aquinas agreed, but reasoned that a higher law is revealed in Christian scripture. Both thought that to be happy in a flourishing society people must be reasonable and virtuous. Aristotle praised *the virtue of moderation* and criticized humility as having too little self-regard. Aquinas endorsed humility and *the virtues of faith, hope, and charity* as crucial for a good and happy life.

In the Tao tradition human flourishing is understood as *harmony* rather than as happiness. The *Tao Te Ching* recommends *the virtues of mercy and humility*, but does not distinguish religious faith from cultural traditions. It invites us to learn from nature by pointing out that the flow of water wears away stone and in doing so both shapes the landscape and nurtures life.

This notion of Tao is also reflected in the teaching of Confucius that *we should respond to unjust leaders by being civil and virtuous*, which will shame them and in this way prompt them to become more civil and virtuous. This seems analogous to Plato's view of Socrates, but differs with the ideal of resisting unjust authority exemplified by Antigone.

Neither the natural law tradition nor the Tao tradition directly addresses the question of how humans should care for nature, which is the concern of environmental ethics. Taoist teaching, however, describes nature in a way that makes it easier to draw inferences about living more ecologically. The natural law and Tao traditions agree that *we should learn from the natural order*, but teach lessons that diverge over the centuries in Western and Eastern cultures.

CHILDREN'S STORIES

Stories in every culture illustrate what it means to be a good person, but the role of nature in these stories varies. In the West, nature is usually the backdrop for a personal drama. The following children's stories illustrate this, but we may also find that the central character of each tale is virtuous in ways that suggest how we may live in harmony with nature.

Cinderella

This popular children's story tells of a girl who endures mean treatment at the hands of her stepmother and stepsisters without becoming a mean person, and who eventually finds love and a new life.

A Greek version of Cinderella published in the first century BCE may be the earliest written example of the story, but it was also popular in a Chinese version after the ninth century CE.[16] This is evidence that Cinderella is not simply a Western tale, and so it may reflect character traits and a hope for a better life that have also been important in East Asian cultures. The contemporary American story follows a French version edited by Charles Perrault in the seventeenth century. In this version Cinderella is described as "of unparalleled goodness and sweetness of temper" and the transforming miracle of the story is performed by Cinderella's fairy godmother.[17]

In all versions, Cinderella is rewarded for her goodness. In the Grimm brothers' tales she is aided by a tree and a bird, and in the Chinese version she is helped by the bones of a fish she fed and loved, before it was killed by her step-mother. The story of Cinderella does not tell us how to care for the earth, but it does offer hope in facing what appears to be a hopeless situation—and a *sense of hope* will be important as we confront the environmental crisis.

Johnny Appleseed

The legend of Johnny Appleseed is based on the life of John Chapman, who traveled barefoot wearing only rags for clothes through the states of Ohio and Indiana in the first half of the nineteenth century. Johnny Appleseed, as Chapman was known by 1806, transported apple seeds to the frontier and planted nurseries for settlers who would come later.[18]

Johnny Appleseed was a frontier Saint Francis.[19] An Ohio newspaper relates this story. "One cool autumnal night, while lying by his camp-fire in the woods, he observed that the mosquitoes flew in the blaze and were burnt. Johnny, who wore on his head a tin utensil which answered both as a cap and a mush pot, filled it with water and quenched the fire, and afterwards remarked, 'God forbid that I should build a fire for my comfort, that should be the means of destroying any of His creatures.'"[20] The story of Johnny Appleseed tells of a man at home in nature who transformed the wilderness by planting apple trees that would feed future generations.[21]

For those who believe environmental ethics should emphasize all life (an *ecocentric* or *biocentric* perspective), stories such as this one that focus on humans (an *anthropocentric* concern) may seem irrelevant or even detrimental. Yet, others may be inspired by Johnny Appleseed to live in nature with greater *simplicity* and *gratitude*—virtues that seem to contribute to a more ecological way of being a good person.

CHRISTIAN STEWARDSHIP

Many well-known stories about being good come from the New Testament. Often these stories do not concern God directly, but illustrate what it means to be a loving person. This is true of the story of the Good Samaritan, which tells of a man helping an injured stranger.[22] This is not a story about doing our duty, as the Samaritan does not have a duty, according to the ethical teachings of his time, to help a stranger in need. Instead, the story urges us to go beyond our duty by being good neighbors.

This may even mean caring for an enemy, which is part of the moral of this parable. For the injured man in the story is a Jew, and in the first century CE Jews and Samaritans had known five centuries of conflict. A contemporary version of this New Testament story might have a Palestinian helping an injured Jew on the road to Jericho, and if we were to tell the parable in this way everyone listening would see its radical implications.

The stories and parables related in the New Testament are about following Jesus by loving God and our neighbors, but concern being good persons rather than loving or respecting nature. To use these religious teachings to promote a more ecological way of life, Christians must argue that keeping the Great Commandment—to be persons who love God and their neighbors—implies a more caring attitude toward the natural world.[23]

Catholic Ethics

Catholic social teaching has transformed the New Testament commandment to be loving persons into a call to reclaim "our vocation as God's stewards of all Creation."[24] For example, a statement by the bishops of New Mexico urges Catholics to consider how they might change their lives in order to end "the destruction of our planetary home and contribute to its fruitfulness and to its restoration."[25]

- We invite our parents to teach their children how to love and respect the earth, to take delight in nature, and to build values that look at long-range consequences so that their children will build a better place for their own children.
- We invite our worshiping communities to incorporate in their prayers and themes our [the church's] confessions of exploitation and our rededication to be good stewards, and to organize occasional celebrations of creation on appropriate feast days.
- We invite our parish leaders to become better informed about environmental ethics so that religious education and parish policies will contain opportunities for teaching these values.
- We invite our public policy makers and public officials to focus directly on environmental issues and to seek the common good, which includes the good of our planetary home.[26]

The bishops conclude by calling on government officials "to eradicate actions and policies which perpetuate various forms of environmental racism, and to work for an economy which focuses more on equitable sustainability rather than unbridled consumption of natural resources and acquisition of goods."[27]

This Catholic statement affirms the authority of Catholic teaching and three passages in Christian scripture. First, it cites *the story of creation* in Genesis 1–2. "The moral challenge begins with recalling the vocation we were given as human beings . . . [when] God created humankind to 'have dominion' over all creation."[28] The statement argues that in Genesis the word *dominion* does not mean unrestrained exploitation. "[R]ather it is a term describing a 'representative' and how that person is to behave on behalf of the one who sends the representative. We are God's representatives. Therefore we are to treat nature as the Creator would, not for our own selfish consumption but for the good of all creation."[29]

The emphasis in this teaching is on who we are, as persons created in "the image and likeness of God" (Gen. 2:15). "This part of the story suggests that we are brought into being to continue the creative work of God, enhancing this place we call home. In addition to representing God's creative love for the earth, humankind is also responsible for ensuring that nature continues to thrive as God intended."[30]

To illustrate what seeing "the universe as God's dwelling" might mean, the statement evokes the story of Saint Francis of Assisi and quotes his well-known prayer: "Praise be my Lord for our mother the Earth, which sustains us and keeps us, and yields diverse fruits, and flowers of many colors, and grass."[31]

A second reference to scripture identifies *the parables of Jesus*, which "indicate quite clearly that we will be called to give an accounting on how we have managed our stewardship responsibilities" as "caretakers of the earth, its living and natural resources."[32] Loving our neighbors by using our resources charitably is part of this stewardship responsibility.

The third reference to scripture comes at the end of the pastoral statement and concerns *renewing the earth*. It points to the biblical promise "of the New Heaven and the New Earth" that "we as faithful stewards either enhance or contradict with our behavior and lifestyle."[33] This now means *reducing our consumption*. "[I]f there is to be a future, if we are truly partners in shaping the promise of the New Jerusalem, the new 'City of Peace' we can do no other. God gives us the courage to pray: 'Send forth thy Spirit, Lord and renew the face of the earth.'"[34]

There are other pastoral letters as well as statements from the US Catholic Conference of Bishops.[35] These calls to stewardship rest on the 1987 encyclical *Solicitude Rei Socialis* by Pope John Paul II, which asserts *three moral considera-*

tions with respect to the environment. The first involves "a growing awareness . . . that one cannot use with impunity the different categories of beings, whether living or inanimate—animals, plants, the natural elements—simply as one wishes, according to one's own economic needs."[36] The second requires admitting that using some natural resources "as if they were inexhaustible, with absolute dominion, seriously endangers their availability not only for the present generation but above all for generations to come."[37] The third moral consideration acknowledges that the "result of industrialization is, ever more frequently, the pollution of the environment, with serious consequences for the health of the population."[38]

Protestant Teaching

A survey conducted in early 2006 by the Pew Forum on Religion and Public Life verifies that "solid majorities of all major American religious groups back stronger measures to protect the environment," but the survey also shows that evangelical Protestants are less likely to support this position.[39] Protestants who see themselves as liberal or progressive[40] take a position on environmental ethics that, despite diverse theological arguments, is for all practical purposes the same as Catholics'.[41] Evangelical Protestants, however, are deeply divided.

Evangelical Protestants emphasize saving souls and, until recently, most believed that a concern for the environment was a distraction from their mission, which they understand as preparing for the coming rapture and return of Jesus. "Scripture teaches that Christ . . . [is] going to make a new heaven and a new earth. So in that sense I am not so concerned with this present world because I know it is going to be replaced with a better, greater one."[42]

Evangelical leader Rev. Richard Cizik[43] acknowledges the strength of this belief among evangelical Protestants, and also their suspicion of environmental arguments that rely on science rather than a Christian view of nature. Nonetheless, Cizik says, "We, as evangelical Christians, have a responsibility to God, who owns this property we call earth. We don't own it. We're simply to be stewards of it."[44]

The recent Evangelical Climate Initiative links climate change with ethical issues that are accepted by evangelical Protestants. "The same love for God and neighbor that compels us to preach salvation through Jesus Christ, protect the unborn, preserve the family and the sanctity of marriage, and take the whole Gospel to a hurting world, also compels us to recognize that human-induced climate change is a serious Christian issue requiring action now."[45]

The statement by the Initiative, "Climate Change: An Evangelical Call to Action," relies on science to demonstrate that the threat of human-induced climate change is real and will most heavily impact the poor of the world. However, it relies on the Bible to affirm three "Christian moral convictions" that require a faithful response to climate change.

- [W]e love God the Creator and Jesus our Lord, through whom and for whom the creation was made. This is God's world, and any damage that we do to God's world is an offense against God Himself. (Gen. 1; Ps. 24; Col. 1:16)
- [W]e are called to love our neighbors, to do unto others as we would have them do unto us, and to protect and care for the least of these as though each was Jesus Christ himself. (Mt. 22:34–40; Mt. 7:12; Mt. 25:31–46)
- [W]hen God made humanity he commissioned us to exercise stewardship over the earth and its creatures. Climate change is the latest evidence of our failure to exercise proper stewardship. . . . (Gen. 1:26–28)[46]

Thus, "Love of God, love of neighbor, and the demands of stewardship are more than enough reason for evangelical Christians to respond to the climate change problem with moral passion and concrete action."[47] The bottom line for evangelical Protestants with respect to global warming seems to be the same as for Catholics, as both argue that the commandment to love our neighbors means *helping the poor* who will be especially disadvantaged by global warming. In addition, both preach *a stewardship ethic based on the story of creation* in Genesis.

Critics point out that Western culture has long taken literally the divine commandment in the Genesis story of creation, which gives humankind "dominion" over the earth, and that this has led to disastrous consequences for other species and the environment. "Both our present science and our present technology," Lynn White, Jr. writes, "are so tinctured with orthodox Christian arrogance toward nature that no solution for our ecological crisis can be expected from them alone."[48]

This judgment was made in 1965, so it does not reflect any consideration of the recent Catholic and Protestant teachings on environmental ethics (nor advances in science and technology that will likely help us to live more ecologically). Yet, Christian teaching must be measured not merely by the words that church leaders use, but by changes in the lives of Christians and in their support for more sustainable economic policies. The environmental crisis is clearly putting Christian virtues to the test.[49]

VIRTUES: INTEGRITY, GRATITUDE, AND FRUGALITY

If the Western story of civilization is about conquering other peoples and making the environment our property, then the virtues of Western culture include courage, industry, and perseverance. People with these virtues can be blind to injustice, but are rarely remembered this way. Think of legendary cowboy heroes, and also of the Laura Ingalls Wilder stories about growing up in the late nineteenth century, which ran as a television serial for about a decade a century later as *Little House on the Prairie*.[50]

We have few stories that depict courage as caring for the environment, and fewer heroes who oppose those who are exploiting and degrading nature.[51] There are, however, some narratives that apply the virtues of industry and perseverance to environmental concerns.

Bob the Builder

I first heard of Bob the Builder stories from my youngest daughter, who as a medical student told me about a party with her friends that involved dressing up in working clothes and singing songs that everyone knew from the television show. These stories are designed to show children that happiness involves developing the virtues of industry and perseverance.

The show's website includes this exuberant affirmation: "Bob the Builder knows that the fun is in getting it done! With his business partner Wendy and his original can-do crew: Scoop the digger, Muck the digger/dumper, Lofty the crane, Roley the steam roller, and Dizzy the cement mixer, Bob has been getting jobs done all over Bobsville and beyond, and no matter what the job, he always has the right tools—teamwork and a positive attitude!"[52]

Of course, all this construction work involves using natural resources and digging up the earth. In this sense, Bob the Builder exemplifies the American myth that nature is there to be improved by our ingenuity and hard work. Until recently in this television program, there was no hint of environmental problems or of any related ethical issues.

That has changed, however, as the section of the website called The Builder's Log now describes a new project in Sunflower Valley. To prevent a city from being built that would pollute the valley, Bob has devised "a plan that would fit in to the environment."[53] Moreover, while watching a recent episode of *Bob the Builder* with my young grandson, I learned that the three Rs now stand for environmental virtues—"reduce, reuse, and recycle."[54]

Frugality, Gratitude, and Integrity

If *reduce* in the three Rs means reducing our consumption and not only our waste, perhaps being more frugal would be the best way today to identify this virtue. Market forecaster Faith Popcorn says being frugal is now chic. "It's the squeeze," she says, "the squeeze in the environment, squeeze in the economy, squeeze on the ethics."[55]

A character like Johnny Appleseed exemplifies frugality, but is probably too ascetic to be our model.[56] We now need examples of how families and communities can live with greater love and respect for nature. Yet, if we see the story of Johnny Appleseed as exemplifying a life of gratitude, the tale may move us to change our lives. I still remember the first line of the song that Johnny sang in the movie I saw almost sixty years ago:

> *The Lord is good to me, and so I thank the Lord*
> *For giving me the things I need: the sun, the rain and the apple-seed,*
> *The Lord is good to me.*
> *And every seed that grows will grow into a tree.*
> *And some day there'll be apples there for everyone in the world to share,*
> *The Lord is good to me![57]*

The first verse may seem self-centered, but the second verse expresses concern for future generations. Gratitude to God for the gifts of nature evokes a reverence for creation that John Chapman lived as he traveled through the wilderness. We might be inspired by his story, and also by the example of Saint Francis, to follow in their footsteps by reducing our "ecological footprint"[58] (our impact on the environment).

Cinderella persevered and escaped her life of deprivation, but we do not hear that she was grateful. If we were to look for a central virtue in her life, we might say that she had *integrity*.[59] She was not corrupted by the meanness of her stepmother and stepsisters. Despite her suffering, Cinderella persevered in being a good person. The moral of her story may be that living with integrity leads to happiness.

In the tale told by the Grimm brothers, Cinderella has a special relationship with birds that help her sort out the peas and lentils her stepmother scatters, to create a task that would have taken Cinderella the evening to complete and prevented her from attending the prince's ball.[60] Might we hope, therefore, that living with integrity will foster a closer relationship with nature?

RESPECTING AND APPRECIATING NATURE

In a critical assessment of the environmental movement, two well-known activists call for a "new politics" that requires a "mood of gratitude, joy, and pride, not sadness, fear, and regret."[61] I agree. To face our environmental crisis we must foster uplifting *character* traits.

"The moral significance of preserving natural environments is not entirely an issue of rights and social utility," Thomas E. Hill, Jr. writes, "for a person's attitude toward nature may be importantly connected with virtues or human excellences. The question is, 'what sort of person would destroy the natural environment—or even see its value solely in cost-benefit terms?' The answer I suggest is that willingness to do so may well reveal the absence of traits which are a natural basis for a proper humility, self-acceptance, gratitude, and appreciation of the good in others."[62]

Hill does not argue for the intrinsic worth of nature, because most philosophers reject this claim and Hill does not need to persuade them otherwise to make his point. He claims that *a love for nature is connected to other human virtues*, which are well accepted in ethics. This, he says, is convincing evidence that loving nature is as reasonable as these other virtues are.

Being Grateful

As a counterargument to those who claim that nature only has use value, Hill affirms that *good persons cherish things for their own sake.* "[I]f someone really took joy in the natural environment, but was prepared to blow it up as soon as sentient life ended, he would lack this common human tendency to cherish what enriches our lives. While this response is not itself a moral virtue, it may be a natural basis of the virtue we call 'gratitude.' People who have no tendency to cherish things that give them pleasure may be poorly disposed to respond gratefully to persons who are good to them."[63]

Another moral philosopher, Bryan G. Norton, addresses the same issue by telling a story of a young girl picking up sand dollars on a beach. When he asked her what she would do with them, she said she was going to bleach them and then sell them to tourists. The sand dollars had only economic (use) value for her, and Norton admits that he was unable to think of a way to persuade her that she might be a better person if she could appreciate the sand dollars just as they are, rather than as commodities that would bring her a little spending money.[64]

Later, Norton realized that he might have encouraged her to give more value to the sand dollars—as wondrous living creatures, rather than as dead market commodities—by talking with her about *using our human freedom wisely.*

The freedom to collect sand dollars "and to propel ourselves about the countryside by burning petroleum are all fragile freedoms," he writes, "that depend on the relatively stable environmental context in which they have evolved. If I could, then, have used the incident on the beach . . . to illustrate for her the way in which our activities—just like the activities of sand dollars—are possible, and gain meaning and value, only in a larger [environmental] context, I would have progressed a good way toward the goal of getting the little girl to put most of the sand dollars back."[65] Then, perhaps, the young girl "might have killed some sand dollars to study them, but she would still have *respected* sand dollars as living things with a story to tell."[66]

This argument for respecting and appreciating nature rests on the virtue of being grateful for a stable environment, because such an environment is crucial for the exercise of our freedom, and freedom is one of our most precious values. If we *see the wonders of the natural world*, Norton argues, we can hardly help but be grateful for the opportunities it offers us, and *this sense of gratitude may motivate us to protect our natural environment.*[67]

Summary

The natural law and Tao traditions look to nature to learn how we should live. Aristotle discerned in the order of nature a "higher law," and Aquinas saw as well a reflection of divine law. There is tension in this tradition between resisting and obeying unjust authority, as a way of affirming natural law, and between promoting the virtue of moderation or the virtues of humility, faith, hope, and love. There is agreement, however, that *good habits make good persons*, and that happiness requires civic virtues and cooperating for the common good.

Harmony, rather than happiness, is the way of life in the Tao tradition. The *Tao Te Ching* finds this goal in the changing patterns of nature, and the key to all virtue is the way that water wears down stone. Confucius agrees that we should respond with humility to those who misuse their power, in order to shame and change them, and he promotes balance in ceremonies to secure the public virtue of civility. The Tao tradition is more attuned to nature than the natural law tradition, and so we may more easily draw on it for support in doing environmental ethics.

The assertive Western virtues of courage, industry, and perseverance have been promoted around the world in stories, philosophical arguments, and Christian preaching. Nonetheless, the natural law tradition affirming higher ethical standards, which is expressed in secular and religious stories that verify *the virtues of integrity, gratitude, and frugality*, is being reinterpreted to support a more ecological way of life.

The Catholic Church and most Protestant denominations and churches now proclaim that we should be responsible stewards, because God has entrusted humanity with care for the earth and its creatures.[68] Christian teaching also expresses a concern for the poor, which is often ignored in discussions of environmental ethics. Many Christians today are active in advocating for global *economic justice* as well as environmentally *sustainable development.*

Stories like Cinderella and Johnny Appleseed, which are not religious in the sense of being part of the teaching of a religious community, often include religious images and may be understood as supporting virtues that bear on our relationship with nature. The hope of Cinderella confirms that goodness and integrity will win out in the end, and the faith of Johnny Appleseed verifies that living with gratitude and frugality may lead to happiness.

Will the creators of *Bob the Builder* succeed in transforming a story about machines and construction into a tale that inspires children to embrace the three Rs—*reduce, reuse, and recycle?* Will this children's program effectively promote the virtues of integrity, gratitude, and frugality? We can at least hope so, and also do our best to promote these environmental virtues.[69]

Some philosophers assert the value of having respect and gratitude for nature, believing that these virtues may strengthen efforts to preserve our environment. They may also affirm that a scientific understanding of the biosphere helps us to appreciate that nature is the source of the freedom we know and enjoy.

These moral arguments, stories, and religious teachings all suggest that, in protecting the environment, "our final appeal may lie, unabashedly, in apprehension, rather than in anything like formal deduction from general principles. With right training we apprehend that a person who cares about nature is a better person, other things being equal, than one who does not."[70]

QUESTIONS—CHARACTER: ECOLOGICAL VIRTUES

1. Summarize in three sentences the ethical presumptions of the natural law tradition, and then do the same for the Tao tradition.

2. Contrast the virtues of *moderation* (Aristotle) and *balance* (Confucius).

3. What lesson for environmental ethics might you draw from the natural law tradition? From the Tao tradition?

4. Pick a story that tells you what being a good person means. What virtue(s) does it illustrate? How might you interpret the story to make it relevant for environmental ethics?

5. Give an example of a story told in more than one culture. What is the moral of this story? How might this story help us address environmental issues?

6. Explain why the story of Johnny Appleseed might be seen as reinforcing an anthropocentric approach to environmental ethics.

7. Identify two reasons in Catholic teaching for being good stewards. Identify two meanings derived from Genesis 1 concerning human "dominion" over the earth.

8. Evangelical Protestant teaching identifies three Christian moral convictions that apply to caring for the environment. Describe two of these.

9. What are the three Rs promoted by Bob the Builder? Give two reasons for promoting these virtues.

10. Is the virtue of gratitude relevant for environmental ethics? Explain your thinking.

11. Do you agree that a person's humility and self-acceptance will likely encourage appreciation of nature? Explain your thinking.

12. Why might we ascribe value to nature apart from its use value?

6
Relationships

EMPATHY AND INTEGRITY

Moral philosophy has long relied on character traits and virtues to describe what is involved in being a good person. This chapter considers what our relationships with others and with nature mean for doing environmental ethics. Living in Africa led Albert Schweitzer to the realization that "a system of values which concerns itself only with our relationship to other people is incomplete and therefore lacking in power for good."[1] Similarly, moral philosopher Joseph R. DesJardins argues: "We can and do exist in relationships with our natural surroundings, and any abstract ethical theory that ignores that will be inadequate."[2]

To understand our moral community in terms of our many relationships, we consider evidence from biology that empathy evolved in primates. Then we reflect on three human cultures that each have a different sense of what our relationships with animals should be. We assess the claims of those promoting "deep ecology" as the only way to save life on earth, and consider the arguments of ecofeminists for resisting the language of domination used to rationalize the mistreatment of women and nature. Finally, we note that the environmental standard of ecosystem integrity is now recognized by law as well as science.

EMPATHY IS NATURAL

Chapter 1 offered evidence that empathy is natural in human development and important for doing ethics.[3] Is our species unique in this respect, or is empathy also natural for at least some other primates? "Chimpanzees, who cannot swim, have drowned in zoo moats trying to save others. Given the chance to get food by pulling a chain that would also deliver an electric shock to a companion, rhesus monkeys will starve themselves for several days."[4]

If observed in humans, these behaviors would be identified as evidence of empathy. Therefore, many scientists argue that what humans understand as morality arose among primates living in social groups, as in these circumstances there is a survival advantage in helping other members of the community. Ethics, it seems, has its roots in evolution.

Origins of Morality

In the 1960s Frans de Waal, now director of the Living Links Center at Emory University, observed that among chimpanzees, "after fights between two combatants, other chimpanzees would console the loser."[5] He suggested that consoling another creature "requires empathy and a level of self-awareness that only apes and humans seem to possess,"[6] and that empathy is the basis for what in humans is identified as morality.

"Though human morality may end in notions of rights and justice and fine ethical distinctions," it begins "in concern for others and the understanding of social rules as to how they should be treated." For "Social living requires empathy, which is especially evident in chimpanzees, as well as ways of bringing internal hostilities to an end. Every species of ape and monkey has its own protocol for reconciliation after fights."[7]

Female intervention is often crucial in maintaining peace among chimps (and, perhaps, among humans). "If two males fail to make up, female chimpanzees will often bring the rivals together, as if sensing that discord makes their community worse off and more vulnerable to attack by neighbors. Or they will head off a fight by taking stones out of the males' hands."[8]

Scientists suggest that these are not simply random acts, but "are undertaken for the greater good of the community," and are "a significant precursor of morality in human societies."[9] Recent studies have also found that monkeys, like humans, have mirror neurons in their brains that enable them to experience what another monkey is experiencing.[10]

Empathy Binds Us

Like these other primates, humans do not live as individuals. We have evolved as a species with a brain containing mirror neurons that directly link us to other persons (and also to members of some other species). "At the root, as humans, we identify the person we're facing as someone like ourselves."[11] As persons, we are members of social groups and communities.

A recent study reveals that damage to the ventromedial prefrontal cortex of the human brain reduces a person's empathy. "Previous studies showed that this region [of the brain] was active during moral decision-making, and that damage to it and neighboring areas from severe dementia affected moral judgments. The new study seals the case by demonstrating that a very specific kind of emotion-based judgment is altered when the region is offline."[12]

The study posed a hypothetical moral problem of whether to divert a runaway boxcar that is about to kill five people by throwing a switch that would result in the death of one man. Both those with damage to the ventromedial prefrontal cortex and persons in the control group favored throwing the switch. Yet, when asked whether they would push someone in front of a train, if doing this was the only way to save the five other people, those with ventromedial injuries were almost twice as likely to say they would, in contrast with the persons in the control group.[13]

A psychologist not involved in this study explains these results as evidence that in our brains "there are at least two systems working when we make moral judgments . . . an emotional system that depends on this specific part of the brain, and another system that performs more utilitarian cost-benefit analyses which in these people is clearly intact."[14]

Empathy is what binds us in our relationships and enables us to feel what others are feeling. Also, it seems clear that those who have a close relationship with an animal, such as a pet dog or cat, feel empathy for their pet. If we have evolved this capacity for empathy, and thus for caring about our relationships with human beings and also nonhuman animals, it seems reasonable to suppose that our empathy contributes to our fitness to survive in our environment.

Ethics of Care

Empathy moves us to involve those who care for us, when we make an ethical decision, instead of simply following a moral rule or calculating the likely consequences of acting on our decision. Moreover, making such a decision engages an area of our brain that relies largely on our feelings, rather than another area of the brain that makes an impersonal assessment of adverse and beneficial outcomes.

Thus, what is known as an *ethics of care* poses a challenge to more traditional forms of ethics that claim to rely only on objective reasoning. "Caring, empathy, feeling with others, being sensitive to each other's feelings, all may be better guides to what morality requires in actual contexts than may abstract rules of reason, or rational calculation," or at least will enrich our moral ethical reflection.[15] An ethics of care is an effort to temper justice with compassion.

Critics argue that an ethics of care does not offer an alternative to abstract principles, as "being sensitive to other's feelings" is an abstract principle, but this response misses the point. An ethics of care legitimates feelings and emphasizes listening. Incorporating this approach into making ethical decisions may help foster relationships marked by respect and mutual concern, which are likely to facilitate greater agreement as to what principles and rules are just and fair.

Our ethical presumption, therefore, is that we should consider not only our duty and our character aspirations, but also how our response to an ethical problem may reflect empathy for all those involved as well as a commitment to maintain the relationships that are likely to be affected by whatever action we take.[16]

CULTURE AND HUMAN NATURE

Like other primates, we are social animals. Our cultural life, however, although natural for us, sets us apart from nature. Human language, literature, science, art, religion, and ethics are unique among the species of the earth. We continue to live in the natural world, but in our cultural lives we also transcend the natural world.

Human culture, however, is also marked by diversity. Ethical presumptions reflect the relationships among people within a culture, and also the relationship between people and nature in that culture. To see what this means for us, as we face environmental issues in our modern and global culture, we consider two very different contexts—an indigenous community and traditional Buddhist culture.

Indigenous Culture

Native American and other indigenous traditions have preserved legends that emphasize close relationships between people and animals. Many of these striking folktales may be found in wonderfully illustrated versions in the children's section of a public library.

An example is a story called Buffalo Woman. In this Native American tale a buffalo hunter finds and falls in love with a woman, who says she comes from the Buffalo Nation. They marry and she bears him a son, but because members of his tribe mistreat the woman and her son, she leaves to return to her relatives. When the hunter follows their trail, hoping to be reunited with his family, he sees that the footprints of his wife and son have slowly taken the shape of buffalo hooves.

The hunter tracks his family to a large herd, where he is confronted by its leader. The hunter professes his love for his family, but the head buffalo says the "Straight-up-Person" will be killed because his tribe has mistreated his wife and son, unless the hunter can pick them out of the herd. The hunter's son secretly tells his father that he will flick his ear and that he has put a burr on his mother's back, so the hunter is able to identify his wife and child among the buffalo.

After the hunter spends three nights sleeping under a buffalo robe with the horns and hoofs attached to it, the buffalo bulls roll the hunter in the dust, pressing the breath from his body and breathing new life into him. As they lick and rub against him, the hunter feels the buffalo robe adhere to his body and finally he stands on his own four legs, as a young buffalo.

"That was a wonderful day!" the story concludes. "The relationship was made between the People and the Buffalo Nation; it will last until the end of time. It will be remembered that a brave young man became a buffalo because he loved his wife and little child. In return the Buffalo People have given their flesh so that little children, and babies still unborn, will always have meat to eat. It is the Creator's wish."[17]

Narratives from hunting and gathering cultures present animals as "persons" and animal herds as communities. Hunting and killing animals is accepted as necessary, but the stories express respect for animals and gratitude that animals allow themselves to be killed. These stories suggest that the line distinguishing humans from other animals is ambiguous and may be crossed by empathy and imagination.

A Sioux boy, for instance, was taught by his grandparents "to shoot your four-legged brother in his hind area, slowing it down but not killing it. Then, take the four legged's head in your hands, and look into his eyes. The eyes are where all the suffering is. Look into your brother's eyes and feel his pain. Then, take your knife and cut the four-legged under his chin, here, on his neck, so that he dies quickly. And as you do, ask your brother, the four-legged, for forgiveness for what you do. Offer also a prayer of thanks to your four-legged kin for offering his body to you just now, when you need food to eat and clothing to wear. And promise the four-legged that you will put yourself back into the earth when you die, to become nourishment for the earth, and for the sister flowers, and for the brother deer."[18]

We fail to understand what this teaching tells us about taking the lives of animals for food, if we reduce it to a statement about our duty or character. In indigenous traditions, life is understood as a natural community. Humans are related to all forms of life, and thus nonhuman organisms are brothers and sisters. Moreover, in this natural community killing animals is not merely a necessity, but also an act that should express reverence and respect for life.[19]

Buddhist Culture

Two and a half millennia ago Gautama Siddhartha, known to history as the Buddha, renounced his privileges as an upper-caste Hindu and, after years of living as a solitary ascetic, "awoke" and embraced a life of simplicity and gratitude. There are many differences among Buddhists, who for centuries have followed the path of the Buddha, but Buddhist culture has a distinctive way of affirming the interdependence of all life.

Buddhists "take refuge in" (entrust themselves to) the Buddha, the *dharma* (his teachings), and the *sangha* (the community). The *dharma* offers a way of embracing *interdependence* by letting go of the desire to separate ourselves from others and from nature. In the *sangha* monks (or nuns) not only meditate, study, chant, and beg, but also garden, clean, cook, bathe, help one another, and receive guests.[20] The ordinary activities of a Buddhist community are also spiritual practices, because the Buddha came to the realization that being awake to life means participating freely in its interrelationships.

Buddhists follow the Eightfold Path to overcome suffering. In addition to right views, right thought, right speech, right action, right effort, right mindfulness, and right concentration, this way of life also requires right livelihood. A traditional Buddhist would not work in a slaughterhouse, or with animal hides in factories making leather. For Buddhists, right livelihood means living from work that does not harm the natural world.

Given the interdependence of reality, and thus the close relationship between humans and other animals, Buddhists try not to harm animals that appear to suffer as humans do. Therefore, for Buddhists, right conduct requires nonviolence, and killing any sentient being is viewed as an act of violence. (By sentient beings, Buddhists mean all animals that seem to try to avoid pain rather than simply behaving according to reflex actions.)[21]

Buddhist monks traditionally obtained their food by begging and ate whatever was given to them, including scraps of meat. Their vow was not to kill, but this did not mean they were necessarily vegetarians. Later in the Buddhist tradition, the vow of nonviolence was broadened by some orders to mean not eating meat. Today Buddhists vary in what they eat, as some are strict vegetarians and others are not.

Buddhist teaching is paradoxical, as care and empathy involve relationships whereas overcoming suffering requires "letting go" of these relationships. For Buddhists, however, this paradox is an illusion. Accepting the transitory nature of life enables us to do both.

Modern Culture

Our culture emphasizes human relationships, rather than our relationship with nature. Unlike indigenous communities, our folktales do not remind us that the distinction between culture and nature is ambiguous. We do not think of ourselves as human animals and of nonhuman animals as "persons."[22] In contrast to cultures influenced by Buddhist teaching, most of us eat hamburgers without any concern for the suffering of cattle in feedlots and slaughterhouses.

We have pets, visit wild animals in zoos, watch nature shows on television, and fund wildlife preserves, but mostly we live apart from wild animals. We are beginning to understand that biodiversity is required for healthy ecosystems. Yet, we are doing very little to preserve natural habitats, and we rely on chemicals to rid our homes and gardens of organisms that we identify as pests and weeds.

Some in modern culture are developing greater empathy for other species and paying more attention to our relationship with the natural world, but most of us would be unwilling to embrace a traditional indigenous or Buddhist ethic concerning animals. Our life is largely urban, and we live apart from the animals we consume as food or enjoy watching in zoos. Moreover, this modern form of human culture has altered the natural environment almost everywhere, so that the survival and well-being of wildlife now requires careful management.

Is the management of wild habitats within national parks as caring as it ought to be? The policy prohibits staff from intervening to protect a wild animal or to reduce its suffering, if an animal's predicament is not the result of human error—unless the animal belongs to a protected or endangered species. This means a buffalo that has fallen through thin ice on the surface of a pond is left to die. Its carcass becomes food for wolves. Yet, a mother bear and her cubs that are stranded on a small island due to melting ice are rescued, because bears are an endangered species and the cubs are too small to swim to shore.[23]

Native American culture recognizes that wolves need to eat as much as humans do, and that buffalo give their lives to both. Traditional Buddhist culture guards against human desire by limiting the impact of human communities on nature. National park policy in the United States expresses a new awareness of our relationships with animals that distinguishes our duty to care for individual animals, which our actions have put at risk, from our duty to preserve the ecosystems that ensure the survival of wildlife and diverse species.

DEEP ECOLOGY

Scholars whose writings define the deep ecology movement[24] reject modern culture. They find the cause of the environmental crisis in the dominant worldview of Western culture, which they claim values only the human use and consumption of natural resources. Advocates of deep ecology see efforts to curb pollution and the rapid depletion of nonrenewable resources as misguided and ineffectual—as anthropocentric and "shallow" rather than biocentric and "deep." Biodiversity will only be saved, they argue, by embracing "an ecological, philosophical, and spiritual approach" that accepts the "unity of humans, plants, animals, the Earth."[25]

Norwegian philosopher Arne Naess writes: "To the ecological field-worker *the equal right to live and blossom* is an intuitively clear and obvious value axiom. Its restriction to humans is an anthropocentrism with detrimental effects upon the life quality of humans themselves. This quality depends in part upon the deep pleasure and satisfaction we receive from close partnership with other forms of life."[26]

Biocentric Equality

This philosophical worldview affirms that "there is no bifurcation in reality between the human and the nonhuman realms."[27] We must ascribe equal value to all organisms. "The intuition of biocentric equality is that all things in the biosphere have an equal right to live and blossom and to reach their own individual forms of unfolding and self-realization within the larger Self-realization. This basic intuition is that all organisms and entities in the ecosphere, as parts of the interrelated whole, are equal in intrinsic worth."[28]

Yet, the claim of *equal worth for all organisms and entities* is hardly self-evident.[29] Every organism has an interest in survival, but we might reasonably distinguish the nature of this interest for persons from the same interest for other organisms. For instance, although elk and humans need to eat, a human who can be educated has a greater interest in eating than an elk: "The eating supports other interests, and the other interests enrich the significance and value of the eating."[30] Elk eat to survive. We also eat to nourish our bodies, but we dine to enjoy the taste of good food in the company of family and friends, and we feast to celebrate harvests and significant historical and religious events.

In addition, defending the right of self-realization for every organism makes it hard to distinguish our duty of care for animals in the wild from our duty to care for our pets and other domesticated animals. We likely agree that we have a duty to help rescue a person who has fallen through the ice on a pond or our dog, if it has fallen through the ice. But do we have a duty to try to rescue a wild buffalo that falls through the ice in Yellowstone National Park?

The deep ecology platform is summarized by Bill Devall and George Sessions in eight general principles:

1. The well-being and flourishing of human and nonhuman Life on Earth have value in themselves (synonyms: intrinsic value, inherent value). These values are independent of the usefulness of the nonhuman world for human purposes.

2. Richness and diversity of life forms contribute to the realization of these values and are also values in themselves.

3. Humans have no right to reduce this richness and diversity except to satisfy *vital* needs.

4. The flourishing of human life and cultures is compatible with a substantial decrease of the human population. The flourishing of nonhuman life requires such a decrease.

5. Present human interference with the nonhuman world is excessive, and the situation is rapidly worsening.

6. Policies must therefore be changed. These policies affect basic economic, technological and ideological structures. The resulting state of affairs will be deeply different from the present.

7. The ideological change is mainly that of appreciating *life quality* (dwelling in situations of inherent value) rather than adhering to an increasingly higher standard of living. There will be a profound awareness of the difference between big and great.

8. Those who subscribe to the foregoing points have an obligation directly or indirectly to try to implement the necessary changes.[31]

Advocates of the fourth principle urge strong measures to limit the number of births in countries like India, and have little patience with "debates over the types of measures to take (contraception, abortion, etc.) consistent with human rights and feasibility."[32] Ecofeminists, however, resist this approach to population control, as we see in the next section of this chapter, and affirm that securing women's rights is more just and effective.

Whether or not the third principle is reasonable depends on what is meant by "vital" needs. What criteria are to be used in deciding whether a need is vital, and who is to make this determination? Chapter 7 argues that fundamental political and economic rights are the necessary social conditions for human dignity, and this would be one way of identifying what our vital needs are. Yet, proponents of deep ecology seem unable to affirm human rights law, as these moral affirmations are anthropocentric and rooted in the cultural tradition that deep ecologists see as causing the environmental crisis.

Spirituality

Advocates of deep ecology reject the use of contemporary science and law to define our vital needs, and look to philosophy and spirituality for guidance. They ignore or condemn, however, the monotheistic traditions of Judaism, Christianity, and Islam, because each of these traditions gives human beings a privileged place in nature. Instead, they affirm that Taoist, Buddhist, and Native American traditions "agree with the basic principles of deep ecology."[33]

Does their claim withstand scrutiny? Chinese culture reflects Confucian as well as Taoist and Buddhist teachings, and the Chinese have long relied on all three schools of thought. The *Tao Te Ching* presents nature as a model for living, but the Chinese turn to the *Analects* of Confucius to learn the virtues required for realizing harmony in a society.[34] Ancient Chinese culture is more urban and agricultural than wild, and Taoist writings are silent about the self-realization of every organism.

In traditional Buddhist culture the life of a monk depended on the support of nearby merchants and farmers, as well as on begging in the market. The setting of a Buddhist temple is always natural, yet this environment is not wild. Gardens are raked, fish ponds are maintained, and trees are trimmed and often given new shapes. Buddhist monks exercise control over nature around their monastery, without having any desire to dominate the natural world.

The claim that Native American traditions agree with the principles of deep ecology is also misleading. A recent analysis of hunting and fishing societies has shown that "their use of the environment is driven by ecological constraints and not by attitudes, such as sacred prohibitions, and that their relatively low environmental impact is the result of low population density, inefficient technology, and the lack of profitable markets, not from conscious efforts at conservation."[35] In modern culture, Native Americans drive cars or trucks most of the time, rather than ride horses and, like most contemporary Buddhist monks I know, carry cell phones.

Advocates of deep ecology also assert a notion of individual salvation that is absent from Eastern cultures. Devall and Sessions proclaim that: "'No one is saved until we are all saved,' where the phrase 'one' includes not only you, an individual human, but all humans, whales, grizzly bears, whole rain forest ecosystems, mountains and rivers, the tiniest microbes in the soil and so on."[36] This is not Taoist, or Buddhist, or Native American spirituality. Using the notion of being saved, which is central to the Jewish, Christian, and Muslim traditions, and expanding this concern to include all organisms and entities, is meant to shock us, and it does.

Why defend such an extreme position against all other arguments for protecting and preserving the environment? Proponents of deep ecology seem to believe that a mass conversion to their way of thinking is required before an ecological world order can be achieved. "The fact that people can consciously change themselves and society, indeed enhance that natural world in a free ecological society, is dismissed as 'humanism.' Deep ecology essentially ignores the social nature of humanity and the social origins of the ecological crisis."[37]

ECOFEMINISM: A SOCIAL ECOLOGY

The social origins of our environmental crisis, ecofeminists argue, involve a "language of domination"[38] concerning both women and nature, which has long been taken for granted in both Western and Eastern traditions. Thus, we can only improve our relationship with nature by changing the way we live together as men and women.

"Women must see that there can be no liberation for them and no solution to the ecological crisis within a society whose fundamental model of relationships continues to be one of domination. They must unite the demands of the women's movement with those of the ecological movement to envision a radical reshaping of the basic socioeconomic relations and the underlying values of this society."[39]

Advocates of ecofeminism differ in many respects, but affirm "the interdependence of all life, humanity's role as part of the earth's ecosystem, and the non-hierarchical nature of a system in which all parts affecting each other are emphasized to counteract relationships dominated by values of control and oppression."[40] The key concerns are environmental sustainability and social justice. Ecofeminism "takes from the green movement a concern about the impact of human activities on the nonhuman world and from feminism the view of humanity as gendered in ways that subordinate, exploit, and oppress women."[41]

Specifically, "ecofeminists point to a number of ways in which environmental degradation causes a decrease in the quality of life for women, children, and people of color," noting the connections "between women's oppression and the oppression of nature by examining global economics, Third World debt, underdevelopment, production and distribution, reproductive rights, militarism, and environmental racism."[42]

A Social Ecology

Seeing how conceptions of justice and culture allowed the domination of women by concealing this reality, and what this concealment has done to the nature of both men and women, should make us suspicious of similar language about our environment and its resources. The task of environmental ethics, therefore, is not simply to use natural resources more efficiently, but to resist the worldview that depicts both nature and women as resources that should be put to good use.

In this sense, ecofeminism "is a social ecology. It recognizes the twin dominations of women and nature as social problems rooted both in very concrete, historical, socioeconomic circumstances and in oppressive patriarchal conceptual frameworks which maintain and sanction these circumstances."[43]

Doing this requires contextual analysis. An ecofeminist approach to industrial farming "would examine the way in which the logic of domination supports this institution not only as it affects animals' lives, but also as it affects workers, women, and nature."[44] Similarly, "ecofeminists have argued for a contextual moral vegetarianism, one that is capable of accounting for the injustice associated with factory farming while at the same time allowing for the moral justifiability of traditional food practices of indigenous people."[45]

Nurturing healthy relationships with others, and with nature, should be our goal. "The primary aims of ecofeminism are not the same as those typically associated with liberal feminism," for ecofeminists "do not seek equality with men as such, but aim for a liberation of women *as* women. Central to this liberation is a recognition of the value of the activities traditionally associated with women; childbirth, nurturing and the whole domestic arena."[46]

Decision-Making

Ecofeminists reject the notion that "experts" should decide what policies are needed to limit population and make the best use of natural and human resources, pointing out that this approach has generally meant that a few men decide what is best for women (and nature). Thus, in contrast to the biocentric egalitarianism of deep ecology, ecofeminists support women's rights and human rights law.

"[W]omen's health advocates argue for a different approach to population policy—one that makes women's health and other basic needs more central to policy and program focus, and by doing so increases human welfare, transforms oppressive gender relations, and reduces population growth rates."[47] As women are able to make their own reproductive decisions, and to pursue livelihoods that will support their families, they choose to have fewer children.

Ecofeminists also hold that poor women have knowledge that is generally unrecognized. "Women in subsistence economies, producing and reproducing wealth in partnership with nature, have been experts in their own right of holistic and ecological knowledge of nature's processes. But these alternative modes of knowing, which are oriented to the social benefits and sustenance needs" are not valued by those concerned only with economic development, who fail to understand our relationship with nature and "the connection of women's lives, work and knowledge with the creation of wealth."[48]

Ecofeminists are committed to social and economic development in poor societies, but demand that this development be environmentally sustainable. They also argue that living ecologically does not simply mean following a new set of rules to protect the environment. Instead, an ecological way of living involves lifting up the various patterns of life, as these emerge, that embody just relationships between men, women, and the earth's ecosystems. It means evolving our culture, so that it may be more just as well as ecologically sustainable.[49]

Ethical Presumptions

Paying attention to these natural relationships, with one another and with our environment, will likely change the lives of both men and women. "Most ecofeminists believe that men have as much potential as women to adopt a deeper environmental awareness, but they will need to work harder to fully embrace those values."[50] Therefore, to renew our relationships with nature and one another, ecofeminists assert that we should: be suspicious of the language

of domination, address feminist and ecological issues together, and support the
rights of women to make their own decisions.

ECOLOGICAL INTEGRITY

Aldo Leopold, whose affirmation of a land ethic has inspired many in the environmental movement, affirms that: "A thing is right when it tends to preserve the integrity, stability, and beauty of the biotic community. It is wrong when it tends otherwise."[51] Not all moral philosophers agree that beauty can serve as a standard for ethical decisions about the environment,[52] and some argue that stability does not adequately reflect the dynamic nature of ecosystems. But *integrity* is now a *standard for measuring the health of an environment.*

The history of the word integrity "has as its primary context descriptions and evaluations of human character, and, by extension, judgments about human societies, institutions, and cultures. Like health [which also may refer to an individual and an environment], integrity conveys the idea of wholeness and of unbroken functioning."[53] There is "dignity and personal worth" in integrity, and "we praise those who achieve it."[54]

Both Catholics and Protestants combine these notions with stewardship, in affirming the "integrity of creation."[55] Ecological integrity, therefore, is best understood as a system of relationships that is dynamic, self-sustaining, and resilient. Natural chaotic events disrupt an ecosystem, but need not destroy its integrity.

Natural systems are, on the whole, "places of adapted fit with many species integrated into long persisting relationships, life perpetually sustained and renewed. There is cycling and re-cycling of energy and materials. The member organisms are flourishing as interrelated fits in their niches. The system is spontaneously self-organizing in the fundamental processes of climate, hydrology, speciation, photosynthesis, and trophic pyramids. There is resistance to, and resilience after, perturbation."[56]

Human changes to the environment need not destroy the integrity of ecosystems, and therefore this scientific and ethical standard gives us a practical way of measuring our impact on the natural environment. "Earth, from here onward, will become increasingly a managed planet. If humans wish a society with integrity, such management, for the foreseeable future, continues to require integrity and health in ecosystems, keeping them stable in the midst of historical change."[57] I apply this standard in chapter 12 to agriculture, in chapter 13 to the conservation and preservation of forests, deserts, and wetlands, and in chapter 14 to urban environments.

Law

The law has begun to protect *ecological integrity*. In 1972 the United States and Canada agreed to the Great Lakes Water Quality Agreement (GLWQA), which was renewed in 1978 and amended by a protocol in 1987.[58] The current version of the GLWQA states: "The purpose of the Parties is to restore and maintain the chemical, physical and biological integrity of the waters of the Great Lakes Basin Ecosystem," and this integrity is defined as "the interacting components of air, land, water and living organisms, including humans within the drainage basin of the St. Lawrence River."[59]

The 1972 US Clean Water Act affirms *ecosystem integrity*, as do statements by the UN Commission on Environmental Development (UNCED).[60] In 1991 the International Council of Scientific Unions and also the Third World Academy of Sciences asserted this environmental standard.[61]

In the new discipline of industrial ecology, *ecological integrity* is defined in terms of "three facets of the self-organization of ecological systems: (a) current wellbeing, (b) resiliency, and (c) capacity to develop, regenerate, and evolve."[62] The well-being of a system is sometimes identified as its health. Resiliency refers to a system's capacity to respond successfully when it is disturbed. The third facet of ecological integrity concerns its emerging complexity.[63] As we see in chapter 14, those supporting *green construction* are working to include the standard of industrial integrity in architectural design criteria and municipal building codes.

Summary

We bring to environmental ethics not merely a capacity to reason about duty, character, and the likely consequences of our actions, but also our feelings of empathy for one another and for many other organisms. This capacity to act morally, relying both on empathy and reason, is natural for humans. Thus, we may conclude that this moral dimension of our human nature has contributed to our survival as a species. It also seems reasonable to expect that our ethical nature will continue to serve us well, as we confront our environmental crisis.

Relying on empathy as well as reason enables us to see and appreciate our relationships in nature and also to discern and define the integrity of ecosystems. This reasoning process leads us to extend our moral community by affirming the following ethical presumptions. We should:

- Protect ecosystems and endangered species.

- Aid animals that our actions have put at risk.
- Respect the rights and the experience of women.

Aldo Leopold wrote: "That land is a community is the basic concept of ecology, but that land is to be loved and respected is an extension of ethics."[64] He challenged us to make ethical decisions about the environment by "thinking like a mountain."[65] A greater awareness of our relationships within nature may help us see that living ethically now means living ecologically.

QUESTIONS—RELATIONSHIPS: EMPATHY AND INTEGRITY

1. Explain why it is important for ethics to consider relationships and not merely individual character traits. How does this emphasis affect our decision-making?

2. Give an example illustrating empathy in nonhuman animals. Why is this evidence relevant for ethics?

3. Identify evidence for empathy in the way that the human brain functions.

4. How might concern for an ethics of care affect our relationship with nature?

5. Contrast the view of animals in Native American culture and modern culture.

6. Explain how animals are protected (and not protected) by Buddhist teaching.

7. Argue for (and against) US park policy that limits intervening to aid wild animals.

8. Why do deep ecologists argue that all organisms have equal rights to life and self-realization? Assess these claims critically.

9. What concerns do ecofeminists have about population control measures? What proposals do they support?

10. Identify two recommendations that ecofeminists make for addressing our environmental crisis and raise a critical argument about one of these recommendations.

11. What is the meaning of "biological integrity" in the Great Lakes Water Quality Agreement? Suggest a problem in enforcing this legal standard.

12. Give your interpretation of what it might mean to "think like a mountain."

7

Rights

HUMANS AND ANIMALS?

The noun *right* has a plural *rights*, and in ethics these nouns refer to moral or legal claims. Laws transform moral rights into legal rights, and yet some moral rights transcend the law. The "right to life" is a moral claim, and the right to the presumption of innocence is a legal right that recognizes a moral right. Human rights are moral rights that are affirmed by international law as legal rights, because these rights are understood as the necessary social conditions for human dignity.

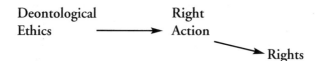

The most widely accepted justification for moral rights relies on Kant's deontological argument that we have a duty to treat every person as an end, and not as a means to our own ends, because every person is autonomous and rational, and thus has intrinsic worth. Our moral right to be respected by others reflects our intrinsic worth, as persons who are able to be rational and moral. On the basis of this reasoning, Kant concluded that only humans have rights.

Advocates of animal rights challenge this conclusion, as we will see, and moral philosophers who extend moral consideration to nature must clarify whether or not this means ascribing rights to animals or ecosystems. This dispute extends beyond the classroom into society, and in this political and economic context concerns what the law should be.

Therefore, this chapter begins by reviewing how moral rights became legal rights through struggles for representative government and the development of international human rights law after World War II. Next we look at environmental rights in international law, as this is the context for the global debate about our duty to protect and preserve the environment. With this background in environmental ethics and law, we consider arguments for animal rights, and then draw conclusions about an environmental rights strategy.

HUMAN RIGHTS LAW

Movements in the eighteenth century for democracy and representative government attributed fundamental moral rights to God or human nature. The American Declaration of Independence asserts that "all men" are "endowed by their Creator with certain inalienable rights," but the French revolution proclaimed that "the rights of man" are natural rights intrinsic to the humanity of each person. In the nineteenth century, as Western societies became more diverse and secular, the claim that rights are God given was largely replaced by the assertion that civil and political rights have intrinsic worth, because these rights are rooted in our human nature as reasoning and autonomous persons.

At the start of the twentieth century, legal rights were conceived as liberties guaranteed to citizens by national governments. This theory of *positive law* prevailed until after World War II, when the victorious Allies faced the terrible fact that Nazi Germany had acted "legally" (under German law) in committing what were characterized after the war as crimes against humanity. The United Nations (UN) and a new era of international law were conceived to embody the ethical presumption that some moral rights transcend the laws of nations. These *human rights* are now asserted in international law as the necessary social conditions for human dignity.[1]

Human rights are clearly anthropocentric, and some moral philosophers see this as a major problem for environmental ethics. To address this question, we look first at international law, which in the past half century has affirmed the right of peoples to economic and social development and also the right of every person to a healthy environment.

International Law

The Charter of the United Nations and the Universal Declaration of Human Rights (UDHR), which was approved without a dissenting vote by the UN

General Assembly in 1948, assert that every nation and citizen have a moral duty to protect international human rights.

The UDHR begins by affirming that "recognition of the inherent dignity and of the equal and inalienable rights of all members of the human family is the foundation of freedom, justice and peace in the world." It states that "disregard and contempt for human rights have resulted in barbarous acts which have outraged the conscience of mankind" and asserts that "a world in which human beings shall enjoy freedom of speech and belief and freedom from fear and want has been proclaimed as the highest aspiration of the common people."[2]

President Franklin D. Roosevelt articulated these "four freedoms," which are affirmed in the UDHR, and after his death his widow, Eleanor Roosevelt, chaired the commission that drafted the UDHR. The UDHR also proclaims: "the peoples of the United Nations have in the Charter reaffirmed their faith in fundamental human rights, in the dignity and worth of the human person and in the equal rights of men and women and have determined to promote social progress and better standards of life in larger freedom."

Traditional religious teachings do not recognize human rights, and until very recently religious leaders have resisted the secularization of society that has fostered human rights. But now that international law affirms universal standards for human dignity, there are leaders in every historic religious tradition who argue that at least some of these rights are implied by the duties and commandments of their ethical and spiritual teachings.[3] Religious institutions, however, have given only limited support to political efforts to protect and progressively realize the civil, economic, and social rights asserted by international human rights law.

Human Rights Treaties

The primary implementing treaties of the UHDR are the International Covenant on Civil and Political Rights (ICCPR) and the International Covenant on Economic, Social, and Cultural Rights (ICESCR), and both of these came into force as international law in 1976. Each begins by affirming the right of self-determination, which is stated as the right of all peoples "to freely determine their political status and freely pursue their economic, social and cultural development" (Article 1.1 in each covenant).

Both covenants assert the right to nondiscrimination. Under international human rights law, men and women have equal rights and are to enjoy equal protection of the law. These two covenants also affirm that some rights, such as the right to enjoy one's culture as a minority community or to participate in a trade union, require protecting group rights and not only individual rights.

These group rights check the individualistic emphasis in asserting rights that dominates the writings of American moral philosophers and lawyers.

Civil and political rights asserted in the ICCPR as human rights include the following moral presumptions:

- Everyone has the right to liberty and security of person. (Article 9.1)
- No one shall be subjected to arbitrary arrest or detention. (Article 9.2)
- Everyone charged with a criminal offense shall have the right to be presumed innocent until proved guilty according to law. (Article 14.2)
- Everyone shall have the right to freedom of expression. . . . (Article 19.2)
- The right of peaceful assembly shall be recognized. (Article 21)
- All persons are equal before the law and are entitled without any discrimination to the equal protection of the law. (Article 26)

The United States has ratified the ICCPR, but with reservations limiting these rights to the standards of US law.[4]

The United States has not ratified the ICESCR,[5] which holds that governments have a duty to realize the following economic, social, and cultural rights:

- The right to work . . . (Article 6)
- The right of everyone to the enjoyment of just and favorable conditions of work which ensure . . . Safe and healthy working conditions. (Article 7)
- The right of everyone to social security . . . (Article 9)
- The right of everyone to an adequate standard of living for himself and his family, including adequate food, clothing, and housing . . . (Article 11)
- The right of everyone to the enjoyment of the highest attainable standard of physical and mental health. (Article 12.1)
- The improvement of all aspects of environmental and industrial hygiene. (Article 12.2)

The ICESCR states that each government should make progress according to its economic development in securing the social and economic conditions necessary for human dignity. This standard of "progressive realization" contrasts with a government's unconditional duty to enforce civil and political rights. The reason for these different standards of duty is that ensuring civil and political rights does not depend on economic development, whereas realizing economic, social, and cultural rights does.

In the United Sates social and economic needs are addressed, more or less, by legislation that provides assistance for the poor who qualify. These "entitlements" have the status of positive law, as the United States has not ratified the ICESCR that makes these economic and social claims "human rights." Yet, it seems reasonable to affirm that the standards of international law, which define the social conditions that most national governments agree are necessary for human dignity, also establish these rights as moral presumptions for Americans.

Regional Treaties

In addition to international human rights instruments, there are regional human rights treaties and organizations in the Americas, Europe, Asia, and Africa. The American Convention on Human Rights was adopted in 1969 and came into force in 1978.[6] Its provisions are administered by the Inter-American Commission on Human Rights and the Inter-American Court of Human Rights, which are organs of the Organization of American States (OAS).

In 1950 the Council of Europe adopted the Convention for the Protection of Human Rights and Fundamental Freedoms, which is generally known as the European Convention on Human Rights.[7] In 1993 the Treaty on European Union (TEU) came into force. The TEU reaffirms the European Convention on Human Rights and makes development and consolidation of "democracy and the rule of law, and respect for human rights and fundamental freedoms" a specific objective of the common foreign and security policy of the European Union (EU).[8]

The treaties of Amsterdam (1999) and Nice (2000) add specificity to the TEU, and a Charter of Fundamental Rights of the European Union (also approved at Nice in 2000) states the civil, political, economic, and social rights of persons residing in the EU. Article 37 of this charter asserts that: "A high level of environmental protection and the improvement of the quality of the environment must be integrated into the policies of the Union and ensured in accordance with the principle of sustainable development."[9]

ENVIRONMENTAL RIGHTS

Neither the ICCPR nor the ICESCR directly protects the environment, but each covenant affirms human rights that affect decisions about the environment. The civil and political rights in the ICCPR protect the due process of law, which supports the ethical presumption that those who are affected by laws have a right to participate in the public process by which these laws are made. These rights are crucial for local communities that depend on natural resources, when land-use decisions are to be made that will affect these communities.

The ICESCR affirms the human rights to adequate food, clothing, housing, and health care, as well as a safe working environment, and the covenant recognizes that realizing these human rights requires economic development in a society. Both the ICCPR and the ICESCR assert the right to self-determination, as the right of peoples not only to govern themselves but also to "pursue their economic, social and cultural development."[10]

Sustainable Development

In 1983 the UN General Assembly established the World Commission on Environment and Development, which came to be known as the Brundtland Commission (in honor of its chair, Gro Harlem Brundtland). The Brundtland Commission Report was published in 1987 under the title *Our Common Future*.[11] This report describes the ethical presumption concerning *sustainable development* as "development that meets the needs of the present without compromising the ability of future generations to meet their own needs."[12]

Five years later in Rio de Janeiro the UN Conference on Environment and Development (often called the Earth Summit) approved a set of recommendations identified as Agenda 21 (referring to the twenty-first century). That same year the UN established the Commission on Sustainable Development (CSD) under the UN Economic and Social Council (ECOSOC) to implement these recommendations.[13]

In 2002 the World Summit on Sustainable Development reaffirmed the UN's commitment to Agenda 21. The fifteenth session of the CSD, held in May 2007, continued the commission's focus on energy, industrial development, air pollution and the atmosphere, and climate change.[14] Subsequent UN texts affirming sustainable development state that this includes *economic development*, *social development*, and *environmental protection*.

For example, the Beijing Declaration of the Fourth World Conference on Women states: "We are deeply convinced that economic development, social development and environmental protection are interdependent and mutually reinforcing components of sustainable development, which is the framework for our efforts to achieve a higher quality of life for all people."[15]

Sustainable development might simply mean choosing a more sustainable course of action from among the options that seem to be feasible for an economic development project. To avoid ambiguity, many environmentalists now promote *green development*, which they define as giving priority to "environmental sustainability over economic and cultural sustainability."[16] They acknowledge, however, that green development "is not necessarily practical in all applications," so they support the lower standard of sustainable development where it may help "to improve overall sustainability when cutting edge green development is unattainable."[17]

Right to a Healthy Environment

In 1972 the UN Conference on the Human Environment (the Stockholm Conference) asserted the "right to a healthy environment." Principle 1 of the Stockholm Declaration identifies protecting the environment with established human rights standards under international law: "Man has the fundamental right to freedom, equality and adequate conditions of life, in an environment of a quality that permits a life of dignity and well being, and he bears a solemn responsibility to protect and improve the environment for present and future generations."[18] The Stockholm Conference led to the UN Environment Programme (UNEP) and the Environment Committee of the Organization for Economic Cooperation and Development (OECD).[19]

The *right to a healthy environment* was inferred in the 1985 Vienna Convention for the Protection of the Ozone Layer, which addresses ozone depletion in the stratosphere. Nations signing the convention agreed to take "appropriate measures . . . to protect human health and the environment against adverse effects resulting or likely to result from human activities which modify or are likely to modify the ozone layer."[20] Two years later the UNEP issued the Montreal Protocol on Substances that Deplete the Ozone Layer, which adds technical changes to the Vienna Convention in order to strengthen it.[21]

The 1992 Earth Summit produced the UN Framework Convention on Climate Change (UNFCCC or FCCC). The treaty is nonbinding, but provides for updates ("protocols") setting mandatory emission limits. One hundred and sixty-nine nations have ratified the Kyoto Protocol to this treaty, and this protocol came into force in 2005. The United States ratified the FCCC, but has refused to ratify the Kyoto Protocol. India and China have ratified the Kyoto

Protocol, but are not required under the protocol to reduce the carbon emissions produced within their countries.[22]

The Rio Declaration, in principle 1, states: "Human beings are at the center of concerns for sustainable development. They are entitled to a healthy and productive life in harmony with nature."[23] The FCCC begins by asserting: "The Parties should protect the climate system for the benefit of present and future generations of humankind. . . ."[24] Both instruments link protecting human health with the right of peoples to sustainable development.

The assertion of the *human right to health* goes back to the Universal Declaration of Human Rights and the ICESCR. Article 12.2 of the ICESCR states: "The steps to be taken by the States Parties to the present Covenant to achieve the full realization of this right shall include those necessary for . . . the improvement of all aspects of environmental and industrial hygiene."[25] The right to health, which some argue implies a right to a healthy environment, is affirmed in other international instruments and in general comments by the committee that enforces the ICESCR, which has emphasized *the right to safe drinking water.*[26]

Regional Enforcement

Latin American countries support the right to a healthy environment. The Additional Protocol to the American Convention on Human Rights, which was approved in 1988 and is generally known at the Protocol of San Salvador, affirms "the right to live in a healthy environment." (Article 11)[27]

To date, this "environmental right" has not been enforced by the Organization of American States (OAS) largely due to opposition by the United States, which opposes the assertion of the right to health in the ICESCR. The right to a healthy environment, however, has been upheld by courts in Latin American countries including Argentina, Chile, Costa Rica, and Guatemala. Some of these decisions extend this right to future generations, whereas other decisions support the right to health protected by international as well as domestic law. To protect indigenous peoples, Latin American courts have affirmed links between the right to a healthy environment and the rights to life and to cultural development.[28]

Some countries have included the right to a healthy environment in their constitutions. The constitution of the Republic of (South) Korea states that "all citizens have the right to a healthy and pleasant environment." Other countries with constitutional protection for the right to a healthy environment include Argentina, Ecuador, Hungary, Peru, Portugal, the Philippines, and South Africa.[29]

The constitution of the Republic of South Africa asserts: "Everyone has the right (a) to an environment that is not harmful to their health or well being; and (b) to have the environment protected, for the benefit of present and future generations, through reasonable legislative and other measures that (i) prevent pollution and ecological degradation; (ii) promote conservation; and (iii) secure ecologically sustainable development and use of natural resources while promoting justifiable economic and social development."[30] This affirmation goes beyond the right to health care, and also beyond the right to a healthy working environment, by specifically referring to ecological degradation and the promotion of conservation.[31]

ANIMAL RIGHTS?

In the 1970s a few environmental activists began to wear a button asserting "Animals Have Rights, Too."[32] Today, the environmental movement is divided over which animals, if any, have rights, and the likely consequences that asserting animal rights may have on protecting the environment. We join the fray by considering humanitarian laws that promote animal welfare, and then assessing the argument for animal rights made by moral philosopher Tom Regan.

Humanitarian Law

The earliest general law in Anglo-American jurisprudence prohibiting cruelty to some animals was the "Body of Liberties" promulgated in the Massachusetts Bay Colony in 1641.[33] The English Parliament did not protect larger domestic animals from cruel treatment until 1822 when the Ill-Treatment of Cattle Act was passed, and this Act only prohibited injuring cattle owned by others. (The law protected the property right of those owning cattle.) To ensure greater protection for animals, English humanitarians in 1824 organized the Society for the Prevention of Cruelty to Animals, and in 1840 it became a "royal society," which is why it is known today is the RSPCA.[34]

In England the humanitarian movement succeeded in securing passage of the 1876 British Cruelty to Animals Act, which did not abolish *vivisection* (the dissection of animals for research purposes), but limited such dissection to licensed medical centers and required using anesthesia to minimize animal pain.[35] Vivisection was not similarly regulated in the United States until Congress passed the 1966 Animal Welfare Act.[36]

In the 1880s the American Ornithologists Union sought to end the killing of wild birds that were not hunted for food. The Audubon Society soon took up this cause, and in 1900 Congress enacted the Lacey Act making transport of illegally killed birds across state lines a federal offense. This act did not recognize the right to life of any bird, yet it did provide some protection to birds that were being killed for their beautiful feathers rather than for food. The law received support because it seemed that the pursuit of economic gain, if left unchecked, would result in the extinction of one or more species.[37]

These initiatives to protect animals asserted ethical presumptions about our *duty* and *character* and, after reformers embraced utilitarian thinking, relied on *consequence* arguments that take animal suffering into account. In modern culture the utilitarian argument is identified with Peter Singer, who asserts that animals have the "right" to "equal consideration of interests."[38] Singer explains, however, that he is not advocating "animal rights" as such, but is arguing "that animals' interests ought to be given equal consideration with the like interests of humans."[39] As chapter 8 considers consequential ethics, we assess Singer's argument there.

Rights Claims

Here we consider arguments for animal rights. In 1867 John Muir wrote: "How narrow we selfish, conceited creatures are in our sympathies! How blind to the rights of all the rest of creation!" A century later David R. Brower, a founder of the Sierra Club, proclaimed, "I believe in the rights of creatures other than man."[40] In 1979 Robert Hunter, one of the founder members of Greenpeace, framed the environmental agenda as a claim for *the rights of nature*: "We must seriously begin to inquire into the rights of rabbits and turnips, the rights of soil and swamp, the rights of the atmosphere, and, ultimately, the rights of the planet."[41]

In statements such as these it seems that the word *rights* is being used in a rhetorical sense "to mean that nature, or parts of it, has intrinsic worth which humans ought to respect."[42] If this is so, the "rights claim" is largely an appealing way to argue for our duty to protect animals and nature.

Arguments explicitly for animal rights are of two kinds. Some moral philosophers argue that many animals have *interests* that may justify rights. For these animals, Joel Feinberg writes, satisfying their interests "constitutes their welfare or good."[43] He also asserts that beings "who *can* have rights are precisely those who have (or can have) interests."[44] Therefore, if animals have interests, it would seem that animals might have rights.

If we hold, Feinberg reasons, "not only that we ought to treat animals humanely but also that we should do so for the animals' own sake, that such treatment is something we owe animals as their due, something that can be claimed for them, something the withholding of which would be an injustice and a wrong, and not merely a harm, then it follows that we do ascribe rights to animals."[45]

Yet, recognizing an animal's interests and our duty to respect these interests does not require affirming that the animal has a right that trumps all interests other than its own.[46] The interest of a rat in living is not a right that necessarily makes it wrong for humans to act in their own interest by using the rat to test a vaccine.

Inherent Value

Tom Regan argues that interests do not justify rights. "What has value for the utilitarian," he writes, "is the satisfaction of an individual's interests, not the individual whose interests they are."[47] Regan asserts that "individuals" have rights because of their inherent value and that some nonhuman animals are "individuals" and thus have rights.

Regan begins his argument by noting that our moral community, in which justice requires giving each individual his due, is comprised of "moral agents" and "moral patients." Moral agents are rational and autonomous individuals and thus morally responsible. Moral patients are individuals who are not moral agents, because they lack rationality or autonomy (such as infants or mentally impaired adults), but are of moral concern.[48] Moral agents have rights and duties, whereas moral patients have only rights.

Next Regan asserts that some animals have lives comparable in significant ways to humans. As these animals have and pursue their own good, although they are not rational or autonomous, they are best understood as "individuals" like moral patients. Therefore, Regan reasons, these animals are "subjects of a life" as humans also are, and deserve to be included in our moral community with rights (like moral patients).

What do some animals and moral patients have in common that makes them "subjects of a life" with rights that should be protected? The short answer is "a unified psychological presence in the world and an experiential welfare,"[49] and the long answer is in this endnote.[50] Children, Regan says, are "each the subject of a life that fares well or ill for them, logically independently of how valuable they are to others."[51] Animals with these same characteristics, he concludes, deserve the same rights.

Which animals does Regan think fit these criteria? He says "that no one knows the exact answer, and I personally have never tried to give one. Instead, I adopt a conservative policy by asking whether a line can be drawn that minimizes otherwise endless disputation."[52] In the 1983 edition of *The Case for Animal Rights*, this line is "mentally normal mammals of a year or more."[53] In the 2004 edition, however, he says that "birds are and fish may be" subjects of a life and thus have rights.[54]

Also, in the 2004 edition Regan leaves unqualified the statement "We simply do not know enough to justify dismissing, *out of hand*, the idea that a frog, say, may be the subject of a life, replete with desires, goals, beliefs, intentions, and the like. When our ignorance is so great, and the possible moral price so large, it is not unreasonable to give these animals the benefit of the doubt, treating them *as if* they are subjects, due our respectful treatment, especially when doing so causes no harm to us."[55]

Finally, he argues that the "subject of a life" criteria are the sole basis for affirming the inherent rights of members of the moral community. This means that every subject of a life has equal rights, whether she is human or not, as anything other than granting equal rights to all would be unreasonable and thus discriminatory.[56]

Regan is an activist in the "animal rights movement"[57] and defends "abolitionist" goals. The philosophy of animal rights calls for an end to:

- The use of animals in cosmetic testing in particular and product testing in general.
- The coercive use of any animal in military research, or in such research topics as the deleterious effects of smoking, maternal deprivation and drug addiction.
- The traditions of "sport" hunting and trapping of wildlife.
- The commerce in the skins of other animals for purposes of human vanity.
- The capture and training of wild animals, for purposes of entertainment.[58]

He acknowledges, however, that utilitarian advocates of animal liberation, who argue for animal interests, reach the same conclusions.[59]

Critical Arguments

I think that these goals are reasonable ethical presumptions, but for three reasons remain unconvinced by arguments for "animal rights." First, Regan concludes that only individuals (subjects of a life) can have rights, because *he assumes only individuals have real inherent value.* His "postulate" that only individual, moral agents have inherent value, which he claims is a reasonable "theoretical assumption,"[60] leads him to extend this value only to individual, moral patients and then to individual animals, which are like moral patients.[61]

Regan does allow that ecosystems, such as forests, "might have inherent value," but he argues that the value of an ecosystem "is incommensurate with any one individual's pleasures, preference-satisfactions, and the like, or with the sum of such goods for any number of individuals."[62] This is not a minor point for Regan, as he condemns assertions of the intrinsic worth of ecosystems and species as "environmental fascism."[63]

There is evidence, however, that makes it reasonable to give moral consideration to species and for an understanding of human rights that transcends individuals. The US Endangered Species Act of 1973 ascribes value to threatened and endangered species, and does not subordinate this good to that of every individual organism.[64] Moreover, international human rights law, which asserts human rights as the necessary social conditions for human dignity, includes *group rights* and *people's rights*, as well as individual rights. Despite the emphasis on individual rights in Western philosophy and jurisprudence, the contemporary practice of law supports a more inclusive perspective.

Second, Regan argues that the inherent rights possessed by human and nonhuman "subjects of a life" are equal, making human culture of no importance for moral consideration. Yet, *human culture is the source of rationality and ethics,* and this is why we can have a discussion about animal rights![65] As explained in chapter 4, we may reasonably conclude that all life has intrinsic value *for itself,* because it has a good of its own, but that human life also has intrinsic value *in itself,* because it is the basis for moral culture. On earth, humans are uniquely capable of ethics, and this is not simply an individual characteristic. It is a social reality.

Third, Regan and other advocates of animal rights (and animal liberation) raise the objection of *speciesism* to the drawing of any line between humans, as a species, and other animals. "To avoid the prejudice of speciesism," Regan says, "we must 'allow that beings which are similar (to humans) in all relevant respects have a similar right to life.'"[66] What distinguishes this issue from the rejection of human culture, as a reason for drawing a line between humans and nonhuman animals, is the analogy to racism and the use of the scientific term *species.*

Regan's claim that race and species are analogous is misleading. Mary Midgley argues that: "Race in humans is not a significant grouping at all, but species in animals certainly is. It is never true that, in order to know how to treat a human being, you must first find out what race he belongs to. (Cases where this might seem to matter always really turn on culture.) But with an animal, to know the species is absolutely essential."[67] A moral distinction based on race is wrong, but this does not mean that a moral distinction based on significant differences among species must be wrong.

A species "consists of all the animals of the same type, who are able to breed and produce young of the same kind."[68] Humans are a species, but animals are a kingdom that is divided into two groups, vertebrates and invertebrates, each of which has various classes, and within each class are species. Fish, amphibians, reptiles, birds, and mammals are classes of vertebrates, and humans are a species within the class of mammals. All talk of "animal rights" is not only scientifically vague but also anthropocentric, as proclaiming such rights relies on an argument about the humanlike characteristics of nonhuman animals.

Two other facts support a critical view of "speciesism." Midgley notes that humans have a "natural preference" for living with other humans in societies, and that this "is not, like race-prejudice, a product of culture."[69] She is well aware that a "species-bond" can "produce terrible misery," but argues that these preferences "are also an absolutely central element in human happiness, and it seems unlikely that we could live at all without them. They are the root from which charity grows."[70]

Furthermore, human societies have domesticated many other species. "It is one of the special powers and graces of our species," Midgley observes, "to draw in, domesticate and live with a great variety of other creatures. No other animal does so on anything like so large a scale."[71] The relationships in human societies between humans and domesticated animals have often been cruel, and in many ways continue to be so, but clearly this is not the whole story.

I think Regan argues that individual animal rights are equal to individual human rights, because be believes this is the only argument that will free animals from the tyranny and the suffering that humans continue to inflict on sentient animals. Regan may be right that an argument for animal interests will not bring about their liberation, but his argument for animal rights is not convincing. There are good reasons for ascribing moral consideration to many species, and for limiting rights to humans, as we are the only species on earth able to protect other species and the natural habitat we share with them.

Rights and Right

Rolston suggests: "Humans do possess rights (that is, they can press claims on other humans about right behavior), and this use of 'rights' may be contagious enough to work rhetorically with higher animals, whose claims can be pressed by sympathetic humans. But environmental ethics uses 'rights' chiefly as a term of convenience; the real convictions here are about what is 'right.'"[72]

This is why laws protecting an endangered species do not grant a *right to life* for every member of a species, but instead define the government's duty to protect the species. This inevitably involves protecting particular organisms, but the focus is preserving habitats.

Whether or not we ascribe rights to *animals in captivity*, we have a duty to consider that it may be wrong to confine the members of some species. More than one zoo has ended its exhibit of elephants, when officials concluded that the elephants were being psychologically damaged by their confinement.[73] After studying dolphins for twelve years in a research facility, John C. Lilly, a neurophysiologist, released them, because he had become convinced that dolphins are too intelligent and sensitive to be kept in captivity.[74]

The US Animal Welfare Act enacted in 1966 has been amended to cover animals in research institutions, but at present excludes "virtually all birds, rats, and mice bred for research" although these species "account for approximately 85 percent of all animals used in laboratories."[75] This exclusion should be ended. It is encouraging that in 2007 the US National Institutes of Health (NIH), which uses animals in biomedical studies, succumbed to moral pressure and agreed to stop breeding chimpanzees for research.[76]

A RIGHTS STRATEGY

International law, as well as the constitutions and laws of nations, assert rights that are intrinsically right, and all these assertions are important for doing ethics. The moral presumptions expressed in international law may provide protection for the environment, if the concept of sustainability is understood ecologically.

The ICCPR asserts *civil and political rights* that guarantee due process. These rights include the right to freedom of expression (Article 19.2) and the right of peaceful assembly (Article 21). In addition, the ICPR affirms that "all persons are equal before the law and are entitled without any discrimination to the equal protection of the law." (Article 26)

These ethical presumptions require that decisions concerning the use of the environment allow public debate and protect the rights of communities likely to be affected. Both the ICCPR and the ICESCR assert *the right of self-determination,*[77] which affirms that it is wrong for one people to exploit another.

In international law, *the right to sustainable development* now means development that:

- Meets the needs of the present without compromising the ability of future generations to meet their own needs. (Brundtland Commission Report)[78]
- Includes economic development, social development, and environmental protection. (Rio Declaration, Beijing Declaration)
- Realizes progressively the social right to health, healthy working conditions, and a healthy environment. (ICESCR, Articles 7 and 12, Stockholm Declaration)

Our ethical presumption should be economic and social development that is *environmentally sustainable.*

We should protect sentient animals in our care by affirming our duty to support public policies that prohibit human acts of cruelty, minimize animal suffering, and provide an environment for animals that is healthy and natural. The more animal interests are like human interests, the more convincing the evidence should be to set aside these presumptions.

For *animals in the wild*, we have a duty to ensure that human activities do not harm the integrity of animal habitats and preserve biodiversity by protecting endangered species. If ecosystem integrity is at risk, compelling evidence should be required to set aside these presumptions.

QUESTIONS—RIGHTS: HUMANS AND ANIMALS?

1. What led to the development of international human rights law after World War II? How is human rights law different than "positive" law?
2. Identify three civil and political rights, and three economic, social, and cultural rights.
3. State the standards for enforcing civil and political rights and for enforcing economic, social, and cultural rights, and explain the difference.
4. Why does the United States oppose the right to a healthy environment? What support is there for this individual human right?
5. Explain what sustainable development in international law now means, and illustrate why enforcing this standard may involve conflicting assertions of human rights.

6. Make an argument for the humanitarian treatment of animals. Does your argument emphasize duty, character, relationships, rights, or consequences?

7. Argue that some animals have rights because of their interests, and raise a critical question about this claim.

8. Summarize Regan's argument for the rights that "subjects of a life" have, and raise a critical question about his argument.

9. Are racism and speciesism morally analogous? Explain your thinking.

10. Argue for extending moral consideration to other species but limiting rights to humans, and raise a critical question about your argument.

11. What is our duty to animals used in research? To animals kept in zoos and aquariums? Explain your thinking.

12. What is our duty to wild animals in their habitats? Explain your reasoning.

8

Consequences

PREDICTING THE FUTURE

In the preceding four chapters of part 2 we have constructed moral presumptions about what we understand to be intrinsically right and good. Now we consider an entirely different way of deciding what is ethical, which involves predicting the likely consequences of taking an action. This approach to ethics does not presume that any action is intrinsically right or wrong, but proposes that the action which will likely have the best consequences is "right."

This shift in moral philosophy—from asserting what actions and ways of being have intrinsic moral worth to predicting consequences—began with a utilitarian argument for maximizing pleasure and minimizing pain. The growing importance of the social sciences led to other ways of assessing consequences, and economics now relies on cost-benefit analysis. In considering environmental issues, however, a consequential prediction of likely economic changes must also take scientific evidence into account, as the impact of economic development on ecosystems and species cannot be reduced to a financial calculation.

UTILITARIANISM

David Hume (1711–1776) first proposed a theory of utilitarianism, but Jeremy Bentham (1748–1832) and John Stuart Mill (1806–1873) became its main proponents. Bentham challenged traditional forms of social and political authority by claiming that moral philosophy should simply involve a factual assessment of our foreseeable experience. "Nature has placed mankind under the governance of two sovereign masters, *pain* and *pleasure*. It is for them alone to point out what we ought to do, as well as to determine what we shall do."[1]

In his book *Utilitarianism*, Mill urged that we act so as to achieve the greatest good for the greatest number of people. "According to the Greatest Happiness Principle . . . the ultimate end, with reference to and for the sake of which all other things are desirable (whether we are considering our own good or that of other people), is an existence exempt as free as possible from pain, and as rich as possible in enjoyments."[2]

We are so accustomed to the utilitarian way of thinking that we may not appreciate how radical this argument was in the nineteenth century, for it meant rejecting the moral authority of established religious teaching and cultural traditions.

Problems

From the beginning, however, there was disagreement as to *how happiness or pleasure is to be measured*. Bentham proposed a quantitative calculation, but Mill argued for a more qualitative assessment. Neither explained how the pleasure or pain experienced by some persons is to be weighed against the pleasure or pain of others.

A second problem with the utilitarian approach is that *no action is prohibited as wrong*. Utilitarian reasoning may be used to ignore significant moral duties and legal rights, if this would increase happiness. Governments that permit corporations to cut down forests and strip minerals from the land, despite devastating impacts on local communities, simply argue that the benefits for the whole economy outweigh the adverse impacts on a minority of the population.[3]

A third problem concerns *future generations*. If these are taken into account, the number of people to consider is so much greater than the people alive that the happiness of "the future" seems clearly to outweigh the happiness of "the present." If, however, we ignore future generations, then there is no reason to limit our consumption of any natural resource unless doing so makes more of us happy.

A fourth problem with the utilitarian approach is that, before we act, *we cannot know the consequences of acting.* Sometimes we know the probabilities of the likely outcomes of an action and can identify its *risks.* When we know the possible outcomes, but have too little information to assign probabilities to these outcomes, our predictions are *uncertain.* When we do not even know the possible outcomes of an action, we are *ignorant* of the consequences.[4]

These distinctions are especially important in environmental ethics. "Estimating stocks of natural resources, or reproductive rates for cultivated species is basically a question of risk. Estimating reproductive rates for wild species is a question of uncertainty, since we cannot accurately predict the multitude of factors that affect these reproduction rates, but we do know the range over which reproduction is possible. Estimating ecological thresholds, conditions beyond which ecosystems may flip into alternative states, is a question of pure uncertainty, since we have limited knowledge of ecosystems and cannot predict the external conditions that affect them. Predicting the alternative state into which an ecosystem might flip when it passes an ecological threshold, and how humans will adapt, are cases of absolute ignorance involving evolutionary and technological change."[5]

Rule and Preference Utilitarianism

Alternative forms of utilitarian reasoning, which may be distinguished from its original formulation now known as *act utilitarianism,* have been devised to try to deal with these difficulties in predicting consequences. *Rule utilitarianism* relies on past events for consequential evidence of what an ethical rule should be. *Preference utilitarianism* assesses the desires of those likely to be affected by a decision, in order to predict whether or not the decision will lead to consequences that yield more happiness.[6]

A rule based on past experience of possible consequences does not remove the uncertainties inherent in making decisions that will affect the environment, as our understanding of its dynamic ecosystems is very limited. Also, making predictions based on individual preferences cannot take into account the actual impact of an action on the environment, but only the desires and hopes of those surveyed. Furthermore, both of these alternative forms of utilitarian reasoning ignore long-term consequences.

Finally, advocates of utilitarianism do not agree about including the suffering of animals in predictions about whether an action will maximize happiness. This is especially relevant in applying utilitarian theory to environmental decisions that will cause animals not only to suffer, but also to lose their habitats and perhaps to die out as a species.

ANIMAL SUFFERING

Bentham was the first utilitarian to express concern about the suffering of animals.

> The day *may* come when the rest of the animal creation may acquire those rights which never could have been witholden from them but by the hand of tyranny. The French have already discovered that the blackness of the skin is no reason why a human being should be abandoned without redress to the caprice of a tormentor . . . What else is it that should trace the insuperable line? Is it the faculty of reason, or perhaps the faculty of disclosure? But a full-grown horse or dog is beyond comparison more rational, as well as a more conversable animal, than an infant of a day, a week, or even a month old. But suppose it were otherwise, what would it avail? The question is not, Can they *reason?* nor Can they *talk?* but, *Can they suffer?*[7]

Among contemporary philosophers Peter Singer is the leading advocate for including animals in consequential calculations of pleasure and pain, and for ending "the tyranny" of humans over animals.[8] Singer specifies that by "animals" he means sentient, nonhuman animals, which "lumps together beings as different as oysters and chimpanzees."[9]

"The animal liberation movement," Singer writes, "is not saying that all lives are of equal worth or that all interests of humans and other animals are to be given equal weight, no matter what those interests may be. [In this respect it differs with deep ecology.] It is saying that where animals and humans have similar interests—we might take the interest in avoiding physical pain as an example, for it is an interest that humans clearly share with other animals—those interests are to be counted equally, with no automatic discount just because one of the beings is not human."[10]

Singer argues that the suffering of animals used in research generally outweighs the benefits for human beings, and he advocates vegetarianism because factory farming causes unnecessary animal suffering.[11] "The case for vegetarianism is at its strongest," he asserts, "when we see it as a moral protest against our use of animals as mere things, to be exploited for our convenience in whatever way makes them most cheaply available to us."[12]

His main concern is ending the intensive rearing of livestock and poultry, for this involves treating animals "like machines that convert low-priced fodder into high-priced flesh, and any innovation that results in a cheaper 'conversion-ratio' is liable to be adopted."[13] Yet, Singer also opposes traditional livestock practices. "Even when animals are roaming freely over large areas, as sheep and cattle do in Australia, operations like hot-iron branding, castration, and dehorning are carried out without any regard for the animals' capacity to suffer."[14]

"The same is true," Singer argues, "of handling and transport prior to slaughter. In the light of these facts, the issue to focus on is not whether there are some circumstances in which it could be right to eat meat, but on what we can do to avoid contributing to this immense amount of animal suffering."[15] Most people are surprised to learn that in the United States alone about thirty-seven million cattle are slaughtered each year for food.[16] Dismayed by these statistics, advocates of animal liberation are committed to changing the way we eat, as the "use and abuse of animals raised for food far exceeds, in sheer numbers of animals affected, any other kind of mistreatment."[17]

Assessing Pain

There are difficulties with including animal suffering in a utilitarian calculation of what actions will yield the greatest happiness. First, we must decide *which animals suffer.* Few doubt that mammals and poultry suffer in our food production system, but what about fish and scallops? Singer identifies suffering with the capacity to feel or sense pain, and ascribes this capacity to vertebrates (fish, amphibians, reptiles, birds, and mammals) and some classes of invertebrates, such as mollusks (including shrimp, oysters, and scallops).[18] Science has yet to settle this question.

Mary Midgley suggests that moral consideration is justified only when we recognize consciousness in an animal. "A conscious being is one which can *mind* what happens to it, which *prefers* some things to others, which can be pleased or pained, can suffer or enjoy."[19] Recognizing an animal as conscious like us, she argues, gives us a reason to include it in our moral community where the Golden Rule applies to all "others." With recognition of consciousness, she says, duties "arise, and if they are to be ignored, some reason is called for."[20]

Midgley thinks this approach also helps to resolve the second difficulty that Singer faces, namely, how to *weigh the suffering of diverse sentient beings*. She notes that his utilitarian approach "allows a principle of selection based on the varying nervous capacities of different animals,"[21] which makes it relevant to consider that "social birds and mammals are upset by solitude, or by the removal of their young, which would have no effect at all on simpler creatures, and how the power to remember and anticipate trouble, which is a specialty though not a monopoly of humans, can increase its impact."[22]

Singer clearly asserts that the moral equality of nonhuman animals and humans should not be understood as minimizing "the obvious differences between most members of our species and members of other species" and that "what harms humans may cause much less harm, or even no harm at all, to some animals."[23] Yet, he does not explain how to weigh these various experiences of suffering in order to maximize the happiness of nonhuman animals and humans.

Given these problems in utilitarian reasoning, Midgley proposes that we need "further principles, say of kinship or intrinsic value," to clarify our moral duty with respect to animals.[24] Anyone with a pet knows that humans can experience empathy for an animal, and this makes attributing emotions to animals reasonable, as our children's stories remind us. In the Grimm brothers version of Cinderella she is aided by a bird, and in the Chinese version she is helped by a fish. These animals care for her, and she attains happiness, in part, because she cares for them.

In fact, most of what we know about the suffering and happiness of an animal comes from our close relationships with mammals and birds. "The degree of mutual understanding which we have," Midgley argues, "is only made possible by attributing moods, motives and so forth to them on the rough model of our own, and constantly correcting the resulting misunderstandings."[25] This process of reasoning supports the moral presumption that *we have a duty to ensure that the feelings of conscious animals are considered*. Those who would cause suffering for animals in our care have the burden of showing that the consequences of such an action outweigh our duty to minimize the suffering of these animals. The more sophisticated the animal's nervous system, the higher the burden.

Wild Animals

A third difficulty with considering animal pain involves animals in the wild. Do we have a duty to protect wild animals from causing more suffering by preying on one another? One utilitarian writes: "Where we can prevent preda-tion without occasioning as much or more suffering than we would prevent, we are obligated to do so. . . ."[26]

Clearly, such thinking is very modern. Hunting and gathering cultures rec-ognized that humans, like other carnivores, are predators. Traditional Native American cultures saw animals as other "persons" who gave their lives when they were killed for food and for use of their skin and bones. Agricultural soci-eties domesticated animals for work and for food, and in these societies moral arguments were constructed for not eating meat. Hindu culture, for instance, justifies the "suffering" of laboring animals as their *karma*, but expects the souls in animals to be reborn in humans. *This sense of relatedness between animals and humans supports a moral argument for being a vegetarian.*

Singer argues that animal suffering is an ethical reason for not eating meat, but he also states that we have no responsibility to interfere in nature to protect animals from one another. "We do enough," he says, "if we eliminate our own unnecessary killing and cruelty toward other animals."[27] His reasoning, of course, is consequential. "Judging by our past record, any attempt to change ecological systems on a large scale is going to do far more harm than good. For that reason, if for no other, it is true to say that, except in a few very limited cases, we cannot and should not try to police all of nature."[28]

Rolston agrees with Singer's conclusion, but for different reasons. "*Environ-mental ethics is not social ethics, nor does it give us any duty to revise nature.* Our attitude toward predation is not just that it is practically difficult to remove, or that removing it is an impossible ideal. We would not want to take predation out of the system if we could (though we take humans out of the predation sys-tem), because pain and pleasure are not the only criteria of value, not even the principal ones."[29]

Rolston agrees with Midgley that our relationship with animals leads to du-ties that recognize intrinsic values. We have a duty to reduce suffering in the world of human culture, and this means minimizing the suffering of domesti-cated animals in our care. We do not have the same duty to try to reduce the suffering of wild animals in their natural habitats.[30]

What does this mean in practice? Rolston argues: "Where humans elect to capture animals for food, domestication, research, or other utility, our duties to them, if any arise, are generated by these animals' encounters with culture; they are not simply a matter of the animals' *capacity* to suffer pains but of their *con-text*."[31] In short, *any suffering that we impose on wild animals should be compara-ble to their suffering in nature.* "Do not cause inordinate suffering, beyond those orders of nature from which the animals were taken."[32]

Singer, Rolston, and Midgley agree that sentience triggers ethical concern, but Rolston and Midgley think that suffering by itself does not justify including animals in the moral community where the Golden Rule applies. Earthworms, Rolston points out, "have nerves, ganglia, brains, even endorphins (natural opiates). But their form of sentience may be so alien to ours that 'Do to others as you would have them do to you' is untranslatable there."[33] Given our knowledge of earthworms, he thinks that we can assess whether our use of them, as bait for catching fish, for example, is analogous to their suffering in nature.

COST-BENEFIT ANALYSIS

Where the predicted consequences of taking an action are probable and may readily be quantified, cost-benefit analysis is useful. For instance, the commercial value of medicinal substances in tropical forests is often greater than the value of using the land for agriculture after logging the forests.[34] To ensure fiscal accountability in the United States the National Policy Act of 1969 mandates cost-benefit analysis for all federal projects related to the environment.[35] Within a decade, cost-benefit analysis was emphasizing the costs of environmental restrictions that would hinder economic growth.[36]

In addition to the likely influence of political lobbying, there are other dangers in using cost-benefit analysis. In making environmental policy we must acknowledge the *nonmarket values* of ecosystems and human rights, our *limited knowledge* of the natural environment, and the danger in using *economic discounting* to estimate future costs and benefits.

Nonmarket Values

There are many consequences not easily assessed by market pricing. Nonmarket values involving *ecosystems* include the depletion of nonrenewable resources, the loss of ecosystem functions, and the extinction of species. Cost-benefit analysis also ignores *human rights*. Relying on cost-benefit analysis, for instance, "will characteristically require placement of toxic wastes near poor people. Such placement usually lowers land values (what people are willing to pay for property). Land that is already cheap, where poor people live, will not lose as much value as land that is currently expensive, where wealthier people live, so a smaller loss of social wealth attends placement of toxic wastes near poor people."[37]

Those who endorse the use of cost-benefit analysis usually agree that some values should not be treated like market costs, but challenge the notion that environmental issues should be exempted from cost-benefit analysis. Even in protecting endangered species, they argue, "we need to know whether a certain approach will be effective, given available resources."[38] In addition, "we need to know whether the cost of saving them involves sacrificing something else we consider equally priceless."[39]

In addition, advocates of cost-benefit analysis point out that social values standing "in the way of important efficiency gains have a way of breaking down and being replaced over time, so that in the long run society manages to accommodate itself to some form of cost-benefit criterion."[40] Certainly, this is true with respect to environmental policy.

It seems reasonable, therefore, that a necessary choice between nonmarket values, such as preserving ecosystem integrity and the human right to food, water, and shelter (all of which require economic development) should be made in a cost-effective way. Yet, this should not be the only consideration. Our ethical presumption is that *ecosystem integrity and human rights are of intrinsic worth*. Protecting these intrinsic values involves economic choices that should be assessed by cost-basis analysis. Nonetheless, we should act on our ethical presumptions to protect ecosystem integrity and human rights unless there is compelling evidence that the likely consequences of doing so would be dire.

Limited Knowledge

Also, our limited knowledge affects the utility of cost-benefit analysis. For example, it is fairly easy to assess the costs of building nuclear power plants, but very hard to know what the *long-term costs* will be if these nuclear power plants are not built, or the financial costs of storing nuclear waste safely for centuries if the power plants are built. Numbers seem precise, but actually are no more accurate than the *assumptions we make* for our calculations.

Therefore, cost-benefit analysis should be conducted in a transparent manner. "In the real world, we must acknowledge that for any actual calculation we perform, there could be some cost or benefit or risk we have overlooked. What can we do to avoid overlooking what in retrospect will become painfully obvious? Although it is no guarantee, the best thing I can think of is to open the process to *public scrutiny*."[41]

Discounting

A third difficulty in cost-benefit analysis involves the use of *economic discounting*, as it may not adequately reflect our moral responsibility to future generations.

To evaluate this issue, we need to understand what economic discounting involves.

"In financial markets, a dollar acquired today is worth more than a dollar we will acquire in a year. The dollar acquired today can be put to work immediately. At worst, it can be put in the bank, and thus be worth perhaps $1.05 in a year [if it earns 5 percent interest annually]. Therefore, if you ask me how much I would pay today to be given a dollar a year from now, I certainly would not pay as much as a dollar. I would pay something less, perhaps about ninety-five cents. Properly valued, then, the future dollar sells at a discount."[42]

This seems reasonable, at least from the perspective of investors. Yet, if we are thinking about the next generations obtaining a dollar of value from a clean environment, discounting this "future dollar" would mean we would invest far less than a dollar now to protect environmental integrity.

To remedy this problem, some economists suggest using a *declining discount rate* for long-term investments. "The costs of taking action to slow climate change are incurred now, while the benefits will only be reaped in the far distant future. With a constant discount rate, the benefits of reducing emissions are discounted to almost nothing and so abatement appears to be poor value for money. However, a declining discount rate results in greater weight being placed on the future benefits, and efforts to slow climate change suddenly become more attractive."[43]

Many economists continue to "assume that money is an adequate substitute for anything, and therefore anything in the future is worth less than the same thing today."[44] Yet, even the most cautious use of economic discounting does not justify applying cost-benefit analysis to all the values at stake in our use of the natural environment.

We have a duty to include externalities in market prices so we are paying the environmental costs that have generally been ignored in our economy. "We have no right to discount the price that *others* will have to pay for our projects. We have no right to discount externalities."[45]

BIOCENTRIC CONSEQUENTIALISM

Singer does not rely on cost-benefit analysis in making utilitarian arguments. For example, his reasoning that our way of raising animals for food causes unnecessary suffering for these animals and for humans as well simply makes a commonsense argument about the consequences of our industrialized food system.

"Intensive animal production is a heavy use of fossil fuels and a major source of pollution of both air and water. It releases large quantities of methane and other greenhouse gases into the atmosphere. We are risking unpredictable changes to the climate of our planet—which means, ultimately, the lives of billions of people, not to mention the extinction of untold thousands of species of plants and animals unable to cope with changing conditions—for the sake of more hamburgers."[46]

States of the World

Moral philosopher Robin Attfield agrees with Singer that ethical decisions can be made without cost-benefit analysis by using reason to predict and weigh likely consequences. Attfield also proposes that claims for intrinsic values are best considered indirectly, as intended consequences, which may be assessed as *states of the world.* He explains the ethical approach of "biocentric consequentialism" in three sentences, which we consider one at a time.

First, Attfield says, the "relevant consequences are the foreseeable consequences of action and inaction upon all bearers of moral standing."[47] Considering only "foreseeable consequences" means ignoring uncertainty, but all those who support a consequential approach to ethics argue that there is no better alternative. We must act on the basis of what we know.

The phrase "all bearers of moral standing" implies that the moral community includes at least some nonhuman organisms, but does not extend moral consideration to ecosystems or species. Attfield argues, however, that a concern for individual organisms requires weighing foreseeable impacts on habitats (in ecosystems) and on populations (which are crucial for species survival). Biocentric consequentialism identifies these impacts as "states of the world."

Second, Attfield explains, a biocentric consequential approach to ethics holds that "impacts on basic needs outweigh lesser impacts, and that impacts on creatures with complex and sophisticated capacities such as autonomy and self-consciousness (in cases where these capacities are themselves at stake) outweigh impacts on creatures lacking them."[48] Distinguishing basic needs from lesser impacts involves qualitative as well as quantitative comparisons. Thus, a survival need, such as adequate food, has more significance than disruption to wild animals caused by tourists or recreational activities.

Attfield's concern for "creatures with complex and sophisticated capacities" gives greater weight to human pleasures and suffering, at least when unique human capacities are at stake. This concern also allows considering human rights, such as the right to participate in land use decisions that affect both human and animal habitats, and distinguishes biocentric consequentialism from the biocentric egalitarianism promoted by deep ecology.

Third, Attfield argues, actions "are right if they maximize the balance of good over bad consequences, or if they uphold practices, general compliance with which would promote such a balance (practices like keeping promises), and obligatory if the difference made by the action or practice is significant and greater than that of alternatives."[49]

This complex sentence is about weighing good and bad results. The first way of doing this involves *specific outcomes.* The second way values *social practices* encouraging good behavior. This second method of considering outcomes allows support for practices that in traditional ethics are valued for their intrinsic worth (like keeping promises) by finding them valuable because of their beneficial results. If these consequential benefits are significant, Attfield argues, we have a duty to adopt the practices that lead to this good *state of the world.*

In short, Attfield's argument for biocentric consequentialism rejects act and preference utilitarianism, and asserts a form of rule utilitarianism that justifies enforcing duties and rights as well as weighing specific outcomes. Attfield argues that this consequential approach to ethics makes other forms of moral reasoning irrelevant.

Our Ethical Approach

Legal scholar Christopher D. Stone reminds us that consequential reasoning originally had a limited focus, as Bentham's goal was reforming social institutions like the prison system. Utilitarian arguments were made "to provide guidance to lawmakers in devising standards for general legislative rules that would apply across broad populations. But once unloosed, the basic idea was generalized to every corner of personal conduct, including, for example, inter-family relations."[50]

Therefore, Stone argues for a pluralist approach to ethics and suggests that anyone arguing for only one form of ethical reasoning should "convince us that all moral conduct, with all its complexities and irregularities, answers to a single index of measurement."[51] Should we rely only on some method of consequential reasoning? Before answering, I suggest that we consider three arguments in defense of a pluralist approach to ethics.

First, our brains have evolved to think about moral issues by relying on feelings of empathy and reasoning about what is intrinsically right and good, as well as on our ability to forecast the possible consequences of our actions.[52] It seems reasonable to assume that we are "fit" for survival, in part, because *our brains have evolved to reason in different ways.*

Second, relying on consequential reasoning alone would mean rejecting our experience that some actions and ways of being are intrinsically right and good, and therefore should be embraced as ethical presumptions. This way of reasoning is the cultural heritage of our biological and evolutionary history. *Humans rely on moral language that reflects not only personal experience, but also literature and religious teachings as well as philosophical, economic, political, and legal discourse.* Does it make sense to replace this heritage with forecasts of the future?

Third, *because our knowledge is limited, there are many difficulties in predicting and measuring consequences.* There is no precise way to assess happiness and pleasure, or pain and suffering, or to compare the quantity or quality of these experiences, and including sentient animals makes these estimates even more speculative. Furthermore, cost-benefit analysis is helpful in making economic decisions, but cannot be used to value nonmarket goods, such as ecosystem integrity and human rights.

Therefore, I propose that we incorporate diverse forms of moral reasoning into our approach to environmental ethics by constructing moral presumptions that reflect arguments for intrinsic values, and then test these presumptions by considering predictions of the likely consequences of acting on them.

This approach to ethical reasoning allows arguments for the intrinsic worth of ecosystems, species, and even some landscapes. Also, it remains open to the possibility that some intrinsic values cannot adequately be taken into account by predicting consequences, and thus should be presumed to be right or good. Finally, our approach puts the burden of proof for overturning a moral presumption on those making consequential arguments, and clarifies that for some intrinsic values this burden requires compelling evidence.

For example, consequential arguments are being used to support the diversion of corn to produce ethanol, despite the unintended consequence of driving up the price of food worldwide. Higher profits, however, are not compelling evidence that justifies setting aside our moral presumption to protect the human right to food. Therefore, in chapters 9, 12, and 15 I argue that the US government should end subsidies for using corn to produce ethanol, and that those who are affluent should reduce their consumption of beef in order to increase the corn available for food.

Responding to global warming offers a second example of how doing environmental ethics differs from a consequentialist approach. If we were to weigh only predicted outcomes that may impact the macro economy, we would probably ignore personal acts of conservation. Yet, decisions by consumers to reduce waste and conserve energy have moral worth—as acts that are right and as virtues that reflect the character of being good persons—apart from any impact assessment as to what these ethical decisions mean for the state of the world.

SCIENTIFIC CONSEQUENCES

Finally, the use of science in predicting consequences is crucial for addressing our environmental crisis. In 2001 the UN Intergovernmental Panel on Climate Change, which was established in 1988 by the World Meteorological Organization and the UN Environment Programme, proposed that human activity was "likely" causing global warming. In 2007, however, the panel "declared that the evidence of a warming trend is 'unequivocal,' and that human activity has 'very likely' been the driving force in that change over the last 50 years."[53] The shift from "likely" to "very likely" as a scientific conclusion has strengthened the argument that governments and their citizens must take action to reduce the amount of carbon dioxide emitted into the atmosphere.

The Limits of Science

We rely on science for predictions of likely consequences, but need to keep in mind that scientific information presents a perspective on the world and does not simply reveal what is. As we saw in chapter 2, *scientific conclusions are limited by what we know, by what we are looking for, and by how we go about it*. The "answers you get depend on the questions you ask."[54]

For instance, if we describe our energy problem as a supply problem, we will likely conclude that we need to find and develop new sources of energy. Then our focus will be on drilling for more oil, considering whether to fund the development of nuclear power plants, and supporting the development of solar and wind technologies. If, however, we define our energy problem as excessive demand, we will focus on ways of reducing our energy use and developing new technologies that increase the efficiency of generating energy. *Science does not give us the whole picture, but only perspectives on it*.[55] So, it would seem best to pursue both inquiries.

Another example of how *scientific facts* depend on what we look for involves measuring the increase in the earth's temperature. The Department of Agriculture (USDA) publishes a hardiness zone map that identifies the lowest winter temperatures in various parts of the country. In December 2006 the National Arbor Day Foundation released a new version of this map showing "that many bands of the country are a full zone warmer, and a few spots are two zones warmer, than they were in 1990, when the map was last updated."[56]

The new Arbor map uses temperature data for fifteen years ending in 2004 to update the USDA map, which was made using thirteen years of data. "The Agriculture Department is in the process of redoing the map itself. But critics have taken issue with the department's decision to use thirty years of temperature data, saying it will result in cooler averages and fail to reflect the warming climate."[57]

The USDA claims that using a longer period will provide a more accurate assessment, as weather varies greatly from year to year. Climatologist Cameron P. Wake disagrees, arguing that a shorter period of study more clearly reveals the impact of global warming. He suggests that "the USDA doesn't want to acknowledge there's been a change."[58]

Science Is Human

Science is done by scientists, who are influenced by funding for their research, their desire to have successful careers, and their personal convictions, as well as by the results of their experiments and observations.[59] Biologist Rupert Sheldrake observes that: "The objective method is supposed to remove all psychic interests of the scientists from what they're doing. In fact, most scientists are heavily engaged in what they're doing if only for reasons of personal ambition."[60]

Scientific reports may be affected by politics. Government officials may delay or withhold scientific reports that contain damaging evidence,[61] or may require changes in scientific reports to weaken the conclusions. In 2003 the White House "altered a climate report by the US Environmental Protection Agency, editing out all references to the dangerous impacts of climate change on the United States."[62] In 2008 two dozen scientists visited Congress to protest "the systematic dismantling of the Endangered Species Act through the manipulation and suppression of science" by political appointees in the Interior Department.[63]

Economic interests may try to confuse the public about scientific conclusions. Claiming only to support "sound science," researchers funded by the coal and oil industry have claimed that there is little scientific evidence of global warming.[64] "There has been an organized campaign," Al Gore notes, "financed to the tune of about $10 million a year from some of the largest carbon polluters, to create the impression that there is disagreement in the scientific community."[65]

Scientific reports about the environment that predict the likely consequences of an action (or inaction) give us probable, possible, or uncertain outcomes. Emphasizing energy supply or demand, or measuring global warming using data from fifteen or thirty years are not simply scientific choices, even though the results of the investigations that follow may be good science. Also, predictions of consequences using scientific data may be manipulated for political ends.

Therefore, *in doing ethics we rely on empathy and critical reasoning to construct moral presumptions before drawing on science and other consequential arguments to test these presumptions.* A worksheet for doing environmental ethics follows this chapter. It offers a way of applying the process of moral reasoning that we have developed in part 2 to specific issues, such as those raised in part 3. Chapter 9 illustrates how this may be done.

QUESTIONS—CONSEQUENCES: PREDICTING THE FUTURE

1. Make a consequential argument for why littering is wrong.
2. How do rule and preference utilitarianism address the problems of utilitarianism?
3. Describe three problems with including animal suffering in a utilitarian calculation.
4. Summarize Singer's position on animal suffering. How does Midgley's reasoning differ? How does Rolston's thinking differ from Singer's and from Midgley's?
5. What assumptions does cost-benefit analysis make about our knowledge of the likely consequences of an action? Raise a critical question about one of these assumptions.
6. What sort of consequences may quite easily be assessed in cost-benefit analysis? Give an example concerning environmental ethics.
7. What are nonmarket goods? Give two examples.
8. Explain why using economic discounting to determine environmental policy is a problem.
9. Give a reason for using a consequentialist approach to ethics, rather than relying on arguments for intrinsic values.
10. Attfield does not directly recognize intrinsic values, but considers these in the form of practices that have consequences for a "state of the world." Explain his reasoning.

11.   Might we reasonably affirm different moral presumptions about the suffering of dogs in our homes and wolves in the wild? Explain your reasoning.

12.   Are scientific facts affected by how we measure them? Give an example. Why is this relevant for deciding how to respond to our environmental crisis?

WORKSHEET FOR DOING ENVIRONMENTAL ETHICS

1. Construct an ethical presumption.*

- Describe the environment issue you are addressing.
- Give *reasons* for responding to this issue based on:
  - *Duty*—To other persons, future generations, nature.
  - *Character*—Virtues of gratitude, integrity, frugality.
  - *Relationships*—The extent of our moral community.
  - *Rights*—Social conditions necessary for human dignity.
- State your reasoning as an *ethical presumption.*

2. Consider the consequences.**

- List the *likely consequences* of acting on this presumption.
  - Are these *probable* or only *possible* consequences?
  - Are the long-term consequences largely *uncertain?*
- Distinguish and *weigh the pro and con arguments*.
  - Rely on reason to assess *nonmarket values*.
  - Use cost-benefit analysis for *market goods*.
  - *Internalize externalities* in market prices.
  - *Avoid passing on costs* to future generations.
- If the pros outweigh the cons, then the presumption is confirmed. If not, challenge the presumption.
- The *evidence* needed *to set aside a presumption*:***
  - Should be *compelling* when the integrity of an ecosystem, or a human right, is at risk.
  - Need only be *convincing* for other presumptions.

3. Make your decision.

- If your analysis confirms your presumption, act on it.
- If not, revise your presumption before acting on it.

* Your reasoning in this process is in part intuitive. You are thinking from your experience about what is right and good, and then constructing an ethical hypothesis as to what action you should take and how you should conduct yourself as you take this action.

** If the likely beneficial consequences (pros) seem to outweigh the likely detrimental consequences (cons) of taking this action, then your thought experiment confirms your presumption. If, however, the cons seem to outweigh the pros, then your thought experiment calls into question the presumption you constructed. In this case, you need to clarify the burden of proof needed to set aside the presumption by deciding how substantial the facts and reasons should be to justify revising or setting aside your ethical hypothesis.

*** If the ethical presumption you constructed affirms a duty to protect the integrity of an ecosystem, or asserts a human right under international law, then a compelling burden of proof should be required to set aside this presumption. Otherwise, the weight of the moral reasoning required to revise or to set aside your ethical presumption only has to be convincing.

PART III
Learning from Nature

Chapter 9 addresses the ethical presumption of *living more ecologically.* International law and equity support the conclusion that members of industrial societies have a duty to reduce their consumption. Arguments about character and relationships, whether religious or secular, encourage sustainable consumption for the sake of future generations as well as nature. We have a legal right to buy and eat what we can afford, but not a moral right to purchase beef at a subsidized price that excludes the social and environmental costs of producing it. As citizens, we should support governmental policies that protect public resources. As consumers, we should use our purchasing power to promote economic development that is environmentally sustainable.

Chapter 10 analyzes the *public policy* initiatives of governments, corporations, and nongovernmental organizations (NGOs). Environmental policy in the United States recognizes our duty to future generations, which is also affirmed in international law. Corporations, such as JPMorgan Chase (financial services) and Interface Incorporated (carpet manufacturing), have pledged to abide by the environmental standards of international law. NGOs, such as Greenpeace, the Sierra Club, World Wildlife Fund (WWF), and the Nature Conservancy, pursue environmental policies worldwide, and collaborative strategies such as the Great Lakes Water Quality Agreement and the Apollo Alliance verify that governments, corporations, and NGOs can work together to protect the environment.

Chapter 11 reviews efforts to reduce *air and water pollution.* In the United States the EPA has banned lead from gasoline, required cars to have catalytic converters to reduce smog, mandated caps on the sulfur dioxide emissions of power plants to reduce acid rain, and phased out refrigeration and aerosol gases that have damaged the ozone layer in the stratosphere. The EPA sets water quality standards for point-source pollution and water treatment facilities, but is using a maximum contaminant level approach that permits lower levels of pollutants, such as pesticides—unlike the European Union, which uses the precautionary principle to ban all pesticides from drinking water. Nonpoint-source water pollution is largely storm water runoff. Groundwater, being pumped from aquifers for agriculture, industry, and drinking water, is being contaminated as well as depleted. Marketing bottled water is creating water scarcity for the poor and adding to the plastic now contaminating 40 percent of the surface of the oceans.

Chapter 12 considers *agriculture.* The industrial agriculture that dominates food production is unsustainable, because it requires cheap fossil fuels, is draining the water from underground aquifers, and causes erosion and loss of soil fertility. In poor countries economic and educational initiatives that empower poor women offer the best hope of controlling population growth and ensuring a sustainable use of agricultural land. In developed economies a transition to sustainable agriculture must be undertaken and is feasible, if those of us who are affluent reduce our consumption of meat by eating "lower on the food chain."

Chapter 13 reviews the debate over *conservation and preservation.* In the twentieth century progressive utilitarian policies dominated US forestry until the Clinton administration initiated an adaptive policy of ecosystem management, which has protected forests, deserts, and wetlands restoration plans negotiated with states, cities, private landowners, and federal agencies. In 2005 the Bush administration dropped (from the forest planning rules) the requirements to sustain viable populations of plants and animals across their natural range, and to prepare an environmental impact statement when a forest plan is significantly revised. In 2006, however, a federal judge ruled that these changes violate the National Environmental Policy Act. In India and Africa, local communities are helping to manage nature reserves and preserve endangered species, as well as benefiting economically from limited hunting and tourism.

Chapter 14 concerns our *urban environment.* Architects and contractors are supporting green standards for retrofitting old buildings and constructing innovative urban habitats. A new discipline of industrial ecology is developing models for buildings that mimic nature in using ecosystem processes to assist in heating and cooling, as well as in treating water and recycling waste. Cities such as Curitiba, Brazil, have creative mass transit systems that are used by large numbers of car owners, and also highly participatory recycling programs. European cities have car-free areas and extensive bicycle lanes, as well as laws that protect bicyclists and pedestrians. Cities in the United States have launched sustainability plans involving business and civic groups, as well as government agencies, and Chicago is planting trees and tending a roof garden on city hall in its quest to be the world's most ecological city.

Chapter 15 considers *global warming*, which is being caused largely by increased greenhouse gas emissions into the atmosphere. Understanding how the carbon cycle has been distorted by industrial society reveals the answer to the problem. We must end deforestation and implement sustainable farming practices, so trees and cover crops can again capture and store more of the carbon in the atmosphere. Also, we have to significantly lower carbon dioxide emissions from the burning of fossil fuels in motor vehicles, airplanes, and power plants. This reduction can be achieved in part by developing more efficient technology, and by switching to alternative sources of energy that do not add greenhouse gases to the atmosphere, such as wind, solar, and geothermal power. These changes will not be enough, however, to stop global warming. So, those of us in societies with the largest ecological footprint, such as the United States, have a moral duty to reduce our driving, flying, and wasteful use of energy—for the sake of nature, future generations, and everyone on earth.

9

Ecological Living

SUSTAINABLE CONSUMPTION

We are all part of a moral community, as well as members of a society. As individuals, we act as citizens and consumers. We fulfill our duty, as citizens, by being informed, voting, and joining with others in groups that support environmental cleanups, or ecosystem restoration projects, or effective legislation and government regulation. Chapter 10 considers how citizens may help shape environmental policy through their involvement in nongovernmental organizations, governments, and businesses.

This chapter addresses our individual ethical decisions as *consumers*, and also the responsibility of businesses and governments to support consumption that is environmentally sustainable. What does this mean for those of us who are affluent? For an answer, we use the worksheet after chapter 8 to construct and test ethical presumptions concerning sustainable consumption.

First, we consider arguments that we have a duty to reduce our consumption. Economists claim that increasing consumption is necessary for a healthy economy, but chapter 3 argues that our growth economy is environmentally unsustainable.[1] If we take both of these concerns into account, what might our ethical presumption be?

Second, we look at a concern for character by comparing the ecological virtues suggested in chapter 5 (gratitude, integrity, and frugality) with what it means today to be a consumer. Are we wasteful? Is our society placing too high a value on consumption?[2] Think about persons you admire for the way they live. What choices, as consumers, do they make?

Third, we evaluate our relationships in our consumer society by recalling the concerns of chapter 6. As consumers, how might we contribute to a healthy environment, for the good of our society, as well as for our own health?[3] Should our tax laws give businesses economic incentives to promote increasing consumption through advertising?

Fourth, we look at rights. International human rights law affirms that we all have a right to a healthy environment. Yet, this right seems to clash with our right to enjoy the benefits of sustainable development. This conflict may be resolved by accepting that the exercise of our rights, as consumers, is constrained by the health of the natural environment.[4]

After constructing presumptions concerning our consumption of goods and services, we test these presumptions by considering the likely consequences of acting on them.

DUTY: TO REDUCE OUR CONSUMPTION

Chapter 4 offers three ethical arguments for the presumption that we should not litter. If we state these as *ethical presumptions about consumption*, our actions as consumers should respect the *intrinsic worth* of nature, reflect moral consideration for the well-being of *future generations*, and protect the *rights of the poor* to an equitable share of the earth's resources. If our present level of consumption as a society is environmentally unsustainable, and if one or more of these presumptions is reasonable, then we have a duty to reduce our consumption.

Chapters 2 and 4 present arguments for respecting the intrinsic worth of organisms, species, and ecosystems. If these arguments are convincing, then we have a *duty to practice the three Rs* promoted by Bob the Builder—*reduce, reuse,* and *recycle.* The moral issue is not merely what changes will protect the environment, but how to allocate fairly the costs of these changes. In this chapter we renew the argument that it is fair to expect industrial countries to assume a greater share of responsibility for funding environmental initiatives.

Chapter 4 also asserts that we have a *duty to future generations* to care for the environment. In the same way that we should leave a public space free of litter so others using it after us may enjoy it as we have, we should reduce our consumption so future generations will be born into an environment as healthy as the environment we now enjoy. As this assertion concerns our *relationship* with future generations, we address it in that part of the chapter.

The third argument in chapter 4 involves *our right to consume the earth's resources.* Most of these natural resources are controlled by corporations, individuals, or governments. If we accept Locke's argument—that persons owning property, and governments holding land in trust for its people, have a duty to ensure conservation among present users *and also* preservation of natural resources for future generations—then, for the sake of the common good, we have a *duty to constrain our use of both private and public land.*

Equity

The Brundtland Report by the UN World Commission on Environment and Development asserts *the right to sustainable development* for every society. The issue of equity concerns *how to apportion responsibility* for achieving economic development and consumption that is environmentally sustainable. For the past twenty years there has been a contentious debate between those who argue that the developed countries should bear a greater burden of the costs for achieving these goals and those who assert that all countries have the same duty to seek environmental sustainability.

This dispute is best understood in the context of recent history. In 1750 the living standards of most people in the world were roughly the same. By the 1980s, however, the average person living in a highly industrialized society was "eight times richer" than a comparable person living in a less industrialized society.[5] Are these simply facts? Or, is the current disparity in living standards between developed and developing societies[6] largely the result of *injustice*?

If the history of Western conquest, colonialism, and imperialism seems to account for much of the present inequity in the world, then developed societies not only have a duty to provide funds for sustainable development in poorer countries, but also have a duty to reduce consumption if this is necessary to realize environmental sustainability.

Agenda 21

Agenda 21, which was approved at the 1992 Earth Summit in Rio, affirms such a duty.[7] Paragraph 4.3 acknowledges that poor people damage the environment, but argues that *unsustainable consumption in developed societies* poses the main threat. "Poverty and environmental degradation are closely interrelated. While poverty results in certain kinds of environmental stress, the major cause of the continued deterioration of the global environment is the unsustainable pattern of consumption and production, particularly in industrialized countries, which is a matter of grave concern, aggravating poverty and imbalances."[8]

Chapter 33 of Agenda 21 states that industrialized countries have a duty to fund sustainable development in developing countries. "Developed countries [should] reaffirm their commitments to reach the accepted United Nations target of 0.7 per cent of GNP" and "to the extent that they have not yet achieved that target, agree to augment their aid programs in order to reach that target as soon as possible and to ensure prompt and effective implementation of Agenda 21."[9]

The United States rejects this moral claim, arguing that using a percentage of GNP to calculate its duty to developing countries would be unfair because the US economy is much larger than that of other countries.[10] Other industrial societies, however, have accepted this ethical presumption; Japan, Germany, and France by 1996 were each giving more than the United States for direct assistance to developing countries.[11]

At a 1996 meeting of the UN Commission on Sustainable Development, which is responsible for implementing Agenda 21, the representative of the US government urged developing countries to look to the private sector for investment capital, rather than to loans from developed countries. This would also mean relying on loans administered by the World Bank, which requires borrowing countries to accept "structural adjustment programs" (SAPs) to force these nations to "implement monetary policy, reduce inefficient subsidies, decrease safety net benefits, divest government holdings, liberalize trade, and implement other export-oriented growth strategies."[12]

Supporters of SAPs claim that these conditions lead to "lower inflation rates, increased savings, lower budget deficits, improved trade balances, higher economic growth rates, employment creation, and poverty reduction."[13] Critics argue that SAPs not only increase wealth disparity, but make it harder for poor countries to protect the environment.[14] Governments of developing countries seeking to attract foreign investment will not pass effective environmental protection laws, as these increase costs for businesses. Also, governments that must reduce expenditures to meet SAP requirements will not spend money on the environment.[15]

Agenda 21 asserts that: "Special attention should be paid to the demand for natural resources generated by unsustainable consumption and to the efficient use of those resources consistent with the goal of minimizing depletion and reducing pollution. Although consumption patterns are very high in certain parts of the world, the basic consumer needs of a large section of humanity are not being met. This results in excessive demands and *unsustainable lifestyles among the richer segments,* which *place immense stress on the environment.* The poorer segments, meanwhile, are unable to meet food, health care, shelter and educational needs."[16]

Agenda 21 not only affirms that nations have a duty to protect the individual right to a healthy environment, but also a *duty to create an equitable inter-*

national order.[17] Although the US government rejects these moral presumptions affirmed by Agenda 21, the European Union has accepted the goal of contributing 0.7 percent of the gross national product (GNP) of its member states to direct assistance for developing countries. Is it reasonable for industrialized countries to accept this duty as an ethical presumption? If so, then the government of the United States bears the burden of showing that the consequences of implementing Agenda 21 are unfair or onerous.

CHARACTER: CONSUMER CHOICES

As consumers, we have a significant choice to make. We can allow ourselves to be persuaded by advertising that consuming more is the way to be happy, and that our increased consumption will support a better world by stimulating economic growth. Or, we can consume less and live more frugally, in a way that is more environmentally sustainable.[18]

Rising prices are prompting many of us to reduce our consumption. But what else might motivate us to consume less?[19] Religious teachings offer an answer that has long been compelling, and some people so love nature that they freely choose to take more responsibility for protecting animal life. Also, many of us are beginning to eat "lower on the food chain" by consuming less meat, especially beef, as a way of reducing animal suffering and conserving natural resources.

Religious Life

The scriptures of Jews and Muslims teach that serving God leads to the joy of salvation, and Christian scripture adds to this Great Commandment that we should love our neighbors as ourselves. In each of these traditions being faithful is now understood to involve caring for the earth. The focus of Buddhist teaching is overcoming desire through mindfulness, because the desire to possess the world through mindless consumption is illusory.

It is no accident, therefore, that the *virtue of frugality* is a goal of religious orders, whether these are Christian, Muslim, or Buddhist. Such orders emphasize living simple lives in natural settings, but promise that such a way of life will awaken a deep sense of gratitude and compassion for all life. Jews reject the ideal of monastic life, but the kibbutz movement in Israel has promoted a vision of frugal, communal life.

Saint Francis is an exemplar in the Christian tradition,[20] the Buddha is the teacher for Buddhists, and Sufis represent this way of life in Islam. The Buddha rejected the ascetic life, but counseled restraint in eating and in other pleasures.

Simple clothing, modest meals and often fasting, physical work, and contemplation are the distinctive practices of a "religious" life.[21] Today, we may hope that millions of people feel called to join such religious disciplines, as these communities care for the land and are low consumers of nature's resources.

Of course, a religious person doesn't have to join a celibate community to live with gratitude, integrity, and frugality. Also, persons not active in religious communities may refrain from excessive consumption in order to protect the beauty and wildlife of nature.

John Muir, founder of the Sierra Club, had a mystical love for the wild and affirmed in his private writings faith in the God of creation. "The Song of God, sounding on forever. So pure and sure and universal is the harmony, it matters not where we are" for "as soon as we are absorbed in the harmony," then "plain, mountain, calm, storm, lilies and sequoias, forests and meadows are only different strands of many-colored Light—are one in the sunbeam!"[22]

Love of Animals

Jane Goodall's research with chimpanzees offers another edifying example of someone with great love for nature. As a child, she was inspired by stories of Dr. Dolittle, and in 1960 began living in Tanzania with chimpanzees and doing research at Gombe Stream National Park. "Where many researchers saw 'primitive' apes living a simple existence, Goodall found highly intelligent, emotional creatures living in complex social groups."[23]

To continue her research and conservation work, she founded the Jane Goodall Institute (JGI), "a global nonprofit that empowers people to make a difference for all living things."[24] Members of the JGI "are creating healthy ecosystems, promoting sustainable livelihoods and nurturing new generations of committed, active citizens around the world."[25]

One JGI initiative gives consumers the ethical choice of purchasing coffee grown in the Gombe ecosystem, which is marketed by Green Mountain Coffee Roasters. "Those who purchase this high-quality coffee are supporting cultivation of a sustainable, chimpanzee-friendly crop grown by farmers in the impoverished Kigoma region of western Tanzania. The coffee is shade-grown (meaning trees aren't cut down). What's more, as chimpanzees don't like coffee beans, they don't raid the fields, thus avoiding human-wildlife conflict—an increasing, life-threatening problem where human and wildlife live in proximity."[26] Fair Trade Certified coffee also supports environmentally friendly, shade-grown coffee in Africa, Asia, and Latin America.[27]

Goodall acknowledges that there is growing despair because of the threat posed by economic development for wildlife, but she says we can trust in the human brain, the determination of young people, the "indomitable human spirit," and the resiliency of nature. "So let us move into the next millennium with hope," she writes. "[L]et us have faith in ourselves, in our intellect, in our staunch spirit. Let us develop respect for all living things. Let us try to replace impatience and intolerance with understanding and compassion. And love."[28]

Eating

Whether we have faith in a Creator, or are moved simply by the wonder of life and the power of love, *we may choose to eat in a more environmentally sustainable way*. This means reducing our consumption of meat and obtaining more of our nutrients lower on the food chain.

The UN Food and Agriculture Organization (FAO) reports that about half of the grains harvested today are fed to livestock. "Feedlot cattle consume 7 kilograms of grain to produce 1 kilogram of live weight. Pork takes nearly 4 kilograms of grain per kilogram of live weight. Poultry and fish are more efficient converters, needing about 2 kilograms of grain for each kilogram of live weight produced. Cheese and egg production are in between, consuming 3 and 2.6 kilograms of grain per kilogram of product respectively."[29] The consequential argument is straightforward. If more people eat less meat, the grain harvested in the world can feed more people. Chapter 12 considers the agricultural implications of this issue.

Today, most of the world's vegetarians are Hindus, for not eating meat is practiced in the Hindu tradition as a way of improving a person's *karma*. "The Vedic and Puranic scriptures of Hinduism assert that animals have souls and the act of killing animals without due course has considerable karmic repercussions (i.e., the killer will suffer the pain of the animal he has killed in this life or the next). The principle of *ahimsa* (nonviolence) compels one to refrain from injuring any living creature, physically, mentally or emotionally without good reason."[30] The moral presumption of the Hindu tradition is a vegetarian diet.

We may choose to eat lower on the food chain without becoming strict vegetarians. Some Jews promote "eco-kosher" cooking.[31] Supporters of "cruelty free diets"[32] assert the right of animals not to be killed by humans, or oppose the suffering inflicted on animals by the industrial food production system. Whatever the motivation, *eating lower on the food chain reduces our per capita consumption of grain*, and this means there is more grain for others to eat.

Consumer Power

Consumers may influence markets in other ways. Fair Trade Certified foods are a small market niche, but demand for *organic food* has had a major impact on retailers.[33] Consumers can now purchase more energy-efficient lightbulbs, appliances, and automobiles, and some cities allow a switch to green sources of electricity. In response to consumer demand, Home Depot sells lumber that is certified to have been cut in sustainably managed forests.[34]

In 2002 Dell made a commitment to recycle and reuse 98 percent of the original materials in its computers, if the consumer pays the shipping costs to return a Dell computer to the nearest recycling center.[35] Consumers can also purchase products and services "where the making and the use of the product are carried out in an environmentally friendly way."[36] Also, consumers "can insist that provisions be made for the recycling and reuse of consumer products."[37] The European Parliament has laws that require manufacturers to bear the costs of recycling electrical appliances. With consumer support, this could also be the ethical presumption in the United States.

RELATIONSHIPS: OUR NATURAL COMMUNITY

What would it mean to "think like a field" of grain? It would mean being aware of planting, growing, harvesting, soil erosion, and fertility loss. It would also mean a sense of life over generations. Those who cultivate and eat the grain harvested from such a field help to sustain its ecosystem and also belong to this natural community.

"We need to respect hydrological cycles; we need to leave room for the plants and other species that help the [natural] community build and retain its valuable soil; we need to leave room for the many forms of wildlife that help the [natural] community resist stress and maintain its ability to recreate. Much of the land's yield needs to stay with the land to promote its health; we cannot assume that all of nature's production is ours for the taking."[38]

Thus, our "overall consumption should be limited by the maximum yield of the land consistent with the continued health of that land."[39] Thinking this way may help us challenge the marketing ideology of our consumer society. We can resist the appeal of advertising to consume more and more by giving priority to living within the ecological community of our habitat.

Local: Control and Consumption

Arguments supporting local control over land clash with current regulations of the World Trade Organization, which prohibit domestic restrictions on "free trade." There are, however, ethical as well as practical reasons for urging greater local control over land-use decisions.

First, outsiders are more likely to sacrifice the environment for *short-term economic gain.* "The outside producer could simply have an economic advantage, and by producing a good more cheaply render the local producer unable to compete, thereby forcing the local producer either to leave the business or, worse, to lower production costs by disrupting the local land's health—by becoming, that is, an irresponsible community member."[40] Or, "the outside producer would gain an advantage over the local producer by misusing distant land in some way, thereby again encouraging the local producer to do the same locally to stay competitive, thus disrupting the local autonomy on which land health depends."[41]

Second, local control encourages *local consumption,* and when local products are consumed locally people are "likely to have a greater attachment to the land, a greater sense of how their lives affect the land and how far they can push the land without diminishing its yields."[42] Current government policies, however, undermine local decision-making by favoring corporate food producers and absentee control.

Third, "all sustainability is local."[43] We cannot simply apply abstract economic or ecological principles to a landscape, but need to *assess the nature of a particular place.* Local people know their environment, and scientific assessments should not ignore their experience.[44] Before intervening, we should consider "what is happening upstream and downstream, how we can create meaningful occupations, enhance the region's economic and physical health, and accrue biological and technical wealth for the future."[45]

Fourth, *participation in decision-making is a human right.* Local people have a civil right under the moral presumptions of international law and domestic laws in most nations to be involved in decisions that affect their environment and access to life-sustaining natural resources.

Advertising: End the Tax Write-Off

Contemporary advertising *promotes greater consumption* and "the link of consumption with happiness, acceptance, and status; the importance of individual freedom as the lack of restraint, and the needlessness of denial and the acceptability of 'instant' gratification."[46] This is thinking "like a mall." Promoting increased consumption, as the path to a fulfilling life, assaults the traditional beliefs of every religious tradition, but few religious leaders in the West have criticized our lifestyle of overconsumption. An exception is Pope Benedict XVI, who has condemned both Marxism and capitalism for being concerned only with material issues.[47]

There is a good reason to be critical of advertising and to oppose the government's subsidy that makes it tax exempt as a business expense. "If advertising convinces us as a society to allocate more resources toward market goods, correspondingly fewer are available to allocate toward non-market goods. And as we know, all resources allocated toward consumer goods are extracted from nature and return to nature as waste. Seen from this light, advertising convinces us to degrade or destroy public goods for private gain. It appears that current levels of consumption in the developed countries are incompatible with a sustainable future; yet reducing consumption levels will be exceedingly difficult in the presence of so much advertising."[48]

Therefore, economists Daly and Farley argue that "it would be more appropriate to *tax advertising as a public bad.* At a minimum we should not allow advertising to be written off as a cost of production."[49] Advertising is not a cost of producing goods, but an expense incurred in stimulating demand. "World advertising spending has doubled over the past twenty years, growing at a rate three times faster than world population."[50] This trend may be beneficial for the bottom line of advertisers, producers, and television networks, but it undermines our sustainable use of natural resources.

Critics of marketing consumer products in less developed countries also argue that the practices of advertising are *destroying traditional values.* "For example, Western marketers have sought to alter the frugality of Indian customers by encouraging them to throw away used goods."[51] Given the scarce resources of most Indians, if Western marketing is successful in transforming Indian culture so that people are less frugal, the consequences will be adverse for many individuals and for the society.

Western marketing practices also undermine traditional systems of economic exchange, by characterizing these "as impediments for the development of market exchange systems, [and] as primitive practices to be broken, rather than as alternative need satisfaction systems."[52] One ethical critic of Western marketing suggests that when it clashes with the "core values of another culture," companies engaged in such marketing "should consider not doing business in that society, or modifying their products and activities to make them compatible with that culture."[53]

RIGHTS: TO A HEALTHY ENVIRONMENT

To enjoy a right to a healthy environment, we must empower the government to ensure that our food supply is safe, adequate, and affordable, as there is no "invisible hand" behind free markets to provide this protection. Therefore, it is reasonable to support laws that regulate agriculture, the raising of livestock,

food processing, and global trade that brings food into the country, and also to support taxes that enable governments to provide these essential services.

Similarly, our right to enjoy the fruits of economic development, by purchasing the food that we like, does not include a right to avoid the costs, as a society, of ensuring that economic development is environmentally sustainable. We can only exercise our rights within the natural constraints of the environment. We cannot reasonably expect to have a healthy life as a people without exercising our rights in a manner that maintains a healthy natural environment.

To put this issue starkly, we should not think of buying a hamburger as our "right," if we have the money to pay the market price, when our present system of raising cattle for beef is devastating the natural environment. Our consumer rights are constrained by the limits imposed on our globalized society by the impact of our consumer lifestyle on the earth's biosphere.

Environmental Impact of Cattle

Raising cattle for food is devastating the earth. "Cattle have arguably caused or are related to the most environmental damage to the globe of any nonhuman species through overgrazing, soil erosion, desertification, and tropical deforestation for ranches."[54] An estimated "30 percent of the earth's ice-free land is directly or indirectly involved in livestock production, according to the United Nation's Food and Agriculture Organization, which also estimates that livestock production generates nearly a fifth of the world's greenhouse gases—more than transportation."[55] And the cattle population, now about 1.3 billion, is growing.[56]

Cattle eat about half the world's grain, and producing a pound of beef takes about seven pounds of grain and 2,700 gallons of water. In contrast, an acre of grains, using much less water and producing no methane, may yield ten times more protein than an acre used to produce beef. An acre of legumes may yield twenty times more protein than an acre used for grazing cattle. If for no other reason than *economic efficiency*, we should reduce our consumption of beef and eat more grains and legumes.

Critics argue that eating fewer hamburgers would be bad for the economy, but fail to take into account the externalities of producing beef.[57] The following *social and environmental costs* of raising cattle, in the way that we do now, are *not included in the price* we pay for a hamburger:

- Erosion and loss of topsoil, deforestation, and loss of biodiversity.
- The subsidized use of surface water and water from aquifers.
- Subsidies paid to agribusiness for growing corn (which is fed to cattle).
- Sewage disposal from cattle feedlots into the surrounding environment.
- Medical costs related to feeding animals in feedlots and eating animal products.
- Antibiotic-resistant infections caused by regularly feeding cattle antibiotics.
- Transport costs including the carbon dioxide emissions into the atmosphere.
- Emissions released in producing fertilizers for growing cattle feed.[58]

Simply removing the subsidies in the United States for the use of water to produce beef would raise the cost of hamburger to about $35 per pound.[59]

Real Cost of Beef

Do we have a right to buy a hamburger at a price that does not cover the social and environmental costs of producing it? Not a moral right, as this leaves these costs to others—to those living near land degraded by cattle ranching, and to future generations that will inhabit a less fertile environment.

Locke argued that the right to private property should not deny good land for the use of others. Today rainforests are being leveled to raise cattle for beef, and aquifers are being drained to grow corn to feed cattle. Thomas Jefferson believed in the right of landowners to improve their land, but argued against inheritance rights on the ground that these rights undermine democracy. Today four meatpacking companies in the United States control over 80 percent of the market,[60] and there is no limit on the "right" of these transnational corporations to lobby Congress for government subsidies on growing corn and raising beef that degrade the environment but provide consumers with a "cheap" burger.

Moreover, eating beef directly affects human welfare. Moral philosopher Mary Midgley writes: "It is enormously extravagant to use grains, beans, pulses and so forth for animal food, and then eat the animals, rather than letting human beings eat the grains, etc. right away. In the present food shortage, and still more in the sharper ones which threaten us, human interests demand most strongly that this kind of waste should be stopped."[61]

What should we do? We should reduce our consumption of beef. If a sufficient number of consumers were to stop buying beef, demand would decline and, over time, the market and food suppliers would reduce the supply of beef and increase the supply of other commodities in response to increased demand for these foods. Eating less beef would also increase the supply of grain available for human consumption. Given the global shortage of grain and rising prices making grain too costly for poor people to purchase, we should take this ethical action immediately.[62]

We should also support legislation that over several years will require producers (of food and other goods as well) to internalize the social and environmental costs of their products. This would not only increase the market price of commodities that are now heavily subsidized, but would also shift consumer demand to more sustainable forms of food production.

CONSEQUENCES: SUSTAINABLE CONSUMPTION

Following the worksheet at the end of chapter 8, we now test the ethical presumptions that we have constructed about our consumption by considering the likely consequences of acting on them. We distinguish probable from possible consequences, and note when long-term consequences are uncertain. We identify the likely pros and cons of acting on an ethical presumption, and then compare these predictions.

We weigh the value of ecosystem integrity and human rights without using cost-benefit analysis, but rely on this analysis for goods that are adequately priced by markets. We attempt to internalize the costs of economic *externalities*— cleaning up and restoring environmental damage, creating substitutes for depleted resources, and treating waste that exceeds the absorption capacity of a habitat. Moreover, we refrain from economic discounting that passes on the costs we are incurring to future generations.

Throughout this assessment we place the burden of proof on those claiming that the likely consequences of acting on ethical presumptions promoting environmental sustainability are sufficiently adverse that we should set these presumptions aside. In our discussion, if the integrity of an ecosystem, or a human right, is at risk, then the evidence to set aside a presumption should be compelling. Otherwise, the evidence only has to be convincing.

Presumptions: Duty

As individuals and as members of developed societies, we have a duty to:

1.   Affirm and maintain the intrinsic worth of a healthy environment.
2.   Care for future generations by consuming no more than is fair for our generation.
3.   Respect the rights of others to use the natural resources we are also consuming.
4.   Abide by Agenda 21 by giving 0.7 percent of GNP to less developed countries.

Pros and Cons.   The first three presumptions would probably help to conserve natural resources, but the long-term consequences are uncertain. Acting on the fourth presumption would possibly stimulate economic development in less developed countries, but under the current system of globalization would probably add to environmental degradation rather than reduce it.

There are economic costs in acting on these presumptions, but the long-term costs and benefits are uncertain. Some of the economic costs can be set by the market and weighed by cost-benefit analysis, but the first three presumptions largely involve nonmarket values.

The strongest argument against acting on these ethical presumptions is the prediction of largely adverse economic consequences. Acting on the first three presumptions would mean reducing our use of natural resources, which would raise the costs of production and the prices for some commodities. The fourth ethical presumption involving aid to developing societies might stimulate economic development, but the international aid could be squandered or stolen. Long-term estimates of all these possible costs are uncertain.

Compelling or Convincing Evidence?   Acting on the first and third presumptions involves, respectively, the integrity of an ecosystem and a human right, so compelling evidence is required to set aside these presumptions. The second and fourth presumptions do not directly involve environmental integrity or a human right, so only convincing evidence is needed to justify setting aside these presumptions.

Presumptions: Character and Relationships

To live with greater character and virtue, as members of a moral community that extends consideration to other organisms, species, and ecosystems, we should:

1.   Live with greater frugality for the sake of present and future generations.
2.   Eat lower on the food chain to attain a more sustainable way of living.
3.   End the tax deduction for advertising because it subsidizes greater consumption.
4.   Support shade-grown coffee and other ecological agricultural practices.

Pros and Cons.   The first two of these presumptions cannot be assessed by cost-benefit analysis, because each involves nonmarket values. Those who live inspiring lives, like John Muir and Jane Goodall, help keep our hopes alive, but this is a nonmarket good that cannot be measured by an economic calculation. Eating lower on the food chain would have economic impacts, but it would also improve our health (which is more than an economic benefit) and might help others see that they belong to an ecological community (with values that are not merely utilitarian).

Also, the long-term consequences of acting on the first two presumptions are uncertain. Those criticizing these choices argue either that each will be of little consequence (merely a lifestyle choice), or if widely adopted would extend our economic recession.[63] The breadth of these predictions is evidence that our ability to foresee the future is uncertain.

The consequences of acting on the third presumption can likely be assessed by cost-benefit analysis. The fourth presumption may be seen, in terms of consequences, as a lifestyle issue (and so of little consequence), or as a way of challenging industrial agriculture (which might have major consequences). Chapter 12 considers what this would mean for farming.

Compelling or Convincing Evidence?   The fourth presumption concerns maintaining ecosystem integrity, therefore compelling consequential arguments are needed to set it aside. Convincing arguments would suffice to overturn the first three presumptions.

Presumptions: Rights

To protect the human right of everyone to a healthy environment, we should:

1.   Support taxes and laws to ensure safe, adequate, and affordable food.
2.   Eat less beef to protect the environment and increase the supply of grain for food.
3.   Support greater control by local people over the use of local land.
4.   Internalize (in the market price) the externalities of food production.

Pros and Cons.   The rights to a healthy environment and to sustainable development depend on laws that protect both nature and the production of food using natural resources. Moreover, we cannot expect to exercise our rights without paying the costs of government to ensure the protection of our rights.

Those who argue against local control, based on a prediction of likely consequences, claim that only a market evaluation will assure the best use of natural resources. Certainly, local people may waste their local resources, or may resist a reasonable use of these resources for the sake of others. Yet, local participation in land use decisions is crucial for human dignity, and this nonmarket value must be protected.

Chapter 3 argues for internalizing externalities in all areas of production and assessing these costs to producers, or, if this is not feasible, to the countries where production takes place. These costs should be included in the market price for goods. Those opposing this presumption on consequential grounds argue that it will raise the price of food and other commodities. Those defending the presumption note that industrial agriculture is heavily subsidized, and that these subsidies conceal the real costs of our agricultural system, which are presently being paid in taxes (that are unfairly distributed as government subsidies) or passed on to future generations.

Compelling or Convincing Evidence?   The first three of these presumptions directly assert human rights, so compelling evidence that the consequences will be more adverse than beneficial should be required to set these presumptions aside. The fourth presumption asserts that cost-benefit analysis should include all the real costs, which seems self-evident. As the last presumption does not assert ecosystem integrity or a human right, only convincing evidence is needed to overcome it.

Predicting Consequences

All these consequential evaluations require a detailed analysis, but these brief comments illustrate the reasoning involved in doing environmental ethics. Subsequent chapters will give greater consideration to some of these issues. We should now realize, however, that it will never be easy to know which consequences are probable, rather than merely possible, and that long-term consequences are usually uncertain. This insight should give us pause, whenever someone claims that predicting consequences is clearly the best way to decide what action is right.

In the following chapters we again construct ethical presumptions based on our duty, character, relationships, and human rights. These chapters, however, will not repeat the explicit format used at the end of this chapter to consider consequence arguments. Instead, throughout each chapter we will "test" presumptions by predicting likely consequences as we consider arguments for what these presumptions ought to be.

QUESTIONS—ECOLOGICAL LIVING: SUSTAINABLE CONSUMPTION

1.   Give an ethical argument for accepting the challenge of Agenda 21 to developed countries. Explain why the US government has rejected this challenge.

2.   Why might choosing to be more frugal be an ethical decision? Does your reasoning concern character or consequences? Or both? Explain your answer.

3.   Argue that those who are affluent today have a duty to eat lower on the food chain, and then raise at least one critical question about this argument.

4.   Explain why you think we do (or do not) have a duty to future generations to restrain our consumption.

5.   Give an example of an ethical issue involving advertising. How might consumers promote a higher ethical standard in advertising?

6.   Argue for and against the assertion, "We have a right to buy what we can afford."

7.   Identify some of the likely consequences of acting on the ethical presumptions of Agenda 21. How would you weigh these pros and cons?

8.   Give an example of nonmarket goods that cannot be assessed by cost-benefit analysis. How are these to be included in testing the likely consequences of acting on a presumption?

9.   Give a reason for buying shade-grown coffee. Does your reason concern duty, character, relationships, or rights? What are the likely consequences of acting on this presumption?

10.   Make an argument for local control over land use. Then weigh the pros and cons of acting on this presumption by considering the likely consequences of taking the action.

11.   Give a reason for supporting taxes to pay for government regulation of food production and trade. Is your argument about rights or consequences? Explain your thinking.

12.   Make a consequential argument for reducing our consumption of beef and raise a critical question about this argument.

13.   Use the worksheet to think through an environmental issue involving consumption.

14.   The chapter gives four reasons for supporting local control over environmental decisions. Identify the two reasons you find most convincing and explain your thinking.

15.   State an environmental presumption, which should be set aside only if there is compelling evidence that acting on it will have dire consequences, and explain your reasoning.

10

Environmental Policy

GOVERNMENTS, CORPORATIONS, NGOs

Effective public action requires clarifying the ethical presumptions of environmental policy and implementing these presumptions. In this chapter we examine the involvement of governments, corporations, and nongovernmental organizations (NGOs) in this process.

GOVERNMENTS: INTERNATIONAL AND US POLICIES

Protecting the environment requires effective action at all levels of government. We have already considered international actions, instruments, and organizations, so here we sum up international environmental policy. Then we look briefly at the National Environmental Policy Act of the United States and actions taken by the Environmental Protection Agency (EPA).

International

Chapters 7 and 9 discussed reports and treaties sponsored by the UN that define environmental policy and create enforcement mechanisms. These include:

- UN Conference on the Human Environment (Stockholm Declaration, 1972)
- UN Environment Programme (UNEP, 1972)
- International Covenant on Civil and Political Rights (ICCPR, in force 1976)

- International Covenant on Economic, Social and Cultural Rights (ICESCR, in force 1976)
- Vienna Convention for the Protection of the Ozone Layer (1985)
- UN World Commission on Environment and Development (Brundtland Report, 1987)
- Montreal Protocol on Substances that Deplete the Ozone Layer (added to the Vienna Convention, 1991)
- Agenda 21 of the Conference on Environment and Development (Earth Summit, 1992)[1]
- Commission on Sustainable Development (1992)
- Environmental Committee of the Organization for Economic Cooperation and Development (1992)
- Framework Convention on Climate Change (FCCC, in force 1994)
- Kyoto Protocol to the FCCC (2005)

On the basis of these instruments, international law affirms that governments and citizens have a duty to support public actions that will realize the right to environmentally sustainable development, protect the right of every person to a healthy environment, and maintain the integrity of the environment for future generations. Of these three moral and legal presumptions, the first two derive our duties from rights and the third asserts a duty on the basis of our character and our relationships with our ancestors and descendants.

Policies of the United States

The National Environmental Policy Act of 1969 (NEPA) defines the duties of the federal government for the environment. The purposes of the NEPA are: "To declare a national policy which will encourage productive and enjoyable harmony between man and his environment; to promote efforts which will prevent or eliminate damage to the environment and biosphere and stimulate the health and welfare of man; to enrich the understanding of the ecological systems and natural resources important to the Nation; and to establish a Council on Environmental Quality."[2]

Title I of the act states that its purposes require the federal government to act in order to:

1.   Fulfill the responsibilities of each generation as trustee of the environment for succeeding generations.

2.   Assure for all Americans safe, healthful, productive, and aesthetically and culturally pleasing surroundings.

3.   Attain the widest range of beneficial uses of the environment without degradation, risk to health or safety, or other undesirable and unintended consequences.

4.   Preserve important historic, cultural, and natural aspects of our national heritage, and maintain, wherever possible, an environment which supports diversity, and variety of individual choice.

5.   Achieve a balance between population and resource use which will permit high standards of living and a wide sharing of life's amenities.

6.   Enhance the quality of renewable resources and approach the maximum attainable recycling of depletable resources.[3]

Title I of NEPA requires all federal agencies to consider the environmental impact of their activities and, if this impact is likely to be significant, to prepare an environmental impact statement (EIS). Title II of the act establishes the Council on Environmental Quality (CEQ) and gives it authority to make recommendations to the president.

On April 22, 1970, twenty million Americans participated in the first Earth Day, and that July President Nixon submitted to Congress a proposal to create an Environmental Protection Agency that would consolidate the environmental programs of other federal agencies.[4]

The initial focus of the EPA was pollution, and passage of the Clean Air Act of 1970 (CAA) gave the EPA the power to regulate the emissions of pollutants. "The Clean Air Act brought dramatic—and substantive—changes to the federal air quality program. The act required EPA to establish national air quality standards as well as national standards for significant new pollution sources and for all facilities emitting hazardous substances. The CAA took dead aim against America's leading source of pollution: the automobile."[5]

Legislation during the 1970s also directed the EPA to set and enforce clean water standards. The EPA initially pursued an enforcement strategy that threatened court action, if compliance was not forthcoming, but in the 1990s began to rely more on incentive programs. In collaboration with the Department of Energy, in 1992 the EPA began Energy Star, a voluntary-labeling program that promotes the use of energy-efficient products in order to reduce greenhouse gas emissions. The Energy Star label now identifies a variety of products using less energy and also new homes and commercial buildings. The EPA claims that the program has delivered savings of about $16 billion in 2007 alone.[6]

In 2001 the EPA launched the Green Power Partnership program, which encourages organizations to buy renewable energy. "EPA defines green power as electricity produced from solar, wind, geothermal, biogas, biomass, and low-impact small hydroelectric sources."[7] The EPA website provides a locator to help consumers find the closest source of green power, and the partnership program presents awards to exemplary users.[8]

In 1980 Congress passed the Comprehensive Environmental Response, Compensation, and Liability Act (CERCLA), which is commonly known as the Superfund law. The EPA administers this fund to clean up hazardous waste sites that have been abandoned and pose a threat to communities. As of 2007, there were over thirteen hundred Superfund sites, but only funds to clean up several of these heavily contaminated areas. CERCLA authorizes the government to order "potentially responsible parties" to clean up sites and to levy fines for noncompliance. The EPA has used this approach, but not as often as critics of the EPA think it should.[9]

In 2003 the head of the EPA ruled that the Clean Air Act did not authorize the EPA to regulate carbon dioxide and other greenhouse gases. This prompted a lawsuit by twelve states, over a dozen nongovernmental organizations, and a few cities; early in 2007 the US Supreme Court in *Massachusetts v. Environmental Protection Agency* held that the EPA "has the authority to regulate heat-trapping gases in automobile emissions. The court further ruled that the agency could not sidestep its authority to regulate the greenhouse gases that contribute to global climate change unless it could provide a scientific basis for its refusal."[10]

In April 2008, after a year of inaction by the EPA, a coalition of states, cities, and environmental NGOs filed a lawsuit in federal court against the EPA, asking "the court to order the agency to publish within 60 days its analysis that found that such emissions endanger humans as well as contribute to climate change. Publication would lay the foundation for the agency to establish rules to control emissions from tailpipes, as the states have long sought."[11]

CORPORATIONS: MORAL LEADERSHIP

Corporations are directly involved in environmental policy in two ways. First, many have environmental policies. Second, corporations not only lobby legislatures and government agencies about laws and the administrative rules for environmental policies, but also influence the election and appointment of public officials who make and administer public policies.

Protecting the environment requires that governments check corporate actions, that corporations support effective governmental policies, and that NGOs effectively stimulate public pressure on both governments and corporations.

Some corporations take their environmental responsibility seriously, and these include the financial services firm of JPMorgan Chase and also the carpet manufacturer Interface Incorporated.

JPMorgan Chase

JPMorgan Chase, which operates in more than fifty countries and has assets of $1.4 trillion, has adopted a "comprehensive environmental policy."[12] In the introduction to its policy entitled "Sustainability Commitment" the company "recognizes that balancing non-financial factors such as environmental and social issues with financial priorities is an essential part of good corporate citizenship."[13] If we were talking about an individual being a good citizen, we would identify this as an argument about character.

JPMorgan Chase accepts its role in realizing sustainable development. "Protecting the natural systems upon which all life depend while lifting people out of poverty and advancing economic development are among the greatest challenges confronting humanity. These three pillars of sustainable development are central to the UN Millennium Development Goals adopted in 2000. We recognize that the policies and practices we adopt today will shape not only our lives but also those of future generations."[14]

Affirming the UN Millennium Development Goals is no small commitment, as these include the following statements on "protecting our common environment."

21. We must spare no effort to free all of humanity, and above all our children and grandchildren, from the threat of living on a planet irredeemably spoilt by human activities, and whose resources would no longer be sufficient for their needs.
22. We reaffirm our support for the principles of sustainable development, including those set out in Agenda 21, agreed upon at the UN Conference on Environment and Development.
23. We resolve therefore to adopt in all our environmental actions a new ethic of conservation and stewardship and, as first steps, we resolve:

- To make every effort to ensure the entry into force of the Kyoto Protocol. . . . and to embark on the required reduction in emissions of greenhouse gases.
- To intensify our collective efforts for the management, conservation and sustainable development of all types of forests.
- To press for the full implementation of the Convention on Biological Diversity and the Convention to Combat Desertification in those Countries Experiencing Serious Drought and/or Desertification, particularly in Africa.
- To stop the unsustainable exploitation of water resources by developing water management strategies at the regional, national and local levels, which promote both equitable access and adequate supplies.[15]

The JPMorgan Chase policy embraces the notion of *environmental stewardship*, which affirms a duty of care for the environment, but acknowledges that exercising such stewardship offers profitable business opportunities involving "innovative financial products and investments in sustainable forestry and renewable energy."[16]

What does this actually mean? "Specifically, we will integrate environmental and social awareness into the credit analysis and financing decision process, and incorporate it, where appropriate, as part of our due diligence review. We will train relevant employees to take responsibility for and implement these policies. Finally, we will publish an annual sustainability report using the Global Reporting Initiative framework."[17] The Global Reporting Initiative (GRI) framework requires internalizing social and environmental externalities as the costs of doing business.[18]

JPMorgan Chase has adopted the Equator Principles[19] for its investment and commercial banks, and has pledged to apply these principles "as appropriate, to all loans, debt and equity underwriting, financial advisories and project-linked derivative transactions where the use of proceeds is designated for potentially [environmentally] damaging projects."[20] The Equator Principles were established by international banks in 2003 to measure and limit the social and environmental impact of new projects costing $10 million or more.[21]

The JPMorgan Chase environmental policy also has sections describing its commitments with respect to climate change, forestry[22] and biodiversity, indigenous communities, and internal resource management. The policy accepts the *precautionary principle* with respect to activities that may influence climate change: "While there remains uncertainty regarding the severity of impacts, we believe that it is appropriate to adopt a precautionary approach to climate protection by working to reduce greenhouse gas emissions today."[23]

The corporation also states that: "If JPMorgan Chase acquires significant amounts of environmentally sensitive land as a result of a default or debt work-out situation, we will work with conservation groups and local stakeholders to consider conservation alternatives, including donation, environmental management plans or protective easements."[24]

For projects that may impact indigenous peoples in sensitive habitats, the corporate environmental policy requires that the borrower or project sponsor demonstrate that:

- They have given indigenous people the opportunity and, if needed, culturally appropriate representation to engage in informed participation and collective decision-making;
- Provided information on the ways in which the project may have a potentially adverse impact on them in a culturally appropriate manner at each stage of project preparation, implementation and operation;
- Given adequate time to study the relevant information; and
- Provided access to a grievance mechanism.[25]

These environmental commitments by JPMorgan Chase, which are shared by some other financial institutions,[26] include rights and duties asserted by international law. The bottom line, of course, is implementation, but this environmental policy demonstrates that corporations may affirm environmental stewardship as intrinsically right and also good for business.[27]

Interface

The environmental policy of Interface, Incorporated, which makes carpets, is also exemplary. In its mission statement Interface affirms that: "We will honor the places where we do business by endeavoring to become the first name in *industrial ecology*, a corporation that cherishes nature and restores the environment. Interface will lead by example and validate by results, including profits, leaving the world a better place than when we began, and we will be restorative through the power of our influence in the world."[28] Interface promises "to eliminate any negative impact our company may have on the environment by the year 2020."[29]

The chairman of Interface, Ray C. Anderson, admits that "sustainability" meant nothing to him a few years ago, but now the company's website addresses the three related issues of economic, social, and environmental sustainability. Interface defines *sustainability* as: "A dynamic process which enables all people to realize their potential and to improve their quality of life in ways that simultaneously protect and enhance the Earth's life support systems."[30] It affirms the ethical presumption in the Brundtland Report that we should meet "the needs of the present without compromising the ability of future generations to meet their own needs."[31]

To become environmentally sustainable, Interface is working on seven fronts:

1. *Eliminate Waste:* Eliminating all forms of waste in every area of business;

2. *Benign Emissions:* Eliminating toxic substances from products, vehicles, and facilities;

3. *Renewable Energy:* Operating facilities with renewable energy sources—solar, wind, landfill gas, biomass,[32] and low-impact hydroelectric;

4. *Closing the Loop:* Redesigning processes and products to close the technical loop using recovered and bio-based materials;

5. *Resource-Efficient Transportation:* Transporting people and products efficiently to reduce waste and emissions;

6. *Sensitizing Stakeholders:* Creating a culture that integrates sustainability principles and improves people's lives and livelihoods;

7.   *Redesign Commerce:* Creating a new business model that
       demonstrates and supports the value of sustainability-based
       commerce.[33]

The progress made by Interface is impressive. "Use of fossil fuels is down 45
percent (and net greenhouse gas production, by weight, is down 60 percent)
. . . while sales are up 49 percent. Globally, the company's carpet-making uses
one-third the water it used to. The company's worldwide contribution to landfills has been cut by 80 percent."[34]

Interface turned to the Natural Step,[35] an international NGO founded in Sweden in 1989, for help in taking the following steps to realize economic sustainability.

1.   *Eliminate our contribution to systematic increases in
       concentrations of substances from the Earth's crust.* This means
       substituting certain minerals that are scarce in nature with
       others that are more abundant, using all mined materials
       efficiently, and systematically reducing dependence on
       fossil fuels.

2.   *Eliminate our contribution to systematic increases in
       concentrations of substances produced by society.* This means
       systematically substituting certain persistent and unnatural
       compounds with ones that are normally abundant or break
       down more easily in nature, and using all substances
       produced by society efficiently.

3.   *Eliminate our contribution to systematic physical degradation
       of nature through over-harvesting, depletion, foreign
       introductions, and other forms of modification.* This means
       drawing resources only from well-managed ecosystems,
       systematically pursuing the most productive and efficient
       use both of those resources and land, and exercising caution
       in all kinds of modification of nature.

4.   *Contribute as much as we can to the goal of meeting human
       needs in our society and worldwide, going over and above all
       the substitution and dematerialization measures taken in
       meeting the first three objectives.* This means using all of our
       resources efficiently, fairly and responsibly so that the needs
       of all people on whom we have an impact, and the future
       needs of people who are not yet born, stand the best chance
       of being met.[36]

These are the ethical presumptions that Interface is trying to realize in its carpet business.

Interface has found, however, that *existing laws and regulations are an obstacle to realizing greater sustainability.* "The current infrastructure subsidizes unsustainable industrial processes. To make significant progress, we will need the cooperation of government and other industrial partners to shift taxation away from economic and social benefits, (labor, income, and investment) to detriments, (pollution, waste, and the loss of primary resources)."[37]

To make the economy more sustainable, Anderson argues, economists should stop underestimating the true cost of doing business by excluding externalities from their accounting, such as damage to the environment due to pollution. Moreover, governments should cut income taxes and raise the gasoline tax (while providing subsidies for the poor).[38]

Other Business Initiatives

Many other corporations are adopting environmental policies. In 2007 Wal-Mart, which has long been criticized by NGOs for its lack of environmental responsibility,[39] began working with the Carbon Disclosure Project (CDP) to measure the energy used to create products throughout its supply chain. CDP chief executive Paul Dickinson says, "Wal-Mart will encourage its suppliers to measure and manage their greenhouse gas emissions, and ultimately reduce the total carbon footprint of Wal-Mart's indirect emissions."[40]

Proctor & Gamble defines its commitment to sustainable development as "ensuring a better quality of life for everyone, now and for generations to come."[41] Therefore, its policy sets a higher safety standard than the law requires: "All P&G ingredients must pass Environmental Risk Assessment before they are safely cleared for the market."[42] P&G has also made substantial gains in eco-efficiency.[43]

The "sustainability business model" of P&G sees addressing poverty not only as a responsibility, but as an opportunity. "For companies such as P&G, the challenge to make sustainable development part of the goods and services we deliver is not business as usual. It means reaching consumers we have never reached in rural villages and urban slums of the developing world. It means developing new products specific to the needs, frustrations and aspirations of those new consumers at an affordable price. It means exploring new business models, often built on volume instead of margin, and with new supply and distribution systems to lower cost and reach where we have ever gone before."[44] It means being profitable as well as responsible in creative new ways.[45]

NONGOVERNMENTAL ORGANIZATIONS: ADVOCACY AND ACTION

JPMorgan Chase uses the reporting framework of the Global Reporting Initiative, an international NGO in the Netherlands.[46] Interface uses an analytical approach created by the Natural Step, an international NGO in Sweden.[47] Wal-Mart is collaborating with the Carbon Disclosure Project (CDP).[48] Nonprofit NGOs like these provide technical assistance to industry and promote the ethical presumptions for sustainable development asserted by international declarations and treaties.

More familiar NGOs taking environmental actions and lobbying for sustainable government and corporate policies include Greenpeace,[49] the Sierra Club,[50] the World Wildlife Fund,[51] and the Nature Conservancy.[52] There are also thousands of smaller international NGOs involved in environmental advocacy,[53] perhaps overall in the world a hundred thousand NGOs engaged in environmental work in most countries,[54] and about ten thousand environmental NGOs in the United States.[55]

Greenpeace and the Sierra Club

Greenpeace is "an independent global campaigning organization" that acts to protect the environment and to work for peace by:

- Catalyzing an energy revolution to address . . . climate change.
- Defending our oceans by challenging wasteful and destructive fishing, and creating a global network of marine reserves.
- Protecting . . . ancient forests and the animals, plants, and people that depend on them.
- Working for disarmament and peace by tackling the causes of conflict and calling for the elimination of all nuclear weapons.
- Creating a toxic free future with safer alternatives to hazardous chemicals. . . .
- Campaigning for sustainable agriculture by rejecting genetically engineered organisms, protecting biodiversity, and encouraging socially responsible farming.[56]

Greenpeace is working in forty countries "to expose environmental criminals, and to challenge government and corporations when they fail to live up to their mandate to safeguard our environment and our future."[57]

Greenpeace USA says it uses "peaceful direct action" to expose environmental problems and promote green solutions. Its executive director, John Passacantando, offers this moral challenge: "In the end, protecting the environment is about very clear *choices*. We can either stand up for what is right—our health, humanity, and heritage on this *planet of ours*—or we can sit by and watch while decisions are made that threaten to destroy our collective *future*."[58] I assume the emphasis on *our* health, heritage, and planet is expressing the right of everyone to live in a healthy environment.[59]

The Sierra Club is primarily a grassroots lobbying organization with a mission to:

- Explore, enjoy, and protect the wild places of the earth.
- Practice and promote the responsible use of the earth's ecosystems and resources.
- Educate and enlist humanity to protect and restore the quality of the natural and human environment.
- Use all lawful means to carry out these objectives.

Its website makes this promise: "When you give to the Sierra Club you will have the satisfaction of knowing that you are helping to preserve irreplaceable wild lands, save endangered and threatened wildlife, and protect this fragile environment we call home. You can be sure that your voice will be heard through congressional lobbying and grassroots action on the environmental issues that matter to you most."[60]

In 1971 the Sierra Club launched the Legal Defense Fund and six years later this became Earthjustice: "a non-profit public interest law firm dedicated to protecting the magnificent places, natural resources, and wildlife of this earth and to defending the right of all people to a healthy environment. We bring about far-reaching change by enforcing and strengthening environmental laws on behalf of hundreds of organizations and communities."[61] Earthjustice seeks to protect both nature and the right to a healthy environment.

WWF and the Nature Conservancy

The World Wildlife Fund, generally identified as WWF, operates in more than a hundred countries and supports about two hundred conservation projects. Its mission is: "To stop the degradation of the planet's natural environment and to build a future in which humans live in harmony with nature, by: conserving the world's biological diversity, ensuring that the use of renewable natural resources is sustainable, and promoting the reduction of pollution and wasteful consumption."[62] To achieve this, WWF pledges to:

- Be global, independent, multicultural, and nonparty political.
- Use the best available science to address issues and critically evaluate all its endeavors.
- Seek dialogue and avoid unnecessary confrontation.
- Build concrete conservation solutions through a combination of field based projects, policy initiatives, capacity building, and education work.
- Involve local communities and indigenous peoples in the planning and execution of its field programs, respecting their cultural as well as economic needs.
- Strive to build partnerships with other organizations, governments, business, and local communities to enhance WWF's effectiveness.
- Run its operations in a cost-effective manner and apply donors' funds according to the highest standards of accountability.[63]

The Nature Conservancy is dedicated to preserving biodiversity: "The Nature Conservancy's mission is to preserve the plants, animals and natural communities that represent the diversity of life on Earth by protecting the lands and waters they need to survive."[64] In 2006 the Nature Conservancy purchased for $231 million from International Paper 212,000 acres of forest in ten southern states, in order to conserve it.[65] The Nature Conservancy is also known for facilitating debt-for-nature swaps, such as the recent agreement by the United States to forgive $24 million in debt owed to it by Guatemala, which instead will be used to fund forest conservation in Guatemala for fifteen years.[66]

In late 2006 the Nature Conservancy joined WWF and Stanford University in a new conservation partnership: "The Natural Capital Project is focused on living natural capital assets—ecosystems that, if properly managed, yield a flow of vital services both to humans and nature. Relative to other forms of capital, natural capital is poorly understood, rarely monitored, and in many cases undergoing rapid degradation and depletion. Often the tremendous importance and economic value of natural capital is appreciated only upon its loss."[67]

Many environmental advocates oppose using economic value to support preservation policies, and instead rely on ecocentric ethical reasoning. The Nature

Conservancy, however, emphasizes *the economic worth of nature's assets and the benefits for human health.* "When we destroy natural ecosystems, we lose these assets and the services they provide us. But putting an accurate value on these ecosystem services could make protecting those services even more attractive to business, policymakers and the public."[68]

Peter Kareiva, chief scientist of the Nature Conservancy, also suggests that "the goals of conservation and the goals of alleviating poverty and improving human health are deeply interwoven. Our best hope for conservation success is to work more closely with poverty and public-health NGOs and to end the extreme compartmentalization among our efforts."[69]

COLLABORATIVE STRATEGIES: GLWQA AND THE APOLLO ALLIANCE

National governments have created environmental policies and enforcement agencies, and within nations there may also be state or provincial as well as municipal governments that are making decisions about what is best for the environment.[70] As all of these actions by governments involve lobbying by corporations and NGOs, distinguishing these three kinds of institutions should not be understood as implying that they function separately.[71]

GLWQA

For instance, the Great Lakes Water Quality Agreement (GLWQA) is a treaty between the governments of Canada and the United States. In Canada the government agency with responsibility for environmental policy is Environment Canada, and in the United States the Environmental Protection Agency is charged with enforcement. However, the province of Ontario and the states of Illinois, Indiana, Michigan, Minnesota, New York, Ohio, Pennsylvania, and Wisconsin are also involved, along with over 150 local NGOs that belong to a coalition NGO, the Great Lakes Union (GLU).[72]

Enforcing the treaty involves doing studies and making recommendations for all the "stakeholders,"[73] which include governments, private organizations, and citizens. In the case of the GLQWA this process is overseen by the International Joint Commission (IJC) established by the Boundary Waters Treaty of 1909. More than four thousand individuals and organizations participated in the most recent IJC review, which also included consultations with the national governments, state governments, and first nations [Canada's Native Americans].[74]

The IJC's Thirteenth Biennial Report, released in February of 2007, recommends that "the governments of Canada and the United States create and apply an uncommonly strong Accountability Framework for Great Lakes restoration and protection under the Great Lakes Water Quality Agreement."[75]

To achieve greater accountability the IJC suggests "a rigorous, coordinated plan that identifies and prioritizes the actions needed to realize the goals of the Agreement, includes measurable targets and sets timelines for completion— such targets and timelines are generally not in the current agreement."[76] In addition, it recommends that a binational entity be given the responsibility of assessing progress, and that action be taken on progress reports. The need for greater accountability seems evident, as aquatic invasive species in the Great Lakes is a major concern and the St. Lawrence Seaway opened for ocean-going traffic in March of 2007.

GLU asserts: "It is time for a moratorium on ocean-going vessel access to the Great Lakes until the Canadian and US governments put in place regulatory solutions that will curb the influx of these devastating invaders."[77] GLU responds to the claim that restricting access of ocean-going vessels to the Great Lakes would cause severe economic losses (a consequential argument) by pointing out that these economic business losses would be about one-tenth of the cost required to control two of the invasive species in the lakes, the zebra and quagga mussels.[78]

The Apollo Alliance

The Apollo Alliance is another example of collaboration between NGOs, government officials, and corporate leaders. The About Us page of its website has as its title, "The Apollo Alliance for Good Jobs and Clean Energy," which reveals a new strategy for protecting the environment.[79] Those endorsing this effort include environmental NGOs, such as Greenpeace USA and the Sierra Club, and also labor unions. The website identifies an advisory board that includes several elected officials and a lengthy list of business partners supporting of Apollo.

Rather than focus on environmental problems, "The Apollo Alliance provides a message of optimism and hope, framed around rejuvenating our nation's economy by creating the next generation of American industrial jobs and treating clean energy as an economic and security mandate to rebuild America."[80] The Apollo Alliance "seeks to spread the benefits of investment into America's energy independence to everyone."[81]

The Alliance supports a ten-point plan to achieve good jobs and energy independence:

1.   Promote Advanced Technology & Hybrid Cars (using tax incentives).

2.   Invest in More Efficient Factories (using tax incentives).

3.   Encourage High Performance Building (invest in "green buildings" and update codes).

4.   Increase Use of Energy Efficient Appliances (use incentives to increase US manufacturing).

5.   Modernize Electrical Infrastructure (research and develop more efficient generating plants).

6.   Expand Renewable Energy Development (create jobs and solar, biomass, and wind energy).

7.   Improve Transportation Options (invest in energy efficient mass transit).

8.   Reinvest in Smart Urban Growth (promote strong cities and good jobs).

9.   Plan for a Hydrogen Future (invest in using hydrogen to power cars and distribute electricity).

10.   Preserve Regulatory Protections (for workers and the environment).[82]

This plan supports investing in more efficient and sustainable ways of producing energy, as this investment will generate a healthy economy as well as a healthy environment.

CONSEQUENCES: INCENTIVES AND TAXES

How can environmental policies be effective? Corporations and NGOs, as well as governments, must act responsibly, and are more likely to do so when under public scrutiny. To its credit, JPMorgan Chase supports the moral presumption asserted by international law that indigenous communities should be involved in decisions affecting their habitats, and WWF has made this its practice as well. The Apollo Alliance has enabled labor unions and environmental NGOs to work together with business leaders in creating jobs as well as a more sustainable economy. The open process of the International Joint Commission in reviewing the GLWQA also is a model of collaboration.

Equity

How can the costs and benefits of environmental policy be allocated fairly? Agenda 21 assesses a greater responsibility to developed countries for these costs, arguing that the industrial countries have promoted the economic development causing the problem and also have enjoyed a greater portion of the economic benefits from the development. The US government rejects this claim, but JPMorgan Chase accepts that Agenda 21 and other international standards reflect what "good corporate citizenship" now means.

Interface affirms language from the Brundtland Report, rather than the stronger presumptions of Agenda 21, but Interface clearly accepts that industry must internalize the social and environmental costs of doing business in order to act "fairly and responsibly so that the needs of all people on whom we have an impact, and the future needs of people who are not yet born, stand the best chance of being met."[83]

The NGOs mentioned in this chapter do not explicitly address the question of equity in allocating the costs and benefits of protecting the environment. The environmental NGOs engaged in direct action and lobbying, such as Greenpeace and the Sierra Club, certainly believe that *multinational corporations should be held accountable* for most of the environmental damage caused by economic development, as these corporations have both caused the damage and persuaded governments to minimize regulations that might have protected the environment. All the NGOs seem to support internalizing social and environmental costs (externalities), and also the principle that the polluter should pay and the precautionary principle.

A concern for responsibility and accountability dominates the ethical arguments presented by some corporations, as well as by governments and NGOs. The right to a healthy environment is affirmed, but largely as a basis for arguing that governments and corporations have a duty to ensure that economic activity is environmentally sustainable.

The personal story of Anderson, the CEO of Interface, offers a *character argument for corporate responsibility*, reminding us that individuals who are motivated to act more responsibly can make a difference. Also, in pledging to pursue "industrial ecology," which Interface says means being "a corporation that cherishes nature and restores the environment,"[84] the carpet company has identified what might be described as a *corporate virtue*. We may hope that good examples, in business practice, will help raise environmental standards.

Apparently, based on the materials we have reviewed in this chapter, a *concern for future generations* is the most persuasive moral argument in support of the presumption that we have a duty to maintain and restore our wild, agricultural, and urban ecosystems.

Ecosystems

None of the environmental NGOs assert animal rights, and most affirm that human needs must be addressed in acting to ensure environmental sustainability.

NGOs emphasize protecting ecosystems and *limiting the impact of human uses*, rather than ending animal suffering. In addition, the Nature Conservancy supports using cost-benefit analysis for decisions about ecosystems, as a way of creating broader political support for effective environmental policies.

In general, there is a clear *shift in emphasis* in environmental policy from regulation and threatening enforcement measures *to investment, partnerships, and incentives*. We would expect to see this in corporate environmental policy, but it is present as well in the EPA's Energy Star and Green Power Partnership programs and in the partnership work of WWF and the Nature Conservancy. It is also the primary strategy of the Apollo Alliance, which has garnered support even from direct action and advocacy NGOs, such as Greenpeace USA and the Sierra Club.[85]

Tax Policy

Among advocates for environmental policy, there is no consensus about *taxes*. The position of Interface is exceptional: "To make significant progress, we will need the cooperation of government and other industrial partners to shift taxation away from economic and social benefits, (labor, income and investment) to detriments, (pollution, waste, and the loss of primary resources)."[86] In the words of economists Daly and Farley, governments should: "Tax bads, not goods."[87]

Does it make sense to *tax activities that harm the environment*, rather than what contributes to our wellbeing? "The idea is to shift the tax burden from value added by labor and capital (something we want more of) to 'that to which value is added'—namely, the throughput and its associated depletion and pollution (something we want less of)."[88] European countries have successfully implemented such tax reform,[89] but so far there is little support in the United States for this change in tax policy.

Unsustainable

Although the threat of disastrous environmental consequences casts a dark cloud over all talk of environmental policy, the ethical arguments do not emphasize consequential calculations. Perhaps this is because these predictions are uncertain, but it may also be that many advocates believe there are strong *arguments for what is inherently right and good*.

For instance, the CEO of Greenpeace USA urges that we "stand up for what is right,"[90] implying that we all know what this means without having to calculate the likely consequences of our conduct. Furthermore, the argument that we should care for the environment because we have a moral duty to future generations appears in government assertions, corporate policies, and also on NGO websites. In the words of the National Environmental Policy Act, we should be "the trustee of the environment for succeeding generations."[91]

Many if not all of the moral presumptions discussed in this chapter should be the basis for environmental policy, unless the consequences of acting on these presumptions are sufficiently adverse to call the presumptions into question. The main *consequence argument opposing these presumptions* is that the economic costs of enforcing such an environmental policy would be severe and politically unsustainable. This counterargument deserves serious consideration, but the burden of proof lies with those who oppose an environmental policy that actually protects ecosystems for future generations. Moreover, given that the integrity of the environment is at stake, compelling evidence should be required to overturn these presumptions.

Also, we must consider the likely economic benefits of enforcing effective environmental policies. JPMorgan Chase affirms that exercising environmental stewardship has led to *new investment opportunities.* Interface reports that one consequence of creating a new business model for "sustainability-based commerce" is *an increase in profits* of almost 50 percent. These are only two corporations, so we cannot generalize about the overall economic impact of "going green." Yet, these results weigh against the common consequential prediction that a social and economic commitment to environmental sustainability is bad for business.

QUESTIONS—ENVIRONMENTAL POLICY:
GOVERNMENTS, CORPORATIONS, NGOs

1. Make an ethical argument for sustainable development, referring to at least one international principle. Is this a duty argument or a rights argument?
2. Identify three duties of the federal government asserted by NEPA and raise a critical question about one of these.
3. What ethical presumption is at stake in the conflict between the EPA and the states that sued it in 2006 and 2008?
4. What UN Millennium Development Goals are affirmed by JPMorgan Chase? What pledge has the corporation made to implement these goals?
5. In what respect does JPMorgan Chase accept the precautionary principle?

6. Interface is committed to addressing sustainability on seven fronts. Identify four of these that you think are most significant, and explain your reasoning.

7. Identify two positive consequences for Interface of acting on its environmental policy.

8. To achieve greater environmental sustainability, Interface has recommended changes in taxation policy and economic practices. Explain two of these recommendations.

9. The Natural Step affirms four ethical presumptions. Summarize two of these and reflect critically on each.

10. Describe Wal-Mart's new environmental initiative, and give an ethical reason supporting it.

11. What evidence is there that sustainable development is an opportunity for business? Why is this relevant for environmental ethics?

12. Choose an NGO mentioned in the chapter and summarize its ethical presumptions. Give an example of what the NGO does.

13. What ethical argument does the GLU make about ocean-going vessels in the Great Lakes? How does the GLU weigh the likely consequences of acting on this ethical presumption?

14. The Apollo Alliance promotes a ten-point plan. Identify five of these ethical presumptions. How is this strategy different from the approach of many environmental NGOs?

15. Do you agree with tax recommendations made by Interface? Explain your reasoning.

11

Air and Water

A HEALTHY ENVIRONMENT

The integrity of ecosystems depends on air quality and both the quality and quantity of water. Access to air and water are also fundamental human rights. Thus, making ethical decisions about our use of air and water requires understanding how nature purifies both, and then relying on this knowledge to provide access for everyone to clean air and clean water.

We begin with the ecology of the atmosphere, and consider how we should respond to air pollution and the increase of greenhouse gases. Then we consider the water cycle, and confront the problems of water pollution and the scarcity of clean water. Finally, we confirm that protecting a healthy environment makes more sense than depending on economic markets to allocate our use of these precious resources.

THE EARTH'S ATMOSPHERE

In the biosphere air and water intermingle almost everywhere. The atmosphere contains water particles, and water in the oceans, lakes, and streams absorbs the gases of the atmosphere. Plants absorb carbon dioxide from the air using solar energy in the process of photosynthesis, which produces needed materials for the plants and releases oxygen into the atmosphere as a waste product. Animals breathe in oxygen, and exhale carbon dioxide. Both plants and animals require water, which is the medium for the metabolism of every organism.

Life on earth also depends on nitrogen, sulfur, and phosphorus compounds[1] as well as chemicals using carbon, oxygen, and hydrogen. A water molecule, which is the most common molecule on earth, is made up of two atoms of hydrogen and one atom of oxygen. Carbon is the sixth most common atom on earth, but carbon dioxide (an atom of carbon plus two atoms of oxygen) makes up only a small fraction of the atmosphere. Nitrogen, which is the second most common element in our bodies, is an essential ingredient for the proteins and nucleic acids needed for life. Nitrogen must be "fixed" (in compounds) to be utilized by plant and animal cells, and this occurs in the atmosphere due to lightning and in the soil because of bacteria.

Sulfur is found in rocks and ocean sediment, and enters the atmosphere with volcanic eruptions, forest fires, and as bacteria decomposes organic matter. Plants and animals require sulfur for proteins and enzymes, but sulfur dioxide in the atmosphere may react with water to form sulfuric acid. (Similarly, nitrous oxides in the atmosphere may react with water to form nitric acid.) Because this is natural, plants have evolved resistance to rain that is slightly acidic.

Phosphorus is essential for life on earth, as it forms part of the structural framework of DNA (deoxyribonucleic acid) and RNA (ribonucleic acid), is used in cell walls and bones, and is involved in energy transfers using ATP (adenosine triphosphate) within cells. Because it is highly reactive, phosphorus is never found as a free element in nature. Where phosphorus is scarce in the natural environment, life will also be scarce.

Ozone (a molecule with three atoms of oxygen) is in the air naturally, as it is produced from oxygen by lightning. In the upper atmosphere, the "ozone layer" prevents ultraviolet light (which damages organic tissue) from reaching the earth's surface. In the lower atmosphere, ozone levels are naturally too low to harm plants and the respiratory organs of animals.

Air and water are only "polluted" by the presence of these substances when the concentration is too high. Too much sulfuric acid in the atmosphere causes "acid rain" that kills plants, and too much ground-level ozone harms plants and animals. Humans are not the only cause of pollution, as natural events such as forest fires and volcanic eruptions contaminate air and water. Nonetheless, as ethical beings, we are responsible for our impact on the biosphere.

AIR: POLLUTION AND GREENHOUSE GASES

The US Congress passed the Clean Air Act in 1963 and the Air Quality Act in 1967. In 1970 it amended these in the Clean Air Act Extension, which charged the newly formed Environmental Protection Agency to develop and enforce regulations to protect the public from airborne contaminants known to be dangerous for human health. These laws reflect a growing awareness of our duty to restore and maintain nature's capacity to purify the atmosphere.

In 1977 Congress again amended the Clean Air Act, this time to require the EPA "to make a special effort to clean the air in national parks, wildlife refuges and other places of 'scenic' and 'historical' value it hoped to leave in somewhat better shape for future generations."[2] Yet, no administration since, "Democratic or Republican, has paid any attention to this mandate."[3] As a result, air pollution has damaged one in three national parks.

There have been efforts, however, to reduce lead poisoning, petrochemical smog in urban areas, acid rain where power plants are burning soft coal, the hole in the ozone layer due to chlorofluorocarbon gases (CFCs) entering the stratosphere (above thirty thousand feet), and the new threat caused by the increase of greenhouse gases in the atmosphere.

Lead

Lead is found naturally in water, but there was little lead in the air until, in the 1920s, lead was added to gasoline to improve the efficiency of the automobile engine. Within two decades the dangers for human health were clear.[4] "Long-term exposure to lead, even in low concentrations, can cause improper brain functioning and development. Scientific studies have clearly established the link between lead intake and the intellectual impairment of children. Unlike some contaminants, lead does not flush out of the body with body fluids. Once ingested, it remains in the fat and body tissue for life."[5]

Public health officials pushed for government regulations that would ban the use of lead in paint, require that lead pipes used to carry drinking water be replaced with copper or plastic pipes, and end the use of lead in gasoline (because particles of lead were introduced into the air with engine emissions). In 1976 the EPA banned the use of lead in gasoline, and since then concentrations of lead in the air have dropped more than 90 percent.[6]

Other sources of lead in the atmosphere are "from solid waste, coal, oil, iron and steel production, lead smelters and tobacco smoke."[7] A recent study endorsed by the EPA's Clean Air Science Advisory Committee (CASAC) concludes that there is no safe human level for exposure to lead.[8] Because of the continuing danger, the EPA monitors not only lead, but also five other air pollutants—ozone, soot,[9] sulfur dioxide, carbon monoxide, and nitrous oxides.[10]

Smog

In the 1950s smog in urban areas began to endanger human health. This "photochemical smog" is due to sunlight causing nitrogen oxides and volatile organic compounds to react, which produces airborne particles and ozone.[11] Scientists created a *catalytic converter* to reduce nitrogen oxides to nitrogen and oxygen, to oxidize carbon monoxide into carbon dioxide, and to oxidize unburned hydrocarbons into carbon dioxide and water.[12]

In 1976 the EPA required all new cars to have catalytic converters, and now these devices neutralize about 90 percent of the harmful emissions produced by automobile engines.[13] Since catalytic converters have been required in the United States, "Emissions of carbon monoxide have dropped by 32 percent even as driving has increased 127 percent."[14]

In 2008 the EPA "lowered the amount of ozone that should be allowed in the air for it to be considered healthy," but the "Clean Air Scientific Advisory Committee, created by Congress to advise the EPA" has protested that the "new air quality standard for smog fails to protect public health as required by law and should be strengthened."[15] Research in 2008 also indicates that high levels of ozone in the lower atmosphere "can decrease forest growth by as much as 30 percent," and interfere with "the ability of bees and other insects to follow the scent of flowers to their source, undermining the essential process of pollination."[16]

Reducing ozone in the lower atmosphere to levels that are harmless will require substantial investment in mass transit; engines for vehicles that produce fewer emissions; lower-cost housing in cities enabling people to live closer to where they work; and higher gasoline prices that motivate people to walk, bicycle, ride mass transit, and use car pools.[17]

Acid Rain

Acid rain is due largely to excess amounts of sulfur dioxide in the atmosphere. It is not only a problem in North America and Europe, but also in Asia and Latin America.[18] In Europe, the Convention on Long-Range Transboundary Air Pollution (CLRTAP) regulates emissions of both sulfur dioxide and nitrogen oxides.[19]

In the United States, utility companies burning coal with a high content of sulfur produce 70 percent of this airborne sulfur dioxide.[20] Acid rain reduces the yield of crops, kills pine trees, and renders lakes sterile by killing the small plants in the water. "The contaminated smoke is sent high into the air by the heat of combustion and the height of the smokestacks. Strong winds can carry the damaging gases for long distances before they fall to the ground."[21]

The Clean Air Act of 1990 directed the EPA to regulate the emissions of power plants. "Under the provisions of this act, regulators were required to study the records of each utility company. From this information, they calculated the amount of sulfur dioxide that had been generated by each factory in

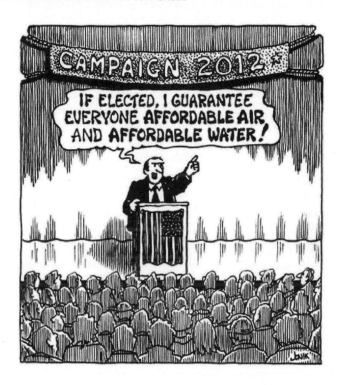

the preceding years. Because sulfur dioxide gas is the most frequent pollutant, this figure determines the tonnage of pollutants, or allowances, allotted to each factory or power plant."[22]

This allowance defines the "cap" (limit) of the sulfur dioxide emissions from a power plant and reduces this amount over time. Power companies that lower their emissions below their cap may sell the "extra allowances" to other companies, and a company exceeding its cap must pay a penalty. Under this regulatory program, "Emissions of sulfur dioxide have dropped by 35 percent even though the gross domestic product has more than doubled."[23]

This "cap-and-trade system" lowers the level of contaminants, but does not end pollution. In 2003, when an overload of the electrical circuits in northeastern North America shut down several power plants, scientists measured the air pollutants a day later. In comparison with measurements made a year earlier, there was "a 90 percent drop in the sulfur oxides that cause acid rain, a 50 percent drop in the nitrogen oxides that generate smog, and an increase of aerial visibility of 40 miles (64 km)."[24]

Laws that limit sulfur dioxide emissions and require catalytic converters have reduced the contaminants in the atmosphere causing acid rain and smog.[25] Yet, acid rain continues to destroy forests, and smog in the United States "causes more than 50,000 hospital cases a year."[26] These economic "externalities" are substantial costs.

Ozone in the Upper Atmosphere

The presence of nitrogen oxides in the upper atmosphere continues to damage the ozone layer protecting life on earth, as nitrogen oxides react with ozone in direct sunlight.[27] In the stratosphere ozone deflects ultraviolet light that, if it reached the earth, would "kill fish and shrimp larvae near the surface of the oceans, stunt the growth of plants, and contribute to vision problems and skin cancer in humans."[28]

The ozone layer in the stratosphere was stable until chlorofluorocarbons (CFCs) were invented in 1930 for use in air conditioners. In the 1940s these synthetic gases, which are odorless, nontoxic, nonflammable, and chemically inert, were also used in aerosol dispensers. In 1973 researchers found that CFC molecules exposed to undiluted light in the stratosphere break up, releasing chlorine gas that reacts with ozone and produces oxygen. Five years later the US Congress banned CFCs in aerosol dispensers, despite arguments by CFC manufacturers that scientific evidence of the danger to the ozone layer was inconclusive.

In 1986 a large hole in the ozone layer was confirmed, and a year later scientists verified the presence of chlorine molecules in this hole. At the end of 1987 the UNEP launched the Montreal Protocol on Substances that Deplete the Ozone Layer, which came into force as international law in 1989. The Montreal Protocol oversees phasing out CFCs.[29] This protocol is an example of successful international regulation. The battle for the Montreal Protocol was won because proponents: were able to define the issue as a serious threat to public health, made the precautionary principle the standard for intervention, gained credibility when the ozone hole over Antarctica was discovered, and had a more effective lobbying network than the opposition.[30] Production of CFCs is to end in 2010, but CFCs will continue to pose a threat, as these gases in refrigerators and air conditioners made before 2000 may be reused.

Greenhouse Gases

Water vapor and other natural gases in the atmosphere act like a glass ceiling, letting the light through and blocking much of the heat radiating from the earth. This is known as the *greenhouse effect*, as this process is how glass warms a greenhouse. Greenhouse gases include carbon dioxide, carbon monoxide, nitrous oxide, methane, fluorocarbons, and hydrofluorocarbons.[31]

The greenhouse effect of the atmosphere is natural and sustains life.[32] Since the industrial era, however, the carbon dioxide in the atmosphere has risen by 30 percent[33] and "the rate of growth increases every year."[34] This increase, which is causing rapid global warming, is largely due to burning fossil fuels (coal, oil, and natural gas).[35] To slow global warming, we must lower carbon dioxide emissions, which requires reducing our consumption of fossil fuels. Chapter 15 considers ways of doing this.

WATER: QUALITY AND SCARCITY

Nature purifies water through the *hydrologic cycle*. Evaporation from streams, lakes, and oceans leaves impurities behind. If the atmosphere is not polluted, then rain will bring clean water back to earth. Impurities added to water in the atmosphere, or picked up in streams from rocks and sediments, are filtered out by plants growing along streams and wetlands that absorb organic material and minerals. Water in underground aquifers has been filtered by the soil and purified by bacteria in the ground that transforms chemicals into nutrients.

What is our duty to maintain these ecosystem processes, and to restore ecosystems when these functions are damaged? We look first at the stress now on surface water and groundwater ecosystems. Then we consider our choices in treating water, and how we might protect access to water where there is scarcity.

Surface Water

In 1972 the US Congress passed the Federal Water Pollution Control Act Amendments, which were later modified and are now known as the Clean Water Act (CWA). The purpose of this act is "to restore and maintain the chemical, physical, and biological integrity of the nation's waters."[36] The CWA requires protecting streams and wetlands, as these provide essential ecosystem services such as filtering out sediment. "Too much sediment can fill up reservoirs and navigation channels, damage commercial and sport fisheries, eliminate recreation spots, harm aquatic habitats and their associated plants and animals, and increase water filtration costs."[37]

Streams and wetlands also filter and process organic material, such as manure, leaves, and dead insects, and chemicals, such as nitrogen and phosphorus compounds in fertilizers that run off fields and golf courses. "In headwater streams and wetlands, more water is in direct contact with the streambed, where most processing takes place. Bacteria, fungi and other microorganisms living on the bottom of a stream consume inorganic nitrogen and phosphorus and convert them into less harmful, more biologically beneficial compounds."[38]

In one study of small streams, nitrogen and phosphorus were removed before traveling less than sixty-five feet (twenty meters).[39] Where the forest surrounding a small stream is replaced by fields or lawns, however, grasses along the bank of the stream trap sediment and expand, shrinking the width of the moving water. This greatly reduces the cleansing capability of a stream, causing nitrogen and phosphorus to travel five to ten times farther.[40]

In Appalachia from 1986 to 1998 more than nine hundred miles of streams were buried because of mining operations, and in Maryland more than half of the streams of the Rock Creek watershed were destroyed when the area was developed.[41] Land development in the twentieth century throughout the United States has destroyed over ninety million acres of wetlands.[42]

Laws concerning water pollution distinguish between *point source* pollution (from factories, mining, landfills, and leaking sewage treatment facilities) and *nonpoint source* pollution.[43] Point source pollution is addressed by efforts to ensure that wastewater released into the environment has been properly treated, so it is safe for the designated uses of the area, such as fishing or agriculture. The direct discharge of wastes from point sources into streams and lakes is regulated by the National Pollutant Discharge Elimination System (NPDES), a permit system established by the Clean Water Act and administered by the EPA.[44]

Prevention is the best way to reduce point source pollution.[45] Remember the three Rs? *Reducing* waste dumped in landfills, for example, means fewer pollutants washed into nearby streams. *Reusing* water in industry lowers demand for clean water, reduces the wastewater requiring treatment, and minimizes the volume of treated wastewater discharged into the environment. *Recycling* paper reduces demand for trees, which means there are more trees maintaining soil and preventing runoff. Also, producing recycled paper takes less water than making paper from raw wood.[46]

Nonpoint source pollution in the United States is largely due to *storm water runoff*, which carries pollutants from surface areas, such as roadways, parking lots, golf courses, farm fields, and construction sites, into storm gutters and streams.[47] The EPA says that nonpoint source pollution is the main cause of contaminants in our water, and that this is largely due to industrial agriculture.[48]

Agricultural runoff contains phosphorus used in fertilizer and animal feeds. Phosphorus is a *limiting nutrient* in plants, as the supply of phosphorus is usually lower than other nutrients. When storm water runoff brings phosphorus into a water system, algae thrive, but too much phosphorus causes *eutrophication*. "When thick blooms of algal growth block sunlight from reaching the plants below, the decay of dead algae uses up the available oxygen in the water, suffocating fish and sometimes causing whole populations of species to be lost."[49]

The intensive use of fertilizer and animal feed (containing phosphorus and nitrogen) has led to a global catastrophe. By 1994, "significant eutrophication problems were being reported in 54 percent of all lakes and reservoirs in Southeast Asia, 53 percent of those in Europe, 48 percent in North America, 41 percent in South America, and 28 percent in Africa."[50]

Nature cleans water in *watersheds* that maintain the natural processes of sedimentation, biodegradation, filtration, and *sorption* (both *absorption* and *adsorption*, when a substance adheres to the surface of another material). When constructing highways or buildings disrupts watersheds, we should restore these natural processes.[51] Sedimentation works best in standing water, so we need to construct storm water runoff ponds that allow surface water to collect.

Biodegradation, filtering, and sorption occur where water is in contact with soil and plants, and is most effective when water is moving slowly across a large surface area. This means developed areas should have grass-lined, flat drainage ditches (called swales). Because surface water runoff not only spreads chemical pollutants but also erodes soil, it is important to reduce the velocity of storm water runoff by using swales, ponds, and boulders where the velocity is great, by planting grass and other vegetation to hold the soil, and by capturing eroded sediments as close to the source as possible.[52]

Dams to produce power and levees to control flooding often interfere with the natural cleansing provided by rivers and streams.[53] Holding water behind a dam expands the surface area and exposes the water to more sunlight. As the water temperature rises, the amount of oxygen in the water decreases, causing a decline in the fish population and an increase in algae. Dams and levees also interfere with the migratory routes of fish.[54]

Our ethical presumption is that sustainable development requires restoring and managing natural systems of water purification, as these ecosystem processes are the most effective (and least costly) way to maintain both the health of the environment and clean water for our use.[55]

Groundwater

Surface water, due to the hydrologic cycle, is a renewable resource. Groundwater, however, for all practical purposes is a *nonrenewable resource*, because on average it takes fourteen hundred years to replenish an underground aquifer.[56] About 97 percent of the liquid freshwater on earth is underground, but these reserves are shrinking.[57] "Today, aquifers supply water to more than half of India's irrigated land. The United States, with the third highest irrigated area in the world, uses groundwater for 43 percent of its irrigated farmland."[58] Groundwater is also the main source of drinking water for 1.5 billion people.[59]

As aquifers are depleted, surface water may decline. A study of fifty-four streams by the US Geological Survey found that groundwater is the source of about half the flow of surface water. Also, aquifers stabilize wetlands by providing water during the dry season and absorbing water when rains are heavy. Pumping water from aquifers tends to remove moisture from the earth's surface, which in agricultural areas increases the need for irrigation and dries up shallow wells.

Because surface water seeps into groundwater, *pollutants in surface water eventually reach aquifers.* DDT has been banned in the United States for more than thirty years,[60] but now is present in groundwater. Nitrate contamination (which may cause cancer) is a problem in Iowa, Kansas, Nebraska, and South Dakota,[61] and the fissured aquifers of southern California, Florida, and Maine are polluted.[62] Chemicals also enter groundwater from landfills and from leaking petroleum storage tanks.

In addition, *the process of extracting groundwater may pollute it.* In the 1970s the World Health Organization (WHO) began a well-drilling program in Bangladesh to reduce the use of contaminated surface water, and today 95 percent of the people there drink groundwater from aquifers. Recently, however, arsenic has been found in this water. It seems that oxygen entering the aquifers during pumping has oxidized iron pyrite sediment around the aquifer, causing the arsenic to dissolve and contaminate the groundwater.[63]

Finally, *an aquifer near a sea may be contaminated by salt.* A full aquifer drains to the sea, but as the aquifer is emptied seawater may flow back into the aquifer. "Because of its high salt content, just 2 percent of seawater mixed with freshwater makes the water unusable for drinking or irrigation."[64] The aquifers under the heavily populated cities of Manila, Jakarta, Madras, and areas of Florida are now threatened by seawater.

Increasingly, therefore, *groundwater will have to be treated before it can be used.* Furthermore, because aquifers offer only a limited supply of water, it will not be long before aquifers are unable to provide the quantity of water now used for agriculture, manufacturing, and drinking. Our ethical presumption, therefore, should be "to improve social and individual well-being *per unit of water used.*"[65]

It is estimated that more than 40 percent of the world's peoples live in river basins suffering from *water stress,* and that more than eighty countries with about 40 percent of the world's population are experiencing *water scarcity.*[66] Countries that have dry ecosystems and sufficient funds often import "virtual water" in the form of grain, as it takes about a thousand tons of water to grow a ton of grain.[67]

Population growth, however, as well as greater consumption of beef, is raising the demand for grain. This means more water will be allocated for cash crops and cattle grazing, and less water for other uses. "Water is available only if water sources are regenerated and used within limits of renewability. When development philosophy erodes community control and instead promotes technologies that violate the water cycle, scarcity is inevitable."[68]

Allowing the market to determine the use of water and its price will not ensure its conservation and best use. "Market assumptions are blind to the ecological limits set by the water cycle and the economic limits set by poverty. Overexploitation of water and disruption of the water cycle create absolute scarcity that markets cannot substitute with other commodities."[69]

In India, for example, "even as capital investment was being poured into water projects [to support irrigation for growing export crops], more and more villages were running out of water [to drink and grow their own food]."[70]

Clearly, public and private investment in recycling wastewater makes sense. "Israel recycles 75 percent of its water," and Orange County, California, "will pump 70 million gallons of treated sewage into the aquifer under the county, thereby replenishing the volume of underground water and ensuring available supplies for the county's growing population."[71]

Water Treatment

Governments must also invest in more effective water treatment systems. *Chemical pollution is pervasive*, as virtually "every industrial facility in the United States that manufactured or used toxic chemicals has historically polluted air, land, and water resources."[72] There are now about eighty-five thousand chemicals in use in the US, and two thousand more are added each year. The EPA does not review every toxic chemical, but only the three thousand chemicals produced or imported into the United States at levels greater than one million pounds annually. A study by the General Accounting Office of 236 facilities manufacturing pulp and paper, pharmaceutical, and pesticides found that 77 percent of the toxic pollutants identified were *not* being controlled through the EPA point-source permit process.[73]

Pesticides are used everywhere but often not regulated. The EPA lists twenty-one pesticides (four of which are banned), and the World Health Organization lists thirty-one pesticides (eleven on the US list and another twenty of concern). The European Union enforces the precautionary principle by requiring that drinking water be free of pesticides,[74] but US water regulation provides less protection. In a 1997 test of ten drinking water sites in California, seventeen of the twenty-five pesticides detected were not being regulated under the EPA's primary drinking water standards.[75]

The Clean Water Act established programs to control water quality in *watersheds* by enforcing "the maximum daily pollutant load allowable" from each

source. This requires *identifying what pollutants are to be measured*, and *what level of contamination is unacceptable*. In effect, CWA regulation makes it acceptable "to pollute the environment up to specified water quality standards and not worry about unregulated chemicals."[76]

In the United States the *permissible pollution* approach also applies to regulating facilities that purify water for human consumption. The EPA sets maximum contaminant levels (MCLs) for the pollutants that must be treated, and there are now about ninety contaminants on this list. Since 1996 the EPA has also been required to publish a list of contaminants that are not subject to MCLs, but are "known or anticipated" to occur in public water systems.[77] This contaminant candidate list (CCL) includes about fifty chemicals and ten microbiological contaminants.[78]

The process of studying and setting an MCL for a chemical that is known to be dangerous can be lengthy. Arsenic, for example, is known to cause cancer, but the EPA did not propose an MCL for arsenic until 2001 (perhaps because it is costly to measure). Then it took five years for the EPA to enforce this MCL in public water systems.[79]

There are also *problems with water treatment techniques.* Two chemicals commonly used to combine small particles (to facilitate their removal from water) have been identified by the US Public Health Service as "reasonably anticipated to be human carcinogens."[80] Also, the use of chlorine and bromine to destroy biological contaminants produces toxic halogenated compounds, most of which are not covered by the EPA's primary drinking water standards.[81]

Pharmaceutical pollutants that are not covered by the primary drinking water standards "have been shown to survive the treatment process," which is generally used in publicly operated treatment systems.[82] In 2001 a report published by the Centers for Disease Control (CDC) found that "virtually all humans have some 'background' level of industrial chemicals in their bodies."[83]

Who has the duty to ensure that chemicals are safe? If we affirm the *precautionary principle*, industries have this responsibility. Some companies have voluntarily accepted this duty,[84] and the FDA requires companies manufacturing drugs to ensure that these chemicals are safe before they are sold. Many of the industrial chemicals in the environment are as dangerous as pharmaceutical drugs. Therefore, it seems reasonable that these substances should meet the same burden of proof before being released into the environment.

Implementing such a system, however, would require government monitoring and would not remove the tens of thousands of chemicals already in our water. So, governments have a duty to provide effective water treatment. Is it sufficient to meet the Environmental Protection Agency's MLC standards? Affirming the precautionary principles, as in Europe, would mean local governments in the United States have a duty to use the *best available technology* (BAT) to make our water as safe as possible. This means using ozone and ultraviolet light now and more effective forms of treatment as these are developed.

As water treatment impacts our human right to safe water, those who argue the BAT standard is too costly bear the burden of showing that this is a compelling reason for setting aside our ethical presumption.[85] In California, water utility managers estimate that using "advanced treatment technologies should add only 15 to 25 percent to a water utility's budget."[86] In areas where there is a shortage of water, treatment programs may find it cost effective to use new techniques for recycling wastewater to supply the drinking water that communities require.[87]

ECONOMIC PREDICTIONS: SHORTSIGHTED

Clear air and water are essential for a healthy environment and for human health, which is why the purpose of the Clean Water Act is "to restore and maintain the chemical, physical, and biological integrity of the nation's waters."[88] In this statement the word *integrity* is used in a scientific sense, but there is an ethical implication as well. We should restore and maintain the integrity of the nation's waters, because we have a duty to care for the ecosystems that sustain life on earth, protect the human right to clean air and water, and preserve these ecosystem functions for future generations. Will doing our duty be cost effective?[89] There is ample evidence that restoring and maintaining natural systems that cleanse water "saves much money, both capital and operating costs."[90]

Nonmarket Goods

Life on earth depends on the atmosphere and the hydrologic cycle.[91] The air is not a commodity to be priced by the market, and no one "has a right to overuse, abuse, waste, or pollute water systems."[92] *Everyone has a human right to clean air and water.*[93]

In 1985 the Supreme Court of India restrained the mining of limestone quarries in the Doon Valley, arguing that the law must protect "the right of the people to live in a healthy environment with minimum disturbance of ecological balance and without avoidable hazards to them and to their cattle, homes and agricultural land and undue affection of air, water and environment."[94] This decision rests on a moral argument that community rights, which secure the necessary social conditions for human dignity, outweigh individual property rights.[95]

Also, to protect human rights, *we must resist the privatization of water.*[96] The World Bank failed to do this in Maharashtra, India, where it subsidized the construction of tube wells and mechanized pumping systems for irrigation, although 80 percent of the water supplied was used to grow sugar cane as a cash crop. This may make "economic sense" for those with the financial capital to invest in sugar cane production, but as a consequence "public wells and shallow wells owned by small farmers have run dry."[97]

As long as the market price of removing groundwater from aquifers is simply the cost of extraction, this water will not be assessed economically as a "scarce" resource. Yet, it is that for billions of people wherever the integrity of ecosystems is being degraded, or where access to water for domestic use is restricted because of irrigation or the privatization of water.

Our ethical presumption, therefore, is that *the cost of using air and water has to increase when the use of the resource is polluting, or wasteful, or violates a human right.* Also, the public costs of monitoring air and water, and treating water to make it safe, must be paid, and these costs should be assessed in a way that is proportional to "bad" uses of air and water. *Good uses should be cheap*, and *bad uses expensive.*

Although the cap-and-trade approach has reduced sulfur dioxide emissions, setting a cap and providing tax credits for companies reducing emissions below their cap might be more effective in providing incentives for companies to invest in conservation.[98] Also, offering tax credits would not encourage trade in a "bad" (pollution), as the cap-and-trade approach does, but instead would reward companies for (the "good" of) reducing pollution.

Certainly, without legal mandates most corporations will not internalize the long-term environmental and social costs of the air and water pollution they create. Therefore, we should support government regulations that impose these long-term costs fairly on manufacturing and agribusiness.

Bottled Water

As a final example, consider the present market in bottled water, which is growing rapidly all over the world. In India, where shallow wells are drying up due to pumping water from aquifers for irrigation, between 1992 and 2000, sales of bottled water increased tenfold. In 1998 alone the number of plastic water bottles sold in India was estimated at 6 billion.[99]

Yet, research in the United States has shown that 25 to 40 percent of bottled water is tap water, and a 1999 study revealed that "one-third of the 103 brands of bottle water tested contained elevated levels of bacteria, inorganic chemicals, and/or organic chemicals."[100] Bottled water is a fraud or an expensive convenience, and this privatization of water undermines support for public access.[101] Selling bottled water raises India's GNP and thus counts as economic development, but the main beneficiaries are those able to invest in the water-bottling industry.

Using plastic to bottle water adds nothing to water quality[102] and adds energy costs to making water available. Marketing bottled water has also increased the global debris of plastic now covering about 40 percent of the surface of the oceans,[103] which threatens these ecosystems.

"[T]he plastic polymers commonly used in consumer products, even as single molecules of plastic, are indigestible by any known organism. Even those single molecules must be further degraded by sunlight or slow oxidative breakdown before their constituents can be recycled in the building blocks of life. There is no data on how long such recycling takes in the oceans—some ecologists have made estimates of five hundred years or more. Even more ominously, no one knows the ultimate consequences of the worldwide dispersion of plastic fragments that can concentrate the toxic chemicals already present in the world's oceans."[104]

The short-term costs of producing bottled water are unnecessary,[105] and the long-term costs of removing this debris from the environment are enormous. To *prevent this pollution,* corporations producing bottled water (or other plastic containers) should be required by law to implement recycling programs that meet a high standard of compliance, or to modify their products so the plastic will degrade and be recycled naturally within a reasonable period of time.

Restoring Ecosystems

I have argued that the likely long-term consequences of restoring and maintaining the earth's air and water ecosystems do not give us reason to set aside these ethical duties, but instead confirm them. At least, I suggest, the following three ethical presumptions meet this test.

Prevention is best. Preventing air and water pollution requires emphasizing point-source intervention. Strategies that tax actions, which are "bad" for the environment and provide incentives for actions that are "good," will likely have the best results.

Polluters should pay. Applying this presumption to every industry ensures competition among companies to reduce their "pollution tax" by reducing their pollution, and allows businesses to pass on to consumers (in the price of each product) the costs of minimizing pollution and cleaning up the environment.

Better safe than sorry. This version of the *precautionary principle* rejects the permissible pollution approach, which puts the burden of proof on governments to show that chemicals are unsafe. As we expect pharmaceutical drugs and our food to be safe, we should also expect that manufactured products will not harm the integrity of the earth's ecosystem or our health. Therefore, we should support laws that make producers liable for the safety of their products. Also, we should support the taxes necessary to ensure that water treatment systems use the best available technology to purify drinking water.

QUESTIONS—AIR AND WATER: A HEALTHY ENVIRONMENT

1. Explain why we all have a duty to preserve the integrity of the ecosystems that provide clean air and water for the earth. Why do governments have such a duty?
2. Summarize the action taken by the EPA with respect to lead pollution, smog, or acid rain. Assess the short-term consequences of the action you identify.

3.   How does the Montreal Protocol protect the ozone layer in the stratosphere? Give three reasons why this international regulation has been successful.

4.   Why is carbon dioxide, a natural gas, now a problem in the atmosphere? What duty might we have to reduce carbon dioxide emissions? Explain your reasoning.

5.   Why are small streams important in the hydrologic cycle? What can be done to protect these streams in watersheds?

6.   Give an example of point-source pollution. How is this kind of pollution addressed by the Clean Water Act and EPA oversight?

7.   What is the major cause of nonpoint-source pollution? What should our ethical presumption be in this case?

8.   Why is groundwater a nonrenewable resource? How is it related to surface water?

9.   Explain the EPA's permissible pollution approach for water treatment. How is this different than the EU's use of the precautionary principle?

10.   Who should be responsible for ensuring that a chemical is safe to be released into the environment? Explain your reasoning. Should the precautionary principle apply?

11.   Compare the EPA standard of MCLs for water treatment and the BAT standard. What are the likely consequences of using these standards?

12.   The CWA asserts a duty to protect the integrity of the nation's waters. What is this duty and who has it? Why? Does this duty require actions that are cost effective? Should it?

13.   Give a reason for taxing the use of groundwater. Should the tax be higher when the water is used to grow cash crops rather than food for local communities? Why or why not?

14.   Construct and argue for an ethical presumption concerning bottled water.

15.   Who should be responsible for the costs of pollution? Explain your reasoning.

12

Agriculture

LAND AND FOOD

"Growing crops is nothing else but a more or less astute management of peculiarly simplified ecosystems."[1] In the last half century, however, agricultural
management has ignored the lessons of nature. The net loss of topsoil annually
may be as much as twenty-five billion tons,[2] which is a catastrophic loss, as it
takes up to five hundred years for nature to create an inch of topsoil.[3] *Deforestation* has increased water runoff and affected rainfall, causing a loss of about
six million hectares (close to fifteen million acres) of fertile land each year to
desertification.[4]

Irrigation has increased crop yields, but has made a quarter of the world's
farmland less fertile due to salt left in the soil by evaporation, or waterlogged if
the land was not properly drained. "Although only 17 percent of the world's
cropland is irrigated, that 17 percent produces 40 percent of the global harvest.
This disproportionate share is largely due to the capability of irrigated lands to
produce two and sometimes three crops in a year."[5] Due to irrigation, however,
water tables are falling,[6] and underground *aquifers are being depleted.*[7] "Modern
agriculture places a severe strain on our water resources. In the United States,
for example, it consumes fully 85 percent of all freshwater resources."[8]

The use of *artificial fertilizer* has produced higher crop yields, but degraded
the soil. In fields watered by rain only about 40 percent of the nitrogen in artificial fertilizer is taken up by the crops, and in rice paddies as little as 20 percent of the nitrogen in the fertilizer is utilized.[9] Agricultural runoff of nitrogen
compounds into streams has led to "at least fifty dead zones in the oceans, one
the size of New Jersey in the Gulf of Mexico."[10] "We have perturbed the global

nitrogen cycle," Czech scientist Vaclav Smil asserts, "more than any other, even carbon."[11]

Moreover, our system of agriculture is precarious. "The world's food supply hangs by a slender thread of biodiversity. Ninety percent is provided by slightly more than a hundred plant species out of a quarter-million known to exist. Twenty species carry most of the load, of which only three—wheat, maize [corn], and rice—stand between humanity and starvation."[12]

What should our ethical presumptions be? I will argue that nature is our model for agriculture, poor farmers can feed themselves and their communities when their human rights are protected, and farming can and must be environmentally sustainable.

NATURE'S CYCLES

Plants depend on nitrogen, phosphorus, and potassium, and the soil's *humus* is rich in these elements. "Humus is what's left of organic matter after it has been broken down by the billions of big and small organisms that inhabit a spoonful of earth."[13] An ecosystem naturally maintains the humus required by plants.

Nitrogen "is the single most important nutrient" for plant growth,[14] but plants can only use nitrogen that is fixed by bacteria. Legumes (members of the bean family) form "symbiotic relationships with nitrogen fixing bacteria. In exchange for some nitrogen, the bacteria receive from the plants carbohydrates and special structures (nodules) in roots where they can exist in a moist environment. Scientists estimate that biological fixation globally adds approximately 140 million metric tons of nitrogen to ecosystems every year."[15]

Nitrogen plays a major role in protein and chlorophyll production, and chlorophyll enables plant cells to carry on photosynthesis, which uses solar energy to transform carbon dioxide into sugars. The *nitrogen cycle* is crucial for agriculture, but adding more fixed nitrogen to the soil will not increase yields without a sufficient amount of phosphorus. Phosphorus is required by the enzymes in plants that accumulate and convert carbon dioxide into sugars in photosynthesis, and is also needed for the construction and reproduction of DNA.[16]

In the *phosphorus cycle* rain removes phosphates from rocks and carries them through the soil, where plants take them up. Phosphates move "from plants to animals when herbivores eat plants and carnivores eat plants or herbivores. The phosphates absorbed by animal tissue through consumption eventually return to the soil through the excretion of urine and feces, as well as from the final decomposition of plants and animals after death."[17]

Potassium regulates the water content in plants and the use of nutrients, resists plant diseases and drought, and increases the efficiency of photosynthesis.[18] The *potassium cycle* takes place in the soil and in plants. "In agricultural ecosystems, potassium uptake by various crops varies, and its content in the soil depends on harvesting and general cultivation methods."[19]

The use of artificial fertilizer raises levels of nitrogen, phosphorus, and potassium in the soil and increases plant growth, but disrupts the natural cycles of these elements. Furthermore, using pesticides with artificial fertilizers, which is standard practice in industrial agriculture, degrades the humus that maintains soil fertility.

INDUSTRIAL AGRICULTURE

"Mother earth never attempts to farm without livestock; she always raises mixed crops; great pains are taken to preserve the soil and to prevent erosion; the mixed vegetable and animals wastes are converted into humus; there is no waste; the processes of growth and the processes of decay balance one another; the greatest care is taken to store the rainfall; both plants and animals are left to protect themselves against disease."[20]

Industrial agriculture ignores these lessons. It replaces farm animals with machines, diverse crops and crop rotation with a single crop, natural fertilizer with artificial fertilizer, and grazing with barns and stockyards where livestock are fed grain laced with hormones and antibiotics to fatten the animals and resist the bacteria that thrive in such artificial environments.

Inputs

Cheap *fossil fuels* (which are only cheap due to government subsidies) have made industrial agriculture feasible. Artificial fertilizer is made from natural gas and pesticides from oil. Gasoline powers tractors and irrigation pumps, equipment in the livestock barns, trucks that transport food to processing plants and markets, and processing and refrigeration for much of the food.[21] "The food industry burns nearly a fifth of all the petroleum consumed in the United States (about as much as automobiles do). Today it takes between seven and ten calories of fossil fuel energy to deliver one calorie of food energy to an American plate."[22]

The development of higher yield *hybrid seeds* led to what is called the Green Revolution. "Between 1950 and 1984, as the Green Revolution transformed agriculture around the globe, world grain production increased by 250 percent."[23] By 1994, however, it took four hundred gallons of oil to feed each US citizen. Since 1994 the *energy input in agriculture* has continued to grow, but this increased input has not meant a higher yield, because the soil has been degraded and pesticides have become less effective.[24]

Artificial fertilizers increase yields,[25] but with great waste. Growing a single crop makes using machinery easier (to cultivate and fertilize), but attracts pests. To fight pests, about 1.2 billion pounds of pesticides are used annually in the US— "about five pounds for every person in the country."[26] But pests have evolved resistance to these chemicals. Despite a tenfold increase in pesticide use since the 1950s, *crop losses to pests have doubled.*[27]

Over "the past three to four decades, losses in all major crops have increased in relative terms,"[28] largely due to:

- Planting crops that are increasingly susceptible to insects.
- Killing the natural enemies of pests by using pesticides.
- The development of greater pesticide resistance in insects.
- Reduced use of crop rotation and diversity that limit pest damage.
- Planting in climatic regions where crops are more susceptible to insects.
- Using pesticides that make crops more susceptible to insects.[29]

To reduce losses due to pests, US farm policy has adopted integrated pest management (IPM). The original goal of IPM was to manage "pests in an ecologically and economically sound way. Pesticides were to be applied only as needed, and decisions to treat were to be based on regular monitoring of pest populations and natural enemies (or antagonists) of pests in the target system."[30] The assumption was that using "a wide range of compatible or nondisruptive practices, such as resistant crop varieties and selective pesticides that preserve antagonists of pests, would ultimately lead to reduced reliance on chemical pesticides."[31]

In 2001, however, a report by the General Accounting Office (GAO) criticized federal efforts to enforce IPM and reduce pesticide use. The report found that the "total use of agricultural pesticides, measured in pounds of active ingredient, has actually increased since the beginning of USDA's IPM initiative."[32] It is the same worldwide.[33]

Agribusiness

The shift to industrial agriculture began in the 1970s. Bankers offered low-interest loans, and farmers were persuaded that they would do better by taking out loans to invest in more land and equipment so they could increase production. When inflation raised interest rates, farmers were unable to repay their loans, as the surplus of food they were producing drove prices down.

In the 1980s thousands of farmers went bankrupt and much of their land was bought up by corporations. Many surviving farmers in the United States have agreed to the "contract growing of chickens, hogs, and cattle owned by or committed to the processing companies,"[34] although this requires that they bear all the risk. Today 95 percent of the chickens in the United States are raised by contract growers, and half of these are owned by four food processors.[35] Four firms—Archer Daniels Midland (ADM), Cargill, Cenex Harvest Services, and General Mills—"own 60 percent of the nation's grain-handling facilities."[36]

When four companies control 40 percent or more of a market, they control the price of goods.[37] In 1996 Archer Daniels Midland (ADM) pled guilty to price fixing and paid an antitrust fine of $100 million.[38] A year before the lawsuit was filed, ADM's chairman admitted that: "The only place you see a free market is in the speeches of politicians."[39]

Federal farm policy has undercut effective market pricing. In the midst of the Depression the federal government began to use price supports and loans to help farmers survive. In the 1970s the Nixon administration changed to direct subsides, primarily for wheat, corn, soybeans, rice, and cotton. Paying farmers "directly for the shortfall in the price of corn was revolutionary, as its proponents surely must have understood."[40] Instead of removing corn and other commodities supported by the federal farm bill "out of a falling market, as the old loan programs and federal granary had done, the new subsidies encouraged farmers to sell their corn [and other commodities] at any price, since the government would make up the difference."[41]

Under this system farmers try to maximize their yield on the land they plant, which makes sense given their fixed costs for loans and equipment. They buy more fertilizer and pesticide, which increases their input costs and also their yield. Higher productivity has generally led to declining market prices, less profit for farmers overall, and the consolidation of agricultural land under corporate ownership—as independent farmers have often been unable to pay their debts.

In 2007, however, there was a dramatic change, at least for those growing corn. Federal subsidies for the production of ethanol drove up the market price of corn[42] and made independent farmers rich and agribusiness richer.[43] Before the financial crisis at the end of 2008, net farm income rose by about 50 percent. Senator Richard Lugar, an Indiana farmer and former chairman of the Senate Agriculture Committee, admits that federal farm subsidies, which are "narrowly focused on certain crops and are excessive," become "ridiculous given the exploding possibilities to grow crops for biofuels production."[44]

Opponents of the US farm bill introduced in Congress in 2007 argue that it "subsidizes the overproduction of corn and soy in the Midwest, which is driving up obesity and diabetes and polluting the land. Instead, they say, the farm bill should put more money into sustainable and organic food production, agricultural conservation and efforts to put a higher priority on fresh, local fruits and vegetables."[45] The farm bill that became law in 2008 "preserves an indefensible program of direct payments amounting to about $5 billion a year that flow in good times and bad. It raises support levels for wheat and soybeans, while adding several new crops to the list in a way that will make it easier for farmers to raid the federal Treasury even when prices go up."[46]

US farm bill subsidies have long favored agribusiness.[47] "Just ten percent of America's largest and richest farms collect almost three-fourths of federal farm subsidies—cash payments that too often promote harmful environmental practices."[48] The top 1 percent of subsidy recipients received 17 percent of payments, between 2003 and 2005, of $34,752,000,000. "In this period eleven agricultural businesses each received more than $4 million in subsidies, and half of the total crop subsidy went to agribusiness owners in only 19 congressional districts."[49]

Agribusiness not only controls federal farm policy, as well as seeds, livestock, and food processing, but even food retailing. In 1992 the top-five retailers—Albertson's, Ahold USA, Kroger, Safeway, and Wal-Mart—had only 19 percent of the national market, but by 2004 these five corporations had captured over 45 percent of the national market and almost 75 percent of the market in the largest cities. Pillsbury and General Mills merged in 2000, and Tyson and IPB in 2001. Today, 80 percent of the beef sold by these retailers is packed by four corporations.[50]

Agribusiness also controls international trade. The North American Free Trade Agreement (NAFTA) has "encouraged concentration in the food processing industry and the expansion of factory farms and agribusiness in all three NAFTA countries [Mexico, Canada, and the United States]."[51] Half of Mexico's small farmers have been pushed off the land, and Mexico now imports more than ten times as much corn from the United States as it did before NAFTA. The gap between rich and poor in Mexico and in the United States has grown, and the number of Mexicans coming illegally into the US to find work has increased.[52]

Trade agreements under the WTO, IMF, and World Bank have had similar results elsewhere. In Tanzania, for instance, "the overall impact on food security of the liberalization of agricultural trade is profoundly negative. Farmer incomes are declining, and, at the same time, school and medical fees have been reintroduced under the Structural Adjustment Program.[53] Farmers have to part with some of the little money they earn, and have less to meet farming costs and to buy food in times of shortage."[54]

In India in the past ten years more than twenty-five thousand farmers in prosperous regions have killed themselves because they were unable to pay their debts—due to the rising input costs of corporate seeds, pesticides, and fertilizers, and the declining market prices for their crops.[55] Kofi Annan, the former UN secretary general concludes that, "the world trading system is not fair."[56]

Corn

Farmers growing corn for ethanol production[57] have recently benefited from higher prices for corn, but these higher profits are unsustainable. Growing *corn takes more fertilizer than other crops.*[58] Fertilizer is made from natural gas, and the price of this fossil fuel is rising due to demand, which will raise the price of growing corn (and all products made using corn). In addition, *growing corn takes a lot of water,* but the aquifers beneath the midwestern states being used to grow corn are being depleted. There will soon be less water and it will cost more, which will also push up the price of corn (and everything using it).

Using *more corn for ethanol is increasing prices* for other goods, making it harder for people with low incomes to buy food. "A startling change is unfolding in the world's food markets. Soaring fuel prices have altered the equation for growing food and transporting it across the globe. Huge demand for biofuels has created tension between using land to produce fuel and using it for food."[59] It seems clear that "shortsighted policies in the United States and other wealthy countries" are largely to blame.[60]

Having water to drink and to use in growing crops to eat cannot be left to supply and demand, nor can access to food, as *markets do not protect human rights.*[61] "A long-held basic human right, the right to adequate food for the world's 854 million hungry people, is being threatened once again—this time by the conversion of wheat, sugar, palm oil and maize into agricultural fuel."[62] The price of palm oil, for instance, which is widely used for cooking in many countries, has jumped nearly 70 percent between 2007 and 2008. "Cooking oil may seem a trifling expense in the West. But in the developing world, cooking oil is an important source of calories and represents one of the biggest cash outlays for poor families, which grow much of their own food but have to buy oil in which to cook it." [63]

Rising corn prices will increase the price of most processed foods, which contain corn syrup. Consider these typical items sold at McDonald's: soda (100 percent corn), milk shake (78 percent corn), salad dressing (65 percent corn), chicken nuggets (56 percent corn), cheeseburger (52 percent corn), and french fries (23 percent corn). In addition to paying higher prices for food, consumers will continue to pay for the health costs that result from eating these high calorie foods—"obesity, type II diabetes, heart disease."[64]

For the global poor, "America's corn-fed food chain" is already a disaster, as the fast-food economy is using up much more than our fair share of the energy being captured by plants and stored as carbohydrates.[65] About half of the grain grown today is fed to livestock,[66] and much of this grain is corn. "To eat corn directly (as Mexicans and Africans do) is to consume all the energy in that corn, but when you feed that corn to a steer or a chicken, 90 percent of its energy is lost—to bones or feathers or fur, to living and metabolizing as a steer or chicken."[67]

Processing food also requires energy and this adds to the inefficiency of food production. So, eating processed food, which has a higher profit margin for the producer than unprocessed food, also makes it harder for billions of poor people to obtain the food they need to survive.

Those who defend industrial agriculture and trade liberalization policies argue that traditional forms of agriculture cannot feed the world's growing population. Yet, as industrial agriculture is unsustainable, its defenders bear the burden of demonstrating it is necessary.[68] Sustainable agriculture is now feeding poor farmers in India and elsewhere, and may be able to feed the world—if population growth levels off and more of us eat lower on the food chain.

POOR FARMERS

The law must ensure that the poor have access to financial capital at fair interest rates, and are able to exercise their civil right to participate in local economic decisions.[69] This enables them to use land and water for sustainable agriculture that produces more food than export crops.

Population Control

Economic and educational initiatives empowering poor women offer the best hope of controlling population growth and ensuring sustainable farming in developing communities.[70] "The declining birthrates in nations where poverty and illiteracy are still widespread defy almost all conventional wisdom. Women are taking charge of their lives—not waiting for the slow processes of education and cultural change."[71] Moreover, these "rural women produce between 60 and 80 percent of the food in most developing countries."[72]

Gita Sen argues that those promoting population control in poor countries have made a mistake in identifying women as "targets" of family planning—"the necessary locus of contraceptive technology, and reproductive manipulation," or as "potential decision-makers"—whose capabilities may be improved through education.[73] For women generally perceive these measures as violating their human rights.

"Population and family-planning programs," therefore, "should be framed in the context of health and livelihood agendas, should give serious consideration to women's health advocates, and be supportive of women's reproductive health and rights."[74] A poor, undernourished woman is more likely to limit the number of her children when she is able to improve her health and provide sufficient food for her family.

Empowering Women

A model for this approach is found in Andhra Pradesh, a state in southern India, on the semiarid Deccan Plateau. Government policies favoring rice and wheat production "led to the near collapse of coarse grain production in the region, such as sorghum and pearl millet. The increasing costs of modern agricultural inputs also made it difficult for small and marginal farmers to continue production. The government has also encouraged the production of sugar cane [for export] by providing loans to dig bore wells and setting up a sugar factory to process the cane. This has resulted in wealthy farmers over-utilizing groundwater at the cost of poor farmers, whose shallow wells go dry."[75]

In 1983 a few professional men set up the Deccan Development Society (DDS) to help poor communities. Initially, the DDS worked with men, but it soon discovered that men's groups are easily split by political affiliations and conflicts over leadership. So, the DDS turned to poor women, who "suffer from the triple burden of caste, class, and gender."[76] With the help of the DDS, women's *sanghams* (voluntary associations) have pooled savings to create revolving loan funds, which lend money to women at 12 percent interest annually (rather than at 60 percent or more that is charged by local money lenders).

The problems that these women face are staggering: "A major impact of the poor conditions of agriculture lands and small family holdings is that they are left fallow. Big landlords also cultivate only part of their holdings to grow sugar cane and other irrigated crops while leaving the rest fallow. This leads to (1) lack of employment; (2) lack of basic food since farm laborers are paid in kind when they harvest crops; (3) high rates of soil erosion; and eventually (4) forced migration of landless, small, and marginal farmers."[77]

"The vulnerability of the poor leads to inhuman practices such as annual bondage of young boys (for a very small wage), which prevents them from going to school. Young women belonging to poor families are considered fair game for sexual harassment, so girls are married at the age of 10–12 years old because the families experience them as burdens."[78] Strategies used by women's groups to solve these problems include working together to improve the quality of land owned by group members, pooling their resources to lease land, and creating seed banks.

Today the women's groups of the DDS are active in seventy-five villages and include over five thousand members. Since 1985 these women's groups have brought into cultivation ten thousand acres of degraded land. "Consequently, they have been raising over three million kilos of grain every year, which is six times more than the half a million kilos of grains they used to produce earlier."[79]

The women do not use artificial fertilizers.[80] "To ensure long-term sustainability, they are working to establish regional federations and cooperatives which will produce and market traditional organic food."[81] In eight special *Dalit* (Untouchable) watersheds, women have enabled "local communities to design and shape small areas of land as watersheds and enshrine strong principles of food production through biodiversity based farming systems. . . . [T]hey have breathed life into all kinds of lands around them: the most degraded forest lands, degraded common lands, and their own cultivable fallows."[82]

These Indian women's groups have demonstrated that even "very poor farmers, once in control of their agriculture and natural resources, with a bit of help and access to financial resources, can feed themselves and the non-food producing members of their community."[83]

The ability of poor women to limit as well as feed their families is also verified by the Grameen Bank, a microcredit initiative for poor women in Bangladesh that has five and a half million members. One of the Sixteen Decisions[84] that participants in the Grameen Bank must memorize and affirm is to keep their families small, and studies have shown that these women are 50 percent more likely than other Bangladeshi women to do so.[85] Two of the other Sixteen Decisions are: "We shall grow vegetables all the year round," and "During the plantation seasons, we shall plant as many seedlings as possible."[86]

The UN Food and Agriculture Organization confirmed in 2002 that poverty, not food scarcity, is the cause of hunger.[87] In 2008, a rapid rise in commodity prices worldwide is evidence that too much grain is being used for cattle feed and ethanol production, rather than for food.[88] Raising the input costs of agriculture, by using more artificial fertilizers and pesticides or expensive seeds, exacerbates this problem.

SUSTAINABLE FARMING

Plants transform solar energy and nutrients into edible leaves, roots, and seeds. Many plants are needed to feed a smaller number of herbivores, and even fewer carnivores are able to live off these herbivores. "In the typical food chain, the energy available declines by a factor of ten at each tropic (feeding) level, although the ratio can vary. Thus the efficiency of agriculture in feeding people depends a great deal on where food is taken from the chain."[89] At each level, energy is lost as heat and waste.

Also, efficiency in farming depends on energy inputs. Traditional agriculture uses solar power, farm labor, and farm animals to plow and fertilize the land. Pests are managed by planting a variety of species in smaller plots and rotating crops, and these practices also replenish the soil as nutrients are removed. Livestock graze on the grasses that grow because of solar energy, and grazing maintains the health of the grasses as well as the fertility of the soil.[90]

Agroecology

Sustainable agriculture, or "farming with nature," is "an agroecology that promotes biodiversity, recycles plant nutrients, protects soil from erosion, conserves and protects water, uses minimum tillage, and integrates crop and livestock enterprises on the farm."[91] There are *three objectives:* economic profit, social benefits to the farm family and the farming community, and environmental conservation.[92]

"Farms become and stay environmentally sustainable by imitating natural systems—creating a farm landscape that mimics as closely as possible the complexity of healthy ecosystems. Nature tends to function in cycles, so that waste from one process or system becomes input for another. Industrial agriculture, in contrast, tends to function in a linear fashion similar to a factory: inputs go in one end, and products and waste come out the other. The wastes of industrial agriculture (nonpoint source pollution) include suspended soil, nitrates, and phosphates in stream water, and nitrates and pesticides in ground water."[93]

Some call this "philosophy of mimicking natural processes"[94] *organic* farming. In 1991 the European Commission (EC) set the first official standards, and the International Federation of Organic Agricultural Movements (IFOAM) was founded a year later. In 2002 the US Department of Agriculture established production standards to regulate the commercial use of the label "organic."[95] Some critics argue that in the United States "organic farming has increasingly come to resemble the industrial system it originally set out to replace."[96] To create an international standard, in 2005 IFOAM published "The Principles of Organic Farming."[97]

Sustainable practices in agriculture are more important than achieving a consensus on what "organic" means. Industrial farming takes a huge risk by producing a single crop (a monoculture), such as wheat, corn, or soybeans, because then the farmer is vulnerable to natural disasters and changes in market prices.

To reduce risk, sustainable farming involves growing a diversity of crops and integrating plant and animal agriculture. The model for sustainable farming is an ecosystem, not a factory.

Sustainable agriculture works with *four natural processes*: energy capture, water cycles, mineral cycles, and ecosystem dynamics. *Energy capture* involves maximizing "the leaf area available for photosynthesis, and efficiently cycling the stored solar energy through the food chain. Off-season cover crops, perennial vegetation, and intercropping are among the tools for capturing more solar energy."[98]

The *water cycle* may be improved by adding ground cover and organic matter to the soil. "A surface mulch layer speeds water intake while reducing evaporation and protecting the soil from erosion. Minimizing or eliminating tillage, growing high-residue crops and cover crops, and adding compost or manure to the soil maintains groundcover and builds organic matter."[99]

The *mineral cycle* involves transferring nutrients from the soil to the crops and animals and then returning these nutrients to the soil. "Conditions and practices that inhibit the natural mineral cycle—erosion, nutrient leaching, organic matter depletion, selling hay or grain off the farm—tend to reduce the farm's sustainability. Practices that enhance the mineral cycle include on-farm feeding of livestock,

careful management of manure and crop residues, use of catch crops to reduce nutrient leaching losses, and practices that prevent erosion."[100]

For sustainable farming *fertilizers* containing anhydrous ammonia and potassium chloride should not be used, as these chemicals harm the soil and organisms in it that are beneficial for crops. Monoammonium phosphate (12-50-0), usually called MAP, offers a more environmentally friendly way to make the transition from industrial agriculture to sustainable agriculture.

Agroecology *relies on* a mixture of organisms with genetic diversity within species to create greater stability and control *pests*. "The first step toward increasing biodiversity on the farm is crop rotation, which helps break weed and pest life cycles and provides complementary fertilization among the crops in the planting sequence. Advancing from rotation to strip intercrops brings a higher level of biodiversity and increases sunlight capture."[101]

"Strip intercropping of corn and soybeans or cotton and alfalfa are two examples. Borders, windbreaks, and special plantings for natural enemies of pests provide habitat for beneficial organisms, further increasing biodiversity and stability. The addition of appropriate perennial crops, shrubs, and trees to the farmscape enhances ecosystem dynamics still further."[102]

Integrated pest management requires *knowing a pest's life cycle and its natural enemies*, so growers can deploy other organisms to control pests. IPM strategies include using insects, mites, bacteria, fungi, viruses, and nematodes.[103] "When IPM tactics are unable to maintain insect pest populations below economic thresholds, insecticide application to control the pests and prevent economic loss is clearly justified. In such cases, farmers concerned with sustainability will usually attempt to obtain satisfactory control using one of the 'biorational' pesticides, which are fairly pest-specific and usually non-persistent, causing a minimal amount of harm to beneficial organisms."[104]

Weed control involves crop rotation, which makes it harder for the seeds of weeds to set or to migrate from outside the field, and planting crops that outgrow weeds. "In northern states, oats are commonly planted as a 'nurse crop' for alfalfa, clover, and legume-grass mixtures—the oats simply take the place of weeds that would otherwise grow between the young alfalfa plants."[105] Using mulch and grazers, such as sheep or goats, also helps to keep weeds down.

Food for Everyone?

The higher yields of the Green Revolution are unsustainable, because of increased input costs for seed, fertilizer, and pesticides, and because of the loss of topsoil, the degradation of the environment due to nutrient and pesticide runoff, and crop losses due to resistant pests.[106] In 2007 and 2008 the price of oil shot up due to demand, speculation in commodity markets by investors,[107] and limited refining capacity. Before the middle of the century oil and natural gas production will peak and begin to decline. Thus, food and everything else that depends on the price of fossil fuels is bound to become more costly. Rising ozone levels in the lower atmosphere are likely to reduce plant productivity, the depletion of aquifers will reduce the water available for irrigation, and climate change will require more drought-resistant plants.[108]

It is impossible to use cost-benefit analysis to weigh the consequences of continuing industrial agriculture versus making a transition to sustainable agriculture. There are, however, estimates of some of the *annual global costs of industrial agriculture*:

- Subsidies for agriculture—$362 billion
- Subsidies for water—$247 billion
- Losses due to soil erosion—150 billion
- Losses due to desertification—$42 billion[109]

There are also estimates of some of the *annual costs of industrial agriculture in the United States*:

- Subsidies for agriculture—$75 billion (or more)[110]
- Higher food prices—$25 billion
- Subsidized grazing fees for use of federal land—$50 million
- Subsidizes to farmers using Bureau of Reclamation water—$2.5 billion
- Irrigation subsidies in the western United States—$4.4 billion[111]

Clearly, the "so-called efficiency of industrial animal production is an illusion, made possible by cheap grain, cheap water and prisonlike confinement systems. In short, animal husbandry has been turned into animal abuse. Manure—traditionally a source of fertilizer—has been turned into toxic waste that fouls the air and adjacent water bodies. Crowding creates health problems, resulting in the chronic overuse of antibiotics. And, because the modest profits in confinement operations require the lowest possible labor costs, including automated feeding, watering and manure-handling systems, these operations have helped empty and impoverish rural America."[112]

Drugs derived from plants now provide health benefits worldwide worth $400 billion, and the total value of goods and services from biodiversity is about

$3 trillion.[113] Thus, only a 10 percent loss in biodiversity could mean a loss in value of $300 billion. Forests are being cut to clear land for cattle grazing. Yet, tropical deforestation leads to less soil cover and all its benefits, which in India alone is worth around $10 billion per year. Moreover, tropical forests absorb carbon dioxide, and the loss of this benefit "could cost as much as $3.7 trillion."[114]

Pollination services are provided by insects, and this ecological process is worth about $117 billion annually. Pesticides are decimating the population of pollinating insects, and losing these species would raise agricultural costs about $54 billion annually. In the United States we are aware of the recent collapse of honeybee populations, but this is a global problem as well.[115]

The likely consequences of maintaining the industrial food production system do not prove that sustainable farming is more cost effective, but confirm that it is reasonable to put the burden of proof on those who argue that factory farming is required to feed the world. Also, there is evidence that sustainable farming is cost effective. For instance, after pesticides used in Indonesia killed the natural enemies of the brown planthopper, rice losses rose to $1.5 billion annually. When the government slashed subsidies for pesticides and banned fifty-seven of sixty-six pesticides, use of the remaining pesticides fell by 60 percent and rice yields rose by 15 percent, for a savings during 1986–1990 of $1 billion.[116]

Genetically modified (GM) food may offer some benefits in productivity or resistance to a disease or pest,[117] but will not solve the problem of increasing costs for herbicides, pesticides, water for irrigation, and the transport of food, and also pose a threat of contaminating other species.[118] GM food will also raise the price of seeds, as corporations seek to maximize the profit from their research and patents. Moreover, these technological innovations do not address the inequitable distribution of food.

Finally, GM food may replace traditional foods that are naturally more healthy and efficient to grow. For instance, "the heavily advertised vitamin A–rich golden rice increases water abuse in agriculture. Golden rice contains 30 micrograms of vitamin A per 100 grams of rice. On the other hand, greens such as amaranth and coriander contain 500 times more vitamin A, while using a fraction of the water needed by golden rice. In terms of water use, genetically engineered rice is 1,500 times less efficient in providing children with vitamin A, a necessary vitamin for blindness prevention."[119]

Farming and Food: An Answer

First, there must be *a transition to agroecological farming.* This requires government policies that phase out commodity subsidies and offer incentives for independent farmers using the methods of sustainable agriculture.[120] There is little political support now for this change in the United States, but pressure will grow as the costs of fossil fuels increase and more people realize that industrial agriculture is economically as well as environmentally unsustainable.

Second, *governments and citizens must support urban farms and markets.* To reduce the fossil fuel costs of transportation, more of our food has to be grown closer to where we live.[121] This change will require political leadership as well as consumer support.[122] We need to revitalize farmers' markets, grow food on city lots and building roofs, and in urban areas treat and return to the soil the nutrients in organic garbage and waste that are now being wasted.[123]

Third, *those who are affluent must eat lower on the food chain.* The average American obtains about 30 percent of his calories from animal sources.[124] If everyone in the world ate this way, there would only be enough food for about half the world's people. "If everyone ate like the average Latin American and consumed a mere 10 percent of their calories from animal sources, only 4 billion people could be fed."[125] To feed the world's nearly 7 billion inhabitants, most people will have to obtain the bulk of their protein from sources other than meat, and those of us now eating a lot of meat will need to reduce our consumption substantially.

QUESTIONS—AGRICULTURE: LAND AND FOOD

1. Argue for and against the efficiency of using artificial fertilizer. How is the cost of fossil fuels relevant for this discussion?

2. Assess the pros and cons with respect to the consequences of using artificial pesticides.

3. Explain IPM and make an ethical argument for it. Why isn't it used more?

4. Describe the role of corporations today in raising livestock and marketing grain. Explain why our present food production system is not a "market economy."

5. How does the federal system of subsidies for commodity crops affect agriculture?

6. How do international institutions affect trade in agricultural products and local farmers in countries like Mexico and Tanzania?

7. Make an ethical argument against using corn to feed livestock. Why is it more efficient for us to eat corn directly rather than eating a hamburger or drinking a soda?

8. Why has a family-planning approach to controlling population been less effective than promoting women's rights and microcredit opportunities for poor women?

9. What are some of the strategies that women's groups in India use to improve their lives and ensure sustainable development?

10. What do the poor in developing countries need in order to feed themselves? Explain your answer.

11. Sustainable agriculture works with four natural processes. Describe two of these.

12. What techniques are used in sustainable agriculture to replenish nutrients in the soil, control weeds, and deal with pests?

13. Why are the higher yields of the Green Revolution unsustainable?

14. Why do women's groups in India resist GM foods?

15. Make an argument for the ethical presumption that those who are affluent should eat lower on the food chain. Then raise a critical question about this argument.

13

Public Land

ADAPTIVE MANAGEMENT

"As recently as 1950 Earth's old-growth woodland occupied 50 million square kilometers, or nearly 40 percent of the ice-free surface of the land. Today its cover is only 34 million square kilometers and is shrinking fast. Half of that surviving has already been degraded, much of it severely. The loss of forest during the past half-century is one of the most profound and rapid environmental changes in the history of the planet."[1]

Forests all over the world have been logged for lumber to support economic development and to clear land for agriculture and cattle grazing. In the United States the debate about logging forests on public land has been cast into a conflict between *conservation* and *preservation*, although the commonsense meaning of these two words is much the same. The reason is history.

At the beginning of the twentieth century US Forest Service policy required *conservation* of forests in order to provide *the best use of natural resources for the public good.* Head of the US Forest Service, Gifford Pinchot, relied on this argument to support the Hetch Hetchy dam, which now provides water for San Francisco. He was opposed by John Muir, founder of the Sierra Club, who argued for *wilderness preservation.* Near the end of the twentieth century defenders of these conflicting views have fought over the policy of *adaptive management.*

We will consider some of these arguments involving forests and parks, and also the restoration of deserts and wetlands. In addition, we will look briefly at the use of public lands in Asia and Africa, where reserves to protect wildlife have been established.

CONSERVATIONISTS VERSUS PRESERVATIONISTS

Pinchot believed that the object of US forest policy "is not to preserve the forests because they are beautiful . . . or because they are refuges for the wild creatures of the wilderness."[2] His view was utilitarian: "Forestry is the art of producing from the forest whatever it can yield for the service of man."[3] For Pinchot, the goal of conservation was "a planned and orderly scheme for national efficiency, based on the elimination of waste, and directed toward the best use of all we have for the greatest good of the greatest number for the longest time."[4]

Preservationists have offered two counter arguments. First, a *character* argument identifying forests as places of beauty and peace that inspire us to be better persons. Second, a *duty* argument asserting we should preserve wilderness, because it has intrinsic worth for itself. Thus, the struggle between conservationists and preservationists is a dispute that pits a utilitarian point of view against two ways of affirming the intrinsic value of nature.

Sustainable Yield

Early in the twentieth century, the conservationist position was supported by political groups that were resisting the inequities of wealth and land ownership in American society. "Pinchot's conservation was part of a more general progressive movement fighting the laissez-faire, monopolistic social Darwinism characteristic of much of nineteenth-century American economic life. Along with President Roosevelt and other progressives, Pinchot held that natural resources should benefit all citizens, not just the wealthy few who privately owned vast amounts of property. Government policy should serve this goal by preventing waste, limiting monopolistic control, providing economic opportunity for the many, and keeping prices low."[5]

In the 1930s the US forestry policy concerned "sustainable yield," and because of the high demand for lumber for construction after World War II the emphasis was on yield. The Sustained-yield Forest Management Act of 1944 made "community stability" an official goal of the US Forest Service, and in practice this meant that forests were to be regulated in order to "provide a steady flow of wood in a sustained and predictable fashion."[6]

At the same time highway construction and a greater use of the automobile brought more people into the forests for recreation. The Multiple Use-Sustained Yield Act of 1960 reflects the growing importance of recreational use of the forests and also reaffirms the emphasis on producing lumber.[7]

Those supporting preservation were generally unable to prevent the use of the forests for logging and recreation, but in 1964 they secured passage of the

Wilderness Act that protects some forest areas from roads. In the 1980s, however, forestry began to respond to the new environmental movement in the United States by embracing the idea of environmental sustainability.

Adaptive Management

In 1993 President Clinton ordered the use of ecosystem management (EM) for public land.[8] "Regulatory negotiation, which actively involves a broad range of stakeholders in the specification and implementation of regulations, has become more widely used for federal pollution control programs. The EPA has developed the Common Sense Initiative (CSI) in league with corporate America, state regulators, national environmentalists, and locally based environmental justice groups. The goal is to encourage innovation by providing flexibility in the use of a place-by-place approach to achieving pollution control standards."[9]

The Clinton administration promoted land-use *adaptive management* that is:

- *Ecologically sustainable*—"directing public lands toward a desired future condition which embodies the complexity of ecosystem interrelationships . . . ,"
- *Economically feasible*—"meeting societal demands for the myriad products of forests and public lands *at a cost that does not exceed the priced and unpriced benefits gained,*"
- *Socially* acceptable—"reflecting a sensitivity toward recreational, aesthetic, spiritual, and other noncommodity values of public lands."[10]

This shift emphasizes *a local process.* "It depends upon local constraints, the present state of local institutions, and the personalities of key people. Any attempt to manage adaptively should transfer knowledge and understanding to local individuals, but it must do more than that. It must also develop institutional flexibility by encouraging the formation of networks of individuals that bridge institutional boundaries. These groups of individuals can act as agents of reform within their institutions, and [as] the nucleus around which new institutions can form."[11]

Forestry policy is crucial worldwide, as "governments own almost 80 percent of the remaining intact forests in developing countries."[12] Too often, timber concessions "have been granted at below market rates and without safeguards of requirements for good management. Government subsidization of projects like road building has further fueled both timber booms and large-scale settlement. Another favorite policy of forest-rich countries is to promote agricultural development and ranching in previously forested areas, often with government subsidies so deep that the enterprises would be totally uneconomical without them."[13]

At times, international intervention has made things worse. "Critics of globalization charge that economic globalization and the World Trade Organization are magnifying the trend toward expanded logging by encouraging high levels of foreign investment, weaker domestic regulation in the face of international competition, and loss of local community controls."[14]

Yet, logging can be both sustainable and profitable. The Menominee tribe in Wisconsin has logged its reservation for over a century, cutting "only the weaker trees, leaving the strong mother trees and enough of the upper canopy for squirrels and other arboreal animals to continuously inhabit."[15] The logging has provided a steady income, and the 1.3 billion standing board feet of timber in 1870 has grown to 1.7 billion standing board feet.

Forests have to be managed now, because the adverse impact of humans on forests is unavoidable.[16] The Forestry Stewardship Council (FSC), an international NGO, certifies "that a forest is responsibly managed. The certification process requires third-party auditing to ensure international standards are met for the rights of indigenous groups and workers, biodiversity conservation, the protection of ecologically important areas, and a range of other environmental, social, and economic criteria."[17]

FSC does not certify clear cutting, but examples on its website confirm that sustainable logging is profitable.[18] Rainforest Alliance, an NGO active in forest preservation, affirms: "FSC certification has helped strengthen business structures, fire prevention measures, and low-impact harvesting practices."[19]

NATIONAL FORESTS AND PARKS

Bruce Babbitt, US secretary of the Interior from 1993 to 2001, played a crucial role in *applying adaptive management to public land use.* He took office soon after a federal judge in Seattle ruled that enforcing the Endangered Species Act, in order to protect the northern spotted owl, would require a halt to logging in the national forests of the Pacific Northwest. After a public meeting in Portland, Oregon, which President Clinton attended, Babbitt was charged with forging a plan that would protect the owl and its habitat and also allow sufficient logging to be economically feasible and socially acceptable.

Babbitt enlisted more than two hundred geologists, hydrologists, biologists, zoologists, and land planners to figure out what area to protect as the owl's habitat. In 1995 the US Fish and Wildlife Service (FWS) exercised its authority under a 1982 amendment to the Endangered Species Act of 1973, which allowed it to accept a "habitat conservation plan," and negotiated an agreement with Weyerhaeuser, one of the world's largest pulp and paper companies, to maintain "areas of forest large enough to sustain groups of spotted owls and close enough to one another to allow movement of the owls among the forested areas."[20]

Babbitt was unsuccessful, however, in persuading Congress to support a bill that would require the process of conducting a "biological survey" in conjunction with enforcing the Endangered Species Act. Opponents, fearing that more endangered species would be identified, argued that the federal government should stay out of land-use planning. Clearly, however, the federal government has an enormous impact on land use. The Army Corps of Engineers and the Bureau of Reclamation have opened lands for development by building flood-control projects and damming rivers. Moreover, the interstate highway program funded by the federal government has directly affected the growth of cities and suburbs.

Babbitt argues that: "Throughout our history land use planning has been a one-way street down which we relentlessly race toward government-subsidized exploitation of every resource. The question we now face is whether and how to create a parallel process that includes a broader consideration of the public interest in our land and resources."[21] Adaptive management is an effort to combine the science of ecology with the realization of intrinsic values. Foresters, who have long seen their work as an applied science, now need to explain their reasoning to communities of interest (industry, local people, environmentalists, and recreation users).

Adaptive Management Areas

Adaptive management areas (AMAs) were created in the Northwest to resolve conflicts concerning logging and the northern spotted owl. "The underlying premise of adaptive management is that knowledge of the ecological system is not only incomplete, but also elusive. Thus, the experience of management itself is a source of learning. Adaptive management includes not only the use of scientific or expert knowledge in decision-making, but also the knowledge and values of stakeholders in an area."[22]

A 1995 statement for the Cispus AMA in Washington State explains that adaptive management is "a continuing process of action-based planning, monitoring, researching, evaluating, and adjusting; with the objective of improving implementation and achieving the goals that have been identified. In forest management, our limited understanding of ecosystem behavior leads to uncertainty about the effects of management activities."[23] Adaptive management is "a strategy for dealing with uncertainty by explicitly designing management activities as experiments and opportunities for learning."[24]

By 1997 a long-range plan for the Cispus AMA was adopted by a committee including staff from the US Fish and Wildlife Service, the EPA, the National Marine Fisheries Service, industry leaders, elected officials, and citizens. "What we had here was true citizen partnerships with government. A variety of perspectives came to the table and we all generally walked away agreeing with a common vision for the future," said David Jennings of the Black Hills Audubon Society. "The path we have set with this decision focuses on protecting the remnants of our native forests while at the same time learning how to sustain logging on public lands."[25]

The Bush Administration

In 2002 the administration of President George W. Bush began to revise the ethical presumptions of forest management by proposing rule changes, which the Wilderness Society argues "erode fundamental safeguards for our forests."[26] In 2005 the Bush administration dropped several regulations from the forest planning rules, including the requirements to sustain viable populations of plants and animals across their natural range,[27] and to prepare an environmental impact statement (EIS) when a forest plan is significantly amended or revised.[28]

In December 2006 the Forest Service released a statement saying that the rules proposed in 2005 would go into effect.[29] Critics, who claimed this change would allow the Forest Service to ignore the planning requirements of the National Environmental Policy Act (NEPA),[30] found support for their position in March 2007 when a federal judge prohibited the use of the 2005 planning rules on the grounds that these changes were not in compliance with the National Environmental Policy Act.[31]

The Bush administration also promoted the Healthy Forests Initiative (HFI), which was created by the Healthy Forest Restoration Act of 2003 "to reduce the risks severe wildfires pose to people, communities, and the environment."[32] The HFI categorically excludes some decisions from the review provisions of the NEPA, and also creates an exception to the Endangered Species Act, which requires federal agencies to consult with the Fish and Wildlife Service and the National Marine Fisheries Service to ensure that an action "will not jeopardize the continued existence of listed species, or adversely modify their designated critical habitat."[33]

The HFI is administered by the US Forest Service and also by the US Bureau of Land Management (BLM), which exercises authority over 30 percent of federal public land. The BLM has added provisions for administering the HFI that make wildfire management decisions effective immediately, if the BLM "determines that vegetation, soil, or other resources on public lands are at substantial risk of wildfire due to drought, fuels buildup, or other reasons, or when public lands are at immediate risk of erosion or other damage due to wildfire."[34]

Critics of the HFI warn that "the law will lead to more cutting of mature and old-growth forests, further damage to wildlife habitat, greater risk of destructive fires, and little additional assistance to communities."[35] The Sierra Club says that HFI is "is based on the false assumption that landscape-wide logging will decrease forest fires."[36] President George W. Bush argued: "[I]n order to have a healthy economy, we've got to have a healthy forest policy. . . . After all, the fires that have devastated the West create a drag on the economy. It costs money to fight these fires. It means people lose property."[37]

He also claimed that thinning is needed to reduce the danger of fire and to prevent lawsuits against the government. "We need to thin, we need to make our forests healthy by using some common sense," he says. "[P]lus, there's just too many lawsuits, just endless litigation . . . there's a fine line between people expressing themselves and their opinions and using litigation to keep the United States of America from enacting common sense forest policy."[38]

Zander Evans, research director of the Forest Guild, an association of more than six hundred professional foresters, disagrees with the president and supports adaptive management: "Based on available data, early and substantial public participation is a much more effective tool for facilitating fuel reduction projects than are administrative attempts to curtail litigation."[39]

Resistance by the Bush administration to the adaptive management approach extends beyond forestry regulations to environmental rules concerning coal mining and wetlands. In September 2007, however, a survey "conducted by the Civil Society Institute found that 65 percent of Americans oppose the Bush Administration's proposal 'to ease environmental regulations to permit wider use of *mountain top removal* [MTR] coal mining in the US.' The study also found that 74 percent of Americans are opposed to the expansion of MTR coal mining in general, and that 90 percent of Americans agree that more mining should be permitted only after the United States government has assessed its impacts on safety and the environment."[40]

In 2008 the Bureau of Land Management wrote new rules for wilderness areas to allow off-road vehicles use of about fifteen thousand miles of designated trails. "The Southern Utah Wilderness Alliance, an environmental group, points out that many of these routes have been lifted straight from maps provided by the off-road vehicle associations and have not been independently surveyed to assess their potential damage to the soil, animal habitat, and archaeological sites."[41]

By the end of 2008, however, Congress plans to put about two million acres of land under federal control as protected wilderness. "A confluence of factors is driving this wilderness renaissance: the shift in Congress from Republican to Democratic control; environmentalists' decision to take a more pragmatic approach in which they enlist local support for their proposals by making concessions to opposing interests; and some communities' recognition that intact ecosystems can often offer a greater economic payoff than extractive industries."[42]

RESTORING DESERTS AND WETLANDS

Many criticize the idea of restoring environments,[43] but Andrew Light believes "that philosophers can make constructive contributions to ecological restoration and to environmental issues in general by helping to articulate the normative foundations for environmental policies in ways . . . that resonate with the moral intuitions most people carry around with them every day."[44]

Perhaps the "relationship between humans and nature imbues restoration with a positive value" even though fully restoring a natural environment is generally impossible: "When we engage in acts of benevolent restoration, we are bound by nature in the sense that we are obligated to respect what it once was attempting to realize before we interfered with it. In addition to the substantial personal and social benefits that accrue to people who engage in benevolent forms of restoration, we can also say that restoration restores the human connection to nature by restoring the part of culture that has historically contained a connection to nature."[45]

Deserts

Under Babbitt, the Department of the Interior wielded federal authority to try to restore and protect desert and wetland environments. In 1993 the US Fish and Wildlife Service recommended that the California gnatcatcher be listed as an endangered species, because its population had shrunk to less than three thousand birds. Listing the gnatcatcher, however, put a land-use moratorium over hundreds of thousands of acres of land between San Diego and Los Angeles.

The political conflict seemed intractable, but federal action under the Endangered Species Act helped the governor enforce the Natural Communities Conservation Program, a 1992 California law giving local communities new powers to draft comprehensive plans in order to preserve open space. It was also helpful that in Orange County a single landowner held title to a hundred thousand acres of coastal plain, and he preferred to negotiate rather than go to court.

In San Diego County, however, there was no single large landowner to work with. The preserves had "to be stitched together from thousands of landholdings through careful use of zoning incentives to protect sufficient area while freeing less critical land for development. On smaller tracts and as a condition of developing them, landowners could opt to purchase other land designated for protection as mitigation. And in some areas outright purchases by the county" were necessary.[46]

After the San Diego Zoo campaigned for community support, both Republican and Democratic members of Congress began to secure federal grants to help pay for the planning process. By 1998 thirty thousand acres in Orange County had been set aside as two permanent reserves, to provide a habitat for the gnatcatcher and thirty-two other species under threat, and both the city of San Diego and San Diego County had approved significant habitat preserves.

"The plans took in nearly two hundred thousand acres of crucial sage habitats, stream corridors, and vernal pools throughout the county, protecting essential habitat for more than one hundred species, including the least Bell's vireo, the ship-tailed lizard, a number of invertebrates, a long list of plants endemic to the region, and of course the gnatcatcher. These plans demonstrated that the Endangered Species Act could be made to work even on complex, partially developed landscapes with highly fragmented ownership."[47] A habitat was not only protected, but "restored" at least in part, by changing land-use patterns over a large portion of the southern California coastal plain.

The Endangered Species Act was also helpful in preserving the habitat of the desert tortoise. This required restricting development around Las Vegas on "the sandy, gently sloping alluvial fans extending outward from the mountains."[48] Business leaders, politicians, and environmentalists collaborated to end grazing on public land and to purchase sufficient private land to create a preserve. (In this case "restoration" meant buying grazing rights so the desert terrain could recover.) The costs for implementing this plan were assessed to the developers in Las Vegas, who agreed to pay a $565 fee for each new subdivision lot they developed.[49]

The Endangered Species Act has been crucial in the southern and western parts of the country, where many species are endangered, whereas few such species exist in the northeast. Babbitt has urged that the act be amended "to include not just endangered species, but to promote the protection of open space and important watersheds, forests, and other threatened ecosystems—before the downward spiral to extinction begins."[50] This would mean applying the *precautionary principle* by shifting the ethical presumption of protection from an endangered species to an endangered ecosystem.

Wetlands

In the 1940s the state of Florida petitioned Congress to help control flooding, and after legislation was passed in 1948 the Army Corps of Engineers in collaboration with the South Florida Water Management District constructed an elaborate system that divided the Everglades ecosystem into three parts: "a third to be drained for the sugar plantations, a third to store water for the cities, and a third for nature."[51]

The Everglades is not only a swamp but a river, miles wide and inches deep, that flows slowly on land with a slope of about two inches per mile.[52] Under the 1948 plan the canals below Lake Okeechobee, which lead southward and eastward to the Atlantic, were enlarged and pumping plants were installed to irrigate the sugar cane fields directly from Lake Okeechobee in times of drought. These changes expanded agricultural land to more than a million acres.

South of this area the plan reserved a million acres for water storage to refill underground aquifers, and the corps built earthen dikes to store water on the surface at a depth of five to six feet. This system was also designed to capture irrigation water draining from the sugar plantations, and all this water was designated for the growing cities on the Atlantic coast. The national park in the southern part of the watershed was to receive the rest of the water. The Florida legislature created the South Florida Water Management Agency to oversee this water system, and its costs were to be split between the federal and state governments.

As development spread in the area south of Lake Okeechobee, more land was drained and the flow of water to the park in the south declined. By the 1990s it became clear that the park could not survive unless the entire ecosystem from Lake Okeechobee to the park was at least partially restored, so water could flow through the region as it once had.

"To restore adequate flows meant taking water back from existing agricultural uses, filling in drainage canals, and allowing some farms to revert to swampland. And it would be necessary to halt further encroachment by purchasing or condemning thousands of undeveloped subdivision lots within the natural floodways that bring water into the park."[53]

Babbitt learned that the Army Corps of Engineers was open to restoring the Everglades watershed and that Florida officials would support a feasibility study. However, the problems could not be resolved without restricting both housing development and the use of water by the sugar plantations. A federal lawsuit filed against the plantation owners in 1989 for phosphorus pollution in the watershed gave the Department of the Interior leverage.

"The obvious solution was to regulate sugar growers and other farms to meet the ten parts per billion discharge standard recommended by scientists as necessary for protection of these waters. Under the complex provisions of the federal Clean Water Act, the state had to be a part to the agreement; that would require legislation, and to get action from the Florida legislature we had to demonstrate that requiring compliance would be economically feasible."[54]

The solution involved reducing by more than half the quantity of fertilizer being used by the sugar growers, as studies revealed this lower level would produce the same yield. In addition, scientists calculated that dedicating about 4 percent of the sugar fields on the downstream side to cattail planting would provide a "filter" and thus reduce the phosphorus moving downstream to acceptable levels. When the federal government agreed to drop the lawsuit and the federal and state governments agreed to share the costs of the changes with the sugar growers, the growers accepted the necessary 4 percent dedication of their land to cattails.

Finally, subdivisions in the watershed area had to be recovered. Congress agreed to help buy out these landowners, and by 1999 the Park Service had purchased or condemned more than two thousand swampland lots for inclusion in the expanded park boundaries. In 2000, as part of the Water Resources Development Act (WRDA), the Comprehensive Everglades Restoration Plan

(CERP) was approved, covering sixteen counties and an area of eighteen thousand square miles.[55]

Restoring the entire ecosystem of southern Florida continues to be a struggle, economically and politically.[56] Implementing CERP will require more than thirty years of collaborative decision-making and will cost at least $8 billion.[57] The success of CERP is needed to protect fifteen endangered species and at least eight distinct habitats.[58] In 2007 President Bush vetoed a bill that included funding for CERP, but Congress overrode the veto.[59] CERP is not the plan most environmentalists wanted, but it did shift the ethical and legal presumption from using water for development and agriculture to restoring and protecting the ecosystem.[60]

After a Supreme Court ruling in 2006 extended the protection of the Clean Water Act of 1972 to wetlands and small streams, the Bush administration fought back by writing new regulations that make such federal intervention less likely.[61] "The EPA will now have to prove on a case-by-case basis a 'significant nexus' between intermittent streams and nearby navigable waterways."[62] This undermines the precautionary principle and puts the burden of proof on those who assert that wetlands are threatened by economic development.

WILDLIFE RESERVES IN ASIA AND AFRICA

International NGOs, such as WWF and the International Union for Conservation of Nature (IUCN), have lobbied governments and raised funds to support the creation of wildlife reserves in Asian and African countries. Surprisingly, some of these efforts to preserve wildlife and biodiversity in endangered habitats have been criticized by local environmentalists in Asia and Africa.

The problem, as Ramachandra Guha sees it, derives from American history, which defines a utilitarian notion of conservation over wilderness preservation. He argues that preserving wildlife habitats in Asia and Africa requires allowing access for local communities that rely on these natural areas for food and other resources.

India

India is a densely populated country with agrarian populations that have a long-standing and balanced relationship with nature. Designating tiger reserves, such as the Project Tiger,[63] has displaced local communities, and thus has generated strong opposition. The effect, Guha asserts, of setting aside wilderness areas for Project Tiger is a direct transfer of resources from the poor to the rich. Identifying environmental action with preservation has meant neglecting "environmental problems that impinge far more directly on the lives of the poor—e.g., fuel, fodder, water shortages, soil erosion, and air and water pollution."[64]

Ecological battles in Asia and Africa involve a "conflict over nature between the subsistence and largely rural sector and the vastly more powerful commercial-industrial sector."[65] In India those most affected by environmental degradation—poor and landless peasants, women, and tribals—are mainly concerned with survival. They only support environmental policies that lead to a more equitable distribution of economic and political power and protection for their human rights.[66]

Third world critics of the American preservationist movement see the distinction between the use and preservation of nature as not only abstract, but as reflecting a lack of awareness among Americans to their "use" of the wilderness areas that they are preserving. Historian Samuel Hays has noted that interest in wilderness is "not a throwback to the primitive, but an integral part of the modern standard of living as people . . . add new 'amenity' and 'aesthetic' goals and desires to their earlier preoccupation with necessities and conveniences."[67]

Despite the harm to the natural environment caused by the automobile, Guha points out that "for most Americans it is perfectly consistent to drive a thousand miles to spend a holiday in a national park."[68] Moreover, he finds support for a critical view of the American preservationist movement among German environmentalists, who argue that "economic growth in the West has historically rested on the economic and ecological exploitation of the Third World."[69] In this analysis the ecological crisis is a result of disproportionate consumption by industrialized societies and the urban elite in less developed societies.[70]

Because adaptive management emphasizes *local involvement in environmental decision-making*, it addresses much of this problem. For adaptive management does not describe the ethical issue as a choice between conservation and preservation, but as a process involving local communities that both preserves wildlife habitats and allows for human uses of the natural resources in these habitats.

Africa

To consider environmental issues in Africa we must appreciate that: "People were once an island in a sea of wildlife. Now wildlife survives in parks that are islands in an ocean of people."[71] This means that: "[T]he hard choice in southern Africa is not so much between people and wildlife as between a pragmatic humanism that benefits both and an idealistic environmentalism that benefits neither."[72]

In the 1970s international environmentalists supported bans on hunting and the sale of wildlife products in an effort to prevent the loss of endangered animal populations. Kenya adopted these policies, but the results were unexpected. Ranchers, who had sold licenses for hunting zebra, had to raise more cattle to make up for the loss of income due to the ban on hunting. They also had to cull more zebras to keep the population down, in order to have room for more cattle.[73]

Also, poaching increased after hunting was banned. Countries that authorized rangers to kill poachers soon discovered that despite many human deaths the number of animals lost to poaching increased, because many rangers were involved in poaching.[74] Tanzania banned hunting in 1973, but rescinded the ban in 1985. "During that twelve year moratorium on hunting, the wildlife virtually disappeared. Why? Without licensed hunters to keep poachers in line, poachers ran amok."[75]

Poachers hunt with snares, which is extremely wasteful. Animals that poachers don't want are caught, and animals in snares may be eaten by vultures or hyena before a poacher returns. After 1985 hunters began to pay local people to pick up snares and turn them in, and this incentive strategy has been effective.[76]

In 1990 Kenya began to distribute a quarter of the tourist fees for visiting wildlife reserves to local Masai tribes so the Masai would have an incentive to help protect migratory wildlife. In Zambia, companies involved in tourism distribute a percentage of their profits in equal shares among their entire staff including janitors and maids. In Botswana tribal chiefs administer a game reserve and limit licenses for doing business in the reserve to five years. Young people being employed in the tourism industry are also being educated abroad, so they soon will be able to run it.[77]

In Zimbabwe, the Communal Areas Management Programme for Indigenous Resources (CAMPFIRE), which was established in 1989 in the northwestern area of Zimbabwe known as Nyaminyami, has involved more than a quarter of a million people in managing wildlife. Local communities benefit by selling photographic or hunting concessions to wildlife tour operators, in consultation with the wildlife department, or by culling animal populations.

CAMPFIRE is a community empowerment initiative, not an environmental project. Nonetheless, as communal lands surround wildlife preserves established by the national government, the care and management of wildlife by CAMPFIRE also protects the animals in the preserves.[78] In 1989 twelve rangers were hired to oversee the reserves, using the funds gained by culling impala. "On their daily patrols the rangers pick up snares that have been laid along the animal trails, and their presence deters would-be poachers of elephants and rhinos."[79]

The CAMPFIRE ethical presumption is: "He who bears the costs gets the benefits."[80] Instead of the benefits going largely to the national government, which has been the downfall of preservation programs in Africa, the benefits should go to local communities. In CAMPFIRE this means selling culled impala meat to local people below market price, distributing profits from hunting and tourism to ward councils, and providing compensation to households for any loss due to wild animals (lions killing goats, or elephants entering the fields of the villagers).[81]

Hunting also creates local jobs. By 1993 more than a third of the households in the village of Masoka in Zimbabwe were receiving their primary income from work related to the safari camps, and this increase in income from hunting has meant that villages are turning their land over to wildlife rather than cattle grazing.[82]

When culling is required to prevent an animal population from outgrowing the environment available to it, hunting may be the best option. In the Lowveld areas of South Africa where the Kruger National Park is located, elephants share the environment with other keystone species including baobab trees and knob-thorn trees, both of which shelter small animals and provide them with food. These trees, however, are eaten by elephants, and when there are too many elephants they destroy these trees in their attempt to satisfy their hunger.

To preserve both elephants and biodiversity, the park is now divided into high elephant-impact zones (where there is no management of elephants) and low elephant-impact zones (where the elephant population is limited by translocations or culling). When the damage to the environment in the high elephant-impact zones reaches a "Threshold of Potential Concern," the management of the zones is switched so the highly impacted zone can recover.[83]

The long-term management of this elephant reserve will almost certainly involve culling by shooting elephants, as only a few elephants can be relocated and the cost of practicing contraception on elephants is prohibitive. Using drugs to kill an elephant contaminates the meat, making it unsafe for animal or human consumption, or causes suffering, because when elephants are paralyzed they suffocate to death while fully conscious.

As an elephant population grows by about 6 percent annually, the number of elephants to be culled will depend on the size of the herd.[84] Therefore, to minimize culling in a wildlife reserve, which is committed to preserving both elephants and the biodiversity of the ecosystem, it would seem best to keep the elephant population smaller rather than allowing elephant herds to grow to the maximum size that a habitat can support.

None of these environmental decisions, however, can be made ethically without adaptive management systems, which take into account the ecosystems and also the livelihoods and human rights of those living in these ecosystems. This is as true in Asia and Africa for managing wildlife reserves, as it is in the United States for managing forests, deserts, and wetlands.

ETHICAL AND LEGAL PRESUMPTIONS

United States policy for forests and wildlife has shifted from a best-use approach to an adaptive management policy emphasizing environmental sustainability and local involvement in decision-making. The best-use position puts the burden of proof on those who argue against a utilitarian calculation. Adaptive management affirms ethical and legal presumptions, such as the Endangered Species Act, that support the precautionary principle and shift the burden of proof to potential users of an environment.

Under the Clinton administration pragmatic decisions were made to restore and preserve diverse ecosystems while allowing various uses of public land. The Bush administration, however, tried to return to the moral and legal presumptions of a best-use policy, which would mean setting aside the precautionary principle and shifting the burden of proof back to advocates of preserving public land. The struggle continues in politics and in the courts.

In Asia and Africa, those committed to preserving wildlife in nature reserves also support social justice for local communities living beside these reserves. On these continents adaptive management means preserving ecosystems and endangered species by ensuring that local people are involved in the decision-making process and are fairly compensated for sharing the responsibilities of preserving wildlife.

Hunting and tourism are generally allowed in nature reserves, but are constrained by moral and legal presumptions. The burden of proof is on those proposing to intervene in a wildlife habitat for economic gain. They must ensure protection for endangered species, and also protect the rights of local people to participate in making decisions and to benefit equitably from the use of wildlife habitats.

QUESTIONS—PUBLIC LAND: ADAPTIVE MANAGEMENT

1. State the ethical presumption of the "sustainable yield" policy of the US Forest Service. Why was this policy characterized as progressive?

2. Summarize an argument that preservationists have made against utilitarian conservation.

3. What are the ethical presumptions of adaptive management? How has this approach changed the role of forestry specialists in environmental decision-making?

4. Why is local involvement important in decision-making about the use of public land? In your answer include a rights argument and also a consequential argument.

5. How have the US Army Corps of Engineers and the Bureau of Reclamation impacted land use? What is Babbitt's view of these impacts?

6. How does an AMA try to deal with uncertainty in predicting consequences? Give an example.

7. What reasons has President Bush given for HFI? Identify three arguments against HFI.

8. Andrew Light makes a relationship argument to support the restoration of damaged environments. State his ethical presumption. Do you agree? Explain your thinking.

9. How did Babbitt use the Endangered Species Act to help preserve a western habitat? Explain how this strategy illustrates adaptive management.

10. Describe how saving the Everglades requires restoring its ecosystem. What changes were agreed to by sugar growers, and why did they agree?

11. Explain why Guha thinks that efforts by US preservationists to save the tiger in India have had the unintended consequence of transferring resources from the poor to the rich.

12. Identify some of the unintended consequences of banning hunting in Africa and sale of its wildlife products. Why did proponents of these bans fail to foresee these consequences?

13. Explain how CAMPFIRE works to improve the lives of Africans and protect wildlife. How is hunting part of its preservation program?

14. Identify a conflict of duties concerning the management of elephants in the Kruger National Park. Explain why you agree or disagree with the park policy.

15. Illustrate how local involvement is important in making decisions about conservation in Africa.

14

Urban Ecology

BUILDING GREEN

For many the phrase "urban ecology" is an oxymoron, as urban development disrupts and destroys ecosystems. Yet, with more than half the world's population living in cities,[1] we must learn to live more ecologically in urban environments. Solving urban problems begins with seeing each city, with its suburbs and surrounding countryside, "as a single, evolving system within nature."[2] This means that: "Nature in the city must be cultivated, like a garden, rather than ignored or subdued."[3]

> The city is a granite garden, composed of many smaller gardens, set in a garden world. Parts of the granite garden are cultivated intensively, but the greater part is unrecognized and neglected. To the idle eye, trees and parks are the sole remnants of nature in the city. But nature in the city is far more than trees and gardens, and weeds in sidewalk cracks and vacant lots. It is the air we breathe, the earth we stand on, the water we drink and excrete, and the organisms with which we share our habitat. Nature in the city . . . is rain and the rushing sound of underground rivers buried in storm sewers. It is water from a faucet, delivered by pipes from some outlying river or reservoir, then used and washed away into the sewer, returned to the waters of river and sea. Nature in the city is an evening breeze, a corkscrew eddy swirling down the face of a building, the sun and the sky. Nature in the city is dogs and cats, rats in the basement,

pigeons on the sidewalks, raccoons in culverts, and falcons crouched on skyscrapers. It is the consequence of a complex interaction between the multiple purposes and activities of human beings and other living creatures and of the natural processes that govern the transfer of energy, the movement of air, the erosion of the earth, and the hydrologic cycle.[4]

A more ecological view of cities requires a new approach to urban planning. "Nature's own ecosystems have an essentially *circular* metabolism in which every output which is discharged by an organism also becomes an input which renews and sustains the continuity of the whole living environment of which it is a part. The whole web of life hangs together in a 'chain of mutual benefit,' through the flow of nutrients that pass from one organism to another."[5]

Unfortunately, the "metabolism" of most cities now "is essentially *linear,* with resources being 'pumped' through the urban system without much concern about their origin or about the destination of wastes."[6] Food is imported into cities, "consumed, and discharged as sewage into rivers and coastal waters. Raw materials are extracted from nature, combined and processed into consumer goods that ultimately end up as rubbish which can't be beneficially reabsorbed into the natural world. More often than not, wastes end up in some landfill site where organic materials are mixed indiscriminately with metals, plastics, glass, and poisonous residues."[7]

Therefore, our goal for urban life is to create "an adaptive, resilient, evolving, self-organizing" system that provides "a sustainable livelihood, whose ecological footprint is minimal, and which interfaces with natural systems in a way that promotes ecological integrity."[8]

THE BUILT ENVIRONMENT

In 1993 the International Union of Architects and the American Institute of Architects at their joint World Congress issued the "Declaration of Interdependence for a Sustainable Future." This declaration begins by recognizing that: "A sustainable society restores, preserves, and enhances nature and culture for the benefit of all life, present and future," and that "today's society is seriously degrading the environment and is not sustainable."[9]

Recognizing that buildings and "the built environment play a major role in the human impact on the natural environment and on the quality of life," the World Congress of Architects pledged to promote "sustainable design" that "integrates consideration of resource and energy efficiency, healthy buildings and materials, ecologically and socially sensitive land-use, and an aesthetic sensitivity that inspires, affirms and ennobles."[10] The declaration also affirms that a sustainable design would improve the "quality of life and economic well being" as well as "significantly reduce adverse human impacts on the natural environment."[11]

Standards

In 1990, in the United Kingdom, the Building Research Establishment published a set of guidelines known as the Building Research Establishment Environmental Assessment Method (BREEAM).[12] In 1996 the US Green Building Council created the Leadership in Energy and Environmental Design (LEED)[13] standards, and two years later countries supporting the Green Building Challenge[14] began to promote the Green Building Assessment Tool (GBTool).[15]

These standards are important because buildings consume about "40 percent of all of the raw materials and energy used on the planet."[16] In the United States, buildings use about 65 percent of the electricity consumed, produce around 30 percent of the greenhouse gas emissions, consume almost 12 percent of the potable water used, and generate approximately 135 million tons of construction and demolition waste per year.[17]

In the United States, "LEED promotes a whole-building approach to sustainability by recognizing performance in five key areas of human and environmental health: sustainable site development, water savings, energy efficiency, materials selection, and indoor environmental quality."[18] The US Green Building Council[19] promotes the LEED standards and seven federal agencies (including the army, navy, and air force) have adopted these standards for new building projects,[20] as have several state and municipal governments.

Green standards are being incorporated in municipal building codes. In Santa Monica "the most recent ordinances require building design features to produce 20 to 25 percent more efficiency than California's fairly strict statewide regulations."[21] In Boulder, Colorado, residential construction has to earn twenty-five "green points" for approval. "Green points are earned according to the amount of insulation (for example, R-24 wall insulation would earn 3 points), the type of windows (high performance glazing would earn between 2 and 8 points), the kind of heating system (radiant floor heating, for example, would earn 5 points), and by positioning new construction so that it has enhanced access to solar heat (2 points)."[22]

San Francisco is imposing "the country's most stringent green building codes, regulations that would require new large commercial buildings and residential high-rises to contain such environmentally friendly features as solar

power, nontoxic paints and plumbing fixtures that decrease water usage."[23] This plan has the support of the San Francisco Building Owners and Managers Association, because it makes sense and will be phased in gradually over four years.

Industrial Ecology

Industrial systems should be modeled on ecosystems, so that excess energy and waste from some manufacturing activities "serve as inputs for industries requiring energy and which can use the waste in their production systems. After their 'birth, life, and death' at one scale, the products of industry would ultimately be metabolized and reutilized at another scale, mimicking the closed, waste-free cycles of natural systems."[24]

This ethical presumption represents a new way of looking at economic development. "Industrial ecology is taken to be the activity of designing and managing human production-consumption systems, so that they interact with natural systems, to form an integrated (eco)system which has ecological integrity and provides humans with a sustainable livelihood."[25]

Traditional "waste" is seen as a resource.[26] Every ton of metal "that is reused, re-manufactured, or recycled—or whose use is avoided by more efficient design—replaces a ton that would otherwise have to be mined and smelted, with all of the intermediate energy and material requirements associated with those activities."[27] It also "eliminates at least a ton of carbon dioxide pollution and significant additional pollution of air and water from coking, pickling, and other associated activities."[28]

This view of industrial ecology "requires a major change in some of the ways in which science and decision making are conducted. Traditional reductionistic disciplinary science and expert predictions, the basis for much of the advice given to decision makers, have limited applicability. Narratives about possible futures . . . [should] capture the richness of possibilities."[29]

Ecological Benefits

Green buildings are rich in ecological benefits. First, a green building *uses less fossil fuel* than a standard building. "Large reductions can be made to conventional energy use by using the tried and true techniques of increased insulation, better windows, passive solar heating, daylighting, and natural cooling. Further reductions to carbon-based energy can be made by using more benign sources of energy, including solar water preheating, photovoltaic panels, wind power, geothermal heat exchange, local microhydro, or fuel cells."[30]

The goal of ecological design "is to eliminate the need to adjust temperatures with fossil fuels or electricity. We avoid this by allowing Nature to do the work of creating the desired temperature. Our job is to create [building] designs that exploit temperatures or temperature differences that naturally occur in various media such as air, earth, and even water."[31]

Second, a green building *conserves water.* "Reductions in water use can start with installing water conserving fixtures, but can also include using biological waste water treatment systems for gray and blackwater; using waterless toilets or urinals; using composting toilets; or capturing on-site rainwater. It can also mean planting a landscape that is native and does not require watering."[32]

In 2000 the American Institute of Architects recognized a building constructed at the University of British Columbia (UBC) that significantly reduces water use. "Its nine composting toilets and three urinals require no water. Gray water and rainwater are used for irrigation. The various water-saving devices save about 1,500 gallons of potable water every day."[33] Construction costs were comparable to a similar building, moreover the operating and maintenance costs of the UBC building are lower.

Third, a green building *creates less waste*. It should "filter water pollution before it leaves the site, recharge groundwater, preserve and encourage biodiversity, and use integrated pest management techniques. It should use materials that are not only durable but salvaged and salvageable, recycled and recyclable. It should make it easy for occupants to recycle and compost, reuse construction and demolition waste, and avoid air pollutants."[34]

Fourth, a green building is not only efficient, but *maximizes the effective use of energy*. "This distinction emphasizes the amount of energy required to perform a particular service, rather than the efficiency with which energy is converted from one form to another."[35] For example, if the waste heat from turbines generating electricity is used to heat a building or, "through the absorption cycle, to cool the building in the summer, the gain from using the waste heat will not show up in the efficiency calculation but will show up in an effectiveness calculation."[36] Also, buildings that "capture heat generated during the day by workers and machines etc. and store it for use to heat the building at night do not have any advantage from an efficiency point of view, but do from an effectiveness perspective."[37]

Sustainable Construction

Building green is a way of recovering our relationship with nature, as these design standards "use only as much energy and resources and create only as much waste as can be sustained by the environment."[38] This is why the emerging discipline of "industrial ecology" has, as its first presumption: "View the human system under consideration as part of its ecosystem and large natural systems."[39] The Calvert Fund and the Institute for Responsible Investment recently ranked US builders "based on their environmental and sustainable practices."[40]

Summing up, the objectives of "building green" standards, industrial ecology, and sustainable construction are to:

1. Reduce resource consumption.
2. Reuse resources to the maximum extent possible.
3. Recycle built environment end-of-life resources and use recyclable resources.
4. Protect natural systems and their function in all activities.
5. Eliminate toxic materials and by-products in all phases of the built environment.
6. Incorporate full-cost accounting in all economic decisions.
7. Emphasize quality in all phases of the life cycle of the built environment.[41]

These principles embrace the three Rs, internalize as economic costs the so-cial and environmental consequences of construction (externalities), and pro-tect as well as mimic natural systems.[42]

"[E]thics and values must be incorporated into any discussion of industrial ecology, if for no other reason than the trade-offs between sustainable livelihoods and ecological integrity [that] will have to be made."[43] Scientific reasoning and best practices must be accepted by the public, which requires a decision-making process like *adaptive management*. Industrial ecology is "another stage in a process of never-ending change in which human-designed systems 'naturally' evolve in a manner similar to natural ecosystems."[44]

"After more than a decade of tightening guidelines, Europe has made green ar-chitecture an everyday reality."[45] In the United States, however, "the federal gov-ernment has yet to establish universal efficiency standards for buildings."[46] This should be a priority, as "buildings consume nearly as much energy as industry and transportation combined. And the average building in the United States uses roughly a third more energy than its German counterpart."[47]

TRANSPORTATION

Economic interests, which have persuaded Congress to keep gasoline taxes low and to support federal subsidies for highway development, are largely responsi-ble for the urban-suburban sprawl of most US cities. Few of these cities have energy-efficient mass transportation systems, and most have substantial traffic congestion that increases travel time, causes a greater consumption of gasoline, and adds to urban air pollution.

Mass Transit

There are, however, more sensible cities. Curitiba, Brazil, a city of 2 million in a metropolitan area of 3.5 million, relies for mass transit on buses that are used by 85 percent of the population.[48] Moreover, "more than a quarter of Curitiba's automobile owners take the bus to work."[49] Why is Curitiba's bus system so effective?

- Buses travel on a dedicated track, like a train, so they are not held up by auto traffic.
- Passengers board through a raised tube bus stop, which allows rapid wheelchair access.
- Passengers pay as they enter the tube, reducing the time required for loading a bus.

- Buses can carry 270 passengers, more than three times the ordinary bus.

These innovations have enabled the city to realize most of the benefits of subways at less than 5 percent of the cost of building an underground train system.

There is only one low price for a bus ticket, no matter how far a passenger travels. Also, the city has contracts with ten private companies for bus service, pays according to the length of a route rather than the number of passengers carried, and buys old buses from the companies to ensure that new buses are regularly brought into service. Finally, the city has not widened highways to facilitate travel by motorized vehicles, and has set aside streets for pedestrians.[50]

There are many other efforts worldwide to reduce the use of cars. In Freiburg, Germany, residents in a new ecological district pay the equivalent of about $1,300 for a space in a nearby parking garage, and "car-free" estates are being created in the Netherlands. London has a traffic-congestion zone and charges motorists driving in the city center between 7:00 a.m. and 6:00 p.m. a daily fee of around $16.[51] Stockholm imposes a congestion tax for vehicles entering the city center,[52] and Singapore has an electronic road-pricing system that charges motorists using the city's roads during peak hours.[53]

Bicycles and Pedestrians

To promote bicycle use European cities have increased bike lanes and made other significant changes. "These include separated bike lanes with their own signaling, separate signaling and priority at intersections, signage and provision of extensive bicycle parking facilities (e.g. at train stations, public buildings), and minimum bicycle storage and parking standards for new development. Many cities are gradually converting spaces for auto parking to spaces for bicycles."[54]

Copenhagen now makes available more than two thousand public bicycles that can be used by depositing a coin.[55] "Paris now has some 20,000 bikes available for rental by credit card, scattered around the city at strategic sites. Six million people used the new rental program during the first three months after it was launched last year."[56]

The United States "lags far behind this emerging trend, with less than 1 percent of workers commuting by bicycle. Overall, bike ridership has dropped by 32 percent since the early 1990s."[57] In the United States and Canada, cyclists generally must ride on busy streets and give way to cars. To encourage cycling, laws need to support the moral presumption that cyclists have precedence over motor vehicles "where both are vying for the same road space and neither clearly has the right of way over the other."[58] As bicycling in the United States will require using city streets for the foreseeable future, municipalities should widen curbside lanes and shoulders, replace drain grates, patch potholes, mark lanes, and install bike-activated traffic signals.[59]

The suburbs, too, need to be redesigned, with pedestrians rather than automobiles in mind. "The alternative to sprawl is simple and timely: neighborhoods of housing, parks, and schools placed within walking distance of shops, civil services, jobs, and transit—a modern version of the traditional town."[60] Realizing this new form of community life will require "fundamentally changing our preconceptions and local regulatory priorities, as well as redesigning the federal programs that shape our cities."[61]

WATER AND WASTE

Cities consume enormous amounts of water. Greater London, with a population of about seven million, uses over one billion tons of water per year, which is about 100 gallons per person each day. In the United States it is estimated that cities use about 150 gallons of water per person each day.[62] Much of this water is used to carry waste away from the city, and only a small fraction of the water treated for city use is consumed as drinking water.

Water Use

A more cost-effective and sustainable way of using water in cities involves "dual-use systems" that deliver drinking water separately to homes and businesses and utilize an alternative system to provide lesser-quality water for manufacturing, urban farming, landscaping, firefighting, and carrying away wastes. This approach can be combined with water quality treatment at the neighborhood level, which minimizes the length of the dual-use delivery system.[63]

Also, recycled water that is not suitable for drinking can be used for watering lawns, gardens, and flushing toilets. A building can be plumbed to collect and use its gray water for these purposes. At least one water district in California now delivers recycled water and drinking water to commercial users that have installed dual-use systems.[64]

As the water pipes in our cities deteriorate, the water pumped from central water treatment systems will decline in quality. Installing a dual system with satellite treatment facilities located in neighborhoods would be most cost effective, if done as deteriorating pipes are replaced. Cleaner drinking water can be provided immediately, however, by installing in-home and workplace water treatment systems. Governments could provide financial incentives for this investment by offering low-interest loans, tax credits, and rebates, as is being done for building renovations that save energy.[65]

Therefore, our ethical presumptions for conserving water in the city include: installing dual-use delivery systems with satellite water treatment facilities, providing recycled water for uses that do not require drinking water, and offering financial incentives for in-home and workplace water treatment systems. These changes increase short-term costs, but are probably cost effective in the long term. Moreover, using less drinking water and recycling gray water not only lowers the demand for water, which reduces the rate at which we are consuming nonrenewable groundwater, but also reduces the need for water treatment facilities.

Natural Wastewater Treatment

Natural wastewater treatment systems should be a priority. In these systems, "The sewage water travels slowly among the roots and stems of aquatic plants, which take up some nutrients and other materials from the water in the process of supporting their own growth. However, the bulk of the work is done by bacteria and other microorganisms living on the roots and stems. Plants and microorganisms are capable of taking almost any materials out of the water, including nutrients, metals, and pathogens."[66]

The system in Arcata, California, "begins with primary settling after which 2 to 3 million gallons of sewage move into three oxidation ponds each day and an equal amount moves out. After that, a 5.3 acre intermediate marsh, planted mostly with the hardstem bulrush (*Scirpus acutus*), reduces suspended solids. Mosquito fish control mosquito populations. Chlorination and dechlorination follow the intermediate marsh; then the water moves into the 154-acre Arcata Marsh and Wildlife Sanctuary and from there into Humboldt Bay [the Pacific Ocean]."[67]

An aquatic system occupies more land than mechanized systems, but in an urban plan natural wastewater treatment facilities can be developed with satellite and dual-use water delivery systems. "Aquatic treatment concepts are not limited to municipal or industrial facilities but can be applied in myriad ways at any scale in any situation where purer water or a richer aquatic environment is desirable."[68] These systems "do not use fossil fuels or pollute the air. Finally, they cost far less than do mechanized systems."[69]

Such a system can be combined with techniques to separate sewage, before purifying it, and then drying and converting it to fertilizer. The city of Bristol in the United Kingdom has invested in this process. "The annual sewage output of 600,000 people is turned into 10,000 tons of fertilizer granules."[70]

Solid Waste

Burial and burning have been the most common ways of "treating" solid waste, but burial results in contaminants seeping into the soil and groundwater, and incineration releases dioxins and poisonous gases into the atmosphere. Also, research has shown "that incinerators compare badly with recycling in terms of energy conservation. Because of the high energy content of many manufactured products that end up in the rubbish bin, recycling paper, plastics, rubber and textiles is three to six [times] more energy-efficient than incineration."[71] Therefore, solid urban waste should be largely recycled or reused—or tapped for methane gas as a source of energy. In 2007 the EPA reported that "about 425 US landfills tap gas for power and an additional 560 dumps hold promising supplies of the fuel."[72]

In Curitiba, The Garbage That Is Not Garbage initiative has drawn more than 70 percent of households to sort recyclable materials for collection. The Garbage Purchase program, designed specifically for low-income areas, helps to clean up sites that are difficult for the conventional waste-management system to serve. More than 34,000 families in 62 poor neighborhoods have exchanged over 11,000 tons of garbage for nearly a million bus tokens and 1,200 tons of surplus food. During the past three years, students in more than 100 schools have traded nearly 200 tons of garbage for close to 1.9 million notebooks."[73]

Generally, *effective recycling requires financial incentives.* Arguments that may help to persuade businesses to recycle include:

- Separating wastes, once institutionalized, can be *cost effective.*
- Recycling removes any *liability* for waste that may be hazardous.
- Increased competition for usable waste makes recycling *convenient.*
- Businesses can receive *media attention* for their recycling efforts.
- Employees and customers respond positively to *corporate responsibility.*[74]

In construction, contracts should ensure that a subcontractor is responsible for disposing of any waste that is the result of his work. Research has shown that waste reduction on the job site may reach 80 percent with such "supply-install-dispose" contracts.[75]

SUSTAINABLE CITIES

A 1993 report of the US National Commission on the Environment (NCE) asserts that sustainable development requires "living within the earth's means."[76] The report offers an economic argument for why we should be "living off interest rather than consuming natural capital," but also affirms our ethical duty to future generations. "Sustainable development mandates that the present generation must not narrow the choices of future generations but must strive to expand them by passing on an environment and an accumulation of resources that will allow its children to live at least as well as, and preferably better than, people today."[77]

Indicators

In the United States the federal government has been slow to act, but many cities are addressing this challenge by identifying "indicators" of sustainability and measuring progress toward realizing these goals.[78] For example, Seattle's indicators include:

Environment

- Wild salmon runs through local streams.
- Number of good air quality days per year.
- Percentage of Seattle streets meeting "Pedestrian-Friendly" criteria.

Population and Resources

- Total population of King County.
- Gallons of water consumed per capita in King County.
- Tons of solid waste generated and recycled per capita per year in King County.
- Vehicle miles traveled per capita and gasoline consumption per capita.
- Renewable and nonrenewable energy (in BTUs) consumed per capita.

Economy

- Percentage of employment concentrated in the top ten employers.
- Hours of paid work at the average wage required to support basic needs.
- Percentage of children living in poverty.
- Housing affordability for median- and low-income households.
- Per capita health expenditures.

Culture and Society

- Percentage of infants born with low birth weight.
- Juvenile crime rate.
- Percent of youth participating in some form of community service.
- Percent of population voting in odd-year (local) primary elections.
- Adult literacy rate.
- Library and community center usage rates.
- Participation in the arts.[79]

The citizens of Seattle understand sustainability as involving *quality of life* concerns as well as conservation. Some communities express this understanding of sustainability as three Es: *environment, economy*, and *equity*.[80]

Cities committed to sustainability promote recycling and the reuse of solid wastes. Household recycling is measured by the proportion of households that put recycle bins out for collection, and many city governments set targets to reduce the amount of waste going to landfills and incinerators.[81] By promoting recycling Jacksonville, Florida, "decreased its per capita solid waste from 1.63 tons per person in 1987 to 0.96 tons per person in 1998."[82]

Plans

A sustainable city plan will need support from business and civic organizations as well as government agencies, and also decision-making procedures, like adaptive management, that are responsive to local concerns. Business leaders or a civic organization may initiate a planning process, but to be effective it must be institutionalized in the municipal government.

Portland, Oregon, has incorporated its sustainability goals into the city's Comprehensive Plan and charged a single municipal agency (the Office of Sustainable Development) with implementation.[83] Austin, Texas, owns its electrical generating company, so it is offering residents the option of receiving energy generated by renewable resources.[84]

Chicago, which hopes to be "the most environmentally friendly city in the world,"[85]

- Has planted over 400,000 trees since 1989, removing the pollution of 31,000 vehicles.
- Has invested in clean-burning fleet vehicles, including 45 hybrid cars.
- Has created 250 miles of bicycle lanes and installed 10,000 bicycle racks.
- Operates nine free trolley routes using bio-diesel fueled trolleys.
- Purchases 10 percent of the energy used in its facilities from renewable sources.
- Replaces every year approximately 50 miles of old leaking water mains.
- Recycles about 25 percent of the waste that previously went to landfills.[86]

In addition, Chicago maintains a garden of twenty thousand plants including more than a hundred species on the roof of its city hall. "The garden's plants reflect heat, provide shade and help cool the surrounding air through evapotranspiration, which occurs when plants secrete or 'transpire' water through pores in their leaves. The water draws heat as it evaporates, cooling the air in the process. Plants also filter the air, which improves air quality by using excess carbon dioxide to produce oxygen."[87]

This rooftop garden "mitigates the urban heat island effect by replacing what was a black tar roof with green plants. The garden absorbs less heat from the sun than the tar roof, keeping City Hall cooler in summer and requiring less energy for air conditioning. The garden also absorbs and uses rain water. It can retain 75 percent of a 1 inch rainfall before there is storm water runoff into the sewers."[88]

CONSEQUENCES

What would be the likely consequences of acting on these ethical presumptions to make our communities more sustainable? In the short term, the costs might outweigh the benefits. Furthermore, if future benefits were discounted, as is often done in cost-benefit analysis, the high front-end costs of investing in long-term economic and environmental sustainability might not seem justified.

Yet, the 1993 report by the US National Commission on the Environment (NCE) requires that we *consider long-term consequences without discounting them.* The report says we have an ethical duty to pass on to future generations an environment and an accumulation of resources that will allow them to live at least as well as we have. The NCE report also requires that the loss of *natural capital* be included in any cost-benefit analysis.[89]

The costs of losing natural capital are immense, for this includes "all forms of resources from the environment, including minerals, water, air, sunlight, heat, plants, animals, and other organic matter."[90] The 1993 NCE report asserts that we should be "living off interest rather than consuming natural capital,"[91] which is a way of reminding us, by using an analogy, that we know it is best to preserve our financial capital by living off its returns. Natural capital does not literally have "interest," but preserving the environment (natural capital) allows us to benefit from its ecosystem functions (benefits analogous to interest) even as we sustain natural capital so that it will also provide these benefits for future generations.

Long Term

The major principles of the Netherlands National Environmental Policy Plan (NEPP) offer a summary of the ethical presumptions required for sustainable urban life:

- *Intergenerational equity:* The current generation is responsible for providing a sustainable environment for the next generation.
- *The precautionary principle:* In light of uncertainties, it is best not to make decisions that may involve serious environmental risks.
- *The standstill principle:* As an absolute minimum, environmental conditions shall not further deteriorate.

- *Abatement at source:* Harmful environmental actions should be prevented at their source.
- *The polluter pays principle:* Internalization of environmental costs through such means as licensing fees, environmental taxes.
- *Use of the best applicable technology* to control pollution and other environmental harms.
- *Prevention* of all unnecessary waste.
- *Isolation, management, and control* of wastes that cannot be processed.
- *Internalization:* Environmental considerations are to be integrated into the actions of all responsible groups.
- *Integrated lifecycle management:* Manufacturers are responsible for all environmental impacts of their products, from manufacture to use to disposal. Waste flows and pollution should be reduced at all stages.
- *Environmental space (footprint):* Recognizes a limit to the level of resources each person can consume if society is to be environmentally sustainable.[92]

Do the likely consequences of acting on these presumptions call them into question? The *standstill* and *polluter pays* principles, as well as the presumptions that it is best to *abate pollution at its source* and to *prevent unnecessary waste* (rather than having to clean it up), are easily justified by cost-benefit analysis, even if the focus is only short term.

The ethical principle of *intergenerational equity,* which means accepting a duty to preserve natural capital for future generations, may be criticized as being "too expensive." From an ecological perspective, however, this objection seems largely self-serving. Certainly, using a utilitarian standard and considering the greatest good for the greatest number over more than one generation would require limiting our consumption of natural capital, so it can continue to provide its life-sustaining ecosystem benefits.

What about requiring use of the *best applicable technology*? Saving money in the short term, by using less expensive but less effective technology to clean water, will likely not be cost effective in the long run. Internalizing environmental and social costs, rather than ignoring these as externalities, will increase the cost of doing business and the prices on goods. Yet, ignoring these real costs is foolish, and simply passes them on to the next generation.

Isolation, management, and control of wastes that cannot be processed and reused would seem, on its face, to yield better consequences than dumping these wastes into the environment. Moreover, assigning this responsibility to manufacturers, along with responsibility for all the likely environmental impacts of their products, gives them a financial incentive to reduce, recycle, or reuse waste in every possible way. Those who argue that governments should be responsible for all these costs, rather than manufacturers, bear the burden of demonstrating that this would be more effective.

The Precautionary Principle

German law adopted this ethical principle in the 1970s, in a provision known as the "foresight" principle, which states that natural resources should be protected and that demands on them should be made with care.[93] This duty extends beyond the responsibility to act (with "hindsight") after environmental damage has taken place, in order to prevent future occurrences, and even beyond acting to prevent an imminent hazard. The ethical presumption is that "the proponent of an activity, rather than the public, should bear the burden of proof."[94]

The strongest argument against the precautionary principle is that it reduces innovation and raises costs.[95] Yet, all the precautionary principle does is shift the responsibility for assessing risks and costs from government regulators to the manufacturer of a product, which must verify that a product is safe before it is used or sold. Imposing this principle on all industrial innovation does not disadvantage any particular business.

Corporations are beginning to adopt the precautionary principle, at least for activities that directly affect environmental integrity or human health. JPMorgan Chase applies the principle in its investment activities that may impact climate change. The Body Shop International, a cosmetics company based in the UK, has included the precautionary principle in its chemicals policy.[96] The World Trade Organization has not recognized this principle, but changes in WTO policies are being demanded by many countries and this change, too, should be made.

Some cities have also adopted the precautionary principle. In 2003 San Francisco passed an ordinance that reads: "The Board of Supervisors encourages all City employees and officials to take the precautionary principle into consideration and evaluate alternatives when taking actions that could impact health and the environment, especially where those actions could pose threats of serious harm or irreversible damage."[97] Two years later the city began to consider the environmental and health costs of every item purchased in its $600 million annual budget.[98]

Nature as Our Model

These ecological policies for urban living embody the ethical principle of *internalizing the environmental costs of our consumption*. Implementing these policies requires research that reveals the loss of natural capital involved in making a product, the environmental impact of using it, and the disposal costs of each item. Combining this with the *integrated lifecycle management* of products by manufacturers and with *supply-install-dispose construction contracts* would help cities be more environmentally sustainable.

How are we to *prevent all unnecessary waste?* We should produce more *consumables* that, "when eaten, used, or thrown away, literally turn back into dirt, and therefore are food for other living organisms. This means that shampoos should be in bottles made of beets that are biodegradable in your compost pile. It means carpets that break down into carbon dioxide and water. It means furniture made of lignin, potato peels and technical enzymes that look just like your manufactured furniture of today except it can be safely returned to the earth."[99]

To eliminate waste in using products that are not consumables, but instead provide a service (cars, computers, etc.), these *durables* should be licensed rather than sold, giving the producer a duty to disassemble, recycle, and reuse the components of the product.[100] "Customers may use them as long as they wish, even sell the license to someone else, but when the end-user is finished with, say, a television, it goes back to Sony, Zenith, or Philips."[101]

Toxins and other hazardous products should not be made at all, and *unmarketables* that have already been made should be stored safely "until we can figure out a safe and non-toxic way to dispose of them."[102]

Keeping these principles in mind, McDonough and Braungart modeled a new building for Oberlin College in Ohio "on the way a tree works. We imagined ways that it could purify the air, create shade and habitat, enrich soil, and change with the seasons, eventually accruing more energy than it needs to operate."[103] In its first summer, "the building began to generate more energy capital than it used."[104]

> Features include solar panels on the roof; a grove of trees on the building's north side for wind protection and diversity; an interior designed to change and adapt to people's aesthetic and functional preferences with raised floors and leased carpeting; a pond that stores water for irrigation; a living machine inside and beside the building that uses a pond full of specially selected organisms and plants to clean the effluent; classrooms and large

public rooms that face west and south to take advantage of solar gain, special windowpanes that control the amount of UV light entering the building, a restored forest on the east side of the building, and an approach to landscaping and grounds maintenance that obviates the need for pesticides or irrigation.[105]

Cities can adopt the circular metabolism of nature. Our built environment can become a "granite and green garden."

QUESTIONS—URBAN ECOLOGY: BUILDING GREEN

1. Contrast the metabolism of nature with the metabolism of most cities today.

2. Describe three beneficial consequences of a green building. Identify two of the objectives of sustainable construction, and give an example of each.

3. Explain why sustainable construction involves value choices and give an example.

4. Distinguish the effective use of energy from efficiency and give an example.

5. Give three reasons why Curitiba's bus system is so effective. Why do you think bus systems in US communities are less effective?

6. Recommend three policy changes that would likely encourage bicycling in your community.

7. Identify two ways of conserving water use in cities, and raise a critical question about each.

8. Write a paragraph encouraging recycling. Raise two critical questions about your statement.

9. What does "living off interest rather than consuming natural capital" actually mean?

10. Identify five indicators in Seattle's sustainability plan that you think should be given priority, and explain your reasoning.

11. Identify two beneficial consequences of recycling metal, and raise a critical question about the ethical presumption that we should recycle.

12. Explain why the consequences of intervening in a self-organizing system are uncertain and what this means

for making scientific and economic predictions about
environmental policy.

13. Select three of the NEPP principles and explain why you
think these are important. Predict the likely consequences of
acting on these ethical presumptions.

14. Explain the precautionary principle and apply it to an urban
environmental issue.

15. Make an ethical argument for encouraging manufacturers to
produce "consumables" and for requiring producers of
"durables" to recycle and reuse these products.

15

Climate Change

GLOBAL WARMING

The evidence for global warming is growing.[1] Glaciers are rapidly melting, and sea ice in the Arctic and Antarctic is shrinking.[2] Species are migrating, when they can, as their environment changes, or dying out.[3] The climate is becoming more erratic, increasing rain in some regions and drought elsewhere, and tropical storms forming over a warmer ocean are more violent.[4]

Critics say humans are not the primary cause of these changes,[5] but the EPA argues for a different understanding of the facts. "Scientists know with virtual certainty that:

- Human activities are changing the composition of Earth's atmosphere. Increasing levels of greenhouse gases like carbon dioxide in the atmosphere since preindustrial times are well-documented and understood.
- The atmospheric buildup of carbon dioxide and other greenhouse gases is largely the result of human activities such as the burning of fossil fuels.
- An 'unequivocal' warming trend of about 1.0 to 1.7°F occurred from 1906 to 2005. Warming occurred in both the Northern and Southern Hemispheres, and over the oceans.[6]
- The major greenhouse gases emitted by human activities remain in the atmosphere for periods ranging from decades to centuries. It is therefore virtually certain that atmospheric

concentrations of greenhouse gases will continue to rise over the next few decades.
- Increasing greenhouse gas concentrations tend to warm the planet."[7]

A recent report of the Intergovernmental Panel on Climate Change (IPCC) adds that: "Most of the observed increase in global average temperatures since the mid-20th century is very likely due to the observed increase in anthropogenic [human made] greenhouse gas concentration."[8] In these assertions "virtual certainty" (or "virtually certain") means a "greater than 99 percent chance that a result is true" and "very likely" means a "greater than 90 percent chance the result is true."[9]

The EPA also states as very likely: "In the coming decades, scientists anticipate that as atmospheric concentrations of greenhouse gases continue to rise, average global temperatures and sea levels will continue to rise as a result and precipitation patterns will change."[10] Yet, "Important scientific questions remain about how much warming will occur, how fast it will occur, and how the warming will affect the rest of the climate system including precipitation patterns and storms."[11]

To respond effectively to global warming, we have to understand the earth's carbon cycle and how it has been distorted by industrial development.

THE CARBON CYCLE

Carbon is stored on earth in rocks, oceans, fossil fuels, and the soil. Rocks account for the bulk of this carbon. Oceans absorb more carbon from the atmosphere than they release, but this carbon is used by marine organisms and ends up in sedimentary deposits, so there is no net gain or loss. The carbon cycle uses carbon dioxide to sustain life. Plants use carbon dioxide to make carbohydrates, and organisms consume carbohydrates, releasing carbon dioxide into the atmosphere.

The earth's carbon cycle maintained a level of about 280 parts per million of carbon dioxide in the atmosphere until the industrial revolution. Now, carbon dioxide has reached the level of 380 parts per million,[12] and is increasing by more than six gigatons per year, largely because of:

- *Fossil fuel emissions.* About four to five gigatons of carbon are being emitted into the atmosphere each year from the burning of oil, coal, and natural gas.[13]
- *Soil organic carbon destruction.* Due to excessive tillage (cultivation) and soil erosion, carbon in the soil is being oxidized and entering the atmosphere.

- *Deforestation.* As forests are burned to clear land or for other reasons, a significant amount of carbon is released into the atmosphere.

To stop global warming, we must address these three distortions of the carbon cycle by removing carbon dioxide from the atmosphere and reducing carbon emissions. Atmospheric carbon is absorbed by the ocean, but this part of the carbon cycle is difficult to manipulate. Plants however, readily absorb carbon dioxide, so reforestation, changing agricultural practices and reclaiming marginal land will reduce carbon emissions into the atmosphere.

This strategy will require long-term adaptive management of forests and sustainable agriculture. Sustainable forestry involves cutting mature trees and removing dead wood, which maximizes the net carbon dioxide absorption of a forest. As plant life decays, part of its carbon is converted by microorganisms into organic matter, and this is easily oxidized and returned to the atmosphere. Unlike industrial agriculture, sustainable farming increases the organic carbon held in the soil.[14] Thus, the answer to global warming requires reducing fossil fuel emissions of carbon dioxide, ending deforestation and instituting sustainable forestry, and replacing industrial agriculture with sustainable agriculture.

Carbon dioxide is not the only greenhouse gas (GHG). Chapter 11 describes efforts to reduce air pollution due to carbon monoxide, fluorocarbons, hydrofluocarbons, and nitrous oxide. Methane, which is also a GHG, is increasing in the atmosphere largely because more cattle are being raised and fed a diet of corn, which gives cattle gas. Chapters 9 and 12 present arguments for reducing our consumption of beef, which would reduce the number of cattle and thus lower methane emissions.

Water vapor also reflects heat rays back to earth, and there is now evidence that its level in the atmosphere is increasing, at least over some continents.[15] The cause, however, is the warming of the earth due to GHGs, so there is no way to address the problem of increasing water vapor without reducing the level of greenhouse gases, which means decreasing our consumption of fossil fuels.

RESPONSIBILITY

To address our environmental crisis, we have constructed ethical presumptions to:

- Do our duty to restore and maintain the integrity of the earth's ecosystems.

- Reduce our ecological footprint by living with greater frugality and gratitude.
- Care for nature and other species by farming, eating, and living sustainably.
- Respect the human rights to sustainable development and to a healthy environment.

Now we apply these presumptions to global warming, and then test these convictions by considering the likely consequences of acting on them.

Duty

From 1960 to 1990 "the richest 20 percent of the world's population increased its share of world income from thirty times greater than the poorest 20 percent to sixty times greater."[16] In this same period, the United States with 5 percent of the world's people was responsible for about 30 percent of the world's carbon emissions.[17] These facts support the equitable argument in chapters 4 and 10 that members of industrial societies, like the United States, should accept their duty to pay more of the costs of reducing fossil fuel emissions than people living in less affluent societies.

The first international attempt to reduce GHG emissions is the *Kyoto Protocol*—an amendment to the 1992 United Nations Framework Convention on Climate Change (FCCC). It accepts the moral argument that developed countries have a greater duty than developing countries to reduce their greenhouse gas emissions, and it *mandates that industrial countries reduce these emissions* by at least 5 percent below 1990 levels before 2012.[18]

As of June 2007 the Kyoto Protocol had been ratified by 174 countries. President Clinton signed the Kyoto Protocol and pledged that the United States would reduce its greenhouse gas emissions by 7 percent before 2012. President George W. Bush rejected the Kyoto Protocol and refused to submit it to the Senate for ratification—arguing that the Kyoto Protocol unfairly "exempts 80 percent of the world, including major population centers such as China and India, from compliance, and would cause serious harm to the US economy."[19]

In support of his position, President Bush claimed: "The Senate's vote, 95–0, shows that there is a clear consensus that the Kyoto Protocol is an unfair and ineffective means of addressing global climate change concerns."[20] This 1997 Senate resolution opposes any international agreement requiring the United States to make reductions in GHG emissions, unless it includes mandatory limitations on developing countries. The Senate also rejected any agreement that "would result in serious harm to the economy of the United States."[21]

Other objections to the Kyoto Protocol include claims that the scientific evidence for global warming is uncertain, the targets for reducing GHG emissions are unrealistic, and an effective strategy to lower carbon emissions would require "replacing the command-and-control regulatory scheme with flexible results-oriented policies, and providing incentives to install state-of-the-art technologies."[22]

Nonetheless, European nations and Japan have accepted the equity argument and also the mandatory regulations of the Kyoto Protocol.[23] Under the Protocol, a cap-and-trade program in carbon emissions began in 2005,[24] and after 2007 became mandatory for all members of the European Union. A country exceeding its cap in carbon emissions can buy emission credits from another country that has more than met its cap, and thus has credits to sell.[25]

The United States has yet to create a federal carbon cap-and-trade program.[26] Seven states (led by California) and two Canadian provinces have formed the Western Climate Initiate (WCI), which "requires partners to set an overall regional goal to reduce emissions, develop a market-based, multi-sector [carbon emissions trading] mechanism to help achieve that goal, and participate in a cross-border greenhouse gas registry."[27] The WCI goal is to reduce GHG emissions by 15 percent from 2005 levels by 2020.[28]

In 2007 the European Union pledged to reduce GHG emissions by 50 percent by the year 2050 from levels measured in 1990,[29] and the Group of Eight industrial nations (G-8) agreed to "consider seriously" this goal.[30] Because of US opposition, the G-8 did not affirm the binding reductions accepted by the EU. Yet, new research suggests that much more rapid reductions in carbon emissions are required to prevent disastrous climate changes around the world.[31]

Character

The United States rejects the equity argument, which allocates greater responsibility to developed nations for environmental costs, for the sake of all peoples and future generations. It acknowledges a duty of fairness to other nations, but gives priority to the duty to promote the well-being of American society. Alternatively, we might resolve this conflict of duties by considering the kind of persons that we believe we should be. As we saw in chapter 5, this way of making ethical decisions often involves telling stories. What story would you like your grandchildren to tell about how you responded to the environmental crisis of global warming?

A story about *facing our ethical challenge to reduce fossil fuel emissions* would likely involve choices, such as these:

- Driving a fuel-efficient car and using mass transit whenever possible.
- Walking more and riding a bicycle, when we can, instead of driving.
- Reducing energy use and waste, recycling more, and consuming less.
- Eating lower on the food chain to increase the supply of grain.
- Supporting public policies that address the causes of global warming.

In chapter 5 we looked at the stories of Cinderella, Johnny Appleseed, and Bob the Builder, which present characters that have integrity, express gratitude for life, and are frugal. Tales like these prompt us to ask, How might we *live with more integrity, gratitude, and frugality?* How might we reduce our *ecological footprint?*[32]

For those who are religious, there are many compelling stories to consider. Jewish scripture tells of God bringing the Israelites out of slavery to a fertile land, and commands their descendents to care for strangers because God cared for their ancestors when they were strangers. Christian scripture tells of the Good Samaritan who cared for an enemy, to explain that God calls everyone to love others as we love ourselves. Islamic scripture tells of Noah calling all people to act justly in order to abide by the will of the one God.

These stories do not concern global warming, but *every religious tradition at its best promotes stewardship of the earth's resources.*

Relationships

Chapter 6 describes the importance of relationships in making ethical decisions. Contemporary science verifies that empathy for others is natural, and child psychology confirms the natural development of empathy in young children.[33] Being ethical involves acting with empathy and reason out of concern for the well-being of others.

Empathy helps us *see the world as others do*, and in facing global warming this means seeing the world through the eyes of people living on low ground near the sea, or in the Arctic on frozen ground that is thawing. Global warming threatens land, livelihoods, and lives, and when we see this with empathy as well as reason, we will more likely be moved to act with greater commitment and compassion.

Concern for relationships also means *a more inclusive way of making decisions.* Facing moral choices about global warming should include all of us in local, state, national, and international decision-making. We have a moral responsibility to consider the welfare of others, and to make the best decisions we can for all those who will be affected by climate change.

Finally, global warming threatens not only human life, but *other species*. We face a tremendous loss in biodiversity due to climate change, and thus have a responsibility to reduce carbon emissions in order to preserve biodiversity.

Rights

Chapter 10 notes that the *right to sustainable development* has been part of international law since the 1987 Brundtland Commission defined sustainable development as "development that meets the needs of the present without compromising the ability of future generations to meet their own needs."[34] Agenda 21 and the Beijing Declaration help to clarify that this should be understood to mean economic and social development that is environmentally sustainable.

The right to health and a healthy working environment is affirmed in the Universal Declaration of Human Rights and in the International Covenant on Economic, Social, and Cultural Rights. The *right to a healthy environment* was first asserted in the 1972 Stockholm Declaration of the UN Conference on the Human Environment. The 1992 Rio Declaration reaffirmed this right, and the UN Framework Convention on Climate Change (FCCC) states: "The Parties should protect the climate system for the benefit of present and future generations of humankind. . . ."[35]

PREDICTING CONSEQUENCES

The virtually certain consequence of failing to decrease GHG emissions is more rapid global warming, and the very likely consequences include climate change that will involve flooding in some places and drought elsewhere. Some organisms will be sufficiently "fit" to survive in these rapidly changing environments, but many species will not. The bacteria causing tropical diseases are already on the move, due to the earth's warming, so we can expect malaria to become endemic in southern Europe and southern regions of the United States.[36]

Our ethical presumptions require actions by individuals, governments, and corporations to reduce GHG emissions, and to secure more carbon dioxide in forests and farmland. This requires ending industrial agriculture and deforestation, and substantially reducing our use of fossil fuels for transportation and generating electricity.[37]

Agriculture

A shift to *sustainable agriculture would hold more carbon in plants and the soil.*
Where a commodity crop (like corn) is grown as a monoculture, as is the case
in industrial agriculture, the soil is left uncovered after the harvest until a new
crop comes up in the spring. Sustainable agriculture, however, uses cover crops
to protect and nourish the soil, which increases the plant and soil absorption of
carbon dioxide. Ending industrial agriculture would also lower the amount of
carbon dioxide released by burning fossil fuels to produce fertilizers and pesticides, run farm machinery, and transport food long distances.

Terminating current government subsidies for commodity crops and reducing the use of artificial fertilizers and pesticides would save billions of dollars.
Relying on sustainable farming, however, would likely mean increased costs for
food producers and higher food prices for consumers. It is not possible to predict all the costs and benefits of a shift to sustainable farming, but the adverse
consequences do not clearly outweigh the benefits.

Forests

What are the likely consequences of reducing deforestation and managing forests
sustainably? *Forests remove carbon dioxide from the atmosphere* and transform this
carbon through photosynthesis into carbohydrates. Forests also release oxygen
into the atmosphere, increase rainfall, cool the earth, hold the soil, prevent erosion, and provide habitats for animals. Therefore, assessing the consequences of
sustainable forestry must include not only the likely short-term costs of logging
fewer trees—a loss of jobs and income in some communities, an increase in the
price of timber and products made of wood, and higher costs to manage forests—
but also the long-term environmental benefits.[38] Sustainable forestry also generates
income from jobs and fees for the recreational use of forests.

JPMorgan Chase limits its lending for logging to sustainable forestry management, and requires proof of decision-making that includes local communities.
Companies, such as Home Depot, verify that the lumber in their stores has been
logged from forests managed in a way that is environmentally sustainable. We may
presume, therefore, that the sustainable management of forests is cost effective.

Transportation

What are the likely consequences of reducing the use of fossil fuels for transportation? First, *reducing waste* is always cost effective. A 2008 congressional report suggests that *ending flight delays* would save "US airlines more than $2

billion in wasted jet fuel" each year,[39] and reducing motor vehicle *traffic conges-tion* in cities would also save costs and reduce carbon emissions. Cargo ships that reduce their average speed by just two knots "could save 5 per cent of fuel use and emissions," which is significant as cargo ships account for up to 4.5 per cent of global emissions of carbon dioxide."[40] Improving *fuel efficiency* (with re-designed engines and lower vehicle weights) will require investment and increase the price of cars and trucks, but might add jobs.[41]

Motor vehicles emit a higher percentage of the greenhouse gases released each year than airplanes. US car companies have resisted tougher Corporate Av-erage Fuel Economy (CAFE) standards, but in 2007 Congress voted to raise *fuel efficiency* by at least 25 percent over the next fifteen years.[42] As European coun-tries and Japan require greater engine efficiency, clearly this change is economi-cally feasible.

Second, as fossil fuels are being depleted, *using alternative fuels for transporta-tion* is a long-term necessity. Scientists are experimenting with solar energy, elec-tric vehicles, and hydrogen, but greater investment is needed to speed up research and development.

GM and Ford, whose vehicles cause over 50 percent of the carbon emissions from cars in the United States, are promoting *the use of ethanol to reduce carbon emissions.* Yet, most biofuels generate "more greenhouse gas emissions than con-ventional fuels if the full emissions costs of producing these 'green' fuels are taken into account."[43] Fossil fuels are burned to irrigate, harvest, process, and transport crops, and producing biofuels by cutting forests or plowing grasslands "releases greenhouse gases into the atmosphere" and "also deprives the planet of natural sponges to absorb carbon emissions."[44]

Using sugar cane, however, is "eight times more productive than corn. It grows year round. It must be processed fast, so CO_2-spewing transport to dis-tant ethanol plants is impossible (unlike for corn). Its leftover biomass can be used to produce electricity, enough, by some estimates, to provide a third of Brazil's power needs by 2030. Ethanol already accounts for about 50 percent of car fuel in Brazil."[45] Yet, Brazil's claim that it is not clearing forests to grow sugar cane is misleading, for cattle ranchers sell pastures to farmers (who will grow sugar care) and then move their herds "into the Amazon where land is cheap and deforesting is easy."[46]

To preserve forests and farmland, there is now a push to make ethanol from "non-food crops like reeds and wild grasses," but most of these species of "weeds" have a "high potential to escape biofuel plantations, overrun adjacent farms and natural land, and create economic and ecological havoc."[47] Sufficient investment, however, will likely create energy-efficient "biofuels made from waste products such as citrus peel, corncobs, and wood chips."[48]

Third, despite the development of greater fuel efficiency and alternative fuels, the reduction in carbon emissions from transportation is not likely to be sufficient or rapid enough to stop global warming. Therefore, *we must reduce our driving and flying*. We should walk and cycle more, do business at a distance using computer technology to share information, utilize conference calls, and take vacations that burn less gasoline.

Airplane emissions are less than 5 percent of the carbon dioxide emitted each year, but airplane travel is growing at 5 percent annually and at this rate will triple the number of miles traveled by passengers by 2030.[49] *Motor vehicle emissions* constitute more than 20 percent of the global carbon dioxide emissions annually.[50] Thus, transportation using fossil fuels for power is producing about a quarter of the carbon dioxide emitted into the atmosphere annually.[51]

In the United States carbon emissions are growing overall at a rate close to 3 percent a year, and at this rate will double the carbon dioxide in the atmosphere in twenty-three years.[52] These consequences are uncertain, but we should not assume that the long-term cost of paying for the effects of global warming will be less than the cost of investing now to cut our carbon emissions.

Power Plants

What are the likely consequences of reducing the use of fossil fuels to produce electrical energy? This is crucial, as *power plants burning fossil fuels produce about a third of the global GHG emissions*.[53] The major source of the world's power continues to be *coal*. The United States has about six hundred coal-burning power plants and more under construction.[54] "Already, China uses more coal than the United States, the European Union and Japan combined. And it has increased coal consumption 14 percent in each of the past two years in the broadest industrialization ever. Every 7 to 10 days, another major coal-fired power plant opens somewhere in China. To make matters worse, India is right behind China in stepping up its construction of coal-fired power plants and has a population expected to outstrip China's by 2030."[55]

Europeans, too, are investing in coal-fired power plants. "Driven by rising demand, record high oil and natural gas prices, concerns over energy security and an aversion to nuclear energy, European countries are slated to build about 50 coal-fired plants over the next five years, plants that will be in use for the next five decades."[56]

The Union of Concerned Scientists has verified that a typical coal-burning power plant produces about 3.7 million tons of carbon dioxide annually—equal to cutting down over 160 million trees.[57] Given the rising demand for energy worldwide, more power plants will be built. To reduce carbon emissions, either these new power plants need to use fuels producing less carbon dioxide than coal, or, if these plants burn coal, the carbon dioxide produced must be sequestered in geological repositories.

The *technology to sequester carbon dioxide* does not yet exist, but German companies investing in this technology hope it will be feasible by 2020 at a cost of about 20 percent more than conventional facilities.[58] Many NGOs, however, argue that investing in carbon capture and storage technology (CCS) should not be used "as an excuse for building new coal-fired power plants. Governments should instead give priority to investing in sustainable energy solutions."[59]

The ethical presumption in Agenda 21, which demands an equitable allocation of the costs of dealing with environmental damage, would support subsidies from developed countries to help developing countries incorporate the best available technology for reducing carbon emissions from power plants. Without such assistance, China says, it can only afford to use older technology, and in its defense it points out that "the average American still consumes more energy and is responsible for the release of 10 times as much carbon dioxide as the average Chinese."[60] The US government, however, rejects a per capita comparison of energy consumption by the two countries.

Natural gas is an alternative to coal for producing electricity. "At the power plant," the EPA says, "the burning of natural gas produces nitrogen oxides and carbon dioxide [both greenhouse gases], but in lower quantities than burning coal or oil."[61] As natural gas (like all fossil fuels) is a nonrenewable resource, burning it to produce power does not fulfill our responsibility to future generations, which will not be able to rely on this source of fuel after we use it up. In the short term, however, generating electricity from natural gas rather than burning coal will reduce carbon emissions and slow global warming.

Nuclear energy generates electricity without emitting carbon into the atmosphere. The British are reviving their nuclear plants, and France relies on nuclear power for 80 percent of its electricity. In contrast, the United States obtains only 20 percent of its electricity from nuclear power, and Germany has turned to alternative sources to meet its growing demand for energy.[62] Congress included "incentives for new nuclear plants in the 2005 Energy Policy Act," but public opinion in the United States is divided.[63]

The Union of Concerned Scientists opposes building more nuclear power plants. "It must be borne in mind that a large-scale expansion of nuclear power in the United States or worldwide under existing conditions would be accompanied by an increased risk of catastrophic events—a risk not associated with any of the non-nuclear means for reducing global warming. These catastrophic events include a massive release of radiation due to a power plant meltdown or terrorist attack, or the death of tens of thousands due to the detonation of a nuclear weapon made with materials obtained from a civilian—most likely non-US—nuclear power system."[64]

Expanding nuclear power would increase radioactive waste, which will remain a significant hazard for centuries. Also, the need to lower carbon emissions is urgent, and even beginning construction of new nuclear plants today would not make a substantial difference in lowering emissions "for at least two decades."[65]

Renewable energy alternatives to fossil fuels include *wind, solar energy*, and *geothermal energy*. "The EU's Renewables Directive has been in place since 2001. It aims to increase the share of electricity produced from renewable energy sources (RES) in the EU to 21% by 2010, thus helping the European Union reach the RES target of overall energy consumption of 12% by 2010." [66] In China, wind power "has experienced tremendous development since early 2005, when the government enacted its landmark national renewable energy law."[67] Moreover, "China is the third largest producer of solar photovoltaic cells and is producing 75 percent of the world's global solar hot water from rooftop solar collectors."[68]

In the United States, between 1994 and 2004, *wind energy* capacity tripled, providing enough electrical power to serve more than 1.6 million households.[69] In 2008 a Department of Energy report predicted that wind energy could "supply 20 percent of US electricity needs" in twenty years at a cost 2 percent greater "than sticking with the current energy mix, which relies more heavily on traditional fossil fuels."[70] The District of Columbia and twenty-one states have enacted *renewable energy standards*. "By 2020, state standards will reduce total annual carbon dioxide emissions by 108.1 million metric tons (MMT)— the equivalent of taking 17.7 million cars off the road or planting 25.9 million acres of trees—an area larger than the Commonwealth of Virginia."[71]

Studies completed in 2008 suggest that "both industrialized and developing nations must wean themselves off fossil fuels by as early as mid-century in order to prevent warming that could change precipitation patterns and dry up sources of water worldwide."[72] In the United States this means per capita carbon emissions need to be reduced by about "90 percent from what they are today."[73] The costs of not reaching this goal (or reaching it) are uncertain, but there is no reason to think that ignoring global warming will cost less than facing it.

Taxes

Cap-and-trade programs create financial incentives to lower carbon emissions and create a market in emission "credits," but many argue that a tax on carbon consumption is needed.[74] Representative John Dingell, who chairs the Energy and Commerce Committee, has supported "some form of carbon emissions fee" in order "to curb carbon emissions and make alternatives economically viable."[75] Now that the price of gasoline is rising, consumers are already motivated to increase their energy efficiency in order to lower their costs. So, it makes sense to add an environmental tax to gasoline, *if* income taxes are generally reduced, *and* the income from an added tax on gasoline is invested in developing alternative sources of energy.

In his 2007 appearance before the Energy and Commerce Committee of the House of Representatives, Al Gore made such a proposal: "We should start using the tax code to reduce taxes on employment and production, and make up the difference with pollution taxes, principally [on] carbon dioxide."[76] Ray Anderson, the founder of Interface Incorporated, agrees, arguing that "the tax code is 'perverse,' in that it puts heavy taxes on good things, like income and capital, and leaves a lot of bad things, like energy use, relatively unscathed."[77]

Economist Amory Lovins suggests that a "feebate"—a fee (tax) when buying a less fuel-efficient car and a rebate (tax credit) for a more efficient car—would be more effective than a gas tax.[78] "Fuel taxes are a much weaker way to affect how efficient a car you buy because they are diluted, roughly seven to one, by the other costs of owning and running the car, and then they are heavily discounted."[79] Fuel taxes are also more regressive (have greater impact on the poor) than a feebate on cars would be.

Perhaps the best strategy is to "tax the industrial emission of carbon and return the revenue to industry through subsidies for research and investment in alternative energy sources, cleaner-burning fuel, carbon-capture technologies and other environmental innovations."[80] This tax and investment policy has "led to a large decrease in emissions in Denmark, whose per capita carbon dioxide emissions were nearly 15 percent lower in 2005 than in 1990. And Denmark accomplished this while posting a remarkably strong economic record and without relying on nuclear power."[81]

Those who oppose any form of carbon tax argue that markets provide a more cost-effective way of shifting investment to alternative fuels as the price of fossil fuels increases. Yet, *we should not rely on markets alone to limit an environmentally damaging activity*, because "the absence of an appropriate price for certain scarce resources (such as clean air and water) leads to their excessive use and results in what is called 'market failure.'"[82]

Economist Wallace E. Oates explains: "Many of our environmental resources are unprotected by the appropriate prices that would constrain their use. From this perspective, it is hardly surprising to find that the environment is overused and abused. A market system simply doesn't allocate the use of these resources properly. In sum, economics makes a clear and powerful argument for public intervention to correct market failure with respect to many

kinds of environmental resources. Markets may work well in guiding the production of private goods, but they cannot be relied upon to provide the proper levels of 'social goods' (like environmental services)."[83]

Markets have not included in the price of fossil fuels the cost of the environmental damage due to global warming, or the cost of developing alternative energy sources to reduce carbon emissions. Governments exacerbate this "market failure" by not supporting energy and environmental policies that will correct it, and by not informing consumers so they will understand the need for effective environmental policies.[84]

Burning coal today to produce electricity, without assessing a fee on these carbon emissions, illustrates this problem. Advocates for solar energy argue that: "If coal remains as cheap as it is today due to its relatively abundant supply, renewables such as photovoltaic cells will never gain enough market share to make the efficiency strides necessary to become competitive. If, however, the environmental externalities were factored into the cost of coal-powered electricity, photovoltaic cells would become competitive as an electricity source."[85]

A major shortcoming in the 2007 energy bill passed by the US Congress "was its failure to extend vital tax credits to producers of wind, solar, and other renewable fuels."[86] The 2008 energy bill included authorization for "a one-year extension of the production tax credit for wind and a multiyear extension of the investment tax credit for solar power,"[87] but was blocked in the US Senate by opponents who claimed that any long-term benefits were outweighed by their prediction of the short-term costs. Four months later, however, the $700 billion Economic Growth and Stabilization Act of 2008 extended existing tax credits for renewable energies and included rebates for those purchasing plug-in hybrid cars.[88]

TAKING ACTION

Environmentalist Bill McKibben writes: "Everyone involved knows what the basic outlines of a deal that could avert catastrophe would look like: rapid, sustained, and dramatic cuts in emissions by the technologically advanced countries, coupled with large-scale technology transfers to China, India, and the rest of the developing world so that they can power up their emerging economies without burning up their coal."[89] But, how is this to be done?

Strategies

Scientists Robert Socolow and Stephen Pacala offer *fifteen strategies using existing technology.* They predict that adopting any twelve of these strategies would cut carbon dioxide emissions in half in the next fifty years and prevent a global warming disaster.

Efficiency and Conservation

1. Improve fuel economy of the two billion cars expected on the road by 2057 to 60 mpg from 30 mpg.
2. Reduce miles traveled annually per car from 10,000 to 5,000.
3. Increase efficiency in heating, cooling, lighting, and appliances by 25 percent.
4. Improve coal-fired power plant efficiency to 60 percent from 40 percent.

Carbon Capture and Storage

5. Introduce systems to capture carbon dioxide and store it underground at 800 large coal-fired plants or 1,600 natural gas–fired plants.

6. Use capture systems at coal-derived hydrogen plants producing fuel for a billion cars.
7. Use capture systems in coal-derived synthetic fuel plants producing 30 million barrels a day.

Low-Carbon Fuels

8. Replace 1,400 large coal-fired power plants with natural gas–fired plants.
9. Displace coal by increasing production of nuclear power to three times today's capacity.

Renewables and Biostorage

10. Increase wind-generated power to 25 times current capacity.
11. Increase solar power to 700 times current capacity.
12. Increase wind power to 50 times current capacity to make hydrogen for fuel-cell cars.
13. Increase biofuel production to 50 times current capacity. About one-sixth of the world's cropland would be needed.[90]
14. Stop all deforestation.
15. Expand conservation tillage to all cropland (normal plowing releases carbon by speeding decomposition of organic matter).[91]

Doing Ethics

Al Gore is encouraging everyone to take the pledge recommended by the Alliance for Climate Protection. This pledge includes many of the ethical presumptions presented in this book, and so I have taken it and recommend it to readers.

1. To demand that my country join an international treaty within the next 2 years that cuts global warming pollution by 90 percent in developed countries and by more than half worldwide in time for the next generation to inherit a healthy earth.

2. To take personal action to help solve the climate crisis by reducing my own carbon dioxide emissions as much as I can and offsetting the rest to become "carbon neutral."[92]

3. To fight for a moratorium on the construction of any new generating facility that burns coal without the capacity to safely trap and store the carbon dioxide.

4. To work for a dramatic increase in the energy efficiency of my home, workplace, school, place of worship, and means of transportation.

5. To fight for laws and policies that expand the use of renewable energy sources and reduce dependence on oil and coal.

6. To plant new trees and to join with others in preserving and protecting forests.

7. To buy from businesses and support leaders who share my commitment to solving the climate crisis and building a sustainable, just, and prosperous world for the twenty-first century.[93]

Commentators, who limit their analysis to predicting consequences, are skeptical about such a pledge. Thomas Friedman, in a column describing the rapidly developing (and polluting) cities of Doha (in Qatar) and Dalian (in China) dismisses as useless many of the ethical presumptions affirmed in this book.

He quotes an EPA report: "Demand for oil has grown 22 percent in the United States since 1990. China's oil demand has grown nearly 200 percent in this same period."[94] Moreover, by 2030, the EPA suggests, "the global thirst for oil is forecast to increase by another 40 percent if we maintain business as usual." Friedman's conclusion is that the "appetite" of developing nations, such as China and India, for fossil fuels "would devour every incremental green initiative" that we might make.[95]

Despite such skepticism, what you do about global warming does matter, even if all our efforts to reduce carbon emissions do not offset the emissions of Doha and Dalian. Before we act we cannot know all the consequences of acting, and we can never know for certain that by trying to resolve a problem we will succeed. Yet, we know that doing what is right and being good persons are worthwhile. Living an ethical life is right. Living more sustainably for the sake of nature and future generations is good. Protecting the rights of others is worth doing.

Acting on ethical presumptions always matters. Acting on your duty to reduce your ecological footprint matters to you and to those who look to you for moral leadership. Being grateful and frugal, and having integrity, is inspiring. Working with neighbors and strangers for sustainable forests, farms, and urban communities matters to them. Struggling to realize the social right to sustainable economic development, and the individual right to a healthy environment, matters to us all.

What you do matters to me, and surely it matters to you, too.

QUESTIONS—CLIMATE CHANGE: GLOBAL WARMING

1. How has industrial society disrupted the carbon cycle?
2. Why has the US government rejected mandatory carbon dioxide reductions? Make an ethical argument for the Kyoto Protocol.
3. How might you reduce your ecological footprint? What would motivate you to do this?
4. Why should everyone be involved in decisions about the environment?
5. In what sense does environmental damage violate human rights? Give an example.
6. Explain how sustainable agriculture would reduce carbon emissions.
7. Make an economic argument for sustainable forestry and give a counterargument.
8. Make a consequential argument for reducing carbon emissions caused by transportation burning fossil fuels. Why is even a small rate of increase in emissions a big problem?
9. How can carbon emissions be reduced from power plants burning fossil fuels?
10. Should the United States invest in building nuclear power plants? Explain your reasoning.
11. Weigh the consequences of a carbon tax on gasoline. Consider the likely consequences of a "feebate" on purchasing a car. Describe Denmark's carbon tax policy.
12. Explain why the market pricing of fossil fuels illustrates a "market failure."
13. Identify five strategies for reducing carbon emissions that you think would be most effective, and explain your reasoning.
14. Describe three problems with relying on biofuels to replace gasoline.
15. Do you think that what we do, and who we are, matters? Explain your reasoning.

Notes

PREFACE

1. "James Schlesinger, the nation's first energy secretary in the 1970s, once said the United States was capable of only two approaches to its energy policy: 'complacency or crisis.'" In the words of Vaclav Smil, a prominent energy expert at the University of Manitoba, the United States "has been living beyond its means" and the "situation is dire." Jad Mouwad, "The Big Thirst," *The New York Times* (Apr. 20, 2008), online at http://www.nytimes.com/2008/04/20/weekinreview/20mouawad.html.

2. See Mary Midgley, *The Ethical Primate: Humans, Freedom and Morality* (London: Routledge, 1994).

3. For a more detailed presentation of this approach, see Robert Traer and Harlan Stelmach, *Doing Ethics in a Diverse World* (Boulder, CO: Westview Press, 2007).

CHAPTER 1: MORAL PHILOSOPHY

1. Socrates in Plato's *Republic* says, "We are discussing no small matter, but how we ought to live." Quoted in James Rachels, *The Elements of Moral Philosophy*, fourth edition (New York: McGraw-Hill, 2003), 1.

2. The word *morality* comes from the Latin *mores*, which refers to custom. The *Stanford Encyclopedia of Philosophy* gives two meanings for morality. First, the word can be used to "refer to a code of conduct put forward by a society or some other group, such as a religion, or accepted by an individual for her own behavior." Second, morality may be used "normatively to refer to a code of conduct that, given specified conditions, would be put forward by all rational persons." Online at http://plato.stanford.edu/entries/morality-definition.

3. "Ethics, or moral philosophy, asks basic questions about the good life, about what is better and worse, about whether there is any objective right and wrong, and how we know it if there is." Barbara MacKinnon, *Ethics: Theory and Contemporary Issues*, fifth edition (Belmont, CA: Thomson Wadsworth, 2007), 3.

4. "[S]omething has **intrinsic value** if it is valuable because of its nature, or because of what it is in itself. Intrinsic value contrasts with **extrinsic** (or derivative) **value**, for example the **instrumental**

value that things (such as tools and machines) have because of their actual or potential usefulness, or the value that (say) works of art have because people are benefited through appreciating them . . . and it is important to avoid the widespread confusions that misrepresent aesthetic value or even all non-instrumental values as intrinsic value." Robin Attfield, *Environmental Ethics: An Overview for the Twenty-First Century* (Cambridge, UK: Polity Press, 2003), 12.

5. Our natural environment may be understood as: "The complex of all external, biotic [living], and abiotic [nonliving] influences on an organism or group of organisms." Bill Freedman, *Environmental Ecology: The Ecological Effects of Pollution, Disturbance, and Other Stresses,* second edition (San Diego, CA: Academic Press, 1995), 551.

6. Online at http://www.merriam-webster.com/dictionary/right.

7. All these nouns may have slightly different meanings, depending on the context in which they are used, but I am using them all to affirm our commonsense meaning for an ethical principle or moral standard.

8. Online at http://www.merriam-webster.com/dictionary/good.

9. It is important in raising children to make this distinction, so that children do not take criticism of their actions to mean that they are bad persons.

10. Andrew Light and Holmes Rolston III, "Introduction: Ethics and Environmental Ethics," in Andrew Light and Holmes Rolston III, eds., *Environmental Ethics: An Anthology* (Malden, MA: Blackwell Publishing, 2003), 3.

11. Sandra Blakeslee and Matthew Blakeslee, *The Body Has a Mind of Its Own: How Body Maps in Your Brain Help You Do (Almost) Everything Better* (New York: Random House, 2007), 191. Research has "emphatically confirmed the network model of the brain as well as a long history of thought and metaphor. Reason and passion, thought and emotion, were indeed linked in a loop rather than stacked in a hierarchy. Neither stood as the other's slave. They engaged in a conversation that, to be healthy, had to be rich and balanced." David Dobbs, "Turning Off Depression," in Floyd E. Bloom, ed., *Best of the Brain from Scientific American* (New York: Dana Press, 2007), 175.

12. The scientific method "changes and transforms its object." Werner Heisenberg, quoted in Jeffrey M. Schwartz, *The Mind and the Brain: Neuroplasticity and the Power of Mental Force* (New York: Regan Books, 2002), 255.

13. Mary Midgley, *Animals and Why They Matter* (Athens, GA: The University of Georgia Press, 1983), 43.

14. "[D]isgust at bloodshed often does have a meaning. It has played a great part in the development of more humane behavior, because it can alert people's imagination to what they are doing and wake their sympathies for the victims. The same thing happens with unthinking revulsions to unfairness, meanness, ingratitude, envy and the like. The revulsion itself is not significant, but it can become so in the context of fuller thought." Ibid.

15. Benedict Carey, "Study Finds Brain Injury Changes Moral Judgment," *The New York Times* (Mar. 21, 2007), online at http://www.nytimes.com/2007/03/21/health/21cnd-brain.html. For the development of empathy and rational thinking, see Michael Schulman and Eva Mekler, *Bringing Up a Moral Child: A New Approach for Teaching Your Child to Be Kind, Just, and Responsible* (Reading, MA: Addison-Wesley Publishing Company, 1985), 8.

16. Evan Thompson, *Mind in Life: Biology, Phenomenology, and the Sciences of Mind* (Cambridge, MA: The Belknap Press of Harvard University Press, 2007), 386.

17. Ibid.

18. Ibid., 401.

19. Frans de Waal, quoted in Evan Thompson, *Mind in Life,* 401.

20. Peter Singer, *Animal Liberation: A New Ethics for Our Treatment of Animals* (New York: A New York Review Book, 1975), x.

21. Online at http://www.merriam-webster.com/dictionary/reason.

22. Ibid.

23. Online at http://www.merriam-webster.com/dictionary/reasonable.

24. Online at http://www.merriam-webster.com/dictionary/rationalize.

25. Online at http://www.merriam-webster.com/dictionary/inference.

26. For a presentation of this argument see James Rachels, *The Elements of Moral Philosophy*, 50–53.

27. Aldo Leopold's land ethics and J. Baird Callicott's interpretation and articulation of this approach have been characterized as *holistic*. In the literature of contemporary moral philosophy, *ecocentric* ethics emphasizes ecosystems and ecology, whereas *biocentric* ethics is focused on individual animals.

28. In a new book, two active environmentalists argue that the environmental movement needs to be more anthropocentric, by supporting investment in alternative energy development that creates new jobs, if it is to be successful. "We are Nature and Nature is us. Nature can neither instruct our actions nor punish them. Whatever actions we choose to take or not to take in the name of the survival of the human species or human societies will be natural." Ted Nordhaus and Michael Shellenberger, *Break Through: From the Death of Environmentalism to the Politics of Possibility* (Boston: Houghton Mifflin, 2007), 142–143.

29. Some moral philosophers have tried to reconcile these conceptions. "Although these ethics are generally considered to be polar opposites, in fact, I believe, both often make use of the same moral theory, namely, preference or 'interest' utilitarianism." Roger Paden, "Two Kinds of Preservationist Ethics," in Louis P. Pojman and Paul Pojman, eds., *Environmental Ethics: Readings in Theory and Application*, fifth edition (Belmont, CA: Thomson Wadsworth, 2008), 209. See also James P. Sterba, "Environmental Justice: Reconciling Anthropocentric and Nonanthropocentric Ethics," Louis P. Pojman and Paul Pojman, eds., *Environmental Ethics*, 252.

30. See http://www.urbandictionary.com/define.php?term=different+strokes+for+different+folks.

31. Andrew Light and Holmes Rolston III, "Introduction: Ethics and Environmental Ethics," in Andrew Light and Holmes Rolston III, eds., *Environmental Ethics*, 5.

32. Chapters in part 3 offer evidence for this claim, as does Robert Traer, *Faith in Human Rights: Support in Religious Traditions for a Global Struggle* (Washington, DC: Georgetown University Press, 1991).

33. Teleological ethics refers to a "theory of morality that derives duty or moral obligation from what is good or desirable as an end to be achieved. It is opposed to deontological ethics . . . which holds that the basic standards for an action's being morally right are independent of the good or evil generated." "Teleological Ethics," *Encyclopedia Britannica*, online at http://www.britannica.com/eb/article-9071587/teleological-ethics.

34. "The Natural Law Tradition in Ethics," *Stanford Encyclopedia of Philosophy*, online at http://plato.stanford.edu/entries/natural-law-ethics.

35. "Deontological Ethics," *Stanford Encyclopedia of Philosophy*, online at http://plato.stanford.edu/entries/ethics-deontological. "In contrast to consequentialist theories, deontological theories judge the morality of choices by criteria different than the states of affairs those choices bring about. Roughly speaking, deontologists of all stripes hold that some choices cannot be justified by their effects—that no matter how morally good their consequences, some choices are morally forbidden."

36. Moral philosophers often identify social contract theory as a fourth main ethical approach. See James Rachels, *The Elements of Moral Philosophy*, 157–159. In his version of this theory John Rawls admits that "no account can be given of right conduct in regard to animals, and the rest of nature." John Rawls, *A Theory of Justice*, 512, quoted in Mary Midgely, "Duties Concerning Islands," *Encounter* 60 (1983): 36–43, reprinted in David Schmidtz and Elizabeth Willott, eds., *Environmental Ethics: What Really Matters, What Really Works* (New York: Oxford University Press, 2002), 73.

37. Mary Midgley, *Animals and Why They Matter,* 142.

38. Andrew Light and Holmes Rolston III, "Introduction: Ethics and Environmental Ethics," in Andrew Light and Holmes Rolston III, eds., *Environmental Ethics,* 3.

39. Karl Popper uses this language in his writings about scientific reasoning. For a summary of his approach, see Derek Stanesby, *Science, Reason and Religion* (London, UK: Croom Helm, 1985).

CHAPTER 2: ETHICS AND SCIENCE

1. Christopher D. Stone, "Should Trees Have Standing?—Towards Legal Rights for Natural Objects," 45 *S.Cal.L.Rev* 450 (1972), reprinted in Christopher D. Stone, *Should Trees Have Standing?—Towards Legal Rights for Natural Objects* (Los Altos, CA: William Kaufmann, 1974). The original article was cited by Justice Douglas in his dissent in *Sierra Club v. Morton,* 405 U.S. 727 (1972), a decision by the Supreme Court upholding a lower court ruling that the Sierra Club did not have legal "standing" in its lawsuit to block a decision by the Forest Service that would allow development in the Mineral King Valley in the Sierra Nevada Mountains, because the Sierra Club itself could not show that it would be adversely affected. Stone proposed that the law should allow someone to represent the interests of trees in the valley, because the trees would be adversely affected by economic development. See also Christopher D. Stone, *Earth and Other Ethics: The Case for Moral Pluralism* (New York: Harper & Row, 1987).

2. "Standing is the ability of a party to bring a lawsuit in court based upon their stake in the outcome. A party seeking to demonstrate standing must be able to show the court sufficient connection to and harm from the law or action challenged. Otherwise, the court will rule that you 'lack standing' to bring the suit and dismiss your case." "Standing Law & Definition," *USLegal,* online at http://definitions.uslegal.com/s/standing.

3. See Claire Andre and Manuel Velasquez, "Who Counts?" Markkula Center for Applied Ethics, Santa Clara University, online at http://www.scu.edu/ethics/publications/iie/v4n1/counts.html. Institutions are seen as representing the interests of persons.

4. Immanuel Kant wrote: "So far as animals are concerned we have no direct moral duties. Animals are not self-conscious and are there merely as a means to an end. That end is man." Immanuel Kant, "Duties to Animals and Spirits," in *Lectures on Ethics,* trans. Louis Infield (New York: Harper and Row, 1963), 239–242, in Tom Regan, *The Case for Animal Rights* (Berkeley, CA: University of California Press, 2004), 177.

5. Aristotle wrote: "Plants exist for the sake of animals, and brute beasts for the sake of man." See Claire Andre and Manuel Velasquez, "Who Counts?" Markkula Center for Applied Ethics, Santa Clara University, online at http://www.scu.edu/ethics/publications/iie/v4n1/counts.html.

6. "Jeremy Bentham on the Suffering of Non-human Animals," online at http://www.utilitarianism.com/jeremybentham.html. Chapter 8 quotes Bentham and considers including the assessment of animal suffering in consequential ethics.

7. By sentient he means animals able to feel pain like humans feel pain. See chapter 6.

8. Henry P. Stapp, *Mindful Universe: Quantum Mechanics and the Participating Observer* (New York: Springer, 2007), 5. "The proposition, foisted upon us by a materialism based on classical physics—that we human beings are essentially mechanical automata, with every least action and thought fixed from the birth of the universe by microscopic clockwork mechanisms—has created enormous difficulties for ethical theory. These difficulties lie like the plague on Western culture, robbing its citizens of any rational basis for self-esteem or self-respect, or esteem or respect for others. Quantum physics, joined to a natural embedding ontology, brings our human minds squarely into the dynamical workings of nature. With our physically efficacious minds now integrated into the unfolding of uncharted and yet-to-be-plumbed potentialities of an intricately interconnected whole, the responsibility that accompanies the power to decide things on the basis

of one's own thoughts, ideas, and judgments is laid upon us. This leads naturally and correctly to a concomitant elevation in the dignity of our persons and the meaningfulness of our lives. Ethical theory is thereby supplied with a rationally coherent foundation that an automaton account cannot match." Ibid., 117.

9. Sandra Blakeslee and Matthew Blakeslee, *The Body Has a Mind of Its Own,* 41. "Thus, everyday observation and many experimental studies make it clear that experience-dependent, learned internal structures filter, select, and otherwise alter our perception and evaluation of sensory inputs. Such processes are so common that they seem only natural, and the excess of input beyond processing capacity makes them necessary. Two points, however, are of current relevance. First, since these internal structures select and value sensory input that is consistent with them, they create an exaggerated sense of agreement between the internal and external worlds. Second, since internal structures shape perceptual experience to be consistent with the structures themselves, they limit further alteration of brain structure by environmental input." Bruce E. Wexler, *Brain and Culture: Neurobiology, Ideology, and Social Change* (Cambridge, MA: The MIT Press, 2006), 154–155.

10. Rita Carter, *Exploring Consciousness* (Berkeley, CA: University of California Press, 2002), 128.

11. Ibid. "Anatomists have found that in most areas of the cortex, for every fiber carrying information up the hierarchy, there are as many as ten fibers carrying processed information back down the hierarchy."

12. Robert Nadeau and Menas Kafatos, *The Non-Local Universe: The New Physics and Matters of the Mind* (New York: Oxford University Press), 175.

13. Anthony O'Hear, *Introduction to the Philosophy of Science* (Oxford: Clarendon Press, 1989), 24.

14. Henry P. Stapp, *Mindful Universe,* 8. "Science is what we know, and what we know is only what our observations tell us. It is unscientific to ask what is 'really' out there, what lies behind the observations." Jeffrey M. Schwartz, *The Mind and the Brain,* 273–274.

15. "[T]he stark division between mind and world sanctioned by classical [Newtonian] physics is not in accord with our [current] scientific worldview. When nonlocality is factored into our understanding of the relationship between parts and wholes in physics and biology, then mind, or human consciousness, must be viewed as an emergent phenomenon in a seamlessly interconnected whole called the cosmos." Robert Nadeau and Menas Kafatos, *The Non-Local Universe,* 5.

16. Erwin Schrödinger explains: "Hence this life of yours which you are living is not merely a piece of the entire existence, but is, in a certain sense, the whole; only this whole is not so constituted that it can be surveyed in one single glance." Quoted in Ken Wilber, ed., *Quantum Questions* (Boulder, CO: Shambala, 1984), 97, in Robert Nadeau and Menas Kafatos, *The Non-Local Universe,* 216.

17. "And no scientific description of the physical substrate of a thought or feeling, no matter how complete, can account for the actual experience of a thought or feeling as an emergent aspect of global brain function." Ibid., 143.

18. This is known as the *principle of complementarity.* "What is dramatically different about this new situation is that we are forced to recognize that our knowledge of the physical system cannot in principle be complete or total. Although we have in quantum mechanics complementary constructs that describe the entire situation, the experimental situation precludes simultaneous application of complementary aspects of the complete description." Robert Nadeau and Menas Kafatos, *The Non-Local Universe,* 93.

19. Evan Thompson, *Mind in Life,* 82. "Objectivism takes things for granted, without asking how they are disclosable to human experience and knowledge, or how they come to be disclosed with the meaning of significance they have. Objectivism in biology, for example, takes the organism for granted as a ready-made object out there in the world. No concern is shown for how the category 'organism' is constituted for us in scientific experience." Ibid., 164.

20. "The point here is not that the world would not exist if not for consciousness. Rather, it is that we have no grip on what reality means apart from what is disclosed to us as real, and such disclosure necessarily involves the intentional activity of consciousness." Ibid., 21.

21. Robert Nadeau and Menas Kafatos, *The Non-Local Universe,* 179.

22. This means that we should not seek "to disclose the real essence of phenomena, but only to track down as far as possible relations between the multifold aspects of our experience." Niels Bohr, quoted in Henry P. Stapp, *Mindful Universe,* 86.

23. Werner Heisenberg, quoted in Henry P. Stapp, *Mindful Universe,* 95.

24. Jeffrey M. Schwartz, *The Mind and the Brain,* 263. Henry Stapp argues: "Quantum theory rehabilitates the basic premise of moral philosophy. It entails that certain actions that a person can take are influenced by his stream of consciousness, which is not strictly controlled by any known law of nature." Quoted in Jeffrey M. Schwartz, *The Mind and the Brain,* 374.

25. Evan Thompson, *Mind in Life,* 158.

26. Moral philosophers often refer to this issue as the social construction of nature. "Weaker forms of constructivism argue that 'nature' and 'the environment' have been interpreted in a variety of different ways at different times; and that 'nature' is inescapably viewed through a cultural lens." Clare Palmer, "An Overview of Environmental Ethics," in Andrew Light and Holmes Rolston III, eds., *Environmental Ethics,* 33. In this chapter I am highlighting changes in science that reflect and shape our cultural worldview.

27. This is the philosophical implication of the scientific principle of complementarity.

28. Many biologists, however, as we see in the discussion of evolution, have yet to accept that the Newtonian view of deterministic causality does not adequately explain life and its emergent properties.

29. A scientific *theory* is our best understanding of natural events, and every theory is open to revision as human knowledge grows. Timothy H. Goldsmith, *The Biological Roots of Human Nature: Forging Links between Evolution and Behavior* (New York: Oxford University Press, 1991), 12–13.

30. Science is always an interpretation: "the fact that there is a strong international consensus among scientists that global warming is caused almost entirely by humans does not make it any less of an interpretation." Ted Nordhaus and Michael Shellenberger, *Break Through,* 142.

31. Twentieth-century biologist Theodosis Dobzhansky asserts: "Nothing in biology makes sense except in the light of evolution." Quoted in Francis S. Collins, *The Language of God: A Scientist Presents Evidence for Belief* (New York: Free Press, 2006), 141.

32. The philosopher was Herbert Spencer. Mary Midgley, *The Ethical Primate,* 6.

33. Also, the eugenics movement adopted this slogan to support human breeding to try to improve and purify the human race. See "Modern History Sourcebook: Herbert Spencer: Social Darwinism, 1857," online at http://www.fordham.edu/halsall/mod/spencer-darwin.html.

34. "Painting a new picture on the conflict side, even before the rise of ecology, biologists concluded that to portray a gladiatorial survival of the fittest was a distorted account; they prefer a model of the better adapted." Holmes Rolston III, *Environmental Ethics: Duties to and Values in the Natural World* (Philadelphia, PA: Temple University Press, 1988), 164.

35. "It seems doubtful that 'plant defenses' are that and nothing more. Plants regulate but do not eliminate the insects and animals that have coevolved with them." Ibid., 165.

36. For example, parasitic wasps lay their eggs in caterpillars, and after these eggs hatch in a caterpillar the larvae feed on it. The wasps find the caterpillars by following the scent of a chemical, which is present in the caterpillar feces but is also secreted by the plant, when caterpillars feed on it. Together, parasitic wasps and the plants that caterpillars feed on have evolved a relationship that benefits the wasps and the plants; the caterpillars, too, survive and reproduce. See Steven Rose, *Lifelines: Biology Beyond Determinism* (Oxford: Oxford University Press), 227.

37. Garrett Hardin, "Lifeboat Ethics: The Case against Helping the Poor," *Psychology Today* (Sep. 1974), online at http://www.garretthardinsociety.org/articles/art_lifeboat_ethics_case _against_helping_poor.html.

38. "Evolution is a *fact* that is now established beyond reasonable doubt. So is its main mechanism by *natural selection* acting on accidental genetic modifications *devoid of intentionality.* The findings of molecular biology can leave no doubt in this respect." Christian de Duve, *Life Evolving: Molecules, Mind, and Meaning* (Oxford: Oxford University Press, 2002), 289.

39. Steven Rose, *Lifelines,* 131.

40. Ibid.

41. Ibid., 140. For a critique of Dawkin's position, see "Genocentrism" in Evan Thompson, *Mind in Life,* 173–194.

42. Richard Dawkins, quoted in Midgley, *The Ethical Primate,* 5. Unfortunately, economic and political influences, "which shape our metaphors, constrain our analogies and provide the foundations for our theories and hypothesis-making" support "biology's currently dominant reductionist mode of thinking." Steven Rose, *Lifelines,* 70.

43. Gary Marcus, *The Birth of the Mind* (New York: Basic Books, 2004), 98.

44. Ibid., 22.

45. Ibid.

46. Ibid., 23.

47. The "language" of bees is transmitted genetically, but the dialects of some birdsongs are transmitted culturally. Timothy Goldsmith, *The Biological Roots of Human Nature,* 103–104.

48. "Each tool-using behavior recorded in Africa is limited to certain populations of chimps but has mostly continuous distribution within its range. This is just the pattern expected if the behavior had been spread culturally." Edward O. Wilson, *On Human Nature* (Cambridge, MA: Harvard University Press, 1978), 30.

49. Bijal Trivedi, "Chimps Shown Using Not Just a Tool but a 'Tool Kit,'" *National Geographic News,* online at http://news.nationalgeographic.com/news/2004/10/1006_041006_chimps.html.

50. "The basic principle is this: genetic signals play a large role in the initial structuring of the brain. The ultimate shape of the brain, however, is the outcome of an ongoing active process that occurs where lived experience meets both the inner and the outer environment." Jeffrey M. Schwartz, *The Mind and the Brain,* 117.

51. "Brain Plasticity: What Is It?" online at http://faculty.washington.edu/chudler/plast.html.

52. Timothy Goldsmith, *The Biological Roots of Human Nature,* 85. "Does the genome specify, in detail, all of the connections a developing nervous system makes within itself? A simple calculation shows that this is not possible. The human brain is estimated to contain about 10^{12} neurons and roughly 10^{15} synapses, but human chromosomes contain about 10^5 genes. Even if these estimates are off by one or two orders of magnitude, one can see that the instructions for wiring together the brain must be quite general in character. There is simply not enough information in the genetic code to specify in advance every synaptic connection, let along the finer details of neuron geometry." Ibid., 74. See also Gerald M. Edelman, *Second Nature: Brain Science and Human Knowledge* (New Haven, CT: Yale University Press, 2006), 22.

53. Ibid. "[C]ertain kinds of competence—perceptual, linguistic, social—do need to develop on schedule, or the deleterious consequences are reversed with difficulty, if at all. This is because the capacity for learning, like the development of body form, is subject to some genetic constraints."

54. The adult brain has "the power to repair damaged regions, to grow new neurons, to rezone regions that performed one task and have them assume a new task, [and] to change the circuitry that weaves neurons into the networks that allow us to remember, feel, suffer, think, imagine, and dream." Sharon Begley, *Train Your Mind, Change Your Brain,* 8.

55. Ibid., 8–9.

56. "[E]xercise increases levels of serotonin, norepinephrine, and dopamine—important neurotransmitters that traffic in thoughts and emotions." The neurons in the brain "connect to one another through 'leaves' on treelike branches, and exercise causes those branches to grow and bloom with new buds, thus enhancing brain function at a fundamental level." John J. Ratey, MD, with Eric Hagerman, *Spark: The Revolutionary New Science of Exercise and the Brain* (New York: Little, Brown, 2008), 5.

57. Jeffrey M. Schwartz, *The Mind and the Brain,* 224. For a pianist, "merely thinking about playing the piano leads to a measurable, physical change in the brain's motor cortex" and patients with depression by "thinking differently about the thoughts that threaten to send them back into the abyss of despair . . . have dialed up activity in one region of the brain and quieted it in another, reducing their risk of relapse." Sharon Begley, *Train Your Mind, Change Your Brain,* 9.

58. "This is particularly obvious in predator-prey relationships and the manner in which different predators have evolved to favor different prey and hunting strategies in a particular ecological niche. What is privileged in the struggle for survival is not competition between parts. It is complementary relationships between parts and wholes that result in emergent self-regulating properties that are greater than the sum of parts and that serve to perpetuate the existence of the whole." Robert Nadeau and Menas Kafatos, *The Non-Local Universe,* 207.

59. The phrase "mind matters" is part of the titles of chapters 8–10 in Robert Nadeau and Menas Kafatos, *The Non-Local Universe.*

60. Bill Freedman, *Environmental Ecology,* 550. This text has the subtitle "The Ecological Effects of Pollution, Disturbance, and Other Stresses." Among the topics discussed are air pollution, eutrophication of fresh water, pesticides, harvesting of forests, oil pollution, biodiversity and extinctions, and the ecological effects of warfare.

61. Writing at the beginning of the final quarter of the twentieth century, Donald Worster argues that the split between an "organic, communal ideal and a more pragmatic utilitarianism remains in doubt." Donald Worster, *Nature's Economy: The Roots of Ecology* (San Francisco, CA: Sierra Club Books, 1977), 257.

62. See Laura Westra, *An Environmental Proposal for Ethics: The Principle of Integrity* (Lanham, MD: Rowman & Littlefield, 1994).

63. "Tree Roots," *Iowa State University Extension,* online at http://www.extension.iastate.edu/Pages/tree/roots.html.

64. "Mycorrhiza," online at http://en.wikipedia.org/wiki/Mycorrhizae.

65. Harold Morowitz asserts that "all evolution is coevolution." Harold J. Morowitz, *The Emergence of Everything: How the World Became Complex* (New York: Oxford University Press, 2002), 137.

66. "Citric Acid Cycle," online at http://en.wikipedia.org/wiki/Citric_acid_cycle.

67. "Cellular Respiration," online at http://users.rcn.com/jkimball.ma.ultranet/BiologyPages/C/CellularRespiration.html.

68. "Mitochondria," online at http://en.wikipedia.org/wiki/Mitochondria. "An estimated 6 trillion reactions are taking place in each cell every second." Deepak Chopra, *The Essential Ageless Body, Timeless Mind: The Essence of the Quantum Alternative to Growing Old* (New York: Harmony Books, 2007), 18.

69. *Yahoo! Education,* online at http://education.yahoo.com/reference/dictionary/entry/ecosystem.

70. *Yahoo! Education,* online at http://education.yahoo.com/reference/encyclopedia/entry/14890;_ylt=ApQPyGKZkvGjcMfSDLN.KsZTt8wF.

71. Edward O. Wilson, *The Future of Life* (London: Abacus, 2003), 11.

72. Encyclopedia Britannica, online at http://www.britannica.com/eb/article-9117266/biosphere.

73. *Wikipedia,* online at http://en.wikipedia.org/wiki/Ecosystem.

74. Lynn Margulis, "Power to the Protoctists," in Lynn Margulis and Dorion Sagan, *Slanted Truths: Essays on Gaia, Symbiosis, and Evolution* (New York: Springer-Verlag 1997), 79.

75. Steven Rose, *Lifelines*, 2.

76. "You yourself are a rainforest of a kind. There is a good chance that tiny spiderlike mites build nests at the base of your eyelashes. Fungal spores and hyphae on your toenails await the right conditions to sprout a Lilliputian forest." Edward O. Wilson, *The Future of Life*, 20.

77. "[O]f all the organisms on Earth today, only prokaryotes (bacteria) are individuals. All other live beings ('organisms'—such as animals, plants, and fungi) are metabolically complex communities of a multitude of tightly organized beings. That is, what we generally accept as an individual animal, such as a cow, is recognizable as a collection of various numbers and kinds of autopoietic [self-organizing] entities that, functioning together, form an emergent entity—the cow." Lynn Margulis, "Big Trouble in Biology: Physiological Autopoiesis versus Mechanistic neo-Darwinism," in *Slanted Truths*, 273.

78. Nicholas Wade, "Bacteria Thrive in Inner Elbow; No Harm Done," *The New York Times* (May 23, 2008), online at http://www.nytimes.com/2008/05/23/science/23gene.html.

79. Ibid.

80. "It now appears that microbes—also called microorganisms, germs, bugs, protozoans, and bacteria, depending on the context, are not only the building blocks of life, but occupy and are indispensable to every known living structure on the Earth today." Lynn Margulis and Dorian Sagan, *Microcosmos: Four Billion Years from Our Microbial Ancestors* (New York: Simon & Schuster, 1986), 16, in Robert Nadeau and Menas Kafatos, *The Non-Local Universe*, 110.

81. Herman E. Daly and Joshua Farley, *Ecological Economics: Principles and Applications* (Washington, DC: Island Press, 2004), 431–432. "The concept of emergence essentially recognizes that an assemblage of parts in successive levels of organization in nature can result in wholes that display properties that cannot be explained in terms of the collection of parts." Robert Nadeau and Menas Kafatos, *The Non-Local Universe*, 118.

82. Also, nonlinear systems are unpredictable. In nature the flow of streams and the weather are good examples. "A system like this, in which the outcome is exquisitely dependent on the details of the initial conditions, is said to be chaotic." James Trefil, *Human Nature: A Blueprint for Managing the Earth—by People, for People* (New York: Henry Holt and Company, 2004), 180–181.

83. Robert Nadeau and Menas Kafatos. *The Non-Local Universe*, 118.

84. Robert Ayers, quoted in Charles J. Kibert, Jan Sendzimir and G. Bradley Guy, "Defining an Ecology of Construction," in Charles J. Kibert, Jan Sendzimir, and G. Bradley Guy, eds., *Construction Ecology: Nature as the Basis for Green Buildings* (New York: Spon Press, 2002), 16.

85. Ecological theories now measure the *resiliency* of ecosystems rather than their *stability*, as disturbances are understood to be natural. See Ned Hettinger and Bill Throop, "Refocusing Ecocentrism: De-emphasizing Stability and Defending Wildness," *Environmental Ethics* (Spring 1999), in Louis P. Pojman and Paul Pojman, eds., *Environmental Ethics*, 187–188.

86. Ernest Lowe, "Foreward," in Charles J. Kibert, Jan Sendzimir, and G. Bradley Guy, eds. *Construction Ecology*, xxiv. Italics added.

87. Ibid. "Even very similar organisms in the same habitat display internal adaptive behaviors that serve to sustain the whole when food and other resources are in short supply. One such adaptive behavior involves the division of the habitat into ecological niches where the presence of one species does not harm the existence of another similar species." Robert Nadeau and Menas Kafatos, *The Non-Local Universe*, 117.

88. "By 'productive,' the scientists mean the amount of plant and animal tissue created each hour or year or any other given unit of time. By 'stability' they mean one or the other or both of two things: first, how narrowly the summed abundances of all species vary through time; and second, how quickly the ecosystem recovers from fire, drought, and other stresses that perturb it. Human beings understandably wish to live in the midst of diverse, productive, and stable ecosystem." Edward O. Wilson, *The Future of Life*, 108.

89. For a more detailed description of this ecological worldview see Fritjof Capra, "The Role of Physics in the Current Change of Paradigms," in Richard F. Kitchener, ed., *The World View of*

Contemporary Physics: Does It Need a New Metaphysics? (Albany, NY: State University of New York, 1988), 163, in Robert Nadeau and Menas Kafatos, *The Non-Local Universe,* 213.

90. Karl Popper: "You cannot predict the future. The future is open." Adam J. Chmielewski and Karl R. Popper, "The Future Is Open: A Conservation with Sir Karl Popper," Ian Jarvie and Sandra Pralong, eds., *Popper's Open Society after Fifty Years: The Continuing Relevance of Karl Popper* (London: Routledge, 1999), 32.

91. Robert Nadeau and Menas Kafatos, *The Non-Local Universe,* 196–197.

92. Stuart Kaufman, *Investigations* (Oxford: Oxford University Press, 2000), 135. For example, see Julie Steenhuysen, "Thousands of New Marine Microbes Discovered," *Reuters* (Oct. 4, 2007), online at http://www.reuters.com/article/scienceNews/idUSN0441498020071004.

93. "When two species are ecologically intimate, closely influencing each other's lives as do predators and prey or hosts and parasites, each normally becomes a major source of selection operating on the other; in such situations, coevolution occurs. As a species, human beings are ecologically intimate with lots of organisms, from cows and crop pests to mackerel and malarial mosquitoes, and coevolution affects us in many ways." Paul R. Ehrlich, *Human Natures: Genes, Cultures, and the Human Prospect* (New York: Penguin Books, 2002), 61.

94. A trophic pyramid, or hierarchy, consists of the steps in a food chain within an ecosystem. "Trophic Level," *Encyclopedia Britannica,* online at http://www.britannica.com/eb/article-9073499/trophic-level.

95. Holmes Rolston III, *Environmental Ethics,* 207.

96. Ibid.

97. Robert Nadeau and Menas Kafatos, *The Non-Local Universe,* 109.

98. Holmes Rolston III, *Environmental Ethics,* 175.

99. Ibid., 174. J. Baird Callicott affirms that "the good of the biotic community is the ultimate measure of the moral value, the rightness of wrongness of actions," and that "the effect upon ecological systems is the decisive factor in the determination of the ethical quality of actions." J. Baird Callicott, "Animal Liberation: A Triangular Affair," *Environmental Ethics* 2 (1980): 320, in Eric Katz, "Is There a Place for Animals in the Moral Consideration of Nature?," Andrew Light and Holmes Rolston III, eds., *Environmental Ethics,* 86. This position is in conflict with ascribing moral consideration to individual animals, which is central to advocacy for "animal rights" or "animal liberation." Chapters 6–8 discuss the ethical arguments for these assertions.

100. Attributing moral consideration to ecosystems is seen as undermining the value of human beings, who must be valued in terms of their contribution to the natural community "since the primary goal of moral action is the good of the natural community, and since human technology and population growth create many of the threats to environmental health, an [ecocentric or biocentric] environmental ethic may demand the elimination of much of the human race and human civilization." Eric Katz, "Is There a Place for Animals in the Moral Consideration of Nature?," in Andrew Light and Holmes Rolston III, eds., *Environmental Ethics,* 87.

101. Ibid., 91. "The appropriate unit for moral concern is the fundamental unit of development and survival. Loving lions and hating jungles is misplaced affection. An ecologically informed society must love lions-in-jungles, organisms-in-ecosystems, or else fail in vision and courage." Holmes Rolston III, *Environmental Ethics,* 176.

102. Moral philosopher Paul W. Taylor argues for the intrinsic worth of nature and that all organisms, including humans, have equal intrinsic worth. "The inherent worth of an entity does not depend on its merits. To consider something as possessing inherent worth . . . is to place intrinsic value on the realization of its good." Paul W. Taylor, "The Ethics of Respect for Nature," in David Schmidtz and Elizabeth Willott, eds., *Environmental Ethics,* 91. As the good of humans includes caring for the earth in a unique way, I do not think it necessarily follows that the human "good" is the same in intrinsic worth as the "good" of every other organism. I do agree with Taylor, however, that extending moral consideration to animals does not necessarily mean granting

them rights, for accepting duties to animals is another way of giving them moral and legal consideration. See Paul W. Taylor, *Respect for Nature* (Princeton, NJ: Princeton University Press, 1986).

103. Mary Midgley, *Animals and Why They Matter,* 91.

104. "The difficulties [of developing a rights-based environmental ethic] include reconciling the *individualistic* nature of moral rights with the more *holistic* view of nature emphasized by many of the leading environmental thinkers. . . . It is difficult to see how the notion of the rights of the individual could find a home within a view that, emotive connotations to one side, might be fairly dubbed 'environmental fascism.'" Tom Regan, *The Case for Animal Rights,* 361–362. I argue in chapter 7 that rights need not be limited to the individualistic view that Regan asserts.

105. Chapter 13 considers protecting endangered species and their habitats, and chapter 5 notes how the standard of ecosystem integrity is now being applied.

106. Lynn Margulis and Dorion Sagan, *What Is Life?* (Berkeley, CA: University of California Press, 1995), 92.

107. Ibid., 90–92.

108. Evan Thompson, *Mind in Life,* 146–147.

109. This is true for all organisms, including human beings. "Every five days you get a new stomach lining. You get a new liver every two months. Your skin replaces itself every six weeks. Every year, ninety-eight percent of the atoms in your body are replaced. This nonstop chemical replacement, metabolism, is a sure sign of life." Lynn Margulis and Dorion Sagan, *What Is Life?,* quoted in Evan Thompson, *Mind in Life,* 150–151.

110. Evan Thompson, *Mind in Life,* 155.

111. "Animals maintain a valued self-identity as they cope through the world. Valuing is intrinsic to animal life." Holmes Rolston III, "Value in Nature and the Nature of Value," in Andrew Light and Holmes Rolston III, eds., *Environmental Ethics,* 145.

112. Ibid. "A plant, like any other organism, sentient or not, is a spontaneous, self-maintaining system, sustaining and reproducing itself, executing its program, making a way through the world, checking against performance by means of responsive capacities with which to measure success. Something more than physical causes, even when less than sentience, is operating; there is information superintending the causes; without it the organism would collapse into a sand heap. The information is used to preserve the plant identity."

113. Hans Jonas, quoted in Evan Thompson, *Mind in Life,* 156.

114. Carol Kaesuk Yoon, "Loyal to Its Roots," *The New York Times* (Jun. 10, 2008), online at http://www.nytimes.com/2008/06/10/science/10plant.html. For instance, if the plant known as "the sea rocket detects unrelated plants growing in the ground with it, the plant aggressively sprouts nutrient-grabbing roots. But if it detects family, it politely restrains itself."

115. Keekok Lee, "The Source and Locus of Intrinsic Value: A Reexamination," Andrew Light and Holmes Rolston IIII, eds., *Environmental Ethics,* 155.

116. Holmes Rolston III, *Environmental Ethics,* 173. "The survival of the fittest shapes the ever more fit in their habitats. Each is for itself, but none is by itself; each is tested for optimal compliance in an intricately disciplined community. Every organism is an opportunist in the system but without opportunity except in the ongoing system." Ibid., 219.

117. Ibid., 167. Eugene Hargrove argues that such ecocentric arguments depreciate anthropocentric reasoning that ascribes value to nature for its beauty. Eugene Hargrove, "Weak Anthropocentric Intrinsic Value," in Andrew Light and Holmes Rolston IIII, eds., *Environmental Ethics,* 181. Christopher D. Stone seems to differ with Hargrove: "A respect for nature may engender a preference for natural processes: for example, the natural flow of a river. Untouchedness strikes me . . . as a plausible good, and so does beauty." Christopher D. Stone, *Earth and Other Ethics,* 96.

118. "A sentient valuer is not necessary for value. Another way is for there to be a value-generating system able to generate value." Holmes Rolston III, "Value in Nature and the Nature of Value," in Andrew Light and Holmes Rolston III, eds., *Environmental Ethics,* 152.

119. "From ecology to ethics: the step is inevitable. . . . [W]e live on a planet where the activities of one species have an impact on all processes of the biosphere. . . . The old injunction against scientists uttering moral assertions, based on the notion that nature is devoid of intrinsic value or purpose, is misguided. Ecologists cannot, and ought not, refrain from making moral judgments." From the "Afterword," in David R. Keller and Frank B. Golley, eds., *The Philosophy of Ecology: From Science to Synthesis* (Athens, GA: The University of Georgia Press, 2000), 320.

120. The fallacy was first identified by David Hume in the eighteenth century and then described by G. E. Moore in his book *Principia Ethics* (1903). "Naturalistic Fallacy," International Society for Complexity, Information, and Design, *ISCID Encyclopedia of Science and Philosophy,* online at http://www.iscid.org/encyclopedia/Naturalistic_Fallacy.

121. Holmes Rolston III, *Environmental Ethics,* 232. "We commit the subjectivist fallacy if we think all values lie in subjective experience, and, worse still, the anthropocentrist fallacy if we think all values lie in human options and preferences." Holmes Rolston III, "Value in Nature and the Nature of Value," in Andrew Light and Holmes Rolston III, eds., *Environmental Ethics,* 146.

CHAPTER 3: ETHICS AND ECONOMICS

1. Herman E. Daly and Joshua Farley, *Ecological Economics,* 396.

2. Jim MacNeill quoted in Norman Myers and Jennifer Kent, *Perverse Subsidies: How Tax Dollars Can Undercut the Environment and the Economy* (Washington, DC: Island Press, 2001), 26.

3. John B. Cobb, Jr. believes "the basic principles that govern the global economy today inherently lead to increasing injustice and unsustainability. Policies based on these principles concentrate wealth in fewer hands, leaving the poor more destitute. They transfer wealth from poorer to richer countries. And they speed the destruction of natural resources, especially in the poorer countries." John B. Cobb, Jr., "Toward a Just and Sustainable Economic Order," in Andrew Light and Holmes Rolston III, eds., *Environmental Ethics,* 359.

4. The full title is *An Inquiry into the Nature and Causes of the Wealth of Nations.*

5. Adam Smith, *The Wealth of Nations,* online at http://en.wikipedia.org/wiki/Adam_Smith.

6. Ibid. Italics added. Smith believed the "invisible hand" would bring about "a distribution of the necessaries of life that is 'nearly the same' as it would have been if the world had been divided up equally among all its inhabitants." Peter Singer, *One World: The Ethics of Globalization* (New Haven, CT: Yale University Press, 2002), 30.

7. Robert Nadeau and Menas Kafatos, *The Non-Local Universe,* 199. Smith thought that "forces external to the individual units function as an invisible hand . . . [that] frees the units to pursue their best interests, moves the economy forward, and in general legislates the behavior of parts in the best interests of the whole."

8. Ibid., 207.

9. Ted Nordhaus and Michael Shellenberger, *Break Through,* 234.

10. Interface Incorporated, "Why Is Striving for Sustainability So Important"?, online at http://www.interfaceinc.com/goals/sustainability_overview.html. Italics added.

11. The statement is reprinted in *Renewable Resource Journal* (Summer 2001): 169, in James Gustave Speth, *Red Sky at Morning,* 17. Italics added.

12. Ibid.

13. Most "recycling" is actually better identified as "downcycling," because it "reduces the quality of a material over time" and may even "increase contamination of the biosphere." For recycling to be effective products must be designed to be reused, which is generally not the case today. William McDonough and Michael Braungart, *Cradle to Cradle: Remaking the Way We Make Things* (New York: North Point Press, 2002), 56–57.

14. "Since industry is the sector of the economy capable of continuing growth, growth-oriented policies emphasize the export of whatever is available in order to bring in the capital needed for industrialization. In many countries the available resource most desired by the global market is lum-

ber. Accordingly, the earth as a whole is being rapidly deforested." John B. Cobb, Jr., "Toward a Just and Sustainable Economic Order," in Andrew Light and Holmes Rolston III, eds., *Environmental Ethics,* 362. See also Juliet Eilperin, "Study Suggests Sharing the Catch Could Save Fisheries," *The Washington Post* (Sep. 22, 2008), A07, online at http://www.washingtonpost.com/wp-dyn/content/article/2008/09/21/AR2008092102417.html.

15. An externality is defined formally as: "An unintended and uncompensated loss or gain in the welfare of one party resulting from an activity by another party." Herman E. Daly and Joshua Farley, *Ecological Economics,* 433.

16. John B. Cobb, Jr., "Toward a Just and Sustainable Economic Order," in Andrew Light and Holmes Rolston III, eds., *Environmental Ethics,* 361.

17. Stock-flow resources are: "Resources materially transformed into what they produce (material cause); can be used at virtually any rate desired (subject to the availability of fund-service resources required for their transformation); their productivity is measured by the number of physical units of the product into which they are transformed; can be stock-piled; are used up, rather than worn out." For example, trees are a stock-flow resource, when logged for timber. Herman E. Daly and Joshua Farley, *Ecological Economics,* 440.

18. Fund-service resources are: "Resources not materially transformed into what they produce (efficient cause); which can only be used at a given rate, and their productivity is measured as output per unit of time; cannot be stockpiled; and are worn out, rather than used up." Forests provide many fund-service resources such as releasing oxygen into the atmospheres, providing habitats for other animals, and preventing soil from being eroded by rainfall. Herman E. Daly and Joshua Farley, *Ecological Economics,* 433.

19. I agree with William McDonough and Michael Braungart that it is best not to call ecological benefits "fund-service resources," as it is misleading to think of these natural processes as "services" for human beings. William McDonough and Michael Braungart, *Cradle to Cradle,* 80.

20. The assumption is flawed because it continues to reflect an uncritical faith in the "invisible hand" of an unregulated marketplace. John B. Cobb, Jr., "Toward a Just and Sustainable Economic Order," in Andrew Light and Holmes Rolston III, eds., *Environmental Ethics,* 359–360.

21. J. R. McNeill, *Something New Under the Sun,* 334–336, in Herman E. Daly and Joshua Farley, *Ecological Economics,* xx.

22. Ibid.

23. Benjamin Barber, "A Failure of Democracy, Not Capitalism," *The New York Times* (Jul. 29, 2002), A23, in James Gustave Speth, *Red Sky at Morning,* 111.

24. "Since the 1960s the environmental movement has changed the world. It is arguably one of the most successful social movements in human history." Louis P. Pojman and Paul Pojman, eds., "Introduction," *Environmental Ethics,* 2.

25. Benjamin Barber, "A Failure of Democracy, Not Capitalism," *The New York Times* (Jul. 29, 2002), A23, in James Gustave Speth, *Red Sky at Morning,* 111.

26. Edward O. Wilson, *The Future of Life,* 150.

27. The International Forum on Globalization (IFG), online at http://www.ifg.org/about.htm. For more information see the United Nations Development Programme's *1999 Human Development Report,* online at http://hdr.undp.org/en/reports/global/hdr1999. In contrast, Peter Singer notes various findings about inequality in the world and concludes: "No evidence that I have found enables me to form a clear view about the overall impact of economic globalization on the poor." Peter Singer, *One World,* 89.

28. Herman E. Daly and Joshua Farley, *Ecological Economics,* 262. Historically, economic growth has been good for workers. "It is the rapid economic growth since the Industrial Revolution that has created a broad middle class in the United States and that accounts for much of what is great about American society today." William Wolman and Anne Colamosca, *The Judas Economy: The Triumph of Capital and the Betrayal of Work* (Reading, MA: Addison-Wesley, 1997), 160.

29. Ibid., 395. "Between 1979 and 1989, the richest 1 percent of American households increased their income from $280,000 to $525,000 per year." Ted Nordhause and Michael Shellenberger, *Break Through,* 165. See Lisa Lambert, "Poor Get Poorer as Recession Threat Looms: Report," *Reuters* (Apr. 9, 2008), online at http://www.reuters.com/article/topNews/idUSN0838901420080409.

30. Editorial, "Is Trade the Problem?" *The New York Times* (Apr. 27, 2008), online at http://www.nytimes.com/2008/04/27/opinion/27sun1.html. "Outrageous executive pay and excesses in financial markets also play a big part. The richest 1 percent of the population has captured more than half of the nation's total income growth since 1993."

31. In his critique of current economic policies, John C. Bogle, founder of Vanguard Mutual Fund, quotes favorably the comment by John Maynard Keynes: "When the capital development of a country becomes the by-product of the activities of a casino, the job is likely to be ill-done." John C. Bogle, *The Battle for the Soul of Capitalism* (New Haven, CT: Yale University Press, 2005), xvii.

32. See Susan Tompor, "Speculation Drives Oil Prices, Not Demand," *Detroit Free Press* (Mar. 23, 2008), online at http://www.freep.com/apps/pbcs.dll/article?AID=/20080323/COL07/803230648/1002/BUSINESS, and David Cho, "Investors' Growing Appetite for Oil Evades Market Limits: Trading Loophole for Wall Street Speculators Is Driving Up Prices, Critics Say," *The Washington Post* (Jun. 6, 2008), A01, online at http://www.washingtonpost.com/wp-dyn/content/article/2008/06/05/AR2008060504322.html. Other economists, however, emphasize rising oil consumption and supply constraints. See Paul Krugman, "Running Out of Planet to Exploit," *The New York Times* (Apr. 21, 2008), online at http://www.nytimes.com/2008/04/21/opinion/21krugman.html.

33. Gary Burtless, economist at the Brookings Institution, quoted in Jenny Anderson, "Wall Street Winners Get Billion-Dollar Paydays," *The New York Times* (Apr. 16, 2008), online at http://www.nytimes.com/2008/04/16/business/16wall.html.

34. William H. Gross, chief investment officer of the Pimco bond fund. Ibid.

35. Robert J. Samuelson, "Trickle-Up Economics?" *Newsweek* (Oct. 2, 2006), 40.

36. See the "Social Contract Theory," *The Internet Encyclopedia of Philosophy,* online at http://www.iep.utm.edu/s/soc-cont.htm.

37. See chapter 4.

38. See, for instance, Jeffrey R. Gates, *Democracy at Risk: Rescuing Main Street from Wall Street—A Populist Visit for the 21st Century* (New York: Perseus Books, 2000).

39. Economist Paul Krugman has observed that: "If there were an Economist's Creed it would surely contain the affirmations 'I believe in the Principle of Comparative Advantage,' and 'I believe in free trade.'" Paul Krugman, "Is Free Trade Passé?" *Journal of Economic Perspectives* 1, no. 2 (1987): 131.

40. Steven M. Suranovic, "The Theory of Comparative Advantage—Overview," *International Trade Theory and Policy,* online at http://internationalecon.com/Trade/Tch40/T40-0.php.

41. Herman E. Daly and Joshua Farley, *Ecological Economics,* 429. A country has comparative advantage "if it can produce the good in question more cheaply relative to other goods it produces than can its trading partners, regardless of absolute costs."

42. "Speaking the language of 'free-trade' and poverty alleviation, organizations like the WTO, the IMF, and the World Bank impose a development model which seems designed to benefit transnational corporations over workers; foreign investors over local businesses; and wealthy countries over developing nations." The International Forum on Globalization (IFG), http://www.ifg.org/about.htm.

43. Editorial, "Cleaning Up China," *The New York Times* (Sep. 24, 2007), online at http://www.nytimes.com/2007/09/24/opinion/24mon1.html.

44. "The progressive reduction of barriers to trade between the United States and Mexico during the 1980s serves as an example of the problem. As tariffs were reduced, many US companies found it more economical to relocate production across the border. One reason they could produce more cheaply there was that they did not have to spend money on expensive waste disposal.

They could dump their wastes into the Rio Grande." The costs of the cleanup are now "to be borne primarily by the taxpayers and concerned citizens of Mexico and the United States, rather than by the polluters." John B. Cobb, Jr., "Toward a Just and Sustainable Economic Order," in Andrew Light and Holmes Rolston III, eds., *Environmental Ethics*, 361–362.

45. Herman E. Daly and Joshua Farley, *Ecological Economics*, 317.

46. Ibid., 323.

47. "Nonetheless, in 1999 the US government approved the merger of the two largest international grain trading corporations, Cargill and Continental Grain . . . [even though] over 80 percent of international trade [in grain] is controlled by ten firms." Ibid., 324.

48. Dwayne Andreas, chairman of Archer Daniels Midland (ADM), quoted by Dan Carney in "Dwayne's World," *Mother Jones* (Jan. 1995), in Francis Moore Lappé and Anna Lappé, *Hope's Edge: The Next Diet for a Small Planet* (New York: Jeremy P. Tarcher/Putnam, 2002), 300.

49. Ibid., 325. See Ronald Coase, "The Nature of the Firm," *Economics* 4:16 (1937): 386–405.

50. The International Monetary Fund, online at http://www.imf.org/.

51. John Maynard Keynes, quoted in Herman E. Daly and Joshua Farley, *Ecological Economics*, 318.

52. "The WTO began life on 1 January 1995, but its trading system is half a century older. Since 1948, the General Agreement on Tariffs and Trade (GATT) had provided the rules for the system." "What Is the World Trade Organization?," The World Trade Organization, online at http://www.wto.org/english/thewto_e/whatis_e/tif_e/fact1_e.htm.

53. Editorial, "Cleaning Up China," *The New York Times* (Sep. 24, 2007), online at http://www.nytimes.com/2007/09/24/opinion/24mon1.html. "Mr. Summers later apologized, saying his words were 'sardonic counterpoint,' meant to spur new thinking about the environment and development." Summers was secretary of the Treasury during the Clinton administration and president of Harvard University from 2001 to 2006.

54. Celia W. Dugger, "World Bank Neglects African Farming, Report Says," *The New York Times* (Oct. 15, 2007), online at http://www.nytimes.com/2007/10/15/world/africa/15worldbank.html.

55. See "Trade Negotiations Cannot Solve Food Crisis Created by WTO and World Bank: Report Shows Export-Oriented Model Eroded Africa's Food Self-Sufficiency," *CommonDreams.org News Center* (Jul. 24, 2008), online at http://www.commondreams.org/news2008/0724-12.htm.

56. Herman E. Daly and Joshua Farley, *Ecological Economics*, 320.

57. Renato Ruggiero, from a speech to the United Conference on Trade and Development's (UNCTAD) Trade and Development board in October 1996, online at http://r0.unctad.org/en/special/tb4305.htm, quoted in Herman E. Daly and Joshua Farley, *Ecological Economics*, 320.

58. Even when an economic development project increases a nation's revenue, the benefits may not aid the poor. In Chad, for instance, the corrupt government has benefitted the most from World Bank investment in an oil pipeline. See Lydia Polgreen, "World Bank Ends Effort to Help Chad Ease Poverty," *The New York Times* (Sep. 10, 2008), online at http://www.nytimes.com/2008/09/11/world/africa/11chad.html.

59. Peter S. Goodman, "World Bank Reports Poverty Programs Ineffective," *The Washington Post* (Dec. 7, 2006), online at http://www.washingtonpost.com/wp-dyn/content/article/2006/12/07/AR2006120700427.html. This internal report of the World Bank verifies the criticism leveled at the World Bank "by activists who accuse it of an ideological bias toward market reforms and a callous disregard for the people bearing the brunt of such policies."

60. "This trade is 'free' in the sense that the firms engaged in it are free from interference or restriction by governments. But the people of each region are *not* free not to trade. They cannot live without importing the necessities for their livelihood, however unfavorable the terms of trade may be." This makes them vulnerable to price increases, especially for the food they need, as is happening in 2007 and 2008. So, what is the answer? "An alternative ideal is one in which relatively small regions are relatively self-sufficient economically. People of such regions can then make basic

decisions about themselves and about the rules by which they are governed. They are free to trade or not according to the terms of trade that are attractive to them. Not to trade means to deny themselves many desirable goods, but it does not threaten their healthy survival." John B. Cobb, Jr., "Toward a Just and Sustainable Economic Order," in Andrew Light and Holmes Rolston III, eds., *Environmental Ethics*, 366.

61. Herman E. Daly and Joshua Farley, *Ecological Economics*, 328.

62. Ibid. The WTO also ruled against the US Endangered Species Act, "which prohibits the import of shrimp from countries that do not mandate turtle excluder devices."

63. Peter Singer argues that the WTO does "place economic consideration ahead of concerns for other issues, such as environmental protection and animal welfare, that arise from how the product is made." He also asserts that "the WTO is undemocratic both in theory and practice, firstly because a procedure requiring unanimous consent to any change is not a form of democracy, secondly because the dispute panels and the Appellate Body are not responsible to either the majority of members or the majority of the planet's adult population, and thirdly because the organization is disproportionately influenced by the major trading powers." Singer does not conclude that the WTO has made "the rich richer and the poor poorer," but thinks that the operations of the WTO "in practice reduce the scope of national sovereignty." Peter Singer, *One World*, 90.

64. Herman E. Daly and Joshua Farley, *Ecological Economics*, 329.

65. James Gustave Speth, *Red Sky at Morning*, 145. Speth also argues that economic globalization stimulates transportation and energy development, contributes to the commodification of natural resources, and spreads invasive species resulting in greater biological homogenization.

66. Peter Steinfels, "Economics: The Invisible Hand of the Market," *The New York Times*, (Nov. 25, 2006), A11.

67. Ibid.

68. Paul Krugman, "Gore's Derangement Syndrome," *The New York Times* (Oct. 15, 2007), online at http://www.nytimes.com/2007/10/15/opinion/15krugman.html.

69. "The solution to such conflicts between self-interest and the common good is to provide individuals with an incentive to do the right thing." Ibid.

70. Chapter 10 discusses the concept of sustainability.

71. This follows, if we extend the reasoning of the Golden Rule to future generations. See chapter 4.

72. John C. Bogle, founder of the Vanguard Mutual Fund, condemns the "shocking misuse of our world's natural resources, as if they were ours to waste rather than ours to preserve as a social trust for future generations." John C. Bogle, *The Battle for the Soul of Capitalism*, xvi.

73. The loss of natural capital may be captured by severance and waste disposal fees on producers, and these funds should be dedicated to seeking substitute resources and more efficient ways of absorbing and recycling waste. Natural capital is: "Stocks or funds provided by nature (biotic or abiotic) that yield a valuable flow into the future of either natural resources or natural services." Herman E. Daly and Joshua Farley, *Ecological Economics*, 437.

74. Herman E. Daly and Joshua Farley, *Ecological Economics*, 333.

75. The International Forum on Globalization (IFG), online at http://www.ifg.org/about.htm.

76. "Recognizing the social and ecological value of [such] a resource leads to its equitable and sustainable use. In contrast, assessing [such] a resource only in terms of market price creates patterns of nonsustainable and inequitable use." Vandana Shiva, *Water Wars: Privatization, Pollution, and Profit* (Cambridge, MA: South End Press, 2002), 6.

77. "Since much of the unsustainability of the present economy stems from the appropriation of the resources of the poor countries by the richer ones, the ending of the present global economic system would counter this." John B. Cobb, Jr., "Toward a Just and Sustainable Economic Order," in Andrew Light and Holmes Rolston III, eds., *Environmental Ethics*, 367.

78. Herman E. Daly and Joshua Farley, *Ecological Economics*, 363. The idea of dealing with problems at the lowest level of decision-making that can solve them is called the *principle of subsidiarity*. The European Union has adopted this principle for implementing policy decisions. See Peter Singer, *One World*, 199–200.

79. For a brief account of the fair trade movement, see Robert Traer and Harlan Stelmach, *Doing Ethics in a Diverse World*, 254–256. Also see http://www.globalexchange.org and Sharon Cullars, "Fair Trade: Spreading the Wealth," *OneWorld.net* (May 27, 2008), online at http://us.oneworld.net/article/view/160684/1.

80. Treaties, such as NAFTA, should be evaluated using these criteria. Trade is on balance beneficial, if it is fair and subject to political constraints that protect the natural environment.

81. John B. Cobb, Jr., "Toward a Just and Sustainable Economic Order," in Andrew Light and Holmes Rolston III, eds., *Environmental Ethics*, 367.

82. Anthony J. McMichael, Colin D. Butler, and Carl Folke, "New Visions for Addressing Sustainability," in Donald Kennedy, ed., *Science Magazine's State of the Planet: 2006–2007* (Washington, DC: Island Press, 2006), 164.

83. Herman E. Daly and Joshua Farley, *Ecological Economics*, 55. For example, "[T]he state of Kerala in India shows that many social needs can be met without significant economic growth. The per capita income of Kerala is about the same as that for India as a whole. But, with regard to infant mortality and life expectancy, it ranks well in comparison with highly industrialized nations. At the same time it has greatly reduced its rate of population growth without resorting to authoritarian measures. It has achieved this by educating its people, and especially its women, about health and population issues, providing inexpensive care to all, and meeting other basic needs." John B. Cobb, Jr., "Toward a Just and Sustainable Economic Order," in Andrew Light and Holmes Rolston III, eds., *Environmental Ethics*, 365.

84. John S. Mill, *Principles of Political Economy*, Book IV, Chapter VI (1848), in Herman E. Daly and Joshua Farley, *Ecological Economics*, 54, and online at http://www.econlib.org/library/Mill/mlPbl.html.

85. D. Hayes, *Repairs, Reuse, Recycling–First Steps to a Sustainable Society* (Washington, DC: The Worldwatch Institute, Paper 23, 1978), in Charles J. Kibert, Jan Sendzimir, and G. Bradley Guy, "Defining an Ecology of Construction," Charles J. Kibert, Jan Sendzimir, and G. Bradley Guy, eds., *Construction Ecology*, 16.

86. "In December 1991, the Bureau of Economic Analysis (BEA), an agency within the Department of Commerce, began to emphasize gross domestic product (GDP) over gross national product (GNP) as the most comprehensive measure of production in the US. The difference between GNP and GDP lies in the treatment of income from foreign sources. GNP measures the value of goods and services produced by US nationals, while GDP measures the value of goods and services produced within the boundaries of the US." "The Difference between GNP and GDP," online at http://www.cals.ncsu.edu/course/are012/readings/gdp&lead.html.

87. "The United States' per capita GNP registered an increase of 38 percent during the period 1980–1998, yet a decline in GPI of 25 percent." Norman Myers and Jennifer Kent, *Perverse Subsidies*, 15.

88. "Genuine Progress Indicator," Redefining Progress: The Nature of Economics, online at http://www.rprogress.org/sustainability_indicators/genuine_progress_indicator.htm.

89. "Improving and Promoting the Index of Sustainable Economic Welfare," International Institute for Sustainable Development, online at http://www.iisd.org/measure/compendium/DisplayInitiative.aspx?id=1.

90. John B. Cobb, Jr., "Toward a Just and Sustainable Economic Order," in Andrew Light and Holmes Rolston III, eds., *Environmental Ethics*, 365.

91. Robert Nadeau and Menas Kafatos, *The Non-Local Universe*, 205.

92. Ibid., 206.

93. William McDonough and Michael Braungart, *Cradle to Cradle*, 87.

94. Ibid., 90–91.

CHAPTER 4: DUTY

1. See Robert Traer and Harlan Stelmach, *Doing Ethics in a Diverse World*, chapter 4, for a more detailed presentation of the opening section of this chapter.

2. Kant's categorical imperative "is often stated in two forms: (1) Act only on that maxim [ethical presumption] through which you can at the same time will that it should become a universal law. (2) Act as to use humanity, both in your own person and in the person of every other, always at the same time as an end, never as a means." Ibid., 57.

3. "The law of cause and effect forms an integral part of Hindu philosophy. This law is termed as 'karma,' which means to 'act.' *The Concise Oxford Dictionary of Current English* defines it as the 'sum of a person's actions in one of his successive states of existence, viewed as deciding his fate for the next.' In Sanskrit karma means 'volitional action that is undertaken deliberately or knowingly.'" Subhamov Das, "What Is Karma?" Online at http://hinduism.about.com/od/basics/a/karma.htm.

4. Gandhi, *Young India* (Mar. 5, 1925), in Robert Traer, *Faith in Human Rights: Support in Religious Traditions for a Global Struggle* (Washington, DC: Georgetown University Press, 1991), 132.

5. This is the crux of the issue that distinguishes what are called anthropocentric ethical theories and biocentric (or ecocentric) ethical theories.

6. Immanuel Kant, "Duties to Animals and Spirits," in *Lectures on Ethics*, quoted in Tom Regan, *The Case for Animal Rights*, 175–176.

7. Immanuel Kant, *Critique of Judgment*, trans. W. S. Pluhar (Indianapolis, IN: Hackett Publishing Company, 1987), in Evan Thompson, *Mind in Life*, 139.

8. Ibid., 134.

9. See "Lectures on Ethics," Immanuel Kant, online at http://faculty.smu.edu/jkazez/animal%20rights/IMMANUEL%20KANT.htm.

10. For a discussion of the sanctity of life in Hindu thought, see O. P. Dwivedi, "*Satyagraha* for Conservation: A Hindu View," in J. Ronald Engel and Joan Gibb Engel, eds., *Ethics of Environment* (London: Bellhaven Press, 1990), in Louis P. Pojman and Paul Pojman, eds., *Environmental Ethics*, 310–318.

11. Quoted at "How We Treat the Animals We Eat," online at http://www.freewebs.com/foodguide/wfad.htm.

12. "The plausibility of viewing animals as having value only if or as they serve human ends lessens as we begin to recognize that, like relevantly similar humans, animals have a life of their own that fares better or worse for them, logically independently of their utility value" for humans. Tom Regan, *The Case for Animal Rights*, 178.

13. Albert Schweitzer says that Gandhi "compels Indian ethics to come to grips with reality" by making exceptions to the rule of *ahimsa:* "And through his feeling for reality, Gandhi also arrives at the admission that the commandment not to kill or injure cannot be carried out in entirety, because man cannot maintain life without committing acts of violence. So with a heavy heart he gives permission to kill dangerous snakes and allows the farmer to defend himself against the monkeys which threaten his harvest." Charles R. Joy, trans. and ed., *The Animal World of Albert Schweitzer: Jungle Insights into Reverence for Life* (Boston, MA: The Beacon Press, 1951), 155.

14. Modern science cannot disprove *karma* or belief in divine justice.

15. Paul Taylor, "Biocentric Egalitarianism," *Environmental Ethics*, 3 (Fall 1981), in Louis P. Pojman and Paul Pojman, eds., *Environmental Ethics*, 142. Once we "begin to look at other species as we look at ourselves, seeing them as beings which have a good they are striving to realize just as we have a good we are striving to realize," we develop "the disposition to view the world from the standpoint of their good as well as from the standpoint of our own good." Ibid., 152. See Paul Taylor, *Respect for Nature*.

16. Luke 6:31 in the New Testament.

17. See Robert Traer and Harlan Stelmach, *Doing Ethics in a Diverse World,* 32.

18. This reasoning also supports the social compact (or contract) theory of ethics, which chapter 3 argues is threatened by growing wealth disparity in our society.

19. Eric Katz, "Faith, God, and Nature: Judaism and Deep Ecology," in David Landis Barnhill and Roger S. Gottlieb, eds., *Deep Ecology and World Religions: New Essays on Sacred Ground* (Albany, NY: State University of New York Press, 2001), 155.

20. Ibid. The US Humane Methods of Slaughter Act (HMSA) requires that animals be stunned before slaughtering, but Jewish and Muslim rules for animal slaughter do not permit this. "Slaughter," online at http://copperwiki.org/index.php/Slaughter.

21. Ibid., 155–156.

22. Ibid. The *Sefer Hahinukh* (529) includes this comment: "in addition (to the cutting down of trees) we include the negative commandment that we should not destroy anything, such as burning or tearing clothes, or breaking a utensil—without purpose."

23. Ibid., 164.

24. Nawal Ammar, "Islam and Deep Ecology," in David Landis Barnhill and Roger S. Gottlieb, eds., *Deep Ecology and World Religions,* 196.

25. Ibid., from Nawal Ammar, "Islam, Population, and the Environment: A Textual and Juristic View," in *Population, Consumption, and the Environment: Religious and Secular Responses,* ed. Harold Coward (Albany, NY: State University of New York, 1995), 130–131.

26. Nawal Ammar, "Islam and Deep Ecology," in David Landis Barnhill and Roger S. Gottlieb, eds., *Deep Ecology and World Religions,* 196.

27. Ibid.

28. Ibid., 198.

29. Ibid., 197.

30. Mawil Y. Izzi Deen (Samarrai), "Islamic Environmental Ethics, Law, and Society," J. Ronald Engel and Joan Gibb Engel, *Ethics of Environment,* in Louis P. Pojman and Paul Pojman, eds., *Environmental Ethics,* 325.

31. Nawal Ammar, "Islam and Deep Ecology," in David Landis Barnhill and Roger S. Gottlieb, eds., *Deep Ecology and World Religions,* 203–204.

32. *The Declaration of Independence,* online at http://www.archives.gov/national-archives-experience/charters/declaration_transcript.html.

33. Ibid.

34. John Locke, *Two Treatises of Government,* ed. Peter Laslett (Cambridge: Cambridge University Press), 1960), II, 135, in Kristin Shrader-Frechette, "Locke and Limits on Land Ownership," in Lynton Keith Caldwell and Kristin Shrader-Frechette, eds., *Policy for Land: Law and Ethics* (Lanham, MD: Rowman & Littlefield, 1993), 73.

35. Ibid., paragraph 27, at 67.

36. Ibid., paragraph 31.

37. "Federal Land and Buildings Ownership," online at http://johnshadegg.house.gov/rsc/Federal Land Ownership—May 2005.pdf.

38. "Public Trust Doctrine," online at http://en.wikipedia.org/wiki/Public_trust_doctrine.

39. "US Constitution: Fifth Amendment," *Findlaw,* online at http://caselaw.lp.findlaw.com/data/constitution/amendment05/.

40. Some commentators argue that adequate environmental protection will require another amendment to the Constitution. Lynton Keith Caldwell, "Concepts of Ownership and Rights of Use," in *Policy for Land,* 85 and 98.

41. *Environmental Quality—The First Annual Report of the Council on Environmental Quality,* Washington, DC: US Government Printing Office (August 1970), xii–xiii, quoted in Lynton Keith Caldwell, "Limits to Policy: Problems of Consensus," in *Policy for Land,* 150–151.

42. Robert Traer and Harlan Stelmach, *Doing Ethics in a Diverse World,* 32.

43. Kristin Shrader-Frechette, "Practical Steps and Ethical Justifications," in *Policy for Land*, 231.

44. Ibid., 236.

45. At a public hearing held during the administration of President Carter, one speaker asked, "Future generations? What have they done for us?" See James Gustave Speth, *Red Sky at Morning*, 139.

46. "The nearer the generations are to us, the more likely it is that our conception of the good life is relevant to them." Martin Golding, "Limited Obligations to Future Generations," *The Monist* 56 (January 1972), in Louis P. Pojman and Paul Pojman, eds., *Environmental Ethics*, 363.

47. Herman E. Daly and Joshua Farley, *Ecological Economics*, 389.

48. Ibid., 390–394. Among developed nations the United States stands alone in not providing universal health care.

49. Ibid., 399.

50. Ibid., 393.

51. Ibid., 404. See B. Flomenhoft, "The Triumph of Pareto: Does Equity matter?" Unpublished working paper, presented at the US Society for Ecological Economics 2003 conference, Saratoga Springs, May 23, 2003.

52. Ronald Munson, *Intervention and Reflection: Basic Issues in Medical Ethics*, eighth edition (Belmont, CA: Thomson Wadsworth, 2008), 521–525.

53. Henry Shue, "Global Environment and International Inequality," *International Affairs* 75 (1999): 531–545, reprinted as "Poverty as an Environmental Problem" in David Schmidtz and Elizabeth Willott, eds., *Environmental Ethics*, 396.

54. "Coping with the ravages of global warming will cost $50 billion a year, and the rich nations who caused most of the pollution must pay most of the bill, aid agency Oxfam said on Tuesday." Jeremy Lovell, "Rich Must Pay Bulk of Climate Change Bill—Oxfam," *Reuters* (May 28, 2007), online at http://www.reuters.com/article/topNews/idUSL28355435200070528.

55. Peter Singer, *One World*, 33–34. Looking ahead, however, he suggests it is fair to support "equal per capita future entitlements to a share of the capacity of the atmospheric sink, tied to the current United Nations projection of population growth per country in 2050." Ibid., 43.

56. Henry Shue, "Global Environment and International Inequality," *International Affairs* 75 (1999): 531–545, reprinted as "Poverty as an Environmental Problem" in David Schmidtz and Elizabeth Willott, eds., *Environmental Ethics*, 398.

57. For an encouraging article, see "Burger King Offers Cage-Free Food," *The Washington Post* (Mar. 28, 2007), online at http://www.washingtonpost.com/wp-dyn/content/article/2007/03/28/AR2007032800118.html.

58. See http://www.yellowstone-natl-park.com/wolf.htm. Federal policy compensates ranchers for livestock killed by wolves. For support for this policy, see Ned Hettinger and Bill Throop, "Refocusing Ecocentrism: De-emphasizing Stability and Defending Wildness," in Louis P. Pojman and Paul Pojman, eds., *Environmental Ethics*, 196.

59. "The dictum that 'rights and duties are correlative' [the one implying the other] is quite misleading, because the two words keep different company, and one may be narrowed without affecting the other." Mary Midgley, "Duties Concerning Islands," *Encounter* 60 (1983): 36–43, in David Schmidtz and Elizabeth Willott, eds., *Environmental Ethics*, 77–78.

CHAPTER 5: CHARACTER

1. These three points are an edited version of four points made by Christopher D. Stone, *Earth and Other Ethics*, 191–192. Stone uses the geometrical notion of different planes to argue for a pluralist approach to ethics. He suggests "that of the several planes on which moral discourse is conducted, some are drawn to accent what is required for actions; others, for character." Ibid., 191.

2. See Robert Traer and Harlan Stelmach, *Doing Ethics in a Diverse World,* chapter 5, for a more detailed presentation of the natural law and Tao traditions.

3. Sophocles, *Antigone,* online at http://classics.mit.edu/Sophocles/antigone.html.

4. Plato, *Apology,* online at http://www.philosophypages.com/hy/2d.htm.

5. A version of Plato's *Apology,* translated by Benjamin Jowett, is online at http://classics .mit.edu/Plato/apology.html.

6. An introduction to Aristotle is online at http://www.ucmp.berkeley.edu/history/aristotle.html.

7. An introduction to Aquinas is online at http://www.philosophypages.com/ph/aqui.htm.

8. Lao Tsu, *Tao Te Ching,* a new translation by Gia-Fu Feng and Jane English (New York: Vintage Books, 1972), number 21.

9. *The Way of Life,* a new translation of the *Tao Te Ching* by R. B. Blakney (New York: Mentor, 1955), 91, number 38.

10. *The Sayings of Confucius,* translated by James R. Ware (New York: New American Library, 1955) 36, number 4:14.

11. Ibid., 47, number 6:18.

12. Lao Tze, *Tao De Ching,* numbers 43 and 8, online at http://www.chinapage.com/gnl.html. This rendition by Peter A. Merel is based on the translations by Robert G. Henricks, Lin Yutang, D.C. Lau, Ch'u Ta-Kao, Gia-Fu Feng and Jane English, Richard Wilhelm, and Aleister Crowley.

13. Ibid., number 37.

14. Ibid., number 5.

15. Lao Tsu, *Tao Te Ching,* a new translation by Gia-Fu Feng and Jane English, number 67.

16. "Cinderella," online at http://en.wikipedia.org/wiki/Cinderella. Ai-Ling Louie, *Yeh-Shen: A Cinderella Story from China* (New York: Putnam Juvenile, 1996) is beautifully illustrated by Ed Young.

17. "Cinderella," online at http://www.pitt.edu/~dash/type0510a.html#perrault. In the German Grimm brothers' versions of the story, the miracles are attributed to God and the spiritual power of Cinderella's dead mother. In the 1812 tale by the Grimm brothers, the tree that Cinderella plants over her mother's grave provides her party dress and slippers, and in the 1857 account a white bird in this tree performs the miracle.

18. Online at http://en.wikipedia.org/wiki/Johnny_Appleseed. "Johnny Appleseed: A Pioneer Hero" appeared in *Harper's New Monthly Magazine* (1871), LXIV, 833.

19. Saint Francis of Assisi (1182–1226) founded the Franciscan order in the Catholic Church, giving up a life of wealth to live among the poor. See Jack Wintz, "St. Francis of Assisi: Why He's the Patron of Ecology," *St. Anthony Messenger,* online at http://www.americancatholic.org/ Messenger/Oct2007/Feature1.asp.

20. Henry Howe, *Richland County: Howe's Historical Collections of Ohio* (New York: Dover, 1903), 485, online at http://en.wikipedia.org/wiki/Johnny_Appleseed.

21. An Indiana obituary notes that John Chapman "devoutly believed that the more he endured in this world the less he would have to suffer and the greater would be his happiness hereafter—[so] he submitted to every privation with cheerfulness." See "Obituaries," *The Fort Wayne Sentinel* 67, no. 81 (Mar. 22, 1845), online at http://en.wikipedia.org/wiki/Johnny_Appleseed.

22. Luke 10:25–37.

23. The story of the Great Commandment is in three of the New Testament gospels— Matthew 22:34–40, Mark 12:28–34, and Luke 10:25–28. The parable of the Good Samaritan is told in Luke 10:29–37, in response to a question from a lawyer: "And who is my neighbor?"

24. "NMCCB Statement on the Environment: Partnership for the Future," (Nov. 14, 1991), online at http://www.archdiocesesantafe.org/ABSheehan/Bishops/BishStatements/98.5.11.Environment .html.

25. Ibid.

26. Ibid.

27. Ibid.

28. Ibid.

29. Ibid.

30. Ibid. Some Christians have a different interpretation. Commenting on the policy in national parks of not intervening to help an animal that might otherwise die because of a natural occurrence (as when a buffalo bull falls through the ice on a river and is unable to extricate himself), radio commentator Paul Harvey argued on Christian grounds for a moral, rather than a scientific, approach. "The reason Jesus came to earth was to keep nature from taking its course." Jim Robbins, "Do Not Feed the Bears?" *Natural History* (Jan. 1984): 12, 14–16, in Christopher D. Stone, *Earth and Other Ethics,* 155–156.

31. Ibid. The full text of the canticle, which is often called the *Canticle of Brother Sun,* is online at http://www.franciscan-archive.org/patriarcha/opera/canticle.html.

32. Ibid.

33. Ibid.

34. To emphasize this moral challenge, the pastoral statement quotes these words from Pope John Paul II: "Faced with the widespread destruction of the environment, people everywhere are coming to understand that we cannot continue to use the goods of the earth as we have in the past." The Pope also confirms that, "The ecological crisis is a moral issue." Quoted from "Renewing the Earth: An Invitation to Reflection and Action on the Environment in Light of Catholic Social Teaching," *A Pastoral Statement of the US Catholic Conference* (Nov. 14, 1991), Justice, Peace and Human Development, US Conference of Catholic Bishops, online at http://www.usccb.org/sdwp/ejp/bishopsstatement.shtml.

35. John D. Carroll, "Catholicism and Deep Ecology," in David Landis Barnhill and Roger S. Gottlieb, eds., *Deep Ecology and World Religions,* 179. See *Global Climate Change: A Plea for Dialogue, Prudence, and the Common Good* (2001), online at http://www.usccb.org/sdwp/international/globalclimate.htm.

36. *Solicitudo Rei Socialis,* online at http://www.saint-mike.org/Library/Papal_Library/John_PaulII/Encyclicals/Sollicitudo_Rei_Socialis.html. See also Phillip Pullella, "Vatican Lists 'New Sins,' Including Pollution," *Reuters* (Mar. 10, 2008), online at http://www.reuters.com/article/topNews/idUSL109602320080310.

37. Ibid.

38. Ibid.

39. "Evangelicals and the Environment," *Religion & Ethics* (Jan. 13, 2006), online at http://www.pbs.org/wnet/religionandethics/week920/cover.html.

40. For example, "Progressive Christian Beliefs," online at http://progressivetheology.wordpress.com.

41. There are, of course, differences among the ethical positions taken by Protestants, as well as distinctions between the way that Protestants and Catholics do theology. For an insightful reflection on these debates, see Lisa H. Sideris, *Environmental Ethics, Ecological Theology, and Natural Selection* (New York: Columbia University Press, 2003).

42. Christine Schwartz, a shopper in a Christian bookstore in Lynchburg, Virginia. Her statement refers to the same text from the Revelation of John in the New Testament that is cited in Catholic teaching, but Catholic teaching understands this passage as referring to a renewal of life on earth, in history and in the midst of nature. Evangelical Protestants interpret this text as a prophecy of a new way of life with God, after history is over and the natural world has come to an end. "Evangelicals and the Environment," *Religion & Ethics* (Jan. 13, 2006), online at http://www.pbs.org/wnet/religionandethics/week920/cover.html.

43. In June 2008, Rev. Richard Cizik was vice president for Governmental Affairs of the National Association of Evangelicals.

44. Ibid.

45. "Evangelical Climate Initiative," online at http://www.christiansandclimate.org.

46. Ibid.

47. Ibid.

48. Lynn White, Jr., "Historical Roots of Our Ecological Crisis," *Science* 155 (1967): 1203–1207, in David Schmidtz and Elizabeth Willott, eds., *Environmental Ethics*, 14. In reply Lewis W. Moncrief wrote: "The forces of democracy, technology, urbanization, increasing individual wealth, and an aggressive attitude toward nature seem to be directly related to the environmental crisis now being confronted in the Western world. The Judeo-Christian tradition has probably influenced the character of each of these forces: However, to isolate religious tradition as a cultural component and to contend that it is the 'historical root of our ecological crisis' is a bold affirmation for which there is little historical or scientific support." Lewis W. Moncrief, "The Cultural Basis of Our Environmental Crisis," *Science* 170 (1970), in Louis P. Pojman and Paul Pojman, *Environmental Ethics*, 27.

49. See Marc Lacey, "US Churches Go 'Green' for Palm Sunday," *The New York Times* (Apr. 1, 2007), online at http://www.nytimes.com/2007/04/01/world/americas/01palm.html.

50. Movies in 2000 and 2002 and a television miniseries in 2005 renewed these stories for a new audience. "Little House on the Prairie," online at http://en.wikipedia.org/wiki/Little_House_on_the_Prairie.

51. The story of Karen Silkwood, who was contaminated by plutonium in the plant where she was working and then tried to expose this environmental danger, was made into a movie staring Meryl Streep. See Karen Silkwood, online at http://en.wikipedia.org/wiki/Karen_Silkwood.

52. Online at http://www.bobthebuilder.com/usa/all_you_need_to_know_about_the_show.htm.

53. Online at http://www.bobthebuilder.com/usa/read_with_bob_the_builder_as_he_builds_sunflower_valley.htm.

54. Watched on PBS, *Bob the Builder* (Apr. 1, 2007).

55. The subheading of a recent report on CBS News reads, "The Big-Spending Ways of the '80s Are Out as Frugality Comes into Fashion." See "Is Cheap Now Chic?" CBS News (Apr. 4, 2008), online at http://www.cbsnews.com/stories/2008/04/03/eveningnews/main3992908.shtml. However, David Brooks argues that, "The social norms and institutions that encouraged frugality and spending what you earn have been undermined." David Brooks, "The Great Seduction," *The New York Times* (Jun. 10, 2008), online at http://www.nytimes.com/2008/06/10/opinion/10brooks.html.

56. Buddhist teaching places this virtue in the context of communal living, as chapter 6 explains. "Buddhism commends frugality as a virtue in its own right." Lily de Silva, "The Buddhist Attitude Toward Nature," K. Sandell, ed., *The Buddhist Attitude Towards Nature* (Sri Lanka: Buddhist Publication Society, 1987), in Louis P. Pojman and Paul Pojman, eds., *Environmental Ethics*, 320.

57. "Johnny Appleseed," *Sing Along with Me: A Collection of Traditional Guide, Scout and Campfire Songs*, online at http://songs-with-music.freeservers.com/JohnnyAppleseed.html. The words in verse two are altered slightly to improve the English.

58. "The Ecological Footprint is an ecological resource management tool that measures how much land and water area a human population requires to produce the resources it consumes and to absorb its wastes under prevailing technology.... Today, humanity's Ecological Footprint is over 23 percent larger than what the planet can regenerate." Global Footprint Network: Advancing the Science of Sustainability, "Ecological Footprint: overview," online at http://www.footprintnetwork.org/gfn_sub.php?content=footprint_overview. Carbonfund.org calculates your carbon emissions and allows you to invest in carbon emission–reducing activities to offset your "carbon footprint." Online at http://www.carbonfund.org.

59. In the mid-1980s Christopher D. Stone asked: "what are the virtues of human character and of the earth? What makes a person or a lake 'good' or whatever else may be significant?"

Christopher D. Stone, *Earth and Other Ethics*, 199. Now the "integrity" of ecosystems is recognized in both environmental ethics and law. See chapter 6.

60. "Cinderella," *Grimms' Fairy Tales*, online at http://www.nationalgeographic.com/grimm/cinderella.html.

61. Ted Nordhaus and Michael Shellenberger, *Break Through*, 153.

62. Thomas E. Hill, Jr., "Ideals of Human Excellence and Preserving Natural Environments, Environmental Ethics 5 (1983): 211–224, in David Schmidtz and Elizabeth Willott, eds., *Environmental Ethics*, 189.

63. "A nonreligious person unable to 'thank' anyone for the beauties of nature may nevertheless feel 'grateful' in a sense; and I suspect that the person who feels no such 'gratitude' toward nature is unlikely to show proper gratitude toward people." Ibid., 197.

64. Bryan G. Norton, "The Environmentalists' Dilemma: Dollars and Sand Dollars," *Toward Unity Among Environmentalists* (New York: Oxford University Press, 1991), 3–13, in David Schmidtz and Elizabeth Willott, eds., *Environmental Ethics*, 494–500.

65. Bryan G. Norton, "Fragile Freedoms," *Toward Unity Among Environmentalists*, in David Schmidtz and Elizabeth Willott, eds., *Environmental Ethics*, 502.

66. Ibid.

67. For an alternative argument that we are more likely to value individual animals for their aesthetic value, rather than as an endangered species, see Lilly-Marlene Russow, "Why Do Species Matter?, *Environmental Ethics* 3 (1981), in Louis P. Pojman and Paul Pojman, eds., *Environmental Ethics*, 269–276. This argument was confirmed during a *Reading Rainbow* program on PBS (Apr. 24, 2008) when a young reader promoting a book on endangered species said, "We need to save endangered species, because all of the animals make our world more beautiful."

68. James Trefil acknowledges that a religious or philosophical appeal to stewardship is, for many people, "the argument that seems to carry the most weight," but adds that it is "impossible to save everything, and that means that hard choices still have to be made. It's difficult to make those choices if you have a belief that, in effect, assigns infinite value to every species on the planet." James Trefil, *Human Nature*, 123.

69. "These days, recycle, reduce and reuse is the new mantra in schools as educators, politicians and parents push for increased environmental education and ecological awareness in California classrooms." Jill Tucker, Three R's Go Green, Starting with Recycle, *San Francisco Chronicle* (Aug. 15, 2008), W-2, online at http://www.sfgate.com/cgi-bin/article.cgi?f=/c/a/2008/08/15/BAC71230JN.DTL.

70. Christopher D. Stone, *Earth and Other Ethics*, 199.

CHAPTER 6: RELATIONSHIPS

1. "Only by means of reverence for life can we establish a spiritual and humane relationship with both people and all living creatures within our reach. Only in this fashion can we avoid harming others, and, within the limits of our capacity, go to their aid whenever they need us." Albert Schweitzer, "Reverence for Life," *Civilization and Ethics*, A. Naish, trans. (London: Black, 1923), in Louis P. Pojman and Paul Pojman, eds., *Environmental Ethics*, 132.

2. Joseph R. DesJardins, *Environmental Ethics: An Introduction to Environmental Philosophy*, fourth edition (Belmont, CA: Thomson Wadsworth, 2006), 250.

3. "The other's emotion is constituted, experienced and therefore directly understood by means of an embodied simulation producing a shared body state. It is the activation of a neural mechanism shared by the observer and the observed to enable direct experiential understanding." Vittorio Gallese, "Intentional Attunement: The Mirror Neuron System and Its Role in Interpersonal Relations," *European Science Foundation: Interdisciplines*, online at http://www.interdisciplines.org/mirror/papers/1.

4. Nicholas Wade, "Scientist Finds the Beginnings of Morality in Primate Behavior," *The New York Times* (Mar. 20, 2007), online at http://www.nytimes.com/2007/03/20/science/20moral.html.

5. Ibid.

6. Ibid.

7. Ibid.

8. Ibid.

9. Ibid. See Nicholas Wade, "How Baboons Think (Yes, Think)," *The New York Times* (Oct. 9, 2007), online at http://www.nytimes.com/2007/10/09/science/09babo.html.

10. Vittorio Gallese, "Intentional Attunement: The Mirror Neuron System and Its Role in Interpersonal Relations," *European Science Foundation: Interdisciplines,* online at http://www.interdisciplines.org/mirror/papers/1.

11. Vittorio Gallese, quoted in Lea Winerman, "The Mind's Mirror," *Monitor on Psychology,* (Oct. 2005), online at http://www.apa.org/monitor/oct05/mirror.html.

12. "Those with ventromedial injuries were about twice as likely as the other participants to say they would push someone in front of the train (if that was the only option), or poison someone with AIDS who was bent on infecting others, or suffocate a baby whose crying would reveal to enemy soldiers where the subject and family and friends were hiding." Benedict Carey, "Study Finds Brain Injury Changes Moral Judgment," *The New York Times* (Mar. 21, 2007), online at http://www.nytimes.com/2007/03/21/health/21cnd-brain.html.

13. Ibid.

14. Ibid. The psychologist making this comment is Joshua Greene.

15. Virginia Held, "Feminist Transformations of Moral Theory," *Philosophy and Phenomenological Research,* 50 (1990): 344, quoted in James Rachels, *The Elements of Moral Philosophy,* 164.

16. Segun Ogungbemi, a Nigerian philosopher, asserts that in Africa this notion of an ethics of care is "traditional moral wisdom" applied to the "proper management" of natural resources. He also identifies this as "the ethics of nature-relatedness" that "leads human beings to seek to co-exist peacefully with nature and treat it with some reasonable concern for its worth, survival and sustainability." Segun Ogungbemi, "An African Perspective on the Environmental Crisis," in Louis P. Pojman and Paul Pojman, eds., *Environmental Ethics,* 336.

17. Paul Goble, *Buffalo Woman* (Scarsdale, NY: Bradbury Press, 1984).

18. In Karen J. Warren, "The Power and the Promise of Ecological Feminism," *Environmental Ethics* 12 (1990): 125–146, in David Schmidtz and Elizabeth Willott, eds., *Environmental Ethics,* 246.

19. J. Baird Callicott, who has written extensively to develop and defend Leopold's *land ethic,* looks to Native American culture as a model. "Algonquian woodland peoples, for instance, represented animals, plants, birds, waters, and minerals as other-than-human persons engaged in reciprocal, mutually beneficial socioeconomic intercourse with human beings. Tokens of payment, together with expressions of apology, were routinely offered to the beings whom it was necessary for these Indians to exploit. Care not to waste the usable parts and care in the disposal of unusable animal and plant remains were also an aspect of the respectful, albeit necessarily consumptive, Algonquian relationships with fellow members of the land community." J. Baird Callicott, "The Conceptual Foundations of the Land Ethic," *Companion to a Sand County Almanac* (Madison, WI: University of Wisconsin Press, 1987), in Louis P. Pojman and Paul Pojman, eds., *Environmental Ethics,* 184.

20. Eshin Nisimura, *Unsui: A Diary of Zen Monastic Life,* Bardwell L. Smith, ed. (Honolulu: The University Press of Hawaii, an East-West Book, 1973).

21. "Who Are the Sentient Beings?" *Buddhist Teaching of the Week,* online at http://www.geocities.com/dharmawood/sentient_beings.htm.

22. Werewolf and vampire stories are an exception, but both are very negative and threatening in contrast to most Native American stories.

23. Holmes Rolston III, "Values in and Duties to the Natural World," in *Ecology, Economics, Ethics: The Broken Circle,* ed., F. Bormann and S. Kellert (New Haven: Yale University Press, 1991), 73–96, in David Schmidtz and Elizabeth Eillott, eds., *Environmental Ethics,* 35.

24. The three most prominent are Arne Naess, Bill Devall, and George Sessions.

25. Bill Devall and George Sessions, *Deep Ecology: Living As If Nature Mattered* (Salt Lake, UT: Peregrine Smith, 1985), ix.

26. Arne Naess, "The Shallow and the Deep, Long-Range Ecological Movement," in Louis P. Pojman and Paul Pojman, eds., *Environmental Ethics,* 216. See Arne Naess, "Deep Ecology," online at http://www.mogensgallardo.com/deepeco/english/deep_ecology_arne.htm.

27. Warwick Fox, "The Intuition of Deep Ecology" (Paper presented at the Ecology and Philosophy Conference, Australian National University, September, 1983), in Bill Devall and George Sessions, "Deep Ecology," *Deep Ecology,* 65–77, in David Schmidtz and Elizabeth Willott, eds., *Environmental Ethics,* 121.

28. Bill Devall and George Sessions, "Deep Ecology," *Deep Ecology,* 65–77, in David Schmidtz and Elizabeth Willott, eds., *Environmental Ethics,* 122.

29. Richard Watson argues that the logic of species egalitarianism means letting humans be, as they are, even if this means vastly reducing biodiversity. To place a special responsibility on humans, as a species, is anthropocentric, not biocentric. "Anti-anthropocentric biocentrists suggest that other species are to be allowed to manifest themselves naturally. They are to be allowed to live out their evolutionary potential in interaction with one another. But man is different. Man is too powerful, too destructive of the environment and other species, too successful in reproducing, and so on. What a phenomenon is man! Man is so wonderfully bad that he is not to be allowed to live out his evolutionary potential in egalitarian interaction with all the other species." Richard Watson, "A Critique of Anti-Anthropocentric Ethics," *Environmental Ethics* 5 (1983), in Louis P. Pojman and Paul Pojman, eds., *Environmental Ethics,* 283.

30. Holmes Rolston III, *Environmental Ethics,* 74.

31. Bill Devall and George Sessions, "Deep Ecology," *Deep Ecology,* 65–77, in David Schmidtz and Elizabeth Willott, eds., *Environmental Ethics,* 123.

32. Ibid. For a well-known ecological argument in support of strict birth control measures, see Garrett Harding, "The Tragedy of the Commons," *Science* 162 (1968): 1243–48.

33. Ibid., 121.

34. For a discussion of Chinese ethics see chapter 5 in Robert Traer and Harlan Stelmach, *Doing Ethics in a Diverse World.*

35. B. S. Low, "Behavioral Ecology of Conservation in Traditional Societies," *Human Nature* 7, no. 4 (1996): 353–379, in Michael Shermer, *The Science of Good and Evil* (New York: Henry Holt and Company, 2004), 96.

36. Bill Devall and George Sessions, "Deep Ecology," in David Schmidtz and Elizabeth Willott, eds., *Environmental Ethics,* 122

37. Murray Bookchin, "Social Ecology Versus Deep Ecology," *Socialist Review* 88 (1988): 11–29, in David Schmidtz and Elizabeth Eillott, eds., *Environmental Ethics,* 130.

38. "Many authors have argued that, ultimately, historical and causal links between the dominations of women and nature are located in conceptual structures of domination that construct women and nature in male-biased ways." Karen J. Warren, "What is Ecofeminism?" in Michael E. Zimmerman, J. Baird Callicott, George Sessions, Karen J. Warren, and John Clark, eds., *Environmental Philosophy: From Animal Rights to Radical Ecology* (Englewood Cliffs, NJ: Prentice-Hall, 1993), 253–267, online at http://www.roebuckclasses.com/texts/modern/warrenecofeminism.htm.

39. Rosemary Radford Reuther, *New Woman/New Earth* (New York: Seabury, 1975), 204.

40. "Ecofeminism," online at http://www.thegreenfuse.org/ecofem.htm.

41. Mary Mellor, *Feminism & Ecology* (New York: New York University Press, 1997), 1, quoted online at "What Is Ecofeminism?" Women and Life on Earth, http://www.wloe.org/what-is-ecofeminism.76.0.html.

42. Greta Gaard and Lori Gruen, "Ecofeminism: Toward Global Justice and Planetary Health," in Andrew Light and Holmes Rolston III, eds., *Environmental Ethics,* 280.

43. Karen J. Warren, "The Power and the Promise of Ecological Feminism," in David Schmidtz and Elizabeth Willott, eds., *Environmental Ethics,* 244.

44. Greta Gaard and Lori Gruen, "Ecofeminism: Toward Global Justice and Planetary Health," in Andrew Light and Holmes Rolston III, eds., *Environmental Ethics,* 286.

45. Ibid.

46. "Ecofeminism," online at http://en.wikipedia.org/wiki/Ecofeminism.

47. Gita Sen, "Women, Poverty, and Population: Issues for the Concerned Environmentalist," in *Environmental Ethics,* 251, originally published in *Feminist Perspectives on Sustainable Development,* W. Harcourt, ed. (London: Zed, 1994), 216–225.

48. Vandana Shiva, *Staying Alive: Women Ecology and Development* (London, UK: Zed Books, 1989), 24, quoted online at http://en.wikipedia.org/wiki/Ecofeminism.

49. "With its emphasis on inclusivity and difference, ecofeminism provides a framework for recognizing that what counts as ecology and what counts as appropriate conduct toward both human and nonhuman environments is largely a matter of context." Karen J. Warren, "The Power and the Promise of Ecological Feminism," in David Schmidtz and Elizabeth Willott, eds., *Environmental Ethics,* 244.

50. Ibid.

51. Aldo Leopold, *A Sand County Almanac* (New York: Oxford University Press, 1949, 1968), 224–225.

52. "Most of us, I believe, are unpersuaded that all moral judgments can be referred to a single psychological state, such as happiness, or to a thinly veiled conventionalism which reduces all questions of value to what the majority favors or fancies. If so, then some other referent, some other 'goods,' are called for. It is not surprising, nor indefensible, that candidates for morally significant goods should include the living, the beautiful, the majestic, the rare, the untouched, the intricately complex, and the profoundly simple." Christopher D. Stone, *Earth and Other Ethics,* 98.

53. Holmes Rolston III, "Forward," in Laura Westra, *An Environmental Proposal for Ethics: The Principle of Integrity* (Lanham, MD: Rowman & Littlefield, 1994), xi.

54. Ibid.

55. Entering "integrity of creation" into an online search engine will produce many examples of the use of this standard by Catholic and Protestant organizations.

56. Holmes Rolston III, "Forward," in Laura Westra, *An Environmental Proposal for Ethics,* xii.

57. Ibid., xiii.

58. In 2008 the US Environmental Protection Agency delayed a report on public health problems due to contaminants in the environment of the Great Lakes. Kari Lydersen, "Delay of Report Is Blamed on Politics," *The Washington Post* (Feb. 18, 2008), online at http://www.washingtonpost.com/wp-dyn/content/article/2008/02/17/AR2008021702186.html.

59. The Great Lakes Water Quality Agreement is online at http://www.ijc.org/rel/agree/quality.html#prot. This passage is quoted in Laura Westra, *An Environmental Proposal for Ethics,* 21. She is quoting Henry Regier, et al, "Integrity and Surprise in the Great Lakes Basin Ecosystem," in *An Ecosystem Approach to the Integrity of the great Lakes in Turbulent Times,* Great Lakes Fisheries Commission Special Publications 90–4 (Ann Arbor, MI: Great Lakes Commission, 1990): 17–36.

60. Laura Westra, *An Environmental Proposal for Ethics,* 24.

61. ICSU (International Council of Scientific Unions), and TWAS (Third World Academy of Sciences, Conference Statement: International Conference on an Agenda of Science for Environment and Development into the 21st Century (Ascend 21), in Laura Westra, *An Environmental Proposal for Ethics,* 71.

62. James J. Kay, "On Complexity Theory, Exergy, and Industrial Ecology," in Charles J. Kibert, Jan Sendzimir, and G. Bradley Guy, eds., *Construction Ecology,* 83.

63. Ibid., 84.

64. The Aldo Leopold Foundation, online at http://www.aldoleopold.org/LandEthicCampaign/campaign.htm.

65. Aldo Leopold, "Thinking Like a Mountain," online at http://www.eco-action.org/dt/thinking.html.

CHAPTER 7: RIGHTS

1. For a more extensive discussion of ethics and human rights law see Robert Traer and Harlan Stelmach, *Doing Ethics in a Diverse Society*, chapter 7.

2. International human rights instruments are online at http://www.unhchr.ch/html/intlinst.htm.

3. See Robert Traer, *Faith in Human Rights: Support in Religious Traditions for a Global Struggle*. Among the religious institutions supporting international human rights law, the World Council of Churches and the Catholic Church have been especially active.

4. Generally, the US standards for civil and political rights are as high or higher than the international standards, but not always.

5. See Robert Traer, "US Ratification of the International Covenant on Economic, Social and Cultural Rights, in Charles S. McCoy, ed., *Promises to Keep: Prospects for Human Rights* (Pinole, CA: Center for Ethics and Social Policy of the Graduate Theological Union and Literary Directions, 2002), 1–47.

6. The American Convention on Human Rights, online at http://www.oas.org/juridico/english/Treaties/b-32.htm.

7. This convention also established the European Court of Human Rights, which allows a citizen of a member state of the Council of Europe to bring a human rights case against his country—a unique provision in international law.

8. "Promotion of Human Rights and Democratisation in the European Union's External Relations," online at http://ec.europa.eu/comm/external_relations/human_rights/intro/index.htm#1.

9. Charter of Fundamental Rights in the European Union, European Parliament, online at http://www.europarl.europa.eu/comparl/libe/elsj/charter/default_en.htm.

10. The right to self-determination can only be exercised by a people, and so it is different than individual and group rights. For this, and other reasons, the requirements of international law may "differ from the requirements of common morality, and constitute a special 'political' morality, or even a peculiarly 'international' one." Marshall Cohen, "Moral Skepticism and International Relations," *Philosophy and Public Affairs* 13 (1984): 299, in Christopher D. Stone, *Earth and Other Ethics*, 233–234. Cohen disagrees with this view, but Stone argues that personal morality and international morality are significantly different: "human morality is created with an eye toward human relationships and woven of human ideals, such as the attributes and possibilities of personhood. What is moral and just among nations [on the other hand] derives from conceptions of a just and fair world order."

11. *Our Common Future* (Oxford: Oxford University Press, 1987).

12. The full text of the Brundtland Report is available online at http://www.anped.org/media/brundtland-pdf.pdf.

13. The Convention on Biological Diversity was adopted in Rio and entered into force in late December 1993. The Convention adopts a "sustainable use" approach by recognizing that biological diversity benefits human life. It does, however, affirm the precautionary principle. Online at http://www.cbd.int. For a critical analysis of what is often referred to as the Convention on Biodiversity, see Niraja Gopal Jayal, "Ethics, Politics, Biodiversity: A View from the South," in Andrew Light and Avner de-Shalit, eds., *Moral and Political Reasoning in Environmental Practice* (Cambridge, MA: The MIT Press, 2003), 295–316.

14. Commission on Sustainable Development, online at http://www.un.org/esa/sustdev/csd/policy.htm. In 1986, however, the UN General Assembly passed the Declaration on the Right to Development without mentioning sustainability. The 1986 declaration merely affirms: "The right to development is an inalienable human right by virtue of which every human person and all peoples are entitled to participate in, contribute to, and enjoy economic, social, cultural and political development, in which all human rights and fundamental freedoms can be fully realized." (Article 1.1)

15. "Equitable social development that recognizes empowering the poor, particularly women living in poverty, to utilize environmental resources sustainably is a necessary foundation for sustainable development." Beijing Declaration, The Fourth World Conference on Women, paragraph 36, online at http://www.un.org/womenwatch/daw/beijing/beijingdeclaration.html.

16. "Sustainable Development," online at http://en.wikipedia.org/wiki/Sustainable_development.

17. This means, for example, that "a cutting edge treatment plant with extremely high maintenance costs may not be sustainable in regions of the world with less financial resources. An ideal plant that is shut down due to bankruptcy is obviously less sustainable than one that is maintainable by the indigenous community, even if it is somewhat less effective from an environmental standpoint." Ibid.

18. Declaration of the United Nations Conference on the Human Environment, online at http://www.unep.org/Documents.multilingual/Default.asp?DocumentID=97&ArticleID=1503.

19. "The Right to a Healthy Environment," Circle of Rights–Economic, Social and Cultural Rights Activism: A Training Resource, online at http://www1.umn.edu/humanrts/edumat/IHRIP/circle/modules/module15.htm.

20. Vienna Convention for the Protection of the Ozone Layer (1985), Principle 1, online at http://www.globelaw.com/Climate/vienna.htm.

21. Online at http://ozone.unep.org/Treaties_and_Ratification/2B_montreal_protocol.shtml.

22. Kyoto Protocol, online at http://en.wikipedia.org/wiki/Kyoto_Accord.

23. Rio Declaration on Environment and Development, online at http://www.unep.org/Documents.Multilingual/Default.asp?DocumentID=78&ArticleID=1163.

24. The FCCC, online at http://unfccc.int/essential_background/convention/background/items/1349.php.

25. "The Right to a Healthy Environment," Circle of Rights—Economic, Social and Cultural Rights Activism: A Training Resource, online at http://www1.umn.edu/humanrts/edumat/IHRIP/circle/modules/module15.htm.

26. International Instruments on the Right to a Healthy Environment, *Center for Economic and Social Rights,* online at http://cesr.org/healthyenvironment/instruments.

27. Additional Protocol to the American Convention on Human Rights in the Area of Economic, Social and Cultural Rights, "Protocol of San Salvador," (1988), online at http://www.oas.org/juridico/english/Treaties/a-52.html.

28. Adriana Fabra and Eva Arnal, "Review of jurisprudence on human rights and the environment in Latin America," *Joint UNEP-OHCHR Expert Seminar on Human Rights and the Environment* (Jan. 14–16, 2002), Geneva: Background Paper No. 6, Office of the United Nations High Commissioner for Human Rights, online at http://www.ohchr.org/english/issues/environment/environ/bp6.htm.

29. "The Right to a Healthy Environment," Circle of Rights—Economic, Social and Cultural Rights Activism: A Training Resource, online at http://www1.umn.edu/humanrts/edumat/IHRIP/circle/modules/module15.htm.

30. Article 12 of the Constitution of the Republic of South Africa, as adopted on May 8, 1996 and amended on Oct. 11, 1996 by the Constitutional Assembly, in "The Right to a Healthy Environment," Circle of Rights—Economic, Social and Cultural Rights Activism: A Training Resource, online at http://www1.umn.edu/humanrts/edumat/IHRIP/circle/modules/module15.htm.

31. Also, the South African constitution modifies the phrase "sustainable development" with the adverb "environmentally" to be clear that, in South Africa, sustainable development means economic activity that is environmentally sustainable.

32. Cleveland Amory, *Man Kind? Our Incredible War on Wildlife* (New York: Harper & Row, 1974), 231–232, in Roderick Frazier Nash, *The Rights of Nature: A History of Environmental Ethics* (Madison, WI: The University ofo Wisconsin Press), 183.

33. Roderick Frazier Nash, *The Rights of Nature,* 25.

34. Ibid. The RSPCA website is online at http://www.rspca.org.uk.

35. Ibid., 26.

36. Ibid., 30.

37. Ibid., 49.

38. Peter Singer, "The Parable of the Fox and the Unliberated Animals," *Ethics* 88, no. 2 (Jan. 1978): 122, quoted in Tom Regan, *The Case for Animal Rights,* 219.

39. Ibid.

40. Roderick Frazier Nash, *The Rights of Nature,* 3.

41. Robert Hunter, *Warriors of the Rainbow: A Chronicle of the Greenpeace Movement* (New York: Holt, Rinehart and Winston, 1979), ix–x, quoted in Roderick Frazier Nash, *The Rights of Nature,* 179–180.

42. Roderick Frazier Nash, *The Rights of Nature,* 4

43. Joel Feinberg, "The Rights of Animals," originally published as "The Rights of Animals and Unborn Generations," in William Blackstone, ed., *Philosophy and Environmental Crisis* (Athens, GA: University of Georgia Press, 1974), 43–68, in David Schmidtz and Elizabeth Willott, eds., *Environmental Ethics,* 54.

44. Ibid., 54–55. Feinberg gives two reasons for this conclusion: "(1) because a right holder must be capable of being represented and it is impossible to represent a being that has no interests, and (2) because a right holder must be capable of being a beneficiary in his own person, and a being without interests is a being that is incapable of being harmed or benefitted, having no good or 'sake' of its own. Thus, a being without interests has no 'behalf' to act in, and no 'sake' to act for."

45. Ibid., 54.

46. Carl Cohen argues that the interest argument for animal rights uses a "shared feature" that animals and humans have "to justify the moral equation of animals and humans. From that equation the absolute protection of the animals [rights] must follow." Carl Cohen and Tom Regan, *The Animal Rights Debate* (Lanham, MD: Rowman & Littlefield, 2001), 50.

47. Tom Regan, "The Case for Animal Rights," in Peter Singer, ed., *In Defense of Animals* (New York: Basil Blackwell, 1985), 19.

48. Tom Regan, *The Case for Animal Rights,* 152. "In contrast to moral agents, moral patients lack the prerequisites that would enable them to control their own behavior in ways that would make them morally accountable for what they do."

49. Tom Regan, *Defending Animal Rights* (Urbana: University of Illinois Press, 2001), 101.

50. By subjects of a life Regan means having "beliefs and desires; perception, memory, and a sense of the future, including their own future; an emotional life together with feelings of pleasure and pain; preference- and welfare-interests; the ability to initiate action in pursuit of their desires and goals; a psychophysical identity over time, and an individual welfare in the sense that their experiential life fares well or ill for them, logically independently of their utility for others and logically independently of their being the object of anyone else's interests." Tom Regan, *The Case for Animal Rights,* 240.

51. Tom Regan, *Defending Animal Rights,* 101.

52. Tom Regan, *The Case for Animal Rights,* xvi.

53. Ibid., 78.

54. Ibid., xvi. For another statement that birds have rights see Tom Regan, *Defending Animal Rights*, 17. He asserts that fish have rights in Tom Regan, *Empty Cages: Facing the Challenge of Animal Rights* (Lanham, MD: Rowman & Littlefield, 2004), 61, but also states that his focus is animals and birds as these are the least controversial cases.

55. Tom Regan, *The Case for Animal Rights*, 367.

56. "[A]ll moral agents and patients have certain basic moral rights. To say that these individuals possess basic (or unacquired) moral rights means that (1) they posses certain rights independently of anyone's voluntary acts, either their own or those of others, and independently of the position they happen to occupy in any given institutional arrangement; (2) these rights are universal—that is, they are possessed by all relevantly similar individuals, independently of those considerations mentioned in (1); and (3) all who possess these rights possess them equally." Ibid., 327.

57. Regan urges the ten million members of the animal rights movement in the US to reject reform compromises, but to support "incremental abolitionist change" that "stops the utilization of nonhuman animals for one purpose or another." Tom Regan, *Defending Animal Rights*, 40 and 148.

58. Tom Regan, "Animal Rights: What's in a Name?" in Andrew Light and Holmes Rolston III, eds., *Environmental Ethics*, 70. In an essay published in 1985 Regan asserts that the goals of the animal rights movement are the total:

- abolition of the use of animals in science,
- dissolution of commercial animal agriculture,
- elimination of commercial and sport hunting and trapping.

Tom Regan, "The Case for Animal Rights," in Peter Singer, ed., *In Defense of Animals*, 13.

59. Ibid.

60. Tom Regan, *The Case for Animal Rights*, 239–240.

61. Carl Cohen argues that Regan's argument confuses two different meanings of inherent value. "The argument for animal rights that is grounded on their 'inherent value' is utterly fallacious, an egregious example of the fallacy of equivocation—that informal fallacy in which two or more meanings of the same word of phrase are confused in the several propositions of an argument." Regan commits this fallacy by simply stating that the inherent value of humans and the inherent value of animals are the same and thus must be protected by equal rights. Carl Cohen, *The Animal Rights Debate*, 54.

62. Ibid., 362.

63. Ibid.

64. Although urging moral consideration for "trees" (note the plural) and animals, Christopher D. Stone is "skeptical" about ascribing rights to them and suggests, instead, that our "whole moral framework" needs to change. Christopher D. Stone, *Earth and Other Ethics*, 107–109.

65. "[I]t is not just because we are subjects-of-a-life that we are both able and morally compelled to recognize one another as beings with equal basic moral rights. It is also because we are able to 'listen to reason' in order to settle our conflicts and cooperate in shared projects. This capacity, unlike the others, may require something like a human language." Mary Anne Warren, "A Critique of Regan's Animal Rights Theory," in Louis P. Pojman and Paul Pojman, eds., *Environmental Ethics*, 94.

66. Tom Regan, *The Case for Animal Rights*, 219. He is quoting Peter Singer, who also writes: "There is no ethical basis for elevating membership of one particular species into a morally crucial characteristic." Peter Singer, "Ethics and the New Animal Liberation Movement," in Peter Singer, ed., *In Defense of Animals*, 6.

67. Mary Midgley, *Animals and Why They Matter*, 98, from a chapter entitled "The Significance of Species."

68. There are only about four to five thousand species of mammals, but probably one million species of insects and fifty to eighty thousand species of mollusks (including shrimp and oysters). "Classifying Animals," online at http://www.factmonster.com/ipka/A0776195.html.

69. Mary Midgley, *Animals and Why They Matter,* 104.

70. Ibid., 103.

71. Ibid., 111.

72. "The issues soon revert to what they always were, issues of right behavior by moral agents; an environmental ethicist, [for concerns] outside of culture, is better advised to dispense with the noun, *rights,* since this concept is not something that attaches to animals in the world, and to use only the adjective, *right,* which applies when moral agents encounter nature and find something there judged to be good (appropriate, valuable) before human moral agents appear." Holmes Rolston III, *Environmental Ethics,* 51.

73. Michael Ellis, "Detroit Zoo to Free Elephants on Ethical Grounds," *Planet Ark* (May 21, 2004) online at http://www.planetark.com/dailynewsstory.cfm/newsid/25192/story.htm. See "Animal Protection Groups Praise City and Residents of SF for Support of Elephants as Zoo Announces Transfer of Pachyderms to California Sanctuary," *IDA New Release* (Jun. 10, 2004), online at http://www.idausa.org/news/currentnews/sf_zoo_victory.html.

74. John C. Lilly, *The Center of the Cyclone: An Autobiography of Inner Space* (New York: Bantam, 1972) and *Lilly on Dolphins: Humans of the Sea* (Garden City, NJ: Anchor Press, 1975).

75. The act also requires institutions doing research to "ensure that any pain and distress caused by experiments be minimized, and that investigators consider any alternatives that are available to them (including non-animal alternatives). Standards regarding amount of space, feeding, bedding, exercise, and transportation are written according to species." "The Animal Welfare Act," The Humane Society of the United States, online at http://www.hsus.org/animals_in _research/general_information_on_animal_research/laws_protecting_animals_in_research/the _animal_welfare_act.html.

76. Will Dunham, "US Stops Breeding Chimps for Research," *Reuters* (May 24, 2007), online at http://www.reuters.com/article/topNews/idUSN2438996920070524.

77. "All peoples may, for their own ends, freely dispose of their natural wealth and resources without prejudice to any obligations arising out of international economic co-operation, based upon the principle of mutual benefit, and international law. In no case may a people be deprived of its own means of subsistence." The International Covenant on Civil and Political Rights, Article 1.2, online at http://www.ohchr.org/english/law/ccpr.htm. Identical language may be found in the International Covenant on Economic, Social and Cultural Rights, Article 1.2, online at http://www.unhchr.ch/html/menu3/b/a_cescr.htm.

78. This is the weakest of these standards, as it does not address the problem of economic growth. John B. Cobb, Jr., "Toward a Just and Sustainable Economic Order," in Andrew Light and Holmes Rolston III, eds., *Environmental Ethics,* 363.

CHAPTER 8: CONSEQUENCES

1. Jeremy Bentham, Introduction to *The Principles of Morals and Legislation* (New York: Oxford University Press, 1789), quoted in Barbara MacKinnon, *Ethics: Theory and Contemporary Issues,* 51.

2. John Stuart Mill, *Utilitarianism* (London, 1861), quoted in James Rachels, *The Elements of Moral Philosophy,* 92.

3. For examples see chapter 15 in Robert Traer and Harlan Stelmach, *Doing Ethics in a Diverse World.*

4. F. H. Knight, *Risk, Uncertainty, and Profit* (Boston, MA: Houghton Mifflin, 1921), quoted in Herman E. Daly and Joshua Farley, *Ecological Economics,* 95.

5. Herman E. Daly and Joshua Farley, *Ecological Economics,* 95.

6. These forms of utilitarianism are illustrated in chapter 8 of Robert Traer and Harlan Stelmach, *Doing Ethics in a Diverse World.*

7. Jeremy Bentham, introduction to *The Principles of Morals and Legislation,* chapter 17, section 1, note, quoted in James Rachels, *The Elements of Moral Philosophy,* 122–123.

8. Peter Singer, *Animal Liberation,* vii.

9. Ibid., xiii, 8–9.

10. Quoted online at http://www.animalsuffering.com/animalrights.html. Chapter 6 considers the ethical theory known as "deep ecology."

11. For an example of changing practice, see Andrew Martin, "Burger King Shifts Policy on Animals," *The New York Times* (Mar. 28, 2007), online at http://www.nytimes.com/2007/03/28/business/28burger.html.

12. Peter Singer, *Writings on an Ethical Life* (New York: HarperCollins, 2000), 70.

13. Peter Singer, *Animal Liberation,* 98. "In short, animal husbandry has been turned into animal abuse." Editorial, "The Worst Way of Farming," *The New York Times* (May 31, 2008), online at http://www.nytimes.com/2008/05/31/opinion/31sat4.html.

14. Peter Singer, *Writings on an Ethical Life,* 70

15. Ibid.

16. "FDA's Approval of Cloned Beef for Human Consumption Ignites Debate," *News Hour,* PBS (May 27, 2008), online at http://www.pbs.org/newshour/bb/science/jan-june08/clonecows_05-27.html.

17. Peter Singer, *Animal Liberation,* 96.

18. Ibid., 171–174, online at http://www.wesleyan.edu/wsa/warn/singer_fish.htm. Research on fish has confirmed that they feel pain. Lynne Sneddon, V. A. Braithwaite, and M. J. Gentle, "Do Fish Have Nociceptors? Evidence for the Evolution of a Vertebrate Sensory System," *Proceedings of the Royal Society* 270, no. 1520 (2003): 1115–1121, in Peter Singer and Jim Mason, *The Way We Eat: Why Our Food Choices Matter* (Emmaus, PA: Rodale, 2006), 130–131.

19. Mary Midgley, *Animals and Why They Matter,* 92.

20. Ibid.

21. Ibid., 96.

22. Ibid., 94–95.

23. Peter Singer, "Ethics and the New Animal Liberation Movement," Peter Singer, ed., *In Defense of Animals,* 6.

24. Mary Midgley, *Animals and Why They Matter,* 96.

25. Ibid., 142.

26. Steve F. Sapontzis, "Predation," *Ethics and Animals* 5, no. 2 (Jun. 1984): 36, quoted in Holmes Rolston III, *Environmental Ethics,* 56.

27. Peter Singer, *Animal Liberation,* 252.

28. Ibid.

29. Italics added. "In the trophic pyramid the omnivores and carnivores regularly and necessarily capture values by imposing pain on others." Holmes Rolston III, *Environmental Ethics,* 57.

30. "The maximum happiness of particular sentient animals is not what ecosystems are all about, though ecosystems select well-adapted member species, which they support with a generally satisfactory life." Ibid.

31. "That context is as natural as it is cultural; it is a hybrid of the two. The animals do not, in their sentient life, participate in human culture; on the other hand, they are not in the wild but domesticated. Judgments about duties are not merely to sentience but to sentience in niche in ecosystem, now overtaken by culture." Ibid., 61.

32. Ibid.

33. Ibid., 62. For a contrary argument that earthworms have a right to life, see Nick Jackson, "We Don't Need to Kill Animals for Meat," *The Independent* (Nov. 23, 2006), online at http://www.wormdigest.org/content/view/329/2.

34. "In 1992 a pair of economic botanists, Michael Balick and Robert Mendelsohn, demonstrated that single harvests of wild-grown medicinals from two tropical forest plots in Belize were worth $726 and $3,327 per hectare [2.5 acres] respectively, with labor costs thrown in. By comparison, other researchers estimated per-hectare yield from tropical forest converted to farmland at $228 in nearby Guatemala and $339 in Brazil." Edward O. Wilson, *The Future of Life*, 126.

35. David Schmidtz, "A Place for Cost-Benefit Analysis," *Philosophical Issues* 11 (2001): 148–71, in David Schmidtz and Elizabeth Willott, eds., *Environmental Ethics*, 480.

36. Ibid. "Throughout the 1970s, the Council on Wage and Price Stability and the Office of Management and Budget pressured the Environmental Protection Agency to pay more attention to the costs of complying with standards the EPA was trying to impose on industry."

37. Peter S. Wenz, "Just Garbage: The Problem of Environmental Racism," in Laura Westra and Peter S. Wentz, eds., *Faces of Environmental Racism* (Lantham, MD: Rowman & Littlefield, 1995), in Louis P. Pojman and Paul Pojman, eds., *Environmental Ethics*, 673.

38. David Schmidtz, "A Place for Cost-Benefit Analysis," *Philosophical Issues* 11 (2001): 148–71, in David Schmidtz and Elizabeth Willott, eds., *Environmental Ethics*, 485–486.

39. Ibid.

40. Herman B. Leonard and Richard J. Zeckhauser, "Cost-Benefit Analysis Defended," Report from the *Institute for Philosophy and Public Policy* 3, no. 3 (Summer 1983), in David Schmidtz and Elizabeth Willott, eds., *Environmental Ethics*, 464.

41. Italics added. David Schmidtz, "A Place for Cost-Benefit Analysis," *Philosophical Issues* 11 (2001): 148–71, in David Schmidtz and Elizabeth Willott, eds., *Environmental Ethics*, 487.

42. Ibid., 489.

43. "Long-Term Discounting," online at http://www.economics.ox.ac.uk/members/cameron.hepburn/longrundiscounting.pdf.

44. Herman E. Daly and Joshua Farley, *Environmental Economics*, 181.

45. David Schmidtz, "A Place for Cost-Benefit Analysis," *Philosophical Issues* 11 (2001): 148–171, in David Schmidtz and Elizabeth Willott, eds., *Environmental Ethics*, 489.

46. Peter Singer, *Writings on an Ethical Life*, 71.

47. Ibid., 52.

48. Ibid.

49. Ibid.

50. Christopher D. Stone, *Earth and Other Ethics*, 118.

51. Ibid., 168–169.

52. Chapter 2 offers evidence to support this conclusion.

53. "Global Warming," *The New York Times* (Feb. 2, 2007), online at http://topics.nytimes.com/top/news/science/topics/globalwarming/index.html.

54. Amory Lovins, "Technology Is the Answer (But What Was the Question?)" published as a guest essay in G. Tyler Miller, *Environmental Science*, third edition (Belmont, CA: Wadsworth, 1991), 56–57, quoted in Joseph DesJardins, *Environmental Ethics*, 10.

55. Amory Lovins develops this point in "Technology Is the Answer (But What Was the Question?)" cited above. DesJardins provides a helpful discussion of "science and ethics." Joseph DesJardins, *Environmental Ethics*, 9–12.

56. Shaila Dewan, "Feeling Warmth, Subtropical Plants Move North," *The New York Times* (May 3, 2007), online at http://www.nytimes.com/2007/05/03/science/03flowers.html.

57. Ibid.

58. Ibid.

59. Steven Rose, *Lifelines*, 70.

60. Matthew Fox and Rupert Sheldrake, *Natural Grace: Dialogues on Creation, Darkness, and the Soul in Spirituality and Science* (New York: Doubleday, 1996).

61. Caitlin G. Johnson, "Toxic Government Report Uncovered," *OneWorld.net* (Feb. 8, 2008), online at http://us.oneworld.net/article/view/157621/1.

62. Ross Gelbspan, *Boiling Point: How Politicians, Big Oil and Coal, Journalists, and Activists Have Fueled the Climate Crisis—and What We Can Do to Avert Disaster* (New York: Basic Books, 2004), 42. In 2008, "An internal investigation by NASA's inspector general concluded that political appointees in the agency's public affairs office had tried to restrict reporters' access to its leading climate scientist, Dr. James Hansen. He has warned about climate change for twenty years and has openly criticized the administration's refusal to tackle the issue head-on. More broadly, the investigation said that politics played a heavy role in the office and that it had presented information about global warming 'in a manner that reduced, marginalized or mischaracterized climate-change science made available to the general public.'" Editorial, "The Science of Denial," *The New York Times* (Jun. 4, 2008), online at http://www.nytimes.com/2008/06/04/opinion/04wed2.html.

63. Scientists claim that political appointees have been altering their reports recommending "critical habitat" preservation, in order "to favor industries whose interests conflict with the findings" of the reports. Elizabeth Williamson, "Scientists Take Complaints about Interference to Hill," *The Washington Post* (Jan 16, 2008), A13, online at http://www.washingtonpost.com/wp-dyn/content/article/2008/01/15/AR2008011503428.html.

64. "By 2001, ExxonMobil had replaced the coal industry as the major funder of the most prominent and visible 'greenhouse skeptics.' By 2003, ExxonMobil was giving more than $1 million a year to an array of ideological, right-wing organizations opposing action on climate change . . . [in] its effort to sabotage the unprecedented scientific consensus of the IPCC. . . ." Ross Gelbspan, *Boiling Point*, 51, 54.

65. Gillian Wong, "Gore: Polluters Manipulate Climate Information," *The San Francisco Chronicle* (Aug. 7, 2007), online at http://sfgate.com/cgi-bin/article.cgi?f=/n/a/2007/08/07/international/i021136D10.DTL. After the UN Intergovernmental Panel on Climate Change "warned that the cause of global warming is 'very likely' man-made, 'the deniers offered a bounty of $10,000 for each article disputing the consensus that people could crank out and get published somewhere,' Gore said."

CHAPTER 9: ECOLOGICAL LIVING

1. A recent study "estimated that the human population exceeded Earth's sustainable capacity around the year 1978. By 2000 it had overshot by 1.4 times that capacity. If 12 percent of land were now to be set aside in order to protect the natural environment, as recommended in the 1987 Brundtland Report, Earth's sustainable capacity will have been exceeded still earlier, around 1972. In short, Earth has lost its ability to regenerate—unless global consumption is reduced, or global production is increased, or both." Edward O. Wilson, *The Future of Life*, 27.

2. "We cannot survive as a species if greed is privileged and protected and the economics of the greedy set the rules for how we live and die." Vandana Shiva, *Water Wars*, xv.

3. Consider fish. Demand is reducing the supply. Ed Stoddard, "Eating Fish: Good for Health, Bad for Environment?" *Reuters* (Aug. 10, 2007), online at http://www.reuters.com/article/environmentNews/idUSN0926310820070810, "Until All the Fish Are Gone," *The New York Times* (Jan. 21, 2008), online at http://www.nytimes.com/2008/01/21/opinion/21mon1.html, and Jane Kay, "Salmon Arriving in Record Low Numbers," *San Francisco Chronicle* (Jan 30, 2008), A-1, online at http://sfgate.com/cgi-bin/article.cgi?f=/c/a/2008/01/30/MNRIUOE8C.DTL. Tuna is often contaminated. Marian Burros, "High Levels of Mercury Are Found in Tuna Sushi," *The New York Times* (Jan. 23, 2008), online at http://www.nytimes.com/2008/01/23/dining/23sushi.html. Intensive fish farming threatens wild populations. Juliet Eilperin and Marc Kaufman, "Salmon Farming May Doom Wild Populations, Study Says," *The Washington Post* (Dec. 17, 2007), online at http://www.washingtonpost.com/wp-dyn/content/article/2007/12/13/AR2007121301190.html.

4. Rights are constrained by reality. "If soil erosion and withdrawal of groundwater continue at their present rates until the world population reaches (and hopefully peaks) at 9 to 10 billion,

shortages of food seem inevitable. There are two ways to stop short of the wall. Either the industrialized populations move down the food chain to a more vegetarian diet, or the agricultural yield of productive land worldwide is increased by more than 50 percent." Such an increase is unlikely, as the "constraints of the biosphere are fixed." Edward O. Wilson, *The Future of Life*, 33.

5. A critical perspective on this change sees it as "a capitalist version of the much-older imperialist exploitation of the weak by the strong." Tom Athanasiou, *Divided Planet: The Ecology of Rich and Poor* (Toronto: Little, Brown, 1996), 53–54, citing Paul Bairoch in Robert Heilbroner, *Twenty-First Century Capitalism* (New York: Norton, 1993), 55–56, in Don Mayer, "Institutionalize Overconsumption," Laura Westra and Patricia H. Werhane, eds., *The Business of Consumption: Environmental Ethics and the Global Economy* (Lanham, MD: Rowman & Littlefield, 1998), 69.

6. "The average rates at which people consume resources like oil and metals, and produce wastes like plastics and greenhouse gases, are about 32 times higher in North America, Western Europe, Japan and Australia than they are in the developing world." Jared Diamond, "What's Your Consumption Factor?" *The New York Times* (Jan. 2, 2008), online at http://www.nytimes.com/2008/01/02/opinion/02diamond.html. "If everyone in the world had the same consumption rates as in the United States it would take 5.3 planet earths to support them. . . . [The figure is] 3.1 for France and Britain, 3.0 for Spain, 2.5 for Germany and 2.4 for Japan. But if everyone emulated China, which is building a coal-fired power station every five days to feed its booming economy, it would take only 0.9 of a planet." Jeremy Lovell, "World Moves into Ecological Red," *Reuters* (Oct. 5, 2007), online at http://www.reuters.com/article/latestCrisis/idUSL04722887.

7. The duty of developed nations to provide financial support for environmental actions in developing nations is explicitly part of the financial agreement in the Convention on Biological Diversity, which was approved in Rio in 1992. See Convention on Biological Diversity, Article 20, online at http://www.cbd.int/convention/articles.shtml?a=cbd-20.

8. United Nations, Agenda 21 (Rio de Janeiro: Report of the United Nations Conference on Environment and Development, 1992), Agenda 21, online at http://www.unep.org/Documents.Multilingual/Default.asp?DocumentID=52&ArticleID=52&l=en.

9. Agenda 21, Chapter 33, online at http://earthwatch.unep.net/agenda21/33.php.

10. "Despite its enormous wealth and phenomenal growth in technological inventions, the United States remains far behind other industrialized countries in trying to help poor nations embark on the path of development, a new study by an independent think tank concludes." Haider Rizvi, "Anti-Poverty Index Scores U.S. Last on Environment Policies," *OneWorld.net* (Oct. 11, 2007), online at http://us.oneworld.net/article/view/154119/1.

11. Donald A. Brown, "The Need to Face Conflicts between Rich and Poor Nations," in Laura Westra and Patricia H. Werhane, eds., *The Business of Consumption*, 35.

12. Ibid., 37.

13. D. Reed, "Introduction" in D. Reed, ed., *Structural Adjustment, the Environment, and Sustainable Development* (New York: Earthscan Publications, 1996), ixx–xxv, in Donald A. Brown, "The Need to Face Conflicts between Rich and Poor Nations," in Laura Westra and Patricia H. Werhane, eds., *The Business of Consumption*, 37.

14. D. Reed, "Global Economic Policy" and "Conclusions: Short-Term Environmental Impacts of Structural Adjustment Programs," in D. Reed, ed., *Structural Adjustment, the Environment, and Sustainable Development*, 299–333, in Donald A. Brown, "The Need to Face Conflicts between Rich and Poor Nations," in Laura Westra and Patricia H. Werhane, eds., *The Business of Consumption*, 38. As noted in chapter 3, a 2006 report by the Independent Evaluation Group of the World Bank concludes that its loan programs imposing SAPs on developing countries have generally not reduced poverty.

15. Donald A. Brown, "The Need to Face Conflicts between Rich and Poor Nations," in Laura Westra and Patricia H. Werhane, eds., *The Business of Consumption*, 39–40.

16. Italics added. Agenda 21, Chapter 4, Section 4.5, online at http://www.unep.org/Documents.Multilingual/Default.asp?DocumentID=52&ArticleID=52&l=en.

17. Holmes Rolston III, "Environmental Protection and the International World Order: Ethics after the Earth Summit," *Business Ethics Quarterly* 5 (1995): 735–752.

18. "We Americans may think of China's growing consumption as a problem. But the Chinese are only reaching for the consumption rate we already have. To tell them not to try would be futile. The only approach that China and other developing countries will accept is to aim to make consumption rates and living standards more equal around the world." Whether or not we agree with this argument, "we shall soon have lower consumption rates, because our present rates are unsustainable. Real sacrifice wouldn't be required, however, because living standards are not tightly coupled to consumption rates. Much American consumption is wasteful and contributes little or nothing to quality of life." Jared Diamond, "What's Your Consumption Factor?" *The New York Times* (Jan. 2, 2008), online at http://www.nytimes.com/2008/01/02/opinion/02diamond .html.

19. Adam Werbach, former head of the Sierra Club, is promoting PSP (personal sustainability promise) among Wal-Mart employees, with permission from the management to extend the program to all its stores, encouraging each person "to commit to a behavioral change that would benefit the earth. It could be the decision to carpool, to plant trees, to eat organic food, to recycle—anything that might reduce pollution and waste and raise environmental awareness." Burr Snider, "Werbach at WalMart," *The San Francisco Chronicle* (Jan. 6, 2008), P-14, online at http://sfgate.com/cgi-bin/article.cgi?f=/c/a/2008/01/06/CM9TTS800.DTL.

20. Despite his love for animals, Saint Francis was not a vegetarian. Peter Singer, *Animal Liberation,* 216.

21. An old meaning of the word *religious* refers to persons who take vows to live a life apart from the world according to a discipline promulgated by the Catholic Church.

22. John Muir, "Mountain Thoughts," Sierra Club, online at http://www.yosemite.ca.us/ john_muir_writings/mountain_thoughts.html. He saw no reason, however, to believe that human beings are more important to God's purpose than other creatures. "Why should man value himself as more than a small part of the one great unit of creation? And what creature of all that the Lord has taken the pains to make is not essential to the completeness of that unit—the cosmos?" John Muir, "Man's Place in the Universe," Sierra Club, online at http://www.sierraclub.org/john_muir _exhibit/frameindex.html?http://www.sierraclub.org/john_muir_exhibit/life/muir_biography.html.

23. "Jane Goodall's Wild Chimpanzees," *Nature,* online at http://www.pbs.org/wnet/nature/ goodall/story.html.

24. "Animals," The Jane Goodall Institute, online at http://www.janegoodall.org.

25. Ibid.

26. "Africa Programs," The Jane Goodall Institute, online at http://www.janegoodall.org/ news/article-detail.asp?Entry_ID=446&Category_ID=5.

27. See chapter 14 in Robert Traer and Harlan Stelmach, *Doing Ethics in a Diverse Society.*

28. "Jane Goodall—My Four Reasons for Hope," The Jane Goodall Institute, online at http://www.janegoodall.org/jane/essay.asp.

29. Lester R. Brown, *Full House: Reassessing the Earth's Population Carrying Capacity* (New York: W. W. Norton, 1994), 163.

30. "Vegetarianism," online at http://en.wikipedia.org/wiki/Vegetarian.

31. Some Jews are combining "traditional Jewish dietary laws with new concerns about industrial agriculture, global warming and fair treatment of workers." Alan Cooperman, "Eco-Kosher Movement Aims to Heed Conscience," *The Washington Post* (Jul. 7, 2007), A01, online at http://www.washingtonpost.com/wp-dyn/content/article/2007/07/06/AR2007070602092.html.

32. "Animal Rights Concerns," online at http://www.animalsuffering.com/index.php. See Kim Severson, "Suddenly the Hunt Is On for Cage-Free Eggs," *The New York Times* (Apr. 12, 2007), online at http://www.nytimes.com/2007/08/12/us/12eggs.html. "'While cage-free certainly does not mean cruelty-free, it's a significant step in the right direction,' said Paul Shapiro of the Humane Society."

33. Tony Cenicola, "Five Easy Ways to Go Organic," *The New York Times* (Oct. 22, 2007), online at http://well.blogs.nytimes.com/2007/10/22/five-easy-ways-to-go-organic.

34. Michael Barbaro, "Home Depot to Display an Environmental Label," *The New York Times* (Apr. 17, 2007), online at http://www.nytimes.com/2007/04/17/business/17depot.html.

35. James Gustave Speth, *Red Sky at Morning,* 168

36. Ibid., 167. See, for example, "Responsible Shopper," Co-op America, online at http://www.coopamerica.org/programs/responsibleshopper.

37. Ibid., 168.

38. Eric T. Freyfogle, "Consumption and the Practice of Land Health," in Laura Westra and Patricia H. Werhane, eds., *The Business of Consumption,* 194.

39. Ibid., 193–194.

40. Ibid., 195.

41. Ibid.

42. Ibid.

43. William McDonough and Michael Braungart, *Cradle to Cradle,* 123.

44. A report by the Rainforest Alliance says that in the Maya Reserve in Guatemala "local communities and companies in the reserve have created fire control and prevention plans, improved living and working conditions for workers, increased the use of safety equipment, and experienced less social conflict as a result of better land-use mapping. The study's findings seem to demonstrate that forests are more likely to be protected and well-managed when communities have a stake in the process and have alternatives to clearing land for cattle grazing, farming, and other less sustainable activities." Haider Rizvi, "Local Control Saves Forests—Report," *OneWorld.net* (Mar. 27, 2008), online at http://us.oneworld.net/article/view/159182/1.

45. Ibid.

46. George C. Brenkert, "Marketing, the Ethics of Consumption, and Less-Developed Countries," in Laura Westra and Patricia H. Werhane, eds., *The Business of Consumption,* 92.

47. Ian Fisher and Larry Rohter, "The Pope Denounces Capitalism and Marxism," *The New York Times* (May 13, 2007), online at http://www.nytimes.com/2007/05/14/world/americas/14pope.html. The Pope also argues that capitalism has failed to overcome the "distance between rich and poor" and is causing "a worrying degradation of personal dignity through drugs, alcohol and deceptive illusions of happiness."

48. Herman E. Daly and Joshua Farley, *Ecological Economics,* 413.

49. Italics added. Ibid.

50. James Gustave Speth, *Red Sky at Morning,* 127.

51. George C. Brenkert, "Marketing, the Ethics of Consumption, and Less-Developed Countries," in Laura Westra and Patricia H. Werhane, eds., *The Business of Consumption,* 100. We may be encouraged to learn that "They have met resistance in this."

52. A. Fuat Firat, Erodogan Kumcu, and Mehmet Karafakiolglu, "The Interface between Marketing and Development: Problems and Prospects," in Erodogan Kumcu and A. Fuat Firat, eds., *Marketing and Development: Toward Broader Dimensions* (Greenwich, CT: JAI Press, 1988), in Laura Westra and Patricia H. Werhane, eds., *The Business of Consumption,* 105.

53. George C. Brenkert, "Marketing, the Ethics of Consumption, and Less-Developed Countries," in Laura Westra and Patricia H. Werhane, eds., *The Business of Consumption,* 107.

54. R. Goodland, "Environmental Sustainability," in Laura Westra and Patricia H. Werhane, eds., *The Business of Consumption,* 204.

55. Mark Bittman, "Rethinking the Meat-Guzzler," *The New York Times* (Jan. 27, 2008), online at http://www.nytimes.com/2008/01/27/weekinreview/27bittman.html.

56. Anup Shah, "Beef," *Behind Consumption and Consumerism* (Nov. 26, 2003), online at http://www.globalissues.org/TradeRelated/Consumption/Beef.asp.

57. "Like oil, meat is subsidized by the federal government. Like oil, meat is subject to accelerating demand as nations become wealthier, and this, in turn, sends prices higher. Finally—like

oil—meat is something people are encouraged to consume less of, as the toll exacted by industrial production increases, and becomes increasingly visible." Mark Bittman, "Rethinking the Meat-Guzzler," *The New York Times* (Jan. 27, 2008), online at http://www.nytimes.com/2008/01/27/weekinreview/27bittman.html.

58. Ibid., 213. For a personal reaction to industrial cattle raising, see Howard F. Lyman with Glen Marzer, *Mad Cowboy: The Cattle Rancher Who Won't Eat Meat* (New York: Simon & Schuster, 1998).

59. Simone Spearman, "Eating More Veggies Can Help Save Energy," *The San Francisco Chronicle* (Jun. 29, 2001), online at http://www.commondreams.org/views01/0629-06.htm.

60. Robert Goodland, Catherine Watson, and George Ledec, *Environmental Management in Tropical Agriculture* (Boulder, CO: Westview Press, 1984), 237, in R. Goodland, "Environmental Sustainability," in Laura Westra and Patricia H. Werhane, eds., *The Business of Consumption*, 214.

61. Mary Midgley, *Animals and Why They Matter*, 27. To cut waste we not only need to change our eating habits, but also our industrial food system. "Inefficient harvesting, transportation, storage, and packaging ruin 50 percent of the food" that is produced. Ben Block, "Conserve Water Through Food Efficiency, Report Says," Worldwatch Institute (May 23, 2008), online at http://www.worldwatch.org/node/5751.

62. "The current food crisis causing hunger and starvation for millions of people across the world is not going to end as long as those who dominate the international grain markets remain unwilling to change their behavior, according to experts specializing in international trade and environmental economics." On the demand side, "the trends include the addition of 70 million people every year, while some 4 billion people are already struggling to move up the food chain and consume more grain-intensive livestock products. At the same time, the amount of grain used for car fuels is also rising immensely." See Haider Rizvi, "Food Crisis Set to Get Worse," *OneWorld.net* (Apr. 19, 2008), online at http://us.oneworld.net/article/view/159936/1.

63. As we consider economic problems, we should remember that there is no "invisible hand" to ensure that markets promote the common good. Only democratic decision-making and laws that check the power of economic interests will make justice and equity possible in the global economy.

CHAPTER 10: ENVIRONMENTAL POLICY

1. The Convention on Biological Diversity, which was approved in Rio along with Agenda 21, is mentioned only in endnotes to chapters 7 and 9.

2. The National Environment Policy of 1969, as amended, online at http://www.fhwa.dot.gov/environment/nepatxt.htm.

3. Ibid.

4. "Reorganization Plan No. 3 of 1970," online at http://www.epa.gov/history/org/origins/reorg.htm. The EPA consolidated the following functions of existing federal agencies:

- Functions with respect to pesticide studies. (Department of the Interior)
- Functions carried out by the Federal Water Quality Administration. (Interior)
- Functions carried out by the Bureau of Solid Waste Management and the Bureau of Water Hygiene, and portions of the functions carried out by the Bureau of Radiological Health of the Environmental Control Administration. (Health, Education, and Welfare).
- Functions carried out by the National Air Pollution Control Administration. (HEW)
- Functions about pesticides carried out by the Food and Drug Administration. (HEW)
- Authority to perform studies relating to ecological systems. (Council on Environmental Quality)
- Some functions concerning radiation criteria and standards. (Atomic Energy Commission and the Federal Radiation Council)
- Functions concerning pesticide registration and related activities carried out by the Agricultural Research Service. (Department of Agriculture)

5. Jack Lewis, "The Birth of EPA," Environmental Protection Agency, online at http://www.epa.gov/history/topics/epa/15c.htm.

6. "History of Energy Star," online at http://www.energystar.gov/index.cfm?c=about.ab_history.

7. "Green Power Partnership," EPA, online at http://www.epa.gov/greenpower/gpmarket/index.htm.

8. Under the Bush administration, however, this voluntary emphasis has been accompanied by a decline in the enforcement of regulations. "The Environmental Protection Agency's pursuit of criminal cases against polluters has dropped off sharply during the Bush administration, with the number of prosecutions, new investigations and total convictions all down by more than a third, according to Justice Department and EPA data." John Solomon and Juliet Eilperin, "Bush's EPA Is Pursuing Fewer Polluters," *The Washington Post* (Sep. 1, 2007), online at http://www.washingtonpost.com/wp-dyn/content/article/2007/09/29/AR2007092901759.html.

9. "Superfund," online at http://en.wikipedia.org/wiki/Comprehensive_Environmental_Response%2C_Compensation%2C_and_Liability_Act.

10. Linda Greenhouse, "Justices Say EPA Has Power to Act on Harmful Gases," *The New York Times* (Apr. 3, 2007), online at http://www.nytimes.com/2007/04/03/washington/03scotus.html. In November 2007 a federal appeals court "rejected the Bush administration's year-old fuel-economy standards for light trucks and sport utility vehicles . . . saying that they were not tough enough because regulators had failed to thoroughly assess the economic impact of tailpipe emissions that contribute to climate change." The court "told the Transportation Department to produce new rules taking into account the value of reducing greenhouse gas emissions." Felicity Barringer and Michelene Maynard, "Court Rejects Fuel Standards on Trucks," *The New York Times* (Nov. 16, 2007), online at http://www.nytimes.com/2007/11/16/business/16fuel.html.

11. Felicity Barringer, "Groups Seeks EPA Rules on Emissions from Vehicles," *The New York Times* (Apr. 3, 2008), online at http://www.nytimes.com/2008/04/03/washington/03pollute.html.

12. "Environment Policy," JPMorganChase, online at http://www.jpmorganchase.com/cm/cs?pagename=Chase/Href&urlname=jpmc/community/env/policy.

13. Ibid.

14. "We therefore have an opportunity to make a positive contribution to environmental and social concerns by enacting policies designed so that our business operations do not degrade the environment or cause social harm." Ibid.

15. United Nations Millennium Declaration, adopted by the General Assembly (Sep. 8, 2000), online at http://www.un.org/millennium/declaration/ares552e.htm.

16. "Environment Policy," JPMorganChase, online at http://www.jpmorganchase.com/cm/cs?pagename=Chase/Href&urlname=jpmc/community/env/policy.

17. Ibid.

18. Global Reporting Initiative, online at http://www.globalreporting.org/Home.

19. "The Equator Principles: A benchmark for the financial industry to manage social and environmental issues in project financing," online at http://www.equator-principles.com.

20. "Environmental Risk Management Policy," JPMorganChase, online at http://www.jpmorganchase.com/cm/cs?pagename=Chase/Href&urlname=jpmc/community/env/policy/risk.

21. As of November 2006 more than forty major lenders have subscribed to these principles. "Leaders Challenge 'Business as Usual,' Guardian," *The Equator Principles,* online at http://www.equator-principles.com/lcb.shtml.

22. In *forest environments* the corporation is committed to applying the Equator Principles and therefore pledges that:

- JPMorgan Chase will not finance commercial logging operations or the purchase of logging equipment for use in primary tropical moist forests.
- JPMorgan Chase will finance plantations only on non-forested areas (including previously planted areas) or on heavily degraded forestland.

- JPMorgan Chase will not finance projects that contravene any relevant international environmental agreement which has been enacted into the law of, or otherwise has the force of law in, the country in which the project is located.

"Forestry and Biodiversity Policy Commitments," JPMorganChase, online at http://www.jpmorganchase.com/cm/cs?pagename=Chase/Href&urlname=jpmc/community/env/policy/forest.

23. "Climate Change Policy and Commitments," JPMorganChase, online at http://www.jpmorganchase.com/cm/cs?pagename=Chase/Href&urlname=jpmc/community/env/policy/clim.

24. Ibid.

25. A project sponsor or borrower must also demonstrate the following:

- Consultation approaches that rely on existing customary institutions, the role of community elders and leaders, and the established governance structure for tribal and indigenous communities;
- Governmental authorities at the local, regional or national level have provided mechanisms for the affected communities to be represented or consulted, and international and local laws have been upheld; and
- Major indigenous land claims are appropriately addressed.

"Indigenous Communities," JPMorganChase, online at http://www.jpmorganchase.com/cm/cs?pagename=Chase/Href&urlname=jpmc/community/env/policy/indig.

26. "Environmental campaigners scored a major victory this week as some of the nation's top banks agreed to link energy sector investment with initiatives to combat climate change. Officials at Citibank, JPMorgan Chase, and Morgan Stanley pledged . . . that they would give priority to investment in clean energy businesses and put coal-fired electricity generation to 'a rigorous review' process for financing." Haider Rizvi, "Banks to Consider Climate Before Investing in Coal," *OneWorld.net* (Feb. 7, 2008), online at http://us.oneworld.net/article/view/157609/1.

27. See Ida Wahlstrom, "Environmental Action Driving Global Economy—Report," *OneWorld.net* (Jan. 10, 2008), online at http://us.oneworld.net/article/view/156724/1.

28. Italics added. "Mission Statement," Interface, online at http://www.interfaceinc.com/goals/mission.html.

29. Ibid.

30. "Interface Sustainability," Interface, online at http://www.interfacesustainability.com/whatis.html.

31. Ibid.

32. "Because of this creation of a 'carbon sink' (a component which solar and wind energy do not have), we believe that bioenergy from closed loop energy crops represents the most effective choice in 'alternative energy' options to address Global Warming." "Planet Power: Energy and the Environment," Biomass Energy Crop and BioEnergy Working Group, online at http://www.treepower.org.

33. "Interface Sustainability," Interface, online at http://www.interfacesustainability.com/commit.html.

34. Cornelia Dean, "Executive on a Mission: Saving the Planet," *The New York Times* (May 22, 2007), online at http://www.nytimes.com/2007/05/22/science/earth/22ander.html.

35. The Natural Step, online at http://www.naturalstep.org/com/nyStart.

36. "The Natural Step," Interface, online athttp://www.interfacesustainability.com/step.html.

37. "Interface Sustainability," Interface, online at http://www.interfacesustainability.com/commit.html.

38. Cornelia Dean, "Executive on a Mission: Saving the Planet," *The New York Times* (May 22, 2007), online at http://www.nytimes.com/2007/05/22/science/earth/22ander.html.

39. "Wal-Mart has made a name for itself over the past year by highlighting various environmental initiatives, which it sees as an easy way to improve its image. While reducing packaging on food products and selling more energy efficient light bulbs are important steps that Wal-Mart

should be applauded for, they must do much more to make amends for an environmentally un-friendly past. In the past, Wal-Mart has been guilty of air pollution, storm water violations, and improper storage of hazardous materials. With millions in fines resulting from these violations, Wal-Mart's environmental record has been blemished." Wal-Mart Watch, online at http://walmartwatch.com/issues/environment.

40. Thomas L. Friedman, "Lead, Follow or Move Aside," *The New York Times* (Sep. 26, 2007), online at http://www.nytimes.com/2007/09/26/opinion/26friedman.html.

41. P&G, online at http://www.pg.com/company/our_commitment/sustainability.jhtml.

42. P&G, online at http://www.pg.com/company/our_commitment/environment.jhtml.

43. "'More from less' products have included compact detergents that achieve a better wash per-formance, while using only 50% of the ingredients and a fraction of the packaging needed for con-ventional 'big box' products." George Carpenter and Peter White, "Sustainable Development: Finding the Real Business Case," *International Journal for Sustainable Business* 11, no. 2 (Feb. 2004), online as a pdf file at http://www.pg.com/content/pdf/01_about_pg/corporate_citizenship/sustainability/reports/Corporate%20Environmental%20Strategy%20Journal%20PRW&GDC.pdf.

44. Carpenter and White make a challenging ethical argument: "The focus has been on elimi-nating pollution, waste and natural resource depletion, or more recently poor working conditions or child labor. When you focus only on being 'less bad,' by definition you can never be 'good.' The best you can be is 'less bad than you used to be, or less bad than others. This is not a positive message, nor a way to grow future business value. One possible way round this conundrum, how-ever, is to link opportunity with responsibility." Ibid.

45. "Several years ago, P&G purchased the PuR brand, a U.S. based in-home water purifica-tion business. We are developing low cost technologies, and business models to bring those tech-nologies to consumers, that will be effective on the more serious water problems in the developing world. Similarly, over 2 billion people are without adequate sanitation, and better hygiene can re-duce deaths caused by diarrhea by up to 33 percent. P&G has been in the bar soap business for decades, and our Safeguard brand, working in developing countries with local health ministries to create awareness about the importance of hygiene, is showing how public-private partnerships can reach far more people with health messages than either the ministry or we could do individually. Individuals will change their consumption practices when they realize they can improve their quality of life." Ibid.

46. The Global Reporting Initiative, online at http://www.globalreporting.org/Home.

47. The Natural Step, online at http://www.naturalstep.org/com/nyStart.

48. The Carbon Disclosure Project, online at http://www.cdproject.net.

49. Greenpeace International, online at http://www.greenpeace.org/usa.

50. The Sierra Club, online at http://www.sierraclub.org.

51. The World Wildlife Fund, online at http://www.wwf.org/ and http://www.worldwildlife.org.

52. The Nature Conservancy, online at http://www.nature.org.

53. *The World Directory of Environmental Organizations,* online at http://www.interenvironment.org/wd3intl/ingo-intro.htm.

54. Ibid., by country, online at http://www.interenvironment.org/wd4countries/index.htm. See also "Environmental NGOs and Citizen Action," online at http://pubs.wri.org/pubs_content_text.cfm?ContentID=1901. At a 2007 meeting of the Conference of Non-Governmental Orga-nizations in Consultative Relationship with the United Nations, CONGO President Renate Bloem asserted that: "Without civil society as the driving force behind the MDGs [Millennium Development Goals], the chances are very slim that we will reach the MDGs." Christi van der Westhuizen, "Chances of Achieving MDGs 'Slim' without Civil Society," *OneWorld.net* (Jan. 28, 2007), online at http://us.oneworld.net/article/view/150788/1.

55. Ibid., online at http://www.interenvironment.org/wd4countries/us.htm.

56. "About Greenpeace," online at http://www.greenpeace.org/international/about.

57. Ibid.

58. "About Us," Greenpeace USA, online at http://www.greenpeace.org/usa/about.

59. I find this language surprisingly anthropocentric.

60. "Join or Give," The Sierra Club, online at https://secure2.convio.net/sierra/site/Donation
2?idb=0&df_id=1300&1300.donation=form1&s_src=J06WOT0200&JServSessionIdr008
=jlwlstls21.app6a.

61. "About Us: A Snapshot of Earthjustice," Earthjustice, online at http://www.earthjustice.org/
about_us/index.html.

62. "WWF–who we are and how we came about," online at http://www.panda.org/about
_wwf/who_we_are/index.cfm.

63. Ibid.

64. The Nature Conservancy, "How We Work," online at http://www.nature.org/aboutus/
howwework/?src=t2.

65. Colin Woodward, "The Sale of the Century," The Nature Conservancy (Autumn 2006),
online at http://www.nature.org/magazine/autumn2006/forests/index.html.

66. "$24 Million of Guatemala's Debt Now Slated for Conservation," The Nature Conservancy,
online at http://www.nature.org/wherewework/centralamerica/guatemala/work/art19052.html.

67. "The Natural Capital Project: Making Conservation Mainstream," The Nature Conservancy, online at http://www.nature.org/partners/partnership/art19494.html.

68. Ibid.

69. Ibid.

70. In the US: "Overall, since 1990, the Defense Department has reduced its use of ozone-
damaging substances by 97 percent—from more than 16 million pounds to less than a half-
million pounds." Stephen Barr, "The Pentagon's Eco-Leaders," The Washington Post (Oct. 1,
2007), D04, online at http://www.washingtonpost.com/wp-dyn/content/article/2007/09/30/
AR2007093001229.html.

71. There are many other examples of collaboration. For instance, the International Union for
Conservation of Nature (IUCN), which "supports scientific research, manages field projects all
over the world and brings governments, non-government organizations, United Nations agencies,
companies and local communities together to develop and implement policy, laws and best practice," has "a democratic membership union with more than 1,000 government and NGO member organizations, and some 10,000 volunteer scientists in more than 160 countries." Online at
http://cms.iucn.org/about/index.cfm.

72. Great Lakes United, online at http://www.glu.org/english/about_glu/our_coalition/index.htm.

73. Environment Canada, online at http://www.on.ec.gc.ca/greatlakes/Stakeholder's_Corner
-WSC20200D4-1_En.htm.

74. "The GLWQA Review: How the Process Works," International Joint Commission, online
at http://www.ijc.org/en/activities/consultations/glwqa/process.php.

75. International Joint Commission, "Media Release" (Feb. 7, 2007), online at http://www.ijc
.org/rel/news/070208_e.htm.

76. Ibid.

77. "Salt Free Great Lakes," Great Lakes United, online at http://www.glu.org/english/invasive
_species/saltfreelakes/index.htm.

78. John C. Taylor and Mr. James L. Roach, "Ocean Shipping in the Great Lakes:Transporta-
tion Cost Increases That Would Result From A Cessation of Ocean Vessel Shipping," Seidman
College of Business, Grand Valley State University (Dec. 6, 2005), online at http://www.gvsu
.edu/business/index.cfm?id=11971F16-DBAF-2179-96B0680A95CC6F83.

79. "The Apollo Alliance for Good Jobs and Clean Energy," Apollo Alliance, online at http://www.apolloalliance.org/about_the_alliance.

80. Ibid. Advocates of a "Green for All" campaign (http://www.greenforall.org) are asking Congress for $125 million to train thirty thousand young people a year in green trades. Thomas L. Friedman, "The Green-Collar Solution," *The New York Times* (Oct. 17, 2007), online at http://www.nytimes.com/2007/10/17/opinion/17friedman.html.

81. "Benefits of the Apollo Alliance's Plan for Energy Independence," Apollo Alliance, online at http://www.apolloalliance.org/about_the_alliance/benefits_of_apollo_s_plan/index.cfm. Ted Nordhaus and Michael Shellenberger are strong supporters of the Apollo Alliance. Ted Nordhaus and Michael Shellenberger, *Break Through*, 113.

82. "The Ten-Point Plan for Good Jobs and Energy Independence," Apollo Alliance, online at http://www.apolloalliance.org/strategy_center/ten_point_plan.cfm.

83. "The Natural Step," Interface, online at http://www.interfacesustainability.com/step.html.

84. "Mission Statement," Interface, online at http://www.interfaceinc.com/goals/mission.html.

85. "The Apollo Alliance for Good Jobs and Clean Energy," Apollo Alliance, online at http://www.apolloalliance.org/about_the_alliance.

86. "Interface Sustainability," Interface, online at http://www.interfacesustainability.com/commit.html.

87. Herman E. Daly and Joshua Farley, *Ecological Economics*, 385.

88. Ibid., 385–386.

89. B. Bosquet, "Environmental Tax Reform: Does It Work? A Survey of the Empirical Evidence," *Ecological Economics* 34, no. 1 (2000): 19–32, in Herman E. Daly and Joshua Farley, *Ecological Economics*, 386.

90. "About Us," Greenpeace USA, online at http://www.greenpeace.org/usa/about.

91. The National Environment Policy of 1969, as amended, online at http://www.fhwa.dot.gov/environment/nepatxt.htm.

CHAPTER 11: AIR AND WATER

1. The importance of nitrogen and phosphorus for life is discussed in more detail in chapter 12.

2. Editorial, "Parks in Peril," *The New York Times* (Mar. 24, 2008), online at http://www.nytimes.com/2008/03/24/opinion/24mon1.html.

3. In March 2008 "the antiregulatory brigade in the Office of Management and Budget killed ozone standards that would have offered stronger protections for plants, trees, crops and wildlife. And the Environmental Protection Agency, ignoring protests from its own regional offices and the National Park Service, is nearing approval of regulations that would make it easier to build coal-fired plants near parks and wilderness areas without installing pollution controls." Ibid.

4. "[S]cientists have long known that smoking while pregnant or exposure to lead, for instance, can damage a fetus and that recent research is broadening the list of hazards." Alister Doyle, "Fetuses, Babies Said at High Risk from Pollutants," *Reuters* (May 24, 2007), online at http://www.reuters.com/article/scienceNews/idUSL2416652320070524.

5. Kenneth M. Vigil, *Clean Water: An Introduction to Water Quality and Water Pollution Control*, second edition (Corvallis, OR: Oregon State University Press, 2003), 128.

6. John Heilprin, "EPA May Drop Lead Air Pollution Limits," *News Center* (Dec. 7, 2006), online at http://www.commondreams.org/headlines06/1207-01.htm. For example, see Michael Milstein, "Unleaded Gas Helps Create an Unleaded Columbia Gorge," *The Oregonian* (Oct. 15, 2007), online at http://www.oregonlive.com/news/oregonian/index.ssf?/base/news/11924151376020.xml. "In the 1990s, scientists found unusually high levels of lead in rock-dwelling lichens, which are used as barometers of air quality in the gorge because they soak up whatever pollution drifts by. But the

United States removed lead from gasoline starting about two decades ago. That has paid off for the gorge: In new analyses, scientists have found that lead has nearly disappeared from gorge lichens."

7. Ibid.

8. "Debate Over Lead in Air," *Environmental Science and Technology* (Jan. 31, 2007), online at http://pubs.acs.org/subscribe/journals/esthag-w/2007/jan/policy/rr_lead_air.html.

9. "Inhaling diesel exhaust triggers a stress response in the brain that may have damaging long-term effects" due to very small particles of soot that "are able to travel from the nose and lodge in the brain." "Diesel Fumes Can Affect Your Brain, Scientists Say," *Reuters* (Mar. 10, 2008), online at http://www.reuters.com/article/healthNews/idUSL1044145320080311.

10. John Heilprin, "EPA May Drop Lead Air Pollution Limits," *News Center* (Dec. 7, 2006), online at http://www.commondreams.org/headlines06/1207-01.htm.

11. "Smog," online at http://en.wikipedia.org/wiki/Smog.

12. "Catalytic Converter," online at http://en.wikipedia.org/wiki/Catalytic_converter.

13. J. S. Kidd and Renee A. Kidd, *Air Pollution: Problems and Solutions* (New York: Chelsea House, 2006), 71.

14. "Clean Air Act," Foundation for Clean Air Progress, online at http://www.cleanair progress.org/clean-air-pollution/clean-air-act.asp.

15. "While business lobbyists wanted the smog requirement unchanged, most health experts had argued that even stronger measures were needed." H. Josef Hebert, "EPA Advisors Slam New Smog Rule," *Bay News 9* (Apr. 10, 2008), online at http://www.baynews9.com/content/88/2008/4/10/339029.html. In early May a federal judge ruled that the EPA had "violated legal deadlines for updating the nation's clean-air standards on carbon monoxide." Bob Egelko, "Judge Orders EPA to Hurry on Carbon Monoxide," *San Francisco Chronicle* (May 7, 2008), A-2, online at http://www.sfgate.com/cgi-bin/article.cgi?f=/c/a/2008/05/08/MNJR10I1HQ.DTL.

16. "[S]cent-bearing hydrocarbon molecules released by flowers can be destroyed when they come into contact with ozone and other pollutants." Juliet Eilperin, "Air Pollution Impedes Bees' Ability to Find Flowers," *The Washington Post* (May 5, 2008), A03, online at http://www .washingtonpost.com/wp-dyn/content/article/2008/05/04/AR2008050401737.html. See also Juliet Eilperin, "Ozone Rules Weakened at Bush's Request," *The Washington Post* (Mar. 14, 2008), A01, online at http://www.washingtonpost.com/wp-dyn/content/article/2008/03/13/AR2008 031304175.html.

17. These issues exist in many cities in the world and in some cases are being effectively addressed. See Thomas Fuller, "Breathing Easier as the Battle for Blue Skies Pays Off," *The New York Times* (Mar. 6, 2007), online at http://www.nytimes.com/2007/03/06/world/asia/06thai.html.

18. James Gustave Speth, *Red Sky at Morning*, 53.

19. United Nations Economic Commission for Europe, online at http://www.unece.org/env/lrtap.

20. See Bernie Woodall, "Texas Leads List of Dirtiest US Power Plants," *Reuters* (Jul. 26, 2007), online at http://www.reuters.com/article/scienceNews/idUSN2645126520070726.

21. J. S. Kidd and Renee A. Kidd, *Air Pollution*, 75.

22. Ibid., 78.

23. "Clean Air Act," Foundation for Clean Air Progress, online at http://www.cleanairprogress .org/clean-air-pollution/clean-air-act.asp.

24. J. S. Kidd and Renee A. Kidd, *Air Pollution*, 83.

25. In late 2007 the EPA joined in settling a lawsuit against American Electric Power (AEP). At issue was "whether the utility had adequately updated its aging plants with new pollution-control technology when it modified them, an issue that falls under the [EPA's] New Source Review rule. Under Tuesday's settlement, the utility has agreed to install controls on the sixteen plants it has expanded over the years, which will effectively remove 1.6 million tons of pollution from the air annually by 2018. The [Bush] administration has repeatedly questioned the value of

enforcing the current rules, and the settlement guarantees that AEP will not face federal prosecution if its activities over the next decade trigger this sort of federal review. Although the nine state attorneys general and thirteen environmental advocacy groups that are party to the lawsuit praised the administration for Tuesday's settlement, they explicitly rejected this prosecutorial amnesty in the consent decree. . . ." Juliet Eilperin, "EPA Joins Settlement of Lawsuit but Adds a Waiver," *The Washington Post* (Oct. 11, 2007), A03, online at http://www.washingtonpost.com/wp-dyn/content/article/2007/10/10/AR2007101002389.html.

26. J. S. Kidd and Renee A. Kidd, *Air Pollution,* 83.

27. Ibid., 94.

28. Ibid., 92.

29. "Montreal Protocol," UNEP, Ozone Secretariat, online at http://ozone.unep.org/Treaties_and_Ratification/2B_montreal_protocol.shtml.

30. Reiner Grundmann, "The Strange Success of the Montreal Protocol," *International Environmental Affairs* 10, no. 3 (1998): 197, in James Gustave Speth, *Red Sky at Morning,* 182.

31. The substitutes for the chlorofluorocarbons (CFCs) prohibited by the Montreal Protocol, which are called HCFCs (hydrochlorofluorocarbons), are now known to be "stronger greenhouse gases than carbon dioxide," so there is an urgent need to develop replacements for HCFCs that "are not toxic, do not deplete the stratospheric ozone layer, and do not contribute to global warming." J. S. Kidd and Renee A. Kidd, *Air Pollution,* 117.

32. "Just like any other planet, the Earth absorbs the sun's heat and radiates it back towards space. But greenhouse gases counteract that heat loss, trapping heat, and reflecting it back towards the Earth. The more greenhouse gases in the atmosphere, the more heat that is trapped. The less the amount of greenhouse gases, the less heat that is trapped. Earth has just the right amount to help life flourish. Too many of these gases, as is the case on Venus, would create a runaway greenhouse and a sizzling hot surface. On the other hand, without any greenhouse gases, much of the sun's heat would be lost, and the Earth would become a frozen wasteland with an average temperature of 0 degrees fahrenheit (-18 degrees celsius)." "Greenhouse—Green Planet," NOVA, online at http://www.pbs.org/wgbh/nova/ice/greenhouse.html.

33. Thomas R. Karl and Kevin E. Trenberth, "Modern Global Climate Change," in Donald Kennedy, ed., *Science Magazine's the State of the Planet: 2006–2007* (Washington, DC: Island Press, 2006), 89.

34. J. S. Kidd and Renee A. Kidd, *Air Pollution,* 152.

35. James Gustave Speth, *Red Sky at Morning,* 16.

36. Federal Water Pollution Control Act, As amended November 27, 2002, Section 101(a), in Joseph Orlins and Anner Wehrly, "The Quest for Clean Water," in Yael Calhoun, ed., *Water Pollution* (Philadelphia, PA: Chelsea House, 2005), 4.

37. Joseph Orlins and Anner Wehrly, "The Quest for Clean Water," in Yael Calhoun, ed., *Water Pollution,* 32.

38. Ibid., 35.

39. Ibid., 34.

40. Ibid., 35.

41. Ibid., 36. Restoration of waterways is very difficult. See Cornelia Dean, "Follow the Silt," *The New York Times* (Jun. 24, 2008), online at http://www.nytimes.com/2008/06/24/science/24stream.html.

42. Kenneth M. Vigil, *Clean Water,* 16.

43. "In 1977, as a result of pressure from industry, the focus in the United States shifted from control-point discharge regulation to water quality standards. Tacitly, this shift marked a move away from pollution as a violation to pollution as permissible." Vandana Shiva, *Water Wars,* 32.

44. EPA regulation, however, has not been effective. In 2005, the latest date for which information was available, "More than half of all industrial and municipal facilities across the country

dumped more sewage and other pollutants into the nation's waterways than allowed under the Clean Water Act. . . ." Zachery Coile, "Pollution Pouring into Nation's Waters Far Beyond Legal Limits," *San Francisco Chronicle* (Oct. 12, 2007), A-1, online at http://sfgate.com/cgi-bin/article.cgi?f=/c/a/2007/10/12/MNIPSOF76.DTL.

45. This is true, of course, throughout the world, where the problems are often greater than in the United States. For instance, "Lake Tai, the center of China's ancient 'land of fish and rice,' succumbed this year to floods of industrial and agricultural waste." Joseph Kahn, "In China, a Lake's Champion Imperils Himself," *The New York Times* (Oct. 14, 2007), online at http://www.nytimes.com/2007/10/14/world/asia/14china.html.

46. Kenneth M. Vigil, *Clean Water*, 61–62. Because paper, like most materials, has not been designed for recycling, the process is more inefficient than it might be. Effective recycling requires products designed for recycling. William McDonough and Michael Braungart, *Cradle to Cradle*, 56–58.

47. Heavy rain and runoff may also contribute to increased point-source pollution. See Peter Fimrite, "Rain Brings Sewage into San Francisco Bay," *San Francisco Chronicle* (Feb. 26, 2008), online at http://sfgate.com/cgi-bin/article.cgi?f=/c/a/2008/02/26/BA6UV906K.DTL.

48. Joseph Orlins and Anner Wehrly, "The Quest for Clean Water," in Yael Calhoun, ed., *Water Pollution*, 48.

49. Elena Bennett and Steve Carpenter, "P Soup: The Global Phosphorus Cycle," in Yael Calhoun, ed., *Water Pollution*, 47.

50. Ibid., 48.

51. The "capital cost of 'natural' stormwater management is about 10 percent of that of concrete and operating costs are similarly less." James J. Kay, "On Complexity Theory, Exergy, and Industrial Ecology," in Charles J. Kibert, Jan Sendzimir, and G. Bradley Guy, eds. *Construction Ecology*, 95.

52. Kenneth M. Vigil, *Clean Water*, 67.

53. "Fifty-year-old levees blew up in a dramatic display of dirt and smoke Tuesday, freeing lake water as part of an unprecedented wetlands restoration effort to save protected fish and cool the water wars that have divided the Klamath Basin for decades." Gail Kinsey Hill, "Levee Blast Signals a Truce in Water Wars," *The Oregonian* (Oct. 31, 2007), online at http://www.oregonlive.com/news/oregonian/index.ssf?/base/news/1193801124304310.xml.

54. Kenneth M. Vigil, *Clean Water*, 56.

55. This will require legislation with incentives and disincentives for producers to design products that are not harmful to the environment, such as soaps that will likely end up in streams. This has been done and has been shown to be cost effective. William McDonough and Michael Braungart, *Cradle to Cradle*, 146–147.

56. Payla Sampat, "Groundwater Shock," in Yael Calhoun, ed., *Water Pollution*, 66.

57. "Research shows that in many parts of the world water tables are continuing to fall and rivers are drying up." Haider Rizvi, "Washington Pressed to Lead as Water Tables Continue to Fall," *OneWorld.net* (Jul. 27, 2007), online at http://us.oneworld.net/article/view/151746/1. In China, "the groundwater of the northern plains has dropped precipitously, reaching an average 1.5 meters (5 feet) per year by the mid-1990s. Between 1965 and 1995 the water table fell 37 meters (121 feet) beneath Beijing itself." Edward O. Wilson, *The Future of Life*, 36.

58. Payla Sampat, "Groundwater Shock," in Yael Calhoun, ed., *Water Pollution*, 68.

59. Ibid., 67.

60. DDT was banned by the EPA in 1972. "United States Environmental Protection Agency," online at http://en.wikipedia.org/wiki/EPA.

61. Kenneth M. Vigil, *Clean Water*, 125.

62. Payla Sampat, "Groundwater Shock," in Yael Calhoun, ed., *Water Pollution*, 73.

63. Ibid., 79.

64. Ibid.

65. Italics added. Donald Kennedy, ed., *Science Magazine's State of the Planet: 2006–2007*, 64.

66. James Gustave Speth, *Red Sky at Morning*, 16. In general, "When water use falls below 1,700 cubic meters per person per year, a country encounters water stress through lack of adequate supply. When water use falls below 1,000 cubic meters, there is water scarcity, meaning a significant and often severe restriction on material welfare at the individual level and on development prospects at the national level." Norman Myers and Jennifer Kent, *Perverse Subsidies*, 122.

67. This is why the Middle East as a whole imports 30 percent of its grain. Norman Myers and Jennifer Kent. *Perverse Subsidies*, 122. "As food prices escalate and water scarcity extends worldwide, the best solution to both issues would be a global reduction in wasted food." Ben Block, "Conserve Water Through Food Efficiency, Report Says," Worldwatch Institute, online at http://www.worldwatch.org/node/5751.

68. Vandana Shiva, *Water Wars*, 12.

69. Ibid., 15.

70. Ibid., 12.

71. James Flanigan, "The Growth Opportunities of Clean Water," *The New York Times* (Jun. 19, 2008), online at http://www.nytimes.com/2008/06/19/business/smallbusiness/19edge.html.

72. Patrick J. Sullivan, Franklin J. Agardy, and James J. J. Clark, *The Environmental Science of Drinking Water* (Burlington, MA: Elsevier Butterworth-Heinemann, 2005), 74.

73. Ibid., 66, 166. See also "Drug Traces Found in Tap Water," *The New York Times* (Mar. 10, 2008), online at http://www.nytimes.com/aponline/us/AP-PharmaWater-I.html.

74. Ibid., 27.

75. Ibid., 117.

76. Ibid., 81.

77. Ibid., 115.

78. Ibid.

79. Ibid. See also "Arsenic in Drinking Water," EPA, online at http://www.epa.gov/safewater/arsenic/index.html.

80. Patrick J. Sullivan, Franklin J. Agardy, and James J. J. Clark, *The Environmental Science of Drinking Water*, 96. Carcinogens are substances known to cause cancer.

81. Ibid. Generally chlorine is added to water being distributed to combat microbes in the pipes of the system.

82. Ibid., 170.

83. Ibid., 181.

84. Proctor & Gamble, for instance. See http://www.pg.com/company/our_commitment/environment.jhtml.

85. The costs of using BAT will vary for many reasons, and in some situations these costs may be sufficiently compelling to justify setting this presumption aside.

86. Patrick J. Sullivan, Franklin J. Agardy, and James J. J. Clark, *The Environmental Science of Drinking Water*, 218.

87. Randall C. Archibold, "From Sewage, Added Water for Drinking," *The New York Times* (Nov. 27, 2007), online at http://www.nytimes.com/2007/11/27/us/27conserve.html.

88. Federal Water Pollution Control Act, as amended Nov. 27, 2002, Section 101(a).

89. In China, "Fuqing is one of the centers of a booming industry that over two decades has transformed this country into the biggest producer and exporter of seafood in the world, and the fastest-growing supplier to the United States.

But that growth is threatened by the two most glaring environmental weaknesses in China: acute water shortages and water supplies contaminated by sewage, industrial waste and agricultural runoff that includes pesticides. The fish farms, in turn, are discharging wastewater that further pollutes the water supply." David Barboza, "In China, Farming Fish in Toxic Waters," *The New York Times* (Dec. 15, 2007), online at http://www.nytimes.com/2007/12/15/world/asia/15fish.html.

90. James J. Kay, "On Complexity Theory, Exergy, and Industrial Ecology," in Charles J. Kibert, Jan Sendzimir, and G. Bradley Guy, eds., *Construction Ecology,* 95.

91. Climate change due to global warming will affect the hydrologic cycle, probably causing more rain in some areas and greater drought in others. Jon Gertner, "The Future Is Drying Up," *The New York Times* (Oct. 21, 2007), online at http://www.nytimes.com/2007/10/21/magazine/21water-t.html.

92. Ibid.

93. Under the ICESCR governments have a "core obligation" to ensure the minimum conditions for health, which includes clean air, and "an adequate supply of safe and potable water." Committee on Economic, Social and Cultural Rights, "The Right to the Highest Attainable Standard of Health," General Comment No. 14, E/C.12/2000/4 (Aug. 11, 2000), 43.c, online at http://www.unhchr.ch/tbs/doc.nsf/(symbol)/E.C.12.2000.4.En?OpenDocument. See also Rebecca Brown, "South African Win Landmark Victory for the Human Right to Water," *OneWorld.net* (May 5, 2008), online at us.oneworld.net/link/gotolink/addhit/83722.

94. Vandana Shiva, *Water Wars,* 7.

95. Ibid., 30–31. Shiva argues that, "Community rights are necessary for both ecology and democracy. Bureaucratic control by distant and external agencies and market control by commercial interests and corporations create disincentives for conservation. Local communities do not conserve water or maintain water systems if external agencies—bureaucratic or commercial—are the only beneficiaries of their efforts and resources."

96. Amit Srivastava of the India Resource Center reminds us that international law affirms: "Access to potable water is a fundamental human right." Aaron Glanz, "Coke Faces New Charges in India, Including 'Greenwashing,'" *OneWorld.net* (Jun. 6, 2007), online at http://us.oneworld.net/article/view/150028/1.

97. Vandana Shiva, *Water Wars,* 10.

98. By putting "a national cap on greenhouse gas emissions and running a national auction for emissions permits under the cap, the federal government could [probably] accrue tens of billions [of dollars] annually," which might be better than simply a cap-and-trade program. "When Europe first tried regulating greenhouse gases under a cap-and-trade program, in 2005, it gave away, or 'grandfathered,' emissions permits to its power generators, which made modest changes in their operations and then sold the permits to others at a premium. The result: windfall profits for the power companies. Europe is now switching to emissions auctions and plans to finance programs promoting climate protection, economic growth and energy security with the proceeds." Ian Bowlers, "Want to Buy Some Pollution?" *The New York Times* (Mar. 15, 2008), online at http://www.nytimes.com/2008/03/15/opinion/15bowles.html.

99. Vandana Shiva, *Water Wars,* 100–101.

100. Patrick J. Sullivan, Franklin J. Agardy, and James J. J. Clark, *The Environmental Science of Drinking Water,* 124.

101. "According to the Washington, DC–based Earth Policy Institute, consumers spend about $100 billion on bottled water each year. By comparison, experts estimate that just $15 billion per year, above and beyond what is already spent, could bring reliable and lasting access to safe drinking water to half a billion people worldwide—fully half of those who lack it." Aaron Glanz, "Coke Faces New Charges in India, Including 'Greenwashing,'" *OneWorld.net* (Jun. 6, 2007), online at http://us.oneworld.net/article/view/150028/1.

102. Ibid. "From the 1970s to 2000 . . . the annual volume of bottled water purchased and sold in the United States has increased by over 7,000 percent. Yet the bottled water industry operates with little or no regulation."

103. "The so-called Great Pacific Garbage Patch, a stewy body of plastic and marine debris that floats an estimated 1,000 miles west of San Francisco, is a shape-shifting mass far too large, delicate, and remote to ever be cleaned up, according to a researcher who recently returned from the area." Justin Berton, "Feds Want to Survey, Possibly Clean Up Vast Garbage Pit in Pacific,"

San Francisco Chronicle (Oct. 21, 2007), A-1, online at http://www.sfgate.com/cgi-bin/article
.cgi?file=/c/a/2007/10/30/MNT5T1NER.DTL.

104. Charles Moor, "Trashed: Across the Pacific Oceans, Plastics, Plastics Everywhere," *Water Pollution,* 151.

105. It takes 1.5 million barrels of oil per year to create enough PET plastic to make the bottles. "The Real Cost of Bottled Water," *WWF News* (May 3, 2001), online at http://www.panda
.org/about_wwf/what_we_do/freshwater/news/index.cfm?uNewsID=2250. "In 2006, more than 900,000 tons of plastic was used to package 8 billion gallons of bottled water. Production of this plastic leads to the release of a variety of chemicals. Most smaller bottles are made from polyethylene terephthalate (PET), which generates more than 100 times more toxic emissions than an equivalent amount of glass (Berkeley Ecology Center)." "Bottled Water," The Sierra Club, online at http://www.sierraclub.org/committees/cac/water/bottled_water/bottled_water.pdf.

CHAPTER 12: AGRICULTURE

1. Vaclav Smil, *Feeding the World: A Challenge for the Twenty-First Century* (Cambridge, MA: The MIT Press, 2000), xvi.

2. William Ophuls and A. Stephen Boyan, Jr., *Ecology and the Politics of Scarcity Revisited* (New York: W. H. Freeman and Company, 1992), 49–50.

3. David Pimentel and Mario Giampietro, *Food, Land, Population and the U.S. Economy* (Carrying Capacity Network Publications, November 1994), in Dale Allen Pfeiffer, *Eating Fossil Fuels: Oil, Food and the Coming Crisis in Agriculture* (Gabriola Island, Canada: New Society Publishers, 2006), 11.

4. William Ophuls and A. Stephen Boyan, Jr., *Ecology and the Politics of Scarcity Revisited,* 50–51.

5. Dale Allen Pfeiffer, *Eating Fossil Fuels,* 15.

6. "Water tables are dropping a meter or more each year beneath a large area of irrigated farmland in north China; they are falling 20 centimeters a year across two-thirds of India's Punjab, that nation's breadbasket." Dale Allen Pfeiffer, *Eating Fossil Fuels,* 16.

7. "The Ogallala Aquifer that supplies agriculture, industry and home use in much of the southern and central plains states has an annual overdraft 130 to 160 percent in excess of replacement. This vitally important aquifer will become unproductive in another thirty years or so." Dale Allen Pfeiffer, *Eating Fossil Fuels,* 17.

8. Dale Allen Pfeiffer, *Eating Fossil Fuels,* 15. See Sandra L. Postel, Gretchen C. Caily and Paul R. Ehrlich, "Human Appropriation of Renewable Fresh Water," *Science* 271 (Feb. 9, 1996): 785.

9. "Prevailing fertilizer applications are accompanied by large nutrient losses; nitrogen leakage is particularly large due to leaching, erosion, volatilization [loss due to evaporation], and denitrification [changing usable oxidized forms of nitrogen into nitrogen gas]." Vaclav Smil, *Feeding the World,* xviii.

10. James Gustave Speth, *Red Sky at Morning,* 16. Des Moines, Iowa, draws its drinking water from the Des Moines River. "In spring, when nitrogen runoff is at its heaviest, the city issues 'blue baby alerts,' warning parents it's unsafe to give children water from the tap. The nitrates in the water bind to hemoglobin, compromising the blood's ability to carry oxygen to the brain." Michael Pollan, *Omnivore's Dilemma: A Natural History of Four Meals* (New York: The Penguin Press, 2006), 46–47.

11. Michael Pollan, *Omnivore's Dilemma,* 47.

12. Edward O. Wilson, *The Future of Life,* 114. Ecosystems are naturally diverse and thus more fit to survive a change in climate or other distressing event. See James Trefil, *Human Nature,* 193.

13. Michael Pollan, *Omnivore's Dilemma,* 147.

14. "Nitrogen: Role in Plant Biology," Kemira-GrowHow, online at http://www.kemira
-growhow.com/UK/TechnicalAdvice/Plant+Growth/Nitrogen.

15. "The Nitrogen Cycle," *Fundamentals of Physical Geography,* online at http://www.physical geography.net/fundamentals/9s.html.

16. "Phosphorus Cycle," *Environmental Literacy Council,* online at http://www.enviroliteracy .org/article.php/480.html.

17. Ibid.

18. "Potassium: Role in Plant Biology," *Environmental Literacy Council,* online at http://www .kemira-growhow.com/UK/TechnicalAdvice/Plant+Growth/Potassium.

19. W. Grzebisz, K. Cyna, and M. Wron´ska, "Disturbances of the Bio-geo-chemical Potassium Cycle," *Journal of Elementology* 9, no. 4 (Supplement; 2004): 67–77, online at http:// www.cababstractsplus.org/google/abstract.asp?AcNo=20053049354.

20. Michael Pollan, *Omnivore's Dilemma,* 149.

21. Dale Allen Pfeiffer, *Eating Fossil Fuels,* 1. Fisheries, as well as agriculture, depend on "cheap seemingly super-abundant fossil fuels." Donald Kennedy, ed., *Science Magazine's State of the Planet: 2006–2007,* 34. This is also true for fish farming (aquaculture), as fishing fleets need to catch the cheap fish to make the fishmeal to feed the fish being farmed. "Peter Tyedmers of Dalhousie University in Nova Scotia has calculated that for every kilogram of Canadian farmed salmon produced, 2.5 to 5 liters of diesel fuel or its equivalent is consumed." John Ryan, "Feedlots of the Sea," *World Watch Magazine,* vol. 16, no. 5 (Sep/Oct 2003), in Peter Singer and Jim Mason, *The Way We Eat,* 123.

22. Michael Pollan, *Omnivore's Dilemma,* 183.

23. Ibid., 7.

24. Ibid., 8–9. In India farmers argue that artificial pesticides have depleted the soil, and doctors find increasing health problems that seem to be related to the use of artificial pesticides. See Daniel Pepper, "Some Indians Fear Green Revolution is a Killer," *San Francisco Chronicle* (Jul. 28, 2008), A-12, online at http://www.sfgate.com/cgi-bin/article.cgi?f=/c/a/2008/07/27/MN3M11LLJQ.DTL.

25. "More than half of all the synthetic nitrogen made today is applied to corn, whose hybrid strains can make better use of it than any other plant. Growing corn, which from a biological perspective had always been a process of capturing sunlight to turn it into food, has in no small measure become a process of converting fossil fuels into food." Michael Pollan, *Omnivore's Dilemma,* 45.

26. Francis Moore Lappé and Anna Lappé, *Hope's Edge,* 258.

27. Ibid., see David Pimentel et. al., "Environmental and Economic Impacts of Reducing U.S. Agricultural Pesticide Use," *Handbook of Pest Management in Agriculture,* Vol. 1, 679–718 (Boca Raton, FL: CRC press, 1991), also printed in Pimentel and Lehmen, eds., *The Pesticide Question: Environment, Economics and Ethics* (Springer, 1993), 223–278, in Francis Moore Lappé and Anna Lappé, *Hope's Edge,* 258.

28. FAO Corporate Document Repository, "Crop Protection in the Context of Agricultural Development," online at http://www.fao.org/WAIRDOCS/TAC/Y4847E/y4847e05.htm.

29. David Pimentel, "Is Silent Spring Behind Us?" G. J. Marco, R. M. Hollingsworth, and E. Durham, eds., *Silent Spring Revisited* (Washington, DC: American Chemical Society, 1987), in Louis P. Pojman and Paul Pojman, eds., *Environmental Ethics,* 536. Pimentel offers three additional reasons for crop losses: "reduced FDA tolerance and increased cosmetic standards of processors and retailers for fruits and vegetables," "reduced field sanitation including less destruction of infected fruit and crop residues," and "reduced tillage, leaving more crop remains on the land surface to harbor pests for subsequent crops."

30. Lester E. Ehler, "Integrated Pest Management: A National Goal?" *Issues in Science and Technology,* online at http://www.issues.org/22.1/stalk.html.

31. Ibid.

32. Ibid.

33. The World Bank requires that agricultural projects "reduce reliance on pesticides and promote farmer-driven, ecologically based integrated pest management." In 1993, however, a World

Bank report concluded that both national governments and agribusiness were promoting "excessive chemical pesticide use." FAO Corporate Document Repository, "Crop Protection in the Context of Agricultural Development," online at http://www.fao.org/WAIRDOCS/TAC/Y4847E/y4847e05.htm.

34. George Pyle, *Raising Less Corn, More Hell: The Case for the Independent Farm and Against Industrial Food* (New York: Public Affairs, 2005), 12.

35. The four main food processors are Gold Kist, Perdue Farms, Pilgrim's Pride, and Tyson. Cargill/Excel, Smithfield, Swift, and Tyson/IBP control 64 percent of the national pork market. Ibid., 13, 16.

36. Four other companies—Monsanto, Novartis, Dow Chemical, and DuPont—sell 75 percent of the corn seed and 60 percent of the soybean seed being sown. Ibid., 17.

37. See chapter 3 for a discussion of the economic reasoning that supports this conclusion.

38. Kurt Eichenwald, "Archer Daniel Midland, Fine-Payer to the US," *The New York Times* (Oct. 20, 1996), in Francis Moore Lappé and Anna Lappé, *Hope's Edge*, 300.

39. Dwayne Andreas quoted by Dan Carney in "Dwayne's World," *Mother Jones* (Jan. 1995), in Francis Moore Lappé and Anna Lappé, *Hope's Edge*, 300.

40. Michael Pollan, *Omnivore's Dilemma*, 52.

41. "Or, as it turned out, make up *some* of the difference, since just about every farm bill since has lowered the target price in order, it was claimed, to make American grain more competitive in world markets." Ibid.

42. Corn "is trading on the market at about twice the price it was just a couple of years ago." Joel Achenbach, "So What's So Bad about Corn?" *The Washington Post* (Nov. 23, 2007), A01, online at http://www.washingtonpost.com/wp-dyn/content/article/2007/11/22/AR200711220 1442.html.

43. Ibid. "The rural prosperity is due in large measure to billions of dollars in federal subsidies and incentives for corn-based energy. These include a 51-cent tax credit that gasoline manufacturers get on every gallon of ethanol they mix with their blends, and more than $500 million in federal cash to ethanol refiners between 2001 and 2006."

44. Dan Morgan, "Corn Farms Prosper, but Subsidies Still Flow," *The Washington Post* (Sep. 27, 2007), A01, http://www.washingtonpost.com/wp-dyn/content/article/2007/09/27/AR20070 92702054.html. The United States is not alone in subsidizing agriculture. In 2002 the WTO reported "that the rich nations subsidize their agricultural producers at a rate of $1 billion a day, or more than six times the level of development aid they give to poor nations." "Background Paper: The WTO's 2-Year Strategy Comes to Fruition," (Jan. 2002), para. 17, online at http://www.wto.org/english/news_e/news_e.htm, in Peter Singer, *One World,* 95.

45. Carol Ness, "The New Food Crusade," *San Francisco Chronicle* (Jul. 10, 2007), A1, online at http://sfgate.com/cgi-bin/article.cgi?f=/c/a/2007/07/10/MNGNUQTQIT1.DTL. See also Michael Pollan, "You Are What You Grow," *The New York Times* (Apr. 22, 2007), online at http://www.nytimes.com/2007/04/22/magazine/22wwlnlede.t.html.

46. Editorial, "A Disgraceful Farm Bill," *The New York Times* (May 16, 2008), online at http://www.nytimes.com/2008/05/16/opinion/16fri3.html. "According to Oxfam, the largest 10 percent of producers receive about 75 percent of the $20 billion in US commodity subsidies each year." Caitlin G. Johnson, "Mixed Reactions to US Farm Bill," *OneWorld.net* (May 22, 2008), online at http://us.oneworld.net/article/view/160644/1.

47. For example, "From 2001 to 2005, the federal government spent nearly $1.2 billion in agricultural subsidies to boost farmers' incomes and invigorate local economies in this poverty-stricken region of the Mississippi Delta.

Most residents are black, but less than 5 percent of the money went to black farmers. They own relatively little land, and so they generally do not qualify for the payments. Ninety-five percent of the money went to large, commercial farms, virtually all of which have white owners." Gilbert M. Gaul and Dan Morgan, "A Slow Demise in the Delta," *The Washington Post* (Jun. 20, 2007), A01, online at http://www.washingtonpost.com/wp-dyn/content/article/2007/06/19/AR2007061902193.html.

48. "Farming: Farm Subsidies," Environmental Working Group, online at http://www.ewg.org/featured/8.

49. "Crop Subsidy Program in United States, 2003–2005," Environmental Working Group, online at http://farm.ewg.org/sites/farmbi112007/top_recips1614.php?fips=00000&progcode=farmprog&enttype=indv&enttype=entity.

50. George Pyle, *Raising Less Corn, More Hell*, 75.

51. Gary Holthaus, *From the Farm to the Table: What All Americans Need to Know about Agriculture* (Lexington, KY: The University Press of Kentucky, 2006), 210. See the Institute for Agriculture and Trade Policy, online at http://www.iatp.org.

52. Gary Holthaus, *From the Farm to the Table*, 216–219.

53. "Through conditionalities, Structural Adjustment Programs [SAPs] generally implement 'free market' programs and policy. These programs include internal changes (notably privatization and deregulation) as well as external ones, especially the reduction of trade barriers. Countries which fail to enact these programs may be subject to severe fiscal discipline. Critics argue that financial threats to poor countries amount to blackmail; that poor nations have no choice but to comply." Online at http://en.wikipedia.org/wiki/Structural_adjustment.

54. John Madeley, ed., *Trade and Hunger: An Overview of Case Studies on the Impact of Trade Liberalisation on Food Security*, Swedish NGOs Forum Synod, Diakonia, Church of Sweden Aid and the Swedish Society for Nature Conservation, in Gary Holthaus, *From the Farm to the Table*, 219. It is much the same in Kenya, where women produce 75 percent of the food: "As a result of the country's SAP and liberalization of agricultural trade, many women cannot afford adequate chemicals and fertilizers, and farm output has declined. Liberalization has led to an increase in food imports into the country and caused food dumping (cheap surplus food from the North) in local markets, hitting the country's own farmers. Liberalization has also led to an increase in the prices of farm inputs, putting them beyond the reach of most small farmers." Ibid., 220.

55. Girish Mishra, "Why Suicides by Farmers?" *ZNet* (Dec. 20, 2005), online at http://www.zmag.org/znet/viewArticle/4785. US cotton subsidies have also had a devastating impact on West African families producing cotton. "More than 1 million children in West Africa would not go to bed hungry if Washington stopped providing subsidies to America's cotton growers, according to a study" by Oxfam International. Haider Rizvi, "US Cotton Subsidies Cost W. Africa Millions—Report," *OneWorld.net* (Jun. 26, 2007), online at http://us.oneworld.net/article/view/150611/1.

56. "I think the average American should know that the world trading system is not fair. You take the area of agriculture. If US farmers are getting huge subsidies, European farmers are getting huge subsidies and are competing on the global market with a farmer from Burkina Faso or Kenya, how do they compete?" Kofi Annan, quoted in "Annan: World Must Help African Nations Tackle Food Crisis," *The NewsHour* (Jun. 11, 2008), online at http://www.pbs.org/newshour/bb/africa/jan-june08/annan_06-11.html.

57. In 2008 "about a quarter of US corn will go to feeding ethanol plants instead of poultry or livestock." Steven Mufson, "Siphoning Off Corn to Fuel Our Cars," *The Washington Post* (Apr. 30, 2008), A01, online at http://www.washingtonpost.com/wp-dyn/content/article/2008/04/29/AR2008042903092.html. "Brazil and the United States account for a total of more than 70 percent of global ethanol production." Edmund L. Andrews and Larry Rohter, "US and Brazil Seek to Promote Ethanol in West," *The New York Times* (Mar. 3, 2007), online at http://www.nytimes.com/2007/03/03/business/worldbusiness/03ethanol.html.

58. Michael Pollan, *Omnivore's Dilemma*, 41.

59. "The demand for ethanol is already pushing up prices, and explains, in part, the 40 percent rise last year in the food price index calculated by the United Nations' Food and Agricultural Organization." Keith Bradsher, "An Oil Quandry: Costly Fuel Means Costly Calories," *The New York Times* (Jan. 19, 2008), online at http://www.nytimes.com/2008/01/19/business/worldbusiness/19palmoil.html. Aditya Chakrabortty editorial, "Secret Report: Biofuel Caused Food Crisis—Internal World Bank Study Delivers Blow to Plant Energy Drive," *The Guardian* (Jul. 4, 2008), online at http://www.guardian.co.uk/environment/2008/jul/03/biofuels.renewableenergy. See also "Man-Made Hunger," *The New York Times* (Jul. 6, 2008), online at http://www.nytimes.com/2008/07/06/opinion/06sun1.html.

60. "Consumption of meat and other high-quality foods—mainly in China and India—has boosted demand for grain for animal feed. Poor harvests due to bad weather in this country and elsewhere have contributed. High energy prices are adding to the pressures. Yet the most important reason for the price shock is the rich world's subsidized appetite for biofuels. In the United States, 14 percent of the corn crop was used to produce ethanol in 2006—a share expected to reach 30 percent by 2010. This is also cutting into production of staples like soybeans, as farmers take advantage of generous subsidies and switch crops to corn for fuel." Editorial, "Priced Out of the Market," *The New York Times* (Mar. 3, 2008), online at http://www.nytimes.com/2008/03/03/opinion/03mon1.html.

61. "The global food crisis is likely to persist if speculative investment by the corporate world is not reined in soon, warned a top expert responsible for reporting to the United Nations on human rights violations." Haider Rizvi, "UN's Food Rights Advocate Warms Speculators," *OneWorld.net* (May 3, 2008), online at http://us.oneworld.net/article/view/160347/1.

62. Talif Deen, "Dash to Convert Food into Fuels Is Recipe for Disaster," *CommonDreams.org* (Nov. 7, 2007), online at http://www.commondreams.org/archive/2007/11/07/5088.

63. "The palm is a highly efficient producer of vegetable oil, squeezed from the tree's thick bunches of plum-size bright red fruit. An acre of oil palms yields as much oil as eight acres of soybeans, the main rival for oil palms; rapeseed, used to make canola oil, is a distant third. Among major crops, only sugar cane comes close to rivaling oil palms in calories of human food per acre. . . . Farmers and plantation companies are responding to the higher prices, clearing hundreds of thousands of acres of tropical forest to replant with rows of oil palms. But an oil palm takes eight years to reach full production." Keith Bradsher, "An Oil Quandry: Costly Fuel Means Costly Calories," *The New York Times* (Jan. 19, 2008), online at http://www.nytimes.com/2008/01/19/business/worldbusiness/19palmoil.html.

64. Michael Pollan, *Omnivore's Dilemma,* 117.

65. Ibid., 118.

66. James Gustave Speth, *Red Sky at Morning,* 72.

67. Michael Pollan, *Omnivore's Dilemma,* 118.

68. This is also true for fish farming (aquaculture). See Peter Singer and Jim Mason, *The Way We Eat,* 122–124.

69. See Jazmine Rodriguez, "Hungry Farmers Urge Local Control Over Food," *OneWorld.net* (Jun. 13, 2008), online at http://us.oneworld.net/node/160879.

70. "Historically, fertility rates have fallen when people, especially women, have access to education, to jobs, and to food to feed their families." Francis Moore Lappé and Anna Lappé, *Hope's Edge,* 298.

71. Barbara Crossette, "Population Estimates Fall as Poor Women Assert Control," *The New York Times* (Mar. 10, 2002), 3, online at http://www.iwhc.org/resources/nyt031002.cfm.

72. Yifat Susskind from MADRE, an international women's human rights organization. Ida Wahlstrom, "Small Farmers 'Underserved' by Rome Summit," *OneWorld.net* (Jun. 5, 2008), online at http://us.oneworld.net/article/view/160811/1.

73. Gita Sen, "Women, Poverty, and Population: Issues for the Concerned Environmentalist," in W. Harcourt, ed., *Feminist Perspectives on Sustainable Development,* (London: Zed, 1994), 216–225, in David Schmidtz and Elizabeth Willott, eds., *Environmental Ethics,* 248.

74. "This has to be more than lip-service; it requires reorienting international assistance and national policy, reshaping programs and rethinking research questions and methodologies." Ibid., 252.

75. V. Rukmini Rao, "Women Farmers of India's Deccan Plateau: Ecofeminists Challenge World Elites," in David Schmidtz and Elizabeth Willott, eds., *Environmental Ethics,* 255.

76. Ibid., 256.

77. Ibid., 257.

78. Ibid.

79. Deccan Development Society, "About Us," online at http://www.ddsindia.com/www/default.asp.

80. The use of fertilizer in Malawi, however, seems to have ended famine there. "Over the past 20 years, the World Bank and some rich nations that Malawi depends on for aid have periodically pressed this small, landlocked country to adhere to free market policies and cut back or eliminate fertilizer subsidies, even as the United States and Europe extensively subsidized their own farmers. But after the 2005 harvest, the worst in a decade, Bingu wa Mutharika, Malawi's newly elected president, decided to follow what the West practiced, not what it preached. Stung by the humiliation of pleading for charity, he led the way to reinstating and deepening fertilizer subsidies despite a skeptical reception from the United States and Britain. Malawi's soil, like that across sub-Saharan Africa, is gravely depleted, and many, if not most, of its farmers are too poor to afford fertilizer at market prices." Celia W. Dugger, "Ending Famine Simply by Ignoring the Experts," *The New York Times* (Dec. 2, 2007), online at http://www.nytimes.com/2007/12/02/world/africa/02malawi.html.

81. V. Rukmini Rao, "Women Farmers of India's Deccan Plateau: Ecofeminists Challenge World Elites," in David Schmidtz and Elizabeth Willott, eds., *Environmental Ethics,* 259–260.

82. The twenty-five childcare centers (balwadis) operated by DDS sanghams provide care for seven hundred children of laboring women, and 60 percent of these children are girls. The food served in the balwadis: "is made up of the crops grown in the same villages: sorghum, millets, a bit of wheat and a range of uncultivated greens. Being highly superior to rice, the millet-based meals provide a nutritional advantage to the children, meeting 70 percent of their nutritional requirement and helping their mental and physical growth. Besides they also enable the children to respect their own food culture by adapting to it at a very young age." Deccan Development Society, "About Us," online at http://www.ddsindia.com/www/default.asp.

83. Ibid.

84. "The 16 Decisions of Grameen Bank," online at http://www.grameen-info.org/bank/the16.html.

85. Ibid. For information on the Grameen Bank see http://www.grameen-info.org/.

86. "The 16 Decisions of Grameen Bank," online at http://www.grameen-info.org/bank/the16.html.

87. George Pyle, *Raising Less Corn, More Hell,* 159. Pyle notes that the Economic Research Service of the US Department of Agriculture "blames hunger on economic, rather than agricultural, factors."

88. As diverting corn to make ethanol has driven up food prices, investors have begun to promote making biofuel from "non-food crops like reeds and wild grasses." But scientists are warning that these "invasive species—that is, weeds—have an extraordinarily high potential to escape biofuel plantations, overrun adjacent farms and natural land, and create economic and ecological havoc." Elisabeth Rosenthal, "New Trends in Biofuels Has New Risks," *The New York Times* (May 21, 2008), online at http://www.nytimes.com/2008/05/21/science/earth/21biofuels.html.

89. William Ophuls and A. Stephen Boyan, Jr., *Ecology and the Politics of Scarcity Revisited,* 38–39.

90. In the United States this might mean investing in irrigation for crops in the eastern part of the country, where there is more water. See Richard T. McNider and John R. Christy, "Let the East Bloom Again," *The New York Times* (Sep. 22, 2007), online at http://www.nytimes.com/2007/09/22/opinion/22mcnider.html.

91. Richard Earles, revised by Paul Williams, "Sustainable Agriculture: An Introduction," National Sustainable Agriculture Information Service (2005), online at http://www.attra.org/attra-pub/sustagintro.html.

92. Preston Sullivan, "Applying the Principles of Sustainable Farming: Fundamentals of Sustainable Agriculture," National Sustainable Agriculture Information Service (2003), online at http://www.attra.org/attra-pub/trans.html.

93. Ibid.

94. Michael Pollan, *Omnivore's Dilemma,* 150.

95. "The National Organic Program," USDA, online at http://www.ams.usda.gov/nop/index IE.htm.

96. Michael Pollan, *Omnivore's Dilemma,* 151.

97. "Principles of Organic Agriculture," IFOAM, online at http://www.ifoam.org/about_ifoam/principles/index.html. "Worldwide, demand for certified organic products is increasing at 10 percent annually." Peter Singer and Jim Mason, *The Way We Eat,* 197.

98. Preston Sullivan, "Applying the Principles of Sustainable Farming: Fundamentals of Sustainable Agriculture," National Sustainable Agriculture Information Service (2003), online at http://www.attra.org/attra-pub/trans.html.

99. Ibid. Industrial agricultural has altered the hydrology of the land, making flooding in places like Iowa more likely. In early June 2008, "the heavy rains fell on a landscape radically reengineered by humans. Plowed fields have replaced tall grass prairies. Fields have been meticulously drained with underground pipes. Streams and creeks have been straightened. Most of the wetlands are gone. Flood plains have been filled and developed." Joel Achenbach, "Iowa Flooding Could Be an Act of Man, Experts Say," *The Washington Post* (Jun. 19, 2008), A01, online at http://www.washingtonpost.com/wp-dyn/content/article/2008/06/18/AR2008061803371.html.

100. Ibid.

101. Ibid.

102. Ibid.

103. "Nematodes are simple roundworms." Biological Control: A Guide to Natural Enemies in North America, online at http://www.nysaes.cornell.edu/ent/biocontrol/pathogens/nematodes.html.

104. Preston Sullivan, "Applying the Principles of Sustainable Farming: Fundamentals of Sustainable Agriculture," National Sustainable Agriculture Information Service (2003), online at http://www.attra.org/attra-pub/trans.html.

105. Ibid.

106. "At a time when philanthropists like Bill Gates have become entranced by the possibility of a Green Revolution for Africa, the New Rices for Africa, as scientists call the wonder seeds, offer a clear warning. Even the most promising new crop varieties will not by themselves bring the plentiful harvests that can end poverty. New ways to get seeds into the hands of farmers are needed, as well as broader investment in the basic ingredients of a farm economy: roads, credit and farmer education, among others." Celia W. Dugger, "In Africa, Prosperity from Seeds Falls Short," *The New York Times* (Oct. 10, 2007), online at http://www.nytimes.com/2007/10/10/world/africa/10rice.html.

107. As grain prices soared in the summer of 2007: "Investors fleeing Wall Street's mortgage-related strife plowed hundreds of millions of dollars into grain futures, driving prices up even

more." Anthony Faiola, "The New Economics of Hunger," *The Washington Post* (Apr. 27, 2008), A01, online at http://www.washingtonpost.com/wp-dyn/content/story/2008/04/26/ST20080 42602333.html. Diana B. Henriques, "A Bull Market Sees the Worst in Speculators," *The New York Times* (Jun. 13, 2008), online at http://www.nytimes.com/2008/06/13/business/13speculate .html, and "Oil Trading's Powerful 'Dark Markets,'" *CBS News* (Jun. 17, 2008), online at http:// www.cbsnews.com/stories/2008/06/17/broadcasts/main4188620.shtml.

108. David Fogarty, "Farmers Face Climate Challenge in Quest for More Food," *Reuters* (May 4, 2008), online at http://www.reuters.com/article/environmentNews/idUSSP28472120080504.

109. Norman Myers and Jennifer Kent, *Perverse Subsidies,* 12, 13, 14, 27.

110. Dan Morgan, "Corn Farms Prosper but Subsidies Still Flow," *The Washington Post* (Sep. 28, 2007), A01, online at http://www.washingtonpost.com/wp-dyn/content/article/2007/09/27/ AR2007092702054.html.

111. Norman Myers and Jennifer Kent, *Perverse Subsidies,* 46, 50, 136. "In this dry region, irrigation accounts for 86 percent of water use. Ironically, irrigation is used to grow crops that are officially in surplus and subject to other expensive federal programs to reduce production."

112. Editorial, "The Worst Way of Farming," *The New York Times* (May 31, 2008), online at http://www.nytimes.com/2008/05/31/opinion/31sat4.html. The report funded by the Pew Charitable Trust "recommends new laws regulating pollution from industrial farms as rigorously as pollution from other industries, a phasing-out of confinement systems that restrict 'natural movement and normal behavior,' a ban on antibiotics used only to promote animal growth, and the application of antitrust laws to encourage more competition and less concentration."

113. Norman Myers and Jennifer Kent, *Perverse Subsidies,* 27.

114. Ibid., 28.

115. Ibid., 29. See Alexei Barrioneuvo, "Honeybees Vanish, Leaving Beekeepers in Peril," *The New York Times* (Feb. 27, 2007), online at http://www.nytimes.com/2007/02/27/business/ 27bees.html. The Natural Resources Defense Council has filed suit against the EPA because it "is refusing to disclose records about a new class of pesticides that could be playing a role in the disappearance of millions of honeybees in the United States." Jane Kay, "Lawsuit Seeks Pesticide Data," *San Francisco Chronicle* (Aug. 19, 2008), A-1, online at http://www.sfgate.com/cgi-bin/ article.cgi?f=/c/a/2008/08/18/BAKR12DBPO.DTL.

116. Norman Myers and Jennifer Kent, *Perverse Subsidies,* 59. In New Zealand subsidies are not necessary for agriculture to be profitable. Wayne Arnold, "Surviving Without Subsidies," *The New York Times* (Aug. 2, 2007), online at http://www.nytimes.com/2007/08/02/business/worldbusiness/ 02farm.html.

117. Even as there are benefits from the Green Revolution, there are also benefits from GM plants. For instance, "Researchers at the University of Washington have genetically altered poplar trees to pull toxins out of contaminated ground water, offering a cost-effective way of cleaning up environmental pollutants. A group of British researchers, meanwhile, has developed genetically altered plants that can clean residues of military explosives from the environment." Julie Steenhuysen, "Genetically Modified Plants Vacuum Up Toxins," *Reuters* (Oct. 15, 2007), online at http:// www.reuters.com/article/scienceNews/idUSN1525312420071015.

118. The Center for Food Safety and the Sierra Club are suing Monsanto. "The groups said the wind-pollinated biotech sugar beets will cross-pollinate and contaminate conventional sugar beets, organic chard and table beet crops. As well, the groups said the biotech sugar beets will increase the recent rise of weeds resistant to herbicide, which have been reported on 2.4 million acres of US cropland." Carey Gillam, "Biotech Critics Challenging Monsanto GM Sugar Beet," *Reuters* (Jan. 23, 2008), online at http://www.reuters.com/article/healthNews/idUSN2359954920080123.

119. Vandana Shiva, *Water Wars,* 115.

120. This means significant changes in developed countries and world trade agreements, as well as in developing countries. See Jazmine Rodriguez, "Hungry Farmers Urge Local Control

Over Food," *OneWorld.net* (Jun. 13, 2009), online at http://us.oneworld.net/article/view/160879/1.

121. We should, however, support international fair trade. A 2002 Oxfam report notes: "History makes a mockery of the claim that trade cannot work for the poor. Participation in world trade has figured prominently in many of the most successful cases of poverty reduction—and, compared with aid, it has far more potential to benefit the poor." Peter Singer and Jim Mason, *The Way We Eat*, 154.

122. See Michael Pollen, "Farmer in Chief," *The New York Times* (Oct. 9, 2008), online at http://www.nytimes.com/2008/10/12/magazine/12policy-t.html.

123. Dale Allen Pfeiffer, *Eating Fossil Fuels*, 70. See Robin Shulman, "Fed Up by Costs, Many Grow It Alone," *The Washington Post (Aug. 3, 2008)*, A03, online at http://www.washington post.com/wp-dyn/content/article/2008/08/02/AR2008080201397.html.

124. William Ophuls and A. Stephen Boyan, Jr., *Ecology and the Politics of Scarcity Revisited*, 44, 49.

125. Ibid.

CHAPTER 13: PUBLIC LAND

1. Edward O. Wilson, *The Future of Life*, 58. A summary of Wilson's recommendations are at 160–164.

2. Samuel Hays, *Conservation and the Gospel of Efficiency* (Cambridge, MA: Harvard University Press, 1959), 41–42, quoted in Joseph R. DesJardins, *Environmental Ethics*, 48.

3. Gifford Pinchot, *The Training of a Forester* (Philadelphia, PA: Lippincott, 1914), 13, quoted in Joseph R. DesJardins, *Environmental Ethics*, 48.

4. Ibid., 50.

5. Joseph R. DesJardins, *Environmental Ethics*, 49.

6. Solange Nadeau, Bruce A. Shinkler, and Christina Kakoyannis, "Beyond the Economic Model: Assessing Sustainability in Forest Communities," in Bruce A. Shindler, Thomas M. Beckley, and Mary Carmel Finley, eds., *Two Paths towards Sustainable Forests: Public Values in Canada and the United States* (Corvallis, OR: Oregon State University Press, 2003), 62.

7. An economic criticism of the US Forest Service is that it "subsidizes logging by selling timber at prices way below its own costs of timber marketing as well as by providing other subsidies, such as the $811 million in tax breaks that the forest industry enjoyed in 1991." Norman Myers and Jennifer Kent, *Perverse Subsidies*, 170.

8. Jack W. Thomas, "Are there lessons for Canadian foresters lurking south of the border?" *Forestry Chronicle* 78, no. 3 (2002): 382–387, in Peter N. Duinker, Gary Z. Bull, and Bruce Shindler, "Sustainable Forestry in Canada and the United States: Developments and Prospects," in Bruce A. Shindler, Thomas M. Beckley, and Mary Carmel Finley, eds., *Two Paths towards Sustainable Forests*, 38.

9. Brent S. Steel and Edward Weber, "Ecosystem Management and Public Opinion in the United States," in Bruce A. Shindler, Thomas M. Beckley, and Mary Carmel Finley, eds., *Two Paths towards Sustainable Forests*, 78.

10. Ibid., 80. The Clinton administration signed the Convention on Biological Diversity, which has a similar emphasis on ecosystem management. "The ecosystem approach is a strategy for the integrated management of land, water, and living resources that promotes conservation and sustainable use in an equitable way. Application of the ecosystem approach will help to reach a balance of the three objectives of the Convention. It is based on the application of appropriate scientific methodologies focused on levels of biological organization which encompass the essential processes, functions, and interactions among organisms and their environment. It recognizes that humans, with their cultural diversity, are an integral component of ecosystems." Online at http://www.cbd.int/ecosystem. The Clinton administration expected that the Senate would ratify

this treaty, but the opposition was so strong that the convention was never put to a vote. See "How the Convention on Biodiversity was Defeated," online at http://www.sovereignty.net/p/land/biotreatystop.htm.

11. Garry Peterson, "Using Ecological Dynamics to Move toward an Adaptive Architecture," in Charles J. Kibert, Jan Sendzimir, and G. Bradley Guy, eds., *Construction Ecology*, 139.

12. James Gustave Speth, *Red Sky at Morning*, 39.

13. Ibid. Forests in Brazil are being logged to plant sugar cane that will be used to produce ethanol. See Sabrina Vale, "Losing Forests to Fuel Cars," *The Washington Post* (Jul. 31, 2007), D01, online at http://www.washingtonpost.com/wp-dyn/content/article/2007/07/30/AR200 7073001484.html. In Niger, however, trees are being planted. See Lydia Polygren, "In Niger, Trees and Crops Turn Back the Desert," *The New York Times* (Feb. 11, 2007), online at http://www.nytimes.com/2007/02/11/world/africa/11niger.html.

14. James Gustave Speth, *Red Sky at Morning*, 40.

15. William McDonough and Michael Braungart, *Cradle to Cradle*, 88.

16. For example, "Except for a few isolated patches, the 31 million acres of California forests, indeed all the forests in the Western United States, have been changed in some way by humans." Peter Fimrite, "Bringing Forests Up to Date," *San Francisco Chronicle* (Feb. 29, 2008), W-2, online at http://sfgate.com/cgi-bin/article.cgi?f=/c/a/2008/02/29/BAJ5UNM1N.DTL.

17. Haider Rizvi, "Local Control Saves Forests—Report," *OneWorld.net* (Mar. 27, 2008), online at http://us.oneworld.net/article/view/159182/1. The largest private landowner in California, Sierra Pacific Industries, relies on the active forest management guidelines of the Sustainable Forest Initiative (SFI), which represents timber and paper interests. Jonathon Curiel, "Getting Clear with Sierra Pacific Industries," *San Francisco Chronicle* (Feb. 29, 2008), W-8, online at http://sfgate.com/cgi-bin/article.cgi?f=/c/a/2008/02/29/BAE7UTPD6.DTL. See Sustainable Forestry Initiative (SFI), online at http://www.aboutsfi.org.

18. Forestry Stewardship Council, "FSC's Case Studies," online at http://www.fsc.org/en/about/case_studies. The European version of FSC is the Programme for the Endorsement Forest Certification (PEFC) in the UK, online at http://www.pefc.org/internet/html.

19. Haider Rizvi, "Local Control Saves Forests—Report," *OneWorld.net* (Mar. 27, 2008), online at http://us.oneworld.net/article/view/159182/1.

20. "Northern Spotted Owl," Endangered, online at http://www.amnh.org/nationalcenter/Endangered/owl/owl.html.

21. Bruce Babbitt, *Cities in the Wilderness: A New Vision of Land Use in America* (Washington, DC: Island Press, 2005), 61.

22. Clare M, Ryan, "The Ecosystem Experiment in British Columbia and Washington State," in Bruce A. Shindler, Thomas M. Beckley, and Mary Carmel Finley, eds., *Two Paths towards Sustainable Forests*, 196.

23. "AMA Strategies—Executive Summary," online at http://www.fs.fed.us/gpnf/forest-research/ama/strategy/frmain.shtml.

24. Ibid.

25. "Press Release Threatened Ancient Forests Gain Reprieve," Northwest Ecosystem Alliance (Jul. 24, 1997), online at http://www.crcwater.org/issues2/gifford072497.html.

26. "Attacks on Forest Management Regulations," The Wilderness Society, online at http://www.wilderness.org/OurIssues/Forests/regulations.cfm?TopLevel=Regulations.

27. "Forest Management Plans," Conservation Northwest, online at http://www.conservationnw.org/oldgrowth/forest-management-plans.

28. "Final National Forest Regulations Take Step Backwards," The Wilderness Society, online at http://www.wilderness.org/OurIssues/Forests/nfma.cfm.

29. Release No. FS- 0627s, "Finalized Forest Service Rule Improves the Forest Planning Process and Increases Public Involvement," USDA Forest Service, online at http://www.fs.fed.us/news/2006/releases/12/ce-statement.shtml.

30. Brodie Farquhar, "New Forest Plan Rule Nukes NEPA," Truthout.org, online at http://www.truthout.org/cgi-bin/artman/exec/view.cgi/67/24496.

31. Dan Berman, "Judge Forbids Forest Service from Using 2005 Planning Regs," E&E News (Mar. 30, 2007), online at http://www.redlodgeclearinghouse.org/news/03_30_07_judge.html.

32. "What Is the Healthy Forests Initiative?," Healthy Forests Initiative, online at http://www.healthyforests.gov/initiative/introduction.html.

33. "HFI Administrative Reforms," Healthy Forests, online at http://www.healthyforests.gov/initiative/admin_actions.html.

34. Ibid.

35. "'Healthy Forests Initiative': A Campaign of Severe Policy Rollbacks," The Environmental Protection Information Center, online at http://www.wildcalifornia.org/publications/article-57.

36. The Sierra Club argues that the HFI will:

• Limit environmental analysis and limit public participation by excluding environmental analysis for any site-specific project the Forest Service and BLM claim will reduce hazardous fuels, including post-fire salvage projects; and by limiting public participation by allowing "hazardous fuels reduction projects" to be categorically excluded and suspends citizen's rights to appeal projects.

• Accelerate aggressive "thinning" across millions of acres of backcountry forests miles away from communities at risk to forest fires.

• Use "Goods for services" as the Funding Mechanism by (a) allowing the Forest Service and BLM to give away trees to logging companies as payment for any management activity, including logging on public lands; and (b) creating a powerful new incentive to log large fire-resistant trees, old growth, and other commercially valuable forests.

"Forest Protection & Restoration: Debunking the 'Healthy Forests Initiative,'" The Sierra Club, online at http://www.sierraclub.org/forests/fires/healthyforests_initiative.asp.

37. Brant Short and Dale C. Hardy-Short, "'Physicians of the Forest': A Rhetorical Critique of the Bush Healthy Forest Initiative," Electronic Green Journal, 19 (Dec. 2003), online at http://egj.lib.uidaho.edu/egj19/short1.html.

38. Ibid.

39. "Forest Guild Analysis of Wildfire Risk Reduction on Federal Lands," The Forest Guild, http://forestguild.org/fuel_reduction_evaluation.html.

40. "Mountain Top Removal," online at http://en.wikipedia.org/wiki/Mountaintop_removal. See also John M. Broder, "Rule to Expand Mountaintop Coal Mining," The New York Times (Aug. 23, 2008), online at http://www.nytimes.com/2007/08/23/us/23coal.html.

41. "Nature Overrun," The New York Times (Jan. 8, 2008), online at http://www.nytimes.com/2008/01/08/opinion/08tue1.html. See also Felicity Barringer and William Yardley, "Surge in Off-Roading Stirs Dust and Debate in West," The New York Times (Dec. 30, 2007), online at http://www.nytimes.com/2007/12/30/us/301ands.html.

42. Juliet Eilperin, "Congress Pushes to Keep Land Untamed," The Washington Post (Jun. 16, 2008), A01, online at http://www.washingtonpost.com/wp-dyn/content/article/2008/06/15/AR2008061502137.html.

43. Two of the best known essays are Robert Elliot, "Faking Nature," and Eric Katz, "The Big Lie: Human Restoration of Nature," in Andrew Light and Holmes Rolston III, eds., Environmental Ethics.

44. Andrew Light, "Ecological Restoration and the Culture of Nature: A Pragmatic Perspective," in Andrew Light and Holmes Rolston III, eds., Environmental Ethics, 399–400.

45. Ibid., 406–409. Restoration, Light concludes, "is an obligation exercised in the interests of forming a positive community with nature and thus is well within the boundaries of a positive, pragmatic environmental philosophy."

46. Bruce Babbitt, Cities in the Wilderness, 72.

47. Ibid., 73–74.

48. Ibid., 82.

49. Ibid.

50. Ibid., 93.

51. Ibid., 24.

52. Marjorie Stoneman Douglas was one of the first to warn of the threats to the Everglades in her famous book, *The Everglades: Rivers of Grass* (Rinehart: 1947).

53. Bruce Babbitt, *Cities in the Wilderness*, 17.

54. Ibid., 34.

55. The CERP goal is: "to capture fresh water that now flows unused to the ocean and the gulf and redirect it to areas that need it most. The majority of the water will be devoted to environmental restoration, reviving a dying ecosystem. The remaining water will benefit cities and farmers by enhancing water supplies for the south Florida economy." "About CERP: Brief Overview," Everglades Restoration, online at http://www.evergladesplan.org/about/about_cerp_brief.aspx. "In fact, the Everglades Restoration Plan is a kind of blueprint for what a managed planet will look like." James Trefil, *Human Nature*, 229.

56. In June 2008 the governor of Florida proposed that the state buy out one of the two largest sugar cane growers in order to protect the restoration project. It is not clear, however, that this purchase would provide the protection that the Everglades needs. Mary Williams Walsh, "Florida Deal for Everglades May Help Big Sugar," *The New York Times* (Sep. 13, 200), online at http://www.nytimes.com/2008/09/14/business/14fanjul.html.

57. "CERP: The Plan in Depth," Everglades Restoration, online at http://www.everglades plan.org/about/rest_plan_pt_01.aspx.

58. Everglades National Park, online at http://www.everglades.national-park.com/info.htm #his.

59. Everglades National Park, online at http://www.everglades.national-park.com/info.htm #his.

60. Efforts to restore a marshland that purifies Lake Tahoe are also encouraging. Peter Fimrite, "Healing the Lake," *San Francisco Chronicle* (Sep. 5, 2007), online at http://sfgate.com/cgi -bin/article.cgi?f=/c/a/2007/09/05/MNLLRLVHU.DTL.

61. John M. Broder, "After Lobbying, Wetlands Rules are Narrowed," *The New York Times* (Jul. 6, 2007), online at http://www.nytimes.com/2007/07/06/washington/06wetlands.html.

62. "New EPA Wetland Regulations a Victory for Private PropertyOwners," E-Team: Providing Accurate Information on Energy & Environment Issues (Jun. 6, 2007), online at http:// eteam.ncpa.org/news/new-epa-wetland-regulations-a-victory-for-private-property-owners.

63. Ministry of Environment & Forests (Government of India), The Official Website of Project Tiger, online at http://projecttiger.nic.in.

64. Ramachandra Guha, "Radical American Environmentalism and Wilderness Preservation: A Third World Critique," *Environmental Ethics* 11 (1989): 71–83, in David Schmidtz and Elizabeth Willott, eds., *Environmental Ethics*, 288.

65. Ibid., 291.

66. In the words of an Indian activist, "environmental protection per se is of least concern to most of these groups. Their main concern is about the use of the environment and who should benefit from it." Anil Agarwal, "Human-Nature Interactions in a Third World Country," *The Environmentalist* 6, no. 3 (1986): 167, quoted in Ramachandra Guha, "Radical American Environmentalism and Wilderness Preservation: A Third World Critique," *Environmental Ethics* 11 (1989): 71–83, in David Schmidtz and Elizabeth Willott, eds., *Environmental Ethics*, 291.

67. Samuel Hayes, "From Conservation to Environment: Environmental Politics in the United States since World War Two," *Environmental Review* 6 (1982): 21, quoted in Ramachandra Guha, "Radical American Environmentalism and Wilderness Preservation: A Third World

Critique," *Environmental Ethics* 11 (1989): 71–83, in David Schmidtz and Elizabeth Willott, eds., *Environmental Ethics*, 290.

68. Ramachandra Guha, "Radical American Environmentalism and Wilderness Preservation: A Third World Critique," *Environmental Ethics* 11 (1989): 71–83, in David Schmidtz and Elizabeth Willott, eds., *Environmental Ethics*, 290.

69. Ibid., 291.

70. Ibid., 292. "Both German and Indian environmental traditions allow for a greater integration of ecological concerns with livelihood and work. They also place a greater emphasis on equity and social justice . . . [And] they have escaped the preoccupation with wilderness preservation so characteristic of American cultural and environmental history."

71. Raymond Bonner, *At the Hand of Man: Peril and Hope for Africa's Wildlife* (New York: Alfred A. Knopf, 1993), 8, in David Schmidtz, "When Preservationism Doesn't Preserve," *Environmental Values* 6 (1997): 327–339, in David Schmidtz and Elizabeth Willott, eds., *Environmental Ethics*, 322.

72. David Schmidtz, "When Preservationism Doesn't Preserve," *Environmental Values*, 6 (1997): 327–39, in David Schmidtz and Elizabeth Willott, eds., *Environmental Ethics*, 323.

73. Ibid., 321.

74. Ibid., 322.

75. Ibid., 325.

76. Ibid.

77. Ibid., 324.

78. Online at http://freespace.virgin.net/jake.madders/Detailed%20info/living%20with %20wildlife.htm. The Nyaminyami district council recently decided to use zoning to designate:
- A conservation corridor to allow animals to move safely between two parks.
- Sites on the shore of Lake Kariba for small rustic camps for nature tourists.
- Unique stands of vegetation and habitats for crocodile breeding as conservation areas.
- Most of the rest of the land for safari hunting.

Online at http://freespace.virgin.net/jake.madders/campfire%20info.htm.

79. Raymond Bonner, "At the Hand of Man: Peril and Hope for Africa's Wildlife," in Raymond Bonner, *At the Hand of Man*, 253–278, in David Schmidtz and Elizabeth Willott, eds., *Environmental Ethics*, 315.

80. Ibid., 317.

81. Ibid., 315–319.

82. David Schmidtz, "When Preservationism Doesn't Preserve," *Environmental Values* 6 (1997): 327–339, in David Schmidtz and Elizabeth Willott, eds., *Environmental Ethics*, 326.

83. Ian J. Whyte, "Headaches and Heartaches: The Elephant Management Dilemma," in David Schmidtz and Elizabeth Willott, eds., *Environmental Ethics*, 303–304.

84. Ibid., 305.

CHAPTER 14: URBAN ECOLOGY

1. Aaron Glantz, "In Historic First, World Population Now Majority Urban," *OneWorld.net* (May 30, 2007), online at http://us.oneworld.net/article/view/149798/1/2091.

2. Anne Whiston Spirn, "City and Nature," in Stephen M. Wheeler and Timothy Beatley, eds., *The Sustainable Urban Development Reader* (London: Routledge, 2004), 115.

3. Ibid., 114.

4. Ibid.

5. Herbert Girardet, "The Metabolism of Cities," in Stephen M. Wheeler and Timothy Beatley, eds., *The Sustainable Urban Development Reader*, 125.

6. Ibid., 125–126.

7. Ibid.

8. James J. Kay, "On Complexity Theory, Exergy, and Industrial Ecology," in Charles J. Kibert, Jan Sendzimir, and G. Bradley Guy, eds., *Construction Ecology*, 96.

9. "Declaration of Interdependence for a Sustainable Future," UIA/AIA World Congress of Architects (Chicago, June 18–21, 1993), Peter Yost, "Construction and Demolition Waste: Innovative Assessment and Management," in Charles J. Kibert, ed., *Reshaping the Built Environment: Ecology, Ethics, and Economics* (Washington, DC: Island Press, 1999), 199.

10. Ibid.

11. Ibid. For more about green designing, see Michael Kimmelman, "The Accidental Environmentalist," *The New York Times* (May 20, 2007), online at http://www.nytimes.com/2007/05/20/magazine/20shigeru-t.html.

12. The Environmental Assessment Consortium, online at http://www.breeam.com.

13. US Green Building Council, online at http://www.usgbc.org.

14. International Green Building Challenge, online at http://www.eere.energy.gov/buildings/highperformance/gbc.html.

15. Raymond J. Cole, "Environmental Performance of Buildings: Setting Goals, Offering Guidance, and Assessing progress," in Charles J. Kibert, ed., *Reshaping the Built Environment*, 283. See Krishnan Gowri, "Green Building Rating Systems: An Overview," (Nov. 2004), online at http://www.energycodes.gov/implement/pdfs/Sustainability.pdf.

16. Jessica Woolliams, "Designing Cities and Buildings as If They Were Ethical Choices," in David Schmidtz and Elizabeth Willott, eds., *Environmental Ethics*, 427.

17. Andreas R. Edwards, *The Sustainability Revolution* (Gabriola Island, Canada: New Society Publishers, 2005), 97.

18. "Leadership in Energy and Environmental Design," US Green Building Council, online at http://www.usgbc.org/DisplayPage.aspx?CategoryID=19.

19. US Green Building Council, online at http://www.usgbc.org. Hotels in the United States are also beginning to use this standard. Gregory Dickum, "Pleasure Without Guilt: Green Hotels With Comfort," *The New York Times* (Dec. 28, 2007), online at http://www.nytimes.com/2007/12/28/travel/escapes/28greenhotels.html.

20. See Andrea Takash, "New Buildings Must Follow 'Green' Construction Standard," Environmental Update, US Army Environmental Command, online at http://aec.army.mil/usaec/publicaffairs/update/sum07/sum0720.html.

21. Kent E. Portney, *Taking Sustainable Cities Seriously: Economic Development, the Environment, and Quality of Life in American Cities* (Cambridge, MA: The MIT Press, 2003), 97.

22. Ibid.

23. Celia M. Vega, "SF Moves to Greenest Building Codes in US," *San Francisco Chronicle* (Mar. 20, 2008), A-1, online at http://sfgate.com/cgi-bin/article.cgi?f=/c/a/2008/03/20/MN7QVMJ5T.DTL.

24. Charles J. Kibert, Jan Sendzimir and G. Bradley Guy, "Defining an Ecology of Construction," in Charles J. Kibert, Jan Sendzimir, and G. Bradley Guy, eds., *Construction Ecology*, 16.

25. James J. Kay, "On Complexity Theory, Exergy, and Industrial Ecology," in Charles J. Kibert, Jan Sendzimir, and G. Bradley Guy, eds., *Construction Ecology*, 82.

26. "People who earn their living by sorting through and reselling municipal waste have reasserted their role as garbage recyclers and productive members of the global economy at an unprecedented event here this week.

The First World Congress of Waste Pickers, which closed Tuesday after four days of discussions among delegates from over 40 countries, included proposals about how waste pickers can form strong associations and even access funds through carbon credits. . . . Although there is no official estimate of the number of waste pickers worldwide, delegates from Colombia, Turkey, and China estimated that their national totals are around 300,000; 200,000; and 6 million respectively."

Henry Mance, "World's Garbage Recyclers Meet in Columbia," *OneWorld.net* (Mar. 5, 2008), online at http://us.oneworld.net/article/view/158501/1.

27. Robert U. Ayres, "Minimizing Waste Emissions from the Built Environment," in Charles J. Kibert, Jan Sendzimir, and G. Bradley Guy, eds., *Construction Ecology*, 165.

28. Ibid.

29. Ibid.

30. Ibid., 428. See also Timothy Gardner, "Cheaper Solar Power Heads Mainstream," *Reuters* (May 22, 2007), online at http://www.reuters.com/article/scienceNews/idUSN2241870 420070522, and Matt Richtel and John Markoff, "A Green Energy Industry Takes Root in California," *The New York Times* (Feb. 1, 2008), online at http://www.nytimes.com/2008/02/01/technology/01solar.html.

31. Jürgen Bisch, "Natural Metabolism as the Basis for 'Intelligent' Architecture," in Charles J. Kibert, Jan Sendzimir, and G. Bradley Guy, eds., *Construction Ecology*, 257.

32. Ibid.

33. Jessica Woolliams, "Designing Cities and Buildings as If They Were Ethical Choices," in David Schmidtz and Elizabeth Willott, eds., *Environmental Ethics*, 428. For another award winning building, see David Rosenfeld, "Now This Will Be Life at Sustainable Edge," *The Oregonian* (Dec. 20, 2007), online at http://www.oregonlive.com/portland/oregonian/index.ssf?/base/portland_news/119750737913900.xml.

34. Ibid.

35. Garry Peterson, "Using Ecological Dynamics to Move Toward an Adaptive Architecture," in Charles J. Kibert, Jan Sendzimir, and G. Bradley Guy, eds., *Construction Ecology*, 144.

36. James J. Kay, "On Complexity Theory, Exergy, and Industrial Ecology," in Charles J. Kibert, Jan Sendzimir, and G. Bradley Guy, eds., *Construction Ecology*, 100. There are already such buildings. Timothy F. H. Allen, "Applying the Principles of Ecological Emergence to Building Design and Construction," in Charles J. Kibert, Jan Sendzimir, and G. Bradley Guy, eds., *Construction Ecology*, 119.

37. Ibid.

38. Ibid.

39. Ernest A. Lowe, "Sustainable New Towns and Industrial Ecology," in Charles J. Kibert, ed., *Reshaping the Built Environment*, 332.

40. Sarah Yaussi, "Fund Ranks Builders by 'Greenness,'" *Tools of the Trade* (May 6, 2008), online at http://www.toolsofthetrade.net/industry-news.asp?articleID=700353&sectionID=1519.

41. Quoted from Charles J. Kibert, "Introduction," in Charles J. Kibert, Jan Sendzimir, and G. Bradley Guy, eds., *Construction Ecology*, 2.

42. It is encouraging that home insurance is beginning to provide for the costs of meeting green standards. Ilana DeBare, "Fireman's Fund Offers Green Rebuilding Option," *San Francisco Chronicle* (Jun. 6, 2008), C-1, online at http://www.sfgate.com/cgi-bin/article.cgi?f=/c/a/2008/07/06/BUTT11JJOU.DTL.

43. James J. Kay, "On Complexity Theory, Exergy, and Industrial Ecology," in Charles J. Kibert, Jan Sendzimir, and G. Bradley Guy, eds. *Construction Ecology*, 100. This includes designing clothing and all kind of consumer products as well as buildings. See Chelsea Emery, "Designers Say 'Green' Fashion Sustainable," *Reuters* (Sep. 10, 2008), online at http://www.reuters.com/article/environmentalNews/idUSN0930626120080910.

44. Charles J. Kibert, Jan Sendzimir and G. Bradley Guy, "Defining an Ecology of Construction," in Charles J. Kibert, Jan Sendzimir, and G. Bradley Guy, eds., *Construction Ecology*, 18. Schools are building green to save money and to improve learning. Ian Shapira, "Titans of Ecology," *The Washington Post* (Sep. 11, 2007), B01, online at http://www.washingtonpost.com/wp-dyn/content/article/2007/09/10/AR2007091002310.html.

45. Nicholai Ouroussoff, "Why Are They Greener Than We Are?" *The New York Times* (May 20, 2007), online at http://www.nytimes.com/2007/05/20/magazine/20europe-t.html.

46. Ibid.

47. Ibid.

48. "Curitiba," online at http://en.wikipedia.org/wiki/Curitiba.

49. Jonas Rabinovitch and Josef Leitman, "Urban Planning in Curitiba," in Stephen M. Wheeler and Timothy Beatley, eds., *The Sustainable Urban Development Reader*, 246. More recently, car traffic is increasing. Arthur Lebow, "The Road to Curitiba," *The New York Times* (May 20, 2007), online at http://www.nytimes.com/2007/05/20/magazine/20Curitiba-t.html.

50. Ibid.

51. Tom Hundley, "London Widens 'Congestion Tax' Area for Cars," *The Seattle Times* (Feb. 24, 2007), online at http://seattletimes.nwsource.com/html/nationworld/2003586878_london24.html. See also Caitlin G. Johnson, "London, Paris Honored for Greening Transit Systems," *OneWorld.net* (Jan. 18, 2008), online at http://us.oneworld.net/article/view/156966/1.

52. "Stockholm Congestion Tax," online at http://en.wikipedia.org/wiki/Stockholm_congestion_tax. Economists differ over the use of such a tax. See "Stockholm's Congestion Tax," *Economist's View* (Oct. 10, 2006), online at http://economistsview.typepad.com/economistsview/2006/10/stockholms_cong.html.

53. "Electronic Road Pricing," Land Transport Authority, Singapore Government, online at http://www.lta.gov.sg/motoring_matters/index_motoring_erp.htm.

54. Timothy Beatley, "Planning for Sustainability in European Cities: A Review of Practice in Leading Cities," in Stephen M. Wheeler and Timothy Beatley, eds., *The Sustainable Urban Development Reader*, 253.

55. Ibid. "The bikes are geared in such a way that the pedaling is difficult enough to discourage theft."

56. Allison Raphael, "Pedaling toward Cleaner Cities," *OneWorld.net* (May 13, 2008), online at http://us.oneworld.net/article/view/160534/1.

57. Ibid.

58. John Pucher, Charles Komanoff, and Paul Shimek, "Bicycling Renaissance in North America?" in Stephen M. Wheeler and Timothy Beatley, eds., *The Sustainable Urban Development Reader*, 108. Portland, Oregon has a higher percentage of people bicycling to work than any other large city in the United States. William Yardley, "Portland, Ore., Acts to Protect Cyclists," *The New York Times* (Jan 10, 2008), online at http://www.nytimes.com/2008/01/10/us/10bike.html.

59. Changes are happening. Robin Shulman, "NY Hopes to Ensure Smooth Pedaling for Bike Commuters," *Washington Post* (May 25, 2008), A02, online at http://www.washingtonpost.com/wp-dyn/content/article/2008/05/24/AR2008052401457.html.

60. Peter Calthorpe, "The Next American Metropolis," in Stephen M. Wheeler and Timothy Beatley, eds., *The Sustainable Urban Development Reader*, 76.

61. Ibid.

62. Herbert Girardet, "The Metabolism of Cities," in Stephen M. Wheeler and Timothy Beatley, eds., *The Sustainable Urban Development Reader*, 126.

63. Patrick J. Sullivan, Franklin J. Agardy, and James J. J. Clark. *The Environmental Science of Drinking Water*, 216.

64. Ibid., 217.

65. Ibid., 224.

66. John Tillman Lyle, "Waste as a Resource," in Stephen M. Wheeler and Timothy Beatley, eds., *The Sustainable Urban Development Reader*, 139.

67. Ibid., 140.

68. Ibid., 139.

69. Ibid.

70. Herbert Girardet, "The Metabolism of Cities," in Stephen M. Wheeler and Timothy Beatley, eds., *The Sustainable Urban Development Reader*, 127.

71. Ibid., 128. The US Postal Service is testing a free recycling program that "provides courtesy envelopes with pre-paid postage for patrons to deposit their unwanted digital cameras, printer cartridges, MP3 players, cell phones, and PDAs. International recycling company Clover Technologies Group processes the devices in its United States and Mexican facilities and then refurbishes and resells them if possible." Ben Block, "US Postal Service Begins E-Waste Recycling," Worldwatch Institute (May 21, 2008), online at http://www.worldwatch.org/node/5750.

72. Timothy Gardner, "Waste Management taps clean power from garbage," *Reuters* (Jun. 27, 2007), online at http://www.reuters.com/article/scienceNews/idUSN2625324820070627. See also David R. Baker, "Methane to Power Vehicles, Not Pollute Air," *San Francisco Chronicle* (Apr. 30, 2008), C-1, online at http://sfgate.com/cgi-bin/article.cgi?f=/c/a/2008/04/30/BUTS10DSNP.DTL.

73. "Another initiative, All Clean, temporarily hires retired and unemployed people to clean up specific areas of the city where litter has accumulated." Jonas Rabinovitch and Josef Leitman, "Urban Planning in Curitiba," in Stephen M. Wheeler and Timothy Beatley, eds., *The Sustainable Urban Development Reader*, 245.

74. For a more detailed explanation see Peter Yost, "Construction and Demolition Waste: Innovative Assessment and Management," in Charles J. Kibert, ed., *Reshaping the Built Environment*, 185–186.

75. Ibid., 186.

76. Kent E. Portney, *Taking Sustainable Cities Seriously*, 8.

77. Ibid.

78. See Nicholai Ouroussoff, "Why Are They Greener Than We Are?" *The New York Times* (May 20, 2007), online at http://www.nytimes.com/2007/05/20/magazine/20europe-t.html, and Carolyn Jones, "It Won't Be Easy Being Green," *San Francisco Chronicle* (May 24, 2007), online at http://sfgate.com/cgi-bin/article.cgi?f=/c/a/2007/05/24/MNGJSQ0N671.DTL.

79. Virginia W. Maclaren, "Urban Sustainability Reporting," in Stephen M. Wheeler and Timothy Beatley, eds., *The Sustainable Urban Development Reader*, 208.

80. Andreas R. Edwards, *The Sustainability Revolution*, 20–23.

81. Ibid., 87.

82. Ibid.

83. Charles J. Kibert, Jan Sendzimir and G. Bradley Guy, "Defining an Ecology of Construction," in Charles J. Kibert, Jan Sendzimir, and G. Bradley Guy, eds., *Construction Ecology*, 208.

84. Andreas R. Edwards, *The Sustainability Revolution*, 97.

85. "Conserve Chicago Together," online at http://egov.cityofchicago.org/city/webportal/portalEntityHomeAction.do?BV_SessionID=@@@@1129796959.1192640401@@@@&BV_EngineID=ccceaddmfhligdlcefecelldffhdfgk.0&entityName=Conserve+Chicago+Together&entityNameEnumValue=144. See "Chicago Ranked Capital of Sustainable Design," *Reuters* (Jun. 27, 2008), online at http://www.reuters.com/article/lifestyleMolt/idUSN2747409620080627.

86. Ibid. These accomplishments are listed on submenus of this main page.

87. "About the Rooftop Garden," online at http://egov.cityofchicago.org/city/webportal/portalContentItemAction.do?BV_SessionID=@@@@1159231088.1192642186@@@@&BV_EngineID=ccceaddmfhligdmcefecelldffhdfhh1.0&contentOID=536908578&contenTypeName=COC_EDITORIAL&topChannelName=Dept&blockName=Environment%2FCity+Hall+Rooftop+Garden%2FI+Want+To&context=dept&channelId=0&programId=0&entityName=Environment&deptMainCategoryOID=-536887205.

88. Ibid. William McDonough and Michael Braungart helped create the garden on the roof of Chicago's City Hall. See William McDonough and Michael Braungart, *Cradle to Cradle*, 83.

89. *Choosing a Sustainable Future: The Report of the National Commission on the Environment* (Washington, DC: Island Press, 1993).

90. "Natural Capital," *The Dictionary of Sustainable Management*, online at http://www.sustainabilitydictionary.com/n/natural_capital.php.

91. Ibid.

92. See Patricia Scruggs, "A Summary of the Dutch NEPP (National Environmental Policy Plan),"online at http://greenplans.rri.org/resources/greenplanningarchives/netherlands/netherlands_1993_nepp.html.

93. Andreas R. Edwards, *The Sustainability Revolution,* 55.

94. Wingspread Statement, in Andreas R. Edwards, *The Sustainability Revolution,* 56.

95. "Precautionary Tale," Reason Online, online at http://www.reason.com/news/show/30977.html.

96. The Body Shop, online at http://www.thebodyshop.com/_en/_ww/services/pdfs/Values/BSI_chemicals_Strategy.pdf.

97. Andreas R. Edwards, *The Sustainability Revolution,* 58.

98. "Precautionary Principle," online at http://www.answers.com/topic/precautionary-principle?cat=health.

99. Michael Braungart, an ecological chemist from Germany, first suggested seeing products as consumables, durables, and unmarketables. See William McDonough, "Design, Ecology, Ethics and the Making of Things," in Stephen M. Wheeler and Timothy Beatley, eds., *The Sustainable Urban Development Reader,* 184. See also Penelope Green, "Biodegradable Home Product Lines, Ready to Rot," *The New York Times* (May 8, 2008), online at http://www.nytimes.com/2008/05/08/garden/08biodegrade.html.

100. William McDonough has characterized "things as either being part of nature—biological nutrients—or being part of technology, which we call technical nutrients. We look at the world through these two lenses and we say, let the things that are designed to go back to soil, like textiles and clothing, be designed in order to be returned safely to soil, to restore it. But the cars and the computers . . . [should be]designed to go back into closed cycles for technology." William McDonough, "Buildings That Can Breathe," *Newsweek* (Aug. 18, 2008): 38.

101. Ibid. The German government already requires "manufactures to create products that are taken back by their producers to become raw materials for new products." Charles J. Kibert, Jan Sendzimir and G. Bradley Guy, "Defining an Ecology of Construction," in Charles J. Kibert, Jan Sendzimir, and G. Bradley Guy, eds., *Construction Ecology,* 14.

102. Ibid., 185.

103. William McDonough and Michael Braungart, *Cradle to Cradle,* 138.

104. Ibid., 139.

105. Ibid., 138–139.

CHAPTER 15: CLIMATE CHANGE

1. See Deborah Zabarenko, "Human Warming Hobbles Ancient Climate Cycle," *Reuters* (Apr. 27, 2008), online at http://www.reuters.com/article/scienceNews/idUSN2541737720080427, and Kenneth R. Weis, "Scientists Blame Ocean Dead Zones on Climate Change," *San Francisco Chronicle* (Feb. 20, 2008), A-6, online at http://sfgate.com/cgi-bin/article.cgi?f=/c/a/2008/02/20/MNQNV50EU.DTL.

2. See Haider Rizvi, "Record Glacier Melt Spurs New Calls for Climate Action," *OneWorld.net* (Mar. 18, 2008), online at http://us.oneworld.net/article/view/158959/1.

3. See Beth Borenstein, "Narwhals More at Risk to Arctic Warming than Polar Bears," *Live Science* (Apr. 25, 2008), online at http://www.livescience.com/animals/080425-ap-narwhal.html. See also Deborah Zaborenko, "Polar Bears Listed as 'Threatened' Species," *Reuters* (May 14, 2008),

online at http://www.reuters.com/article/oilRpt/idUSN1452119020080514, and David Pearlman, "Greenhouse Gases Called Threat to Pacific Life," *San Francisco Chronicle* (Jul. 4, 2008), B-1, online at http://www.sfgate.com/cgi-bin/article.cgi?f=/c/a/2008/07/03/BA9011IG0Q.DTL.

4. See Keith Bradsher, "A Drought in Australia, A Global Shortage of Rice," *The New York Times* (Apr. 17, 2008), online at http://www.nytimes.com/2008/04/17/business/worldbusiness/17warm.html.

5. See Andrew C. Rivkin, "Skeptics on Human Climate Impact Seize on Cold Spell," *The New York Times* (Mar. 2, 2008), online at http://www.nytimes.com/2008/03/02/science/02cold.html, and Nicholas D. Kristof, "Our Favorite Planet," *The New York Times* (Apr. 20, 2008), online at http://www.nytimes.com/2008/04/20/opinion/20kristof.html.

6. "Contribution of Working Group I to the Fourth Assessment Report of the Intergovernmental Panel on Climate Change," IPCC, online at http://ipcc-wg1.ucar.edu/wg1/wg1-report.html.

7. "State of Knowledge," Climate Change—Science, US Environmental Protection Agency, online at http://www.epa.gov/climatechange/science/stateofknowledge.html.

8. "Contribution of Working Group I to the Fourth Assessment Report of the Intergovernmental Panel on Climate Change," IPCC, online at http://ipcc-wg1.ucar.edu/wg1/wg1-report.html.

9. "State of Knowledge," Climate Change—Science, US Environmental Protection Agency, online at http://www.epa.gov/climatechange/science/stateofknowledge.html.

10. Ibid.

11. Ibid.

12. Bill McKibben, "Carbon's New Math," *National Geographic* 212, no. 4 (Oct. 2007): 33.

13. "What Is the Carbon Cycle?" Soil Carbon FAQ, online at http://faqsoilcarbon.blogspot.com/2007/03/what-is-carbon-cycle.html.

14. Ibid.

15. "Global Warming Supercharged by Water Vapor?" *National Geographic News* (Nov. 10, 2005), online at http://news.nationalgeographic.com/news/2005/11/1110_051110_warming.html.

16. Sara van Gelder, "Environmental Ethics," Charles J. Kibert, ed., *Reshaping the Built Environment,* 64.

17. Peter Singer, *One World,* 32.

18. "Kyoto Protocol to the UN Framework Convention on Climate Change," online at http://unfccc.int/resource/docs/convkp/kpeng.html.

19. "Text of a Letter from the President to Senators Hagel, Helms, Craig, and Roberts," The White House, online at http://www.whitehouse.gov/news/releases/2001/03/20010314.html.

20. Ibid.

21. "Byrd-Hagel Resolution," 105 Congress, 1st Session, Senate Resolution 98, online at http://www.nationalcenter.org/KyotoSenate.html. Ted Nordhaus and Michael Shellenberger argue that the carbon emission reductions by signatories to the Kyoto Protocol are not going to be met and that the protocol "epitomizes the environmentalist obsession with limits." Ted Nordhaus and Michael Shellenberger, *Break Through,* 114, 120.

22. Charlie E. Coon, "Why President Bush Is Right to Abandon the Kyoto Protocol," The Heritage Foundation (May 11, 2001), online at http://www.heritage.org/Research/Energyand Environment/BG1437.cfm.

23. Most Americans do not realize that the Kyoto Protocol is being implemented in many parts of the world. See "UN Approves Thousandth Kyoto Clean Energy Project," *Reuters* (Apr. 14, 2008), online at http://uk.reuters.com/article/environmentNews/idUKL1426496820080414.

24. "Cap-and-Trade Systems," *Catalyst* 4, no. 1 (Spring 2005), Union of Concerned Scientists, online at http://www.ucsusa.org/publications/catalyst/page.jsp?itemID=27226959. In a cap-and-trade program "an aggregate cap on all sources is established and these sources are then allowed to trade amongst themselves to determine which sources actually emit the total pollution load. An

alternative approach with important differences is a baseline and credit program. In a baseline and credit program a set of polluters that are not under an aggregate cap can create credits by reducing their emissions below a baseline level of emissions. These credits can be purchased by polluters that are under a regulatory limit. Many of the criticisms of trading in general are targeted at baseline & credit programs rather than cap type programs." "Emissions Trading," online at http://en.wikipedia.org/wiki/Cap_and_trade.

25. The UN supports carbon emissions trading, but indigenous groups are very critical. See Haider Rizvi, "Carbon Trading Blasted by Indigenous Groups," *OneWorld.net* (May 7, 2008), online at http://us.oneworld.net/article/view/160386/1.

26. Ted Nordhaus and Michael Shellenberger argue that a carbon emissions cap-and-trade program "could, if done right, generate billions of dollars in private investment for cleaner sources of energy." Ted Nordhaus and Michael Shellenberger, *Break Through,* 120. "Although some may think that emissions trading allows the United States to avoid its burdens too easily, the point is not to punish nations with high emissions, but to produce the best outcome for the atmosphere. Permitting emissions trading gives us a better hope of doing this than prohibiting emissions trading does." Peter Singer, *One World,* 46.

27. "Western Climate Initiative," online at http://en.wikipedia.org/wiki/Western_Regional _Climate_Action_Initiative. In the fall of 2008 ten states from Maine to Maryland initiated the Regional Greenhouse Gas Initiative (RGGI) that creates a cap-and-trade system for carbon emissions from 233 power plants. Felicity Barringer and Kate Galbaith, "States Aim to Cut Gases by Making Polluters Pay," *The New York Times* (Sep. 15, 2008), online at http://www.nytimes.com/ 2008/09/16/us/16carbon.html.

28. "Jumping ahead of state and federal regulators, a Bay Area air quality district today became the first in the nation to impose fees on businesses which pump some of the highest levels of carbon dioxide into the air each year." Kelly Zito, "Air Quality Agency Approves First-in-the-Nation Fees for Emissions," *San Francisco Chronicle* (May 21, 2008), online at http://sfgate.com/ cgi-bin/article.cgi?f=/c/a/2008/05/21/BADN10QD60.DTL.

29. "Environmental Groups Slam German Climate Plans," online at http://news.yahoo.com/s/ afp/20070821/sc_afp/germanywarmingpolitics. For critical arguments about trading carbon emissions, see "Emissions Trading," online at http://en.wikipedia.org/wiki/Carbon_emissions_trading.

30. David Jackson, "Greenpeace, Others Pan G-8 Warming Deal," *USA Today* (Jun. 7, 2007), online at http://www.usatoday.com/news/world/environment/2007-06-07-bush-g8-warming_N .htm.

31. Two new studies conclude that "both industrialized and developing nations must wean themselves off fossil fuels by as early as mid-century in order to prevent warming that could change precipitation patterns and dry up sources of water worldwide." Juliet Eilperin, "Carbon Output Must Near Zero to Avert Danger, New Studies Say," *The Washington Post* (Mar. 10, 2008), A01, online at http://www.washingtonpost.com/wp-dyn/content/article/2008/03/09/AR2008030901867.html.

32. To assess your ecological footprint, see "Ecological Footprint Quiz," online at http:// www.earthday.net/footprint/info.asp. To consider using carbon offsets to reduce your ecological footprint, see "Why Carbon Offsets?" online at http://www.carbonfund.org/site/pages/why _offset/, and also "Voluntary Carbon Offsets," Voluntary Carbon Offset Information Portal, Stockholm Environmental Institute, Tufts Climate Initiative, online at http://www.tufts.edu/tie/ tci/carbonoffsets/.

33. Michael Schulman and Eva Mekler, *Bringing Up a Moral* Child, 8.

34. *Our Common Future,* online at http://ringofpeace.org/environment/brundtland.html.

35. The FCCC, online at http://unfccc.int/essential_background/convention/background/ items/1349.php.

36. Elisabeth Rosenthal, "As Earth Warms, Virus from Tropics Moves to Italy," *The New York Times* (Dec. 23, 2007), online at http://www.nytimes.com/2007/12/23/world/europe/23virus

.html. "After a month of investigation, Italian public health officials discovered that the people of Castiglione di Cervia were, in fact, suffering from a tropical disease, chikungunya, a relative of dengue fever normally found in the Indian Ocean region. But the immigrants spreading the disease were not humans but insects: tiger mosquitoes, who can thrive in a warming Europe. Aided by global warming and globalization, Castiglione di Cervia has the dubious distinction of playing host to the first outbreak in modern Europe of a disease that had previously been seen only in the tropics."

37. See Steven Mufson, "Is This Green Enough? We Can Clean Up Our Act but It'll Cost Us," *The Washington Post* (Apr. 20, 2008), B01, online at http://www.washingtonpost.com/wp-dyn/content/article/2008/04/18/AR2008041802664.html.

38. "Once the forest is mature and an old tree dies and rots for every new tree that grows, the forest no longer soaks up significant amounts of carbon from the atmosphere." Peter Singer, *One World,* 33.

39. John Crawley, "Wasted Fuel from US Flight Delays Cost Billions," *Reuters* (May 22, 2008), online at http://www.reuters.com/article/domesticNews/idUSN2250451020080522.

40. Juliette Jowit, "Cargo Ships Told to Go Green by Slowing Down," *The Observer* (Jun. 15, 2008), http://www.guardian.co.uk/environment/2008/jun/15/travelandtransport.carbonemissions.

41. "The FCX Clarity, which runs on hydrogen and electricity, emits only water and none of the noxious fumes believed to induce global warming. It is also two times more energy efficient than a gas-electric hybrid and three times that of a standard gasoline-powered car," the company says. "A breakthrough in the design of the fuel cell stack, which powers the car's motor, allowed engineers to lighten the body." "Honda rolls out its new zero-emission car," *San Francisco Chronicle* (Jun. 17, 2008), online at http://www.sfgate.com/cgi-bin/article.cgi?f=/c/a/2008/06/17/BUTE11A08H.DTL.

42. Nicole Olsen, "Automakers Back Higher Fuel-Economy Standards," *OneWorld.net* (Jul. 31, 2007), online at http://us.oneworld.net/article/view/151819/1.

43. "It does not matter if it is rain forest or scrubland that is cleared, the greenhouse gas contribution is significant. More important . . . taken globally, the production of almost all biofuels resulted, directly or indirectly, intentionally or not, in new lands being cleared, either for food or fuel." The only possible exception seems to be "sugar cane grown in Brazil, which takes relatively little energy to grow and is readily refined into fuel." Governments should focus on developing biofuels using agricultural waste products, rather than crops. Elisabeth Rosenthal, "Studies Deem Biofuels a Greenhouse Threat," *The New York Times* (Feb. 8, 2008), online at http://www.nytimes.com/2008/02/08/science/earth/08wbiofuels.html.

44. Ibid. See also Sabrina Valle, "Losing Forests to Fuel Cars," *The Washington Post* (July 31, 2007), D01, online at http://www.washingtonpost.com/wp-dyn/content/article/2007/07/30/AR2007073001484.html. Nonetheless, the European Union remains committed to the use of biofuels. "EU Defends Biofuel Goals Amid Food Crises," *AFP* (Apr. 14, 2008), online at http://afp.google.com/article/ALeqM5gp1nkJeC-IhlYkVtsvPfp3u7mOWQ.

45. Roger Cohen, "Energy Lessons," *The New York Times* (Jun. 5, 2008), online at http://www.nytimes.com/2008/06/05/opinion/05cohen.html.

46. Andrew Downie, "Brazil Defends Ethanol in Food-Versus-Fuel Fight," (May 5, 2008), *The Christian Science Monitor,* online at http://www.csmonitor.com/2008/0505/p04s01-woam.html.

47. Elizabeth Rosenthal, "New Trend in Biofuels Has High Risks," *The New York Times* (May 21, 2008), online at http://www.nytimes.com/2008/05/21/science/earth/21biofuels.html.

48. Andrew Downie, "Brazil Defends Ethanol in Food-Versus-Fuel Fight," (May 5, 2008), *The Christian Science Monitor,* online at http://www.csmonitor.com/2008/0505/p04s01-woam.html.

49. Mark Rice-Oxley, "Air Travel Latest Target in Climate Change Fight," *The Christian Science Monitor* (Aug. 17, 2007), online at http://www.csmonitor.com/2007/0817/p01s01-woeu.html. A recent, unpublished report reveals that the carbon emissions from airplanes are higher

than previously reported. "Growth of CO_2 emissions on this scale will comfortably outstrip any gains made by improved technology and ensure aviation is an even larger contributor to global warming by 2025 than previously thought. Governments must take action to put a cap on air transport's unrestrained growth." Cahal Milno, "Airline Emissions 'Far Higher than Previous Estimates,'" *The Independent* (May 6, 2008), online at http://www.independent.co.uk/environment/climate-change/airline-emissions-far-higher-than-previous-estimates-821598.html.

50. Nick Hopwood and Jordan Cohen, "Greenhouse Gases and Society," online at http://www.umich.edu/~gs265/society/greenhouse.htm.

51. Higher prices for petroleum will reduce travel by airplane and motor vehicles, and will also increase incentives for airplane and motor vehicle manufacturers to improve energy efficiency.

52. "If something is growing at a steady rate, and you want to know how long before it will double, divide the growth rate into sixty-nine." James Gustave Speth, *Red Sky at Morning,* 137.

53. Nick Hopwood and Jordan Cohen, "Greenhouse Gases and Society," online at http://www.umich.edu/~gs265/society/greenhouse.htm.

54. "Claims about a 250-year supply of coal won't stand up to scrutiny for long, either. Yes, the United States has more coal than any other nation. But we've been mining coal in this country for 150 years—all the simple, high-quality, easy-to-get stuff is gone. What's left is buried beneath towns and national parks, or places that are difficult, expensive, and dangerous to mine." Mining "hard-to-get coal will also devastate Appalachia, where huge mountaintop-removal mines have already buried 700 miles of streams and 400,000 acres of forests." Jeff Goodell, "What It Costs Us," *The Washington Post* (Aug. 26, 2007), B01, online at http://www.washingtonpost.com/wp-dyn/content/article/2007/08/24/AR2007082401206.html.

55. Keith Bradsher and Kenneth Barboza, "China's Burning of Coal Casts a Global Cloud," *The New York Times* (Jun. 11, 2006), online at http://www.nytimes.com/2006/06/11/business/worldbusiness/11chinacoal.html. "Between 2007 and 2020, China will invest 128 billion in coal." Ted Nordhaus and Michael Shellenberger, *Break Through,* 117.

56. Elisabeth Rosenthal, "Despite Climate Worry, Europe Turns to Coal," *The New York Times* (Apr. 23, 2008), online at http://www.nytimes.com/2008/04/23/world/europe/23coal.html.

57. "Environmental Impacts of Coal Power: Air Pollution," Union of Concerned Scientists, online at http://www.ucsusa.org/clean_energy/coalvswind/c02c.html.

58. David Archer, *Global Warming: Understanding the Forecast* (Malden, MA: Blackwell, 2007), 178. "German utility RWE, Europe's largest polluter, said on Friday it plans to develop a new process to remove carbon-dioxide from the emissions of coal-fired power plants as countries throughout Europe make it more expensive to emit the greenhouse gas. Germany's largest power producer will spend 80 million euros ($113.5 million) on the process, which it is devising with industrial-gases producer Linde and chemicals firm BASF, and plans to use it commercially by 2020." The three German companies said "they were aiming to remove 90 percent of CO_2 from their pilot plant's combustion gas, and ultimately bury it underground." "RWE to Develop New Process to Cut Pollution," *Reuters* (Sep. 28, 2007), online at http://www.reuters.com/article/scienceNews/idUSL2880603120070928.

59. "New Greenpeace Report Labels 'Carbon Capture and Storage' a 'Scam,'" online at http://www.greenpeace.org/international/press/releases/new-greenpeace-report-labels. Scientists are also concerned about the consequences of affecting microbes underground. "It's a very risky prospect just putting gases into geological formations and not considering there could be a feedback response because of the organisms down there." Alister Doyle, "Microbes Found Living at Record 1.6km Below Seabed," *Reuters* (May 22, 2008), online at http://www.reuters.com/article/scienceNews/idUSL2273980520080522.

60. Ibid. "But China is also quietly emerging as a global force in renewable energy technologies, from big-ticket items such as wind and solar power to small products. . . . This is being driven by strong government policies, its own vast market, and businesses seizing opportunities in

a fast-growing global industry." "China Offers Surprise Hope in Climate Change Fight," (Oct. 2, 2007), online at http://afp.google.com/article/ALeqM5jZz8YWsNjJOUeh8Y20vuuTXG7zgQ. See also Emma Graham-Harrison, "China Could Be Top Wind Market in Three Years: Vestas," *Reuters* (Sep. 21, 2007), online at http://www.reuters.com/article/scienceNews/idUSPEK21257 420070921.

61. "Clean Energy: Electricity from Natural Gas," EPA, online at http://www.epa.gov/cleanenergy/natgas.htm.

62. Roger Cohen, "American Needs France's Atomic Annie," *The New York Times* (Jan. 24, 2008), online at http://www.nytimes.com/2008/01/24/opinion/24cohen.html.

63. Ibid.

64. "Global Warming: UCS Position on Nuclear Power and Global Warming," Union of Concerned Scientists, online at http://www.ucsusa.org/global_warming/solutions/nuclear-power-and -climate.html.

65. Ibid. See John Vidal, "Nuclear Expansion is a Pipe Dream, Says Report," *The Guardian* (Jul. 4, 2007), online at http://business.guardian.co.uk/story/0,,2117711,00.html.

66. "Europe," Global Wind Energy Council, online at http://www.gwec.net/index.php?id=11.

67. Junfeng Li, "China's Wind Power Development Exceeds Expectations," Worldwatch Institute (Jun. 2, 2008), online at http://www.worldwatch.org/node/5758.

68. Jazmine Rodriguez, "'Tipping Point' for Renewable Energy," *OneWorld.net* (Jun. 19, 2008), online at http://us.oneworld.net/article/view/160914/1.

69. In 2007 "onshore wind power added more than 5,200 megawatts of new electrical capacity to the grid—or nearly a third of America's new generating capacity, surpassing all other forms of new generation except natural gas and amounting to enough electric capacity to power one and a half million homes. While it's true that wind is still a tiny part of the energy picture—just 1 percent of the total electricity portfolio in the United States and 3.3 percent in Europe—more than a quarter of the 20,000 megawatts of the world's new wind capacity last year was installed in North America, where all the global wind-energy players have set up shop, lured by the low US dollar and the high rate of returns." Mark Svenvold, "Wind-Power Politics," *The New York Times* (Sep. 12, 2008), online at http://www.nytimes.com/2008/09/14/magazine/14wind-t.html.

70. Ben Block, "Study Supports US Wind Expansion," Worldwatch Institute (May 19, 2008), online at http://www.worldwatch.org/node/5748. "The United States is the only developed nation without set energy targets." Jazmine Rodriguez, "'Tipping Point' for Renewable Energy," *OneWorld.net* (Jun. 19, 2008), online at http://us.oneworld.net/article/view/160914/1.

71. "Clean Energy: Renewable Energy–Mitigating Global Warming," Union of Concerned Scientists, online at http://www.ucsusa.org/clean_energy/clean_energy_policies/RES-climate -strategy.html. These changes will require updating the US energy transmission system. See Matthew L. Wald, "Wind Energy Bumps Into Power Grid's Limits," *The New York Times* (Aug. 26, 2008), online at http://www.nytimes.com/2008/08/27/business/27grid.html.

72. Juliet Eilperin, "Carbon Output Must Near Zero to Avert Danger, New Studies Say," *The Washington Post* (Mar. 10, 2008), A01, online at http://www.washingtonpost.com/wp-dyn/content/article/2008/03/09/AR2008030901867.html.

73. Ted Nordhaus and Michael Shellenberger, *Break Through,* 115.

74. Gregg Easterbrook, "Al Gore's Outsourcing Solution," *The New York Times* (Mar. 9, 2007), online at http://www.nytimes.com/2007/03/09/opinion/09easterbrook.html. See also Jim Robbins, "Sale of Carbon Credits Helping Land Rich, but Cash Poor Tribes," *The New York Times* (May 8, 2007), online at http://www.nytimes.com/2007/05/08/science/earth/08carb.html.

75. John B. Dingell, "The Power in the Carbon Tax," *The Washington Post* (Aug. 2, 2007), online at http://www.washingtonpost.com/wp-dyn/content/article/2007/08/01/AR2007080102 051.html.

76. See also "Market Forces Essential to Halting Global Warming: Gore," (Dec. 9, 2007), online at http://afp.google.com/article/ALeqM5jTgqt91jaTdJt5-5dSWGwnEXY41A.

77. Cornelia Dean, "Executive on a Mission: Saving the Planet," *The New York Times* (May 22, 2007), online at http://www.nytimes.com/2007/05/22/science/earth/22ander.html. See chapter 10 to learn what Interface is doing to be a "restorative enterprise," that is, "a sustainable operation that takes nothing out of the earth that cannot be recycled or quickly regenerated, and that does no harm to the biosphere."

78. Alternatively, or in addition, vehicle registration fees imposed by a state could be higher for less fuel-efficient vehicles. "Californians support the idea of charging 'green' vehicle fees that would make drivers of gas guzzlers pay higher taxes and offer discounts for those driving less-polluting vehicles, according to a survey by a transportation researcher at San Jose State University." Michael Cabanatuan, "Poll: Make Gas Guzzlers Pay Higher Fees," *San Francisco Chronicle* (Apr. 3, 2008), A-1, online at http://sfgate.com/cgi-bin/article.cgi?f=/c/a/2008/04/03/MNI MVUPFF.DTL.

79. Farid Zakaria, "A Cure for Oil Addicts," *Newsweek* (Aug. 6, 2007): 34.

80. Monica Prasad, "On Carbon, Tax and Don't Spend," *The New York Times* (Mar. 25, 2008), online at http://www.nytimes.com/2008/03/25/opinion/25prasad.html. Denmark was successful because it overcame the temptation to maximize tax revenues, and invested these revenues in renewable energy development that was also good for the economy.

81. Ibid. See Thomas Friedman, "Flush with Energy," *The New York Times* (Aug. 9, 2008), online at http://www.nytimes.com/2008/08/10/opinion/10friedman1.html.

82. James Gustave Speth, *Red Sky at Morning,* 133. Economist Arthur C. Pigou addressed the problem of "unpriced goods" early in the twentieth century.

83. Wallace E. Oates, "An Economic Perspective on Environmental and Resources Management," in Wallace E. Oates, ed., *The RFF Reader in Environmental and Resources Management* (Washington, DC: Resources for the Future, 1999), xiv, quoted in James Gustave Speth, *Red Sky at Morning,* 134. Economist Theo Panayotou writes: "A combination of institutional, market and policy failures results in underpricing of scarce natural resources and environmental assets, which is then translated into underpricing of resource-based and environmental-intensive goods and services. . . . As a direct result producers and consumers of products and services do not receive correct signals about the true scarcity of resources they use up or the cost of environmental damage they cause. This leads to the socially wrong mix of economic output: overproduction and over-consumption of commodities that are resource-depleting and environment-polluting, and underproduction and underconsumption of commodities that are resource-saving and environment-friendly. Thus, the emerging pattern of economic growth and structure of the economy is one that undermines its own resource base, and is ultimately unsustainable, since relative scarcities are not respected." Theodore Panayotou, *Instruments of Change: Motivating and Financing Sustainable Development* (London: Earthscan, 1998), 6, quoted in James Gustave Speth, *Red Sky at Morning,* 135.

84. Michael R. Bloomberg, Mayor of New York City, has called for a tax on carbon emissions, as opposed to relying on a cap-and-trade program to lower emissions. Sewell Chan, "Bloomberg Calls for Tax on Carbon Emissions," *The New York Times* (Nov. 2, 2007), online at http://city room.blogs.nytimes.com/2007/11/02/bloomberg-calls-for-tax-on-carbon-emissions/index.html.

85. Rachel Waldemer, "A proposal to generate 50% of the United States' electricity needs from solar power by the year 2100," (Jul. 24, 2003), online at http://www.ese.ogi.edu/~waldemer/solarpaper.htm. Waldemer has proposed that "an 'externality tax' of 7.6 cents/kWh (phased in over 20 years) be added to the price of coal-powered electricity. Such a tax would generate almost 5 trillion dollars in 20 years." These funds could be used to purchase and install photovoltaic cells in all federal buildings, which would stimulate solar manufacturers to invest in greater production. Funds raised by the tax could also be spent to further research and development into solar technology. Waldemer estimates that implementing this plan would prevent about 200 billion tons of carbon from CO_2 being released into the atmosphere, and that the United States "could be generating 50 percent of its electricity with photovoltaic cells by the year 2020."

86. "This was entirely the doing of the Senate, which caved in to the oil companies and their White House friends." Editorial, "The Senate Shills for Big Oil," *The New York Times* (Mar. 3, 2008), online at http://www.nytimes.com/2008/03/03/opinion/03mon4.html.

87. Editorial, "Big Oil's Friends in the Senate," *The New York Times* (May 5, 2008), online at http://www.nytimes.com/2008/05/05/opinion/05mon2.html. In California, however, utility companies must "generate 20 percent of their energy from renewable sources such as solar, wind and geothermal power by 2010." See Ilana DeBare, "PG&E Plans Big Investment in Solar Power," *San Francisco Chronicle* (Aug. 15, 2008), D-1, online at http://www.sfgate.com/cgi-bin/article.cgi?f=/c/a/2008/08/15/BUP412B774.DTL.

88. "The Senate bill, if passed, would have required that total US emissions of greenhouse gases be cut to 19 percent below 2005 levels by 2020 and up to 71 percent by the year 2050 primarily through a 'cap-and-trade' system that would give companies financial incentives to reduce their emissions. The United States currently accounts for about 25 percent of the world's total greenhouse emissions. The legislation also proposed the creation of a 40-year, $800-billion 'tax relief fund' to encourage energy consumers to switch to cleaner technologies." Jim Lobe, "As Climate Bill Dies, Greens Express Hope," *OneWorld.net* (Jun. 9, 2008), online at http://us.oneworld.net/article/view/160824/1/45. "Bailout Extends Solar Tax Credit," *The Green Technocrat* (Oct. 6, 2008), online at http://thegreentechnocrat.com/?p=181.

89. Bill McKibben, "Carbon's New Math," *National Geographic* 212, no. 4 (Oct. 2007): 34.

90. Using this much cropland for fuel would substantially reduce the production of food and raise food prices, unless affluent societies at the same time substantially reduced their consumption of beef, which would allow land now used to grow corn for cattle feed to be planted with crops for human consumption.

91. This means ending industrial agriculture as we know it today.

92. The ClimateSmart program of Pacific Gas and Electric Company in California enables customers to reduce their impact on climate change. PG&E calculates the amount needed to make the GHG emissions associated with a customer's home energy use "neutral," adds this amount to the customer's monthly energy bill, and then invests these funds in new GHG emission reduction projects. "ClimateSmart—How It Works," PG&E, online at http://www.pge.com/myhome/environment/whatyoucando/climatesmart/climatesmarthowitworks/index.shtml.

93. "Take the Pledge," The Alliance for Climate Protection, online at http://www.climate protect.org/pledge. The Alliance is supporting a plan to repower America with 100 percent electricity within 10 years. Online at http://www.repoweramerica.org/. See also Al Gore, "The Climate for Change," *The New York Times* (Nov. 9, 2008), online at http://www.nytimes.com/2008/11/09/opinion/09gore.html.

94. Thomas Friedman, "Doha and Dalian," *The New York Times* (Sep. 19, 2007), online at http://www.nytimes.com/2007/09/19/opinion/19friedman.html.

95. Ibid. See Joseph Kahn and Jim Yardley, "As China Roars, Pollution Reaches Deadly Extremes," *The New York Times* (Aug. 26, 2007), online at http://www.nytimes.com/2007/08/26/world/asia/26china.html, and Joseph Kahn and Mark Landler, "China Grabs West's Smoke-Spewing Factories," *The New York Times* (Dec. 21, 2007), online at http://www.nytimes.com/2007/12/21/world/asia/21transfer.html.

Bibliography

Amory, Cleveland. *Man Kind? Our Incredible War on Wildlife* (New York: Harper & Row, 1974).

Archer, David. *Global Warming: Understanding the Forecast* (Malden, MA: Blackwell, 2007).

Athanasiou, Tom. *Divided Planet: The Ecology of Rich and Poor* (Toronto: Little, Brown, 1996).

Attfield, Robin. *Environmental Ethics: An Overview for the Twenty-First Century* (Cambridge, UK: Polity Press, 2003).

Babbitt, Bruce. *Cities in the Wilderness: A New Vision of Land Use in America* (Washington, DC: Island Press, 2005).

Baker, Catherine and James B. Miller, eds. *The Evolution Dialogues: Science, Christianity, and the Quest for Understanding* (New York: American Association for the Advancement of Science, 2006).

Barnhill, David Landis and Roger S. Gottlieb, eds. *Deep Ecology and World Religions: New Essays on Sacred Ground* (Albany, NY: State University of New York Press, 2001).

Begley, Sharon. *Train Your Mind, Change Your Brain* (New York: Ballantine Books, 2007).

Bentham, Jeremy. *The Principles of Morals and Legislation* (New York: Oxford University Press, 1789).

Blackburn, Simon. *Truth: A Guide* (Oxford: Oxford University Press, 2005).

Blackstone, William, ed. *Philosophy and Environmental Crisis* (Athens, GA: University of Georgia Press, 1974).

Blakeslee, Sandra and Matthew Blakeslee. *The Body Has a Mind of Its Own: How Body Maps in Your Brain Help You Do (Almost) Everything Better* (New York: Random House, 2007).

Blakney, R. B., trans. *The Way of Life*, a new translation of the *Tao Te Ching* (New York: Mentor, 1955).

Bloom, Floyd E., ed. *Best of the Brain from Scientific American* (New York: Dana Press, 2007).

Bogle, John C. *The Battle for the Soul of Capitalism* (New Haven, CT: Yale University Press, 2005).

Bonner, Raymond. *At the Hand of Man: Peril and Hope for Africa's Wildlife* (New York: Alfred A. Knopf, 1993).

Bookchin, Murray. *The Ecology of Freedom: The Emergence and Dissolution of Hierarchy* (Oakland, CA: AK Press, 2005).

Bormann, F. Herbert and Stephen R. Kellert, eds. *Ecology, Economics, Ethics: The Broken Circle* (New Haven: Yale University Press, 1991).

Brown, Lester R. *Full House: Reassessing the Earth's Population Carrying Capacity* (New York: W. W. Norton, 1994).

Bryant, Raymond L. and Sinéad Bailey. *Third World Political Ecology* (London: Routledge, 1997).

Burstyn, Varda. *Water Inc.* (London: Verso, 2005).

Caldwell, Lynton Keith and Kristin Shrader-Frechette, eds. *Policy for Land: Law and Ethics* (Lanham, MD: Rowman & Littlefield, 1993).

Calhoun, Yael, ed. *Water Pollution* (Philadelphia, PA: Chelsea House, 2005).

Callicott, J. Baird. *Earth's Insights: A Multicultural Survey of Ecological Ethics from the Mediterranean Basin to the Australian Outback* (Berkeley, CA: University of California Press, 1994).

Capra, Fritjof. *The Tao of Physics: An Exploration of the Parallels between Modern Physics and Eastern Mysticism,* fourth edition, updated (Boston, MA: Shambala Publications, 2000).

Carter, Rita. *Exploring Consciousness* (Berkeley, CA: University of California Press, 2002).

Chopra, Deepak. *The Essential Ageless Body, Timeless Mind: The Essence of the Quantum Alternative to Growing Old* (New York: Harmony Books, 2007).

Cohen, Carl and Tom Regan. *The Animal Rights Debate* (Lanham, MD: Rowman & Littlefield, 2001).

Collins, Francis S. *The Language of God: A Scientist Presents Evidence for Belief* (New York: Free Press, 2006).

Coward, Harold, ed. *Population, Consumption, and the Environment: Religious and Secular Responses* (Albany, NY: State University of New York, 1995).

Dalai Lama. *The Universe in a Single Atom: The Convergence of Science and Spirituality* (New York: Morgan Road Books, 2005).

Daly, Herman E. and Joshua Farley. *Ecological Economics: Principles and Applications* (Washington, DC: Island Press).

Damasio, Antonio R. *Descartes' Error: Emotion, Reason, and the Human Brain* (New York: Grosset/ Putnam, 1994).

_____. *The Feeling of What Happens: Body and Emotion in the Making of Consciousness* (New York: Harcourt Brace & Company, 1999).

_____. *Looking for Spinoza: Joy, Sorrow, and the Feeling Brain* (New York: Harcourt, 2003).

Darwin, Charles. *The Descent of Man, and Selection in Relation to Sex,* with an introduction by John Tyler Bonner and Robert M. May (Princeton, NJ: Princeton University Press, 1981).

Dawkins, Richard. *The God Delusion* (Boston, MA: Houghton Mifflin, 2006).

de Duve, Christian. *Life Evolving: Molecules, Mind, and Meaning* (Oxford: Oxford University Press, 2002.)

de Waal, Frans, Robert Wright, Christine M. Korsgaard, Philip Kitcher, and Peter Singer, edited by Stephen Macedo and Josiah Ober. *Primates and Philosophers: How Morality Evolved* (Princeton, NJ: Princeton University Press, 2006).

Dennett, Daniel C. *Breaking the Spell: Religion as a Natural Phenomenon* (New York: Penguin Group, 2006).

DesJardins, Joseph R. *Environmental Ethics: An Introduction to Environmental Philosophy,* fourth edition (Belmont, CA: Thomson Wadsworth, 2006).

Devall, Bill and George Sessions. *Deep Ecology: Living As If Nature Mattered* (Salt Lake, UT: Peregrine Smith, 1985).

Dover, Gabriel. *Dear Mr. Darwin: Letters on the Evolution of Life and Human Nature* (Berkeley, CA: University of California Press, 2000).

Driessen, Paul. *Eco-Imperialism: Green Power, Black Death* (Bellevue, WA: Free Enterprise Press, 2003–2004).

Edelman, Gerald M. *Second Nature: Brain Science and Human Knowledge* (New Haven, CT: Yale University Press, 2006).

_____ and Giulio Tononi. *A Universe of Consciousness: How Matter Becomes Imagination* (New York: Basic Books, 2000).

Edwards, Andreas R. *The Sustainability Revolution* (Gabriola Island, Canada: New Society Publishers, 2005).

Ehrlich, Paul R. *Human Natures: Genes, Cultures, and the Human Prospect* (New York: Penguin Books, 2002).

Eldredge, Niles. *The Pattern of Evolution* (New York: W. H. Freeman and Company, 1999).

_____. *The Triumph of Evolution* (New York: W. H. Freeman and Company, 2000).

Engel, J. Ronald and Joan Gibb Engel, eds., *Ethics of Environment* (London: Bellhaven Press, 1990).

Feinberg, Todd E. *Altered Egos: How the Brain Creates the Self* (New York: Oxford University Press, 2001).

Feng, Gia-Fu and Jane English, trans. *Tao Te Ching,* a new translation by Gia-Fu Feng and Jane English (New York: Vintage Books, 1972).

Fox, Matthew and Rupert Sheldrake. *Natural Grace: Dialogues on Creation, Darkness, and the Soul in Spirituality and Science* (New York: Doubleday, 1996).

Freedman, Bill. *Environmental Ecology: The Ecological Effects of Pollution, Disturbance, and Other Stresses,* second edition (San Diego, CA: Academic Press, 1989).

Freeman, Walter J. *How Brains Make Up Their Minds* (New York: Columbia Press, 2000).

Freyfogle, Eric T. *Bounded People, Boundless Lands* (Washington, DC: Island Press, 1998).

_____, ed. *The New Agrarianism: Land, Culture, and the Community of Life* (Washington, DC: Island Press, 2001).

Gallagher, Kevin P. *Free Trade and the Environment: Mexico, NAFTA, and Beyond* (Sanford, CA: Stanford University Press, 2004).

Gates, Jeffrey R. *Democracy at Risk: Rescuing Main Street from Wall Street—A Populist Visit for the 21st Century* (New York: Perseus Books, 2000).

Gelbspan, Ross. *Boiling Point: How Politicians, Big Oil and Coal, Journalists, and Activists Have Fueled the Climate Crisis—and What We Can Do to Avert Disaster* (New York: Basic Books, 2004).

Gerdes, Louise I., ed. *Pollution* (Detroit, MI: Thomson Gale, 2006).

Goble, Paul. *Buffalo Woman* (Scarsdale, NY: Bradbury Press, 1984).

Goldsmith, Timothy H. *The Biological Roots of Human Nature: Forging Links between Evolution and Behavior* (New York: Oxford University Press, 1991).

Goodland, Robert, Catherine Watson, and George Ledec. *Environmental Management in Tropical Agriculture* (Boulder, CO: Westview Press, 1984).

Greider, William. *The Soul of Capitalism: Opening Paths to a Moral Economy* (New York: Simon and Schuster, 2003).

Harcourt, W., ed. *Feminist Perspectives on Sustainable Development* (London: Zed, 1994).

Harré, Rom, David Clark, and Nicola De Carlo. *Motives and Mechanisms: An Introduction to the Psychology of Action* (London: Methuen, 1985).

Haught, John F. *God After Darwin: A Theology of Evolution* (Boulder, CO: Westview, 2000).

Hays, Samuel. *Conservation and the Gospel of Efficiency* (Cambridge, MA: Harvard University Press, 1959).

Heilbroner, Robert. *Twenty-First Century Capitalism* (New York: Norton, 1993).

Heisenberg, Werner. *Physics and Philosophy: The Revolution in Modern Science.* (New York: Harper Torchbooks, 1958).

Holland, John H. *Emergence: From Chaos to Order* (Reading, MA: Addison-Wesley, 1998).

Holthaus, Gary. *From the Farm to the Table: What All Americans Need to Know about Agriculture* (Lexington, KY: The University Press of Kentucky, 2006).

Hunter, Robert. *Warriors of the Rainbow: A Chronicle of the Greenpeace Movement* (New York: Holt, Rinehart and Winston, 1979).

Jarvie, Ian and Sandra Pralong, eds. *Popper's Open Society after Fifty Years: The Continuing Relevance of Karl Popper* (London: Routledge, 1999).

John, DeWitt. *Civic Environmentalism: Alternatives to Regulation in States and Communities* (Washington, DC: Congressional Quarterly Press, 1994).

Johnson, Steven. *Mind Wide Open: Your Brain and the Neuroscience of Everyday Life* (New York: Scribner, 2004).

Joy, Charles R., trans., ed. *The Animal World of Albert Schweitzer: Jungle Insights into Reverence for Life* (Boston, MA: The Beacon Press, 1951).

Kant, Immanuel. *Critique of Judgment,* trans. W. S. Pluhar (Indianapolis, IN: Hackett Publishing Company, 1987).

Kaufman, Stuart. *Investigations* (Oxford: Oxford University Press, 2000).

Keller, David R. and Frank B. Golley, eds. *The Philosophy of Ecology: From Science to Synthesis* (Athens, GA: The University of Georgia Press, 2000).

Kennedy, Donald, ed. *Science Magazine's State of the Planet: 2006–2007* (Washington, DC: Island Press, 2006).

Kibert, Charles J., ed. *Reshaping the Built Environment: Ecology, Ethics, and Economics* (Washington, DC: Island Press, 1999).

_____, Jan Sendzimir, and G. Bradley Guy, eds. *Construction Ecology: Nature as the Basis for Green Buildings* (New York: Spon Press, 2002).

Kidd, J. S. and Renee A. Kidd. *Air Pollution: Problems and Solutions* (New York: Chelsea House, 2006).

Kitchener, Richard F., ed. *The World View of Contemporary Physics: Does It Need a New Metaphysics?* (Albany, NY: State University of New York, 1988).

Knight, Frank H. *Risk, Uncertainty, and Profit* (Boston, MA: Houghton Mifflin, 1921).

Kohák, Erazim. *The Green Halo: A Bird's-Eye View of Ecological Ethics* (Chicago, IL: Open Court, 2000).

Kumcu, Erodogan and A. Fuat Firat, eds. *Marketing and Development: Toward Broader Dimensions* (Greenwich, CT: JAI Press, 1988).

Lappé, Francis Moore and Anna Lappé. *Hope's Edge: The Next Diet for a Small Planet* (New York: Jeremy P. Tarcher/Putnam, 2002).

Laszlo, Ervin, ed. *The Consciousness Revolution: A Transatlantic Dialogue—Two Days with Stanislav Grof, Ervin Laszlo, and Peter Russell* (Shaftesbury, Dorset: Element, 1999).

Laughlin, Robert B. *A Different Universe: Reinventing Physics from the Bottom Down* (New York: Basic Books, 2005).

Lee, Robert G. and Donald R. Field, eds. *Communities and Forests: Where People Meet the Land* (Corvallis, OR: Oregon State University Press, 2005).

Light, Andrew and Holmes Rolston III, eds. *Environmental Ethics: An Anthology* (Malden, MA: Blackwell Publishing, 2003).

_____ and Avner de-Shalit, eds. *Moral and Political Reasoning in Environmental Practice* (Cambridge, MA: The MIT Press, 2003).

Louie, Ai-Ling. *Yeh-Shen: A Cinderella Story from China,* illus. by Ed Young (New York: Putnam Juvenile, 1996).

Low, Nicholas, Brendan Gleeson, Ray Green, and Darko Radovic. *The Green City: Sustainable Homes, Sustainable Suburbs* (New York: Routledge, 2005).

Lyman, Howard F. with Glen Marzer. *Mad Cowboy: The Cattle Rancher Who Won't Eat Meat* (New York: Simon & Schuster, 1998).

Lynch, Michael P. *True to Life: Why Truth Matters* (Cambridge, MA: The MIT Press, 2004).

MacKinnon, Barbara. *Ethics: Theory and Contemporary Issues,* fifth edition (Belmont, CA: Thomson Wadsworth, 2007).

Marco, Gino J., Robert M. Hollingsworth, and William Durham, eds. *Silent Spring Revisited* (Washington, DC: American Chemical Society, 1987).

Marcus, Gary. *The Birth of the Mind* (New York: Basic Books, 2004).

Margulis, Lynn and Dorion Sagan. *Acquiring Genomes: A Theory of the Origins of Species* (New York: Basic Books, 2002).

_____. *Slanted Truths: Essays on Gaia, Symbiosis, and Evolution* (New York: Springer-Verlag, 1997).

_____. *What Is Life?* (Berkeley, CA: University of California Press, 1995).

Masson, Jeffrey Moussaieff and Susan McCarthy. *When Elephants Weep: The Emotional Lives of Animals* (New York: Delacorte Press, 1995).

McDonough, William and Michael Braungart. *Cradle to Cradle: Remaking the Way We Make Things* (New York: North Point Press, 2002).

Mellor, Mary. *Feminism & Ecology* (New York: New York University Press, 1997).

Midgley, Mary. *Animals and Why They Matter* (Athens, GA: The University of Georgia Press, 1983).

_____. *The Ethical Primate: Humans, Freedom and Morality* (London: Routledge, 1994).

Miller, G. Tyler. *Environmental Science,* third edition (Belmont, CA: Wadsworth, 1991).

Morowitz, Harold J. *The Emergence of Everything: How the World Became Complex* (New York: Oxford University Press, 2002).

Munson, Ronald. *Intervention and Reflection: Basic Issues in Medical Ethics,* eighth edition (Belmont, CA: Thomson Wadsworth, 2008).

Myers, Norman and Jennifer Kent. *Perverse Subsidies: How Tax Dollars Can Undercut the Environment and the Economy* (Washington, DC: Island Press, 2001).

Nadeau, Robert and Menas Kafatos. *The Non-Local Universe: The New Physics and Matters of the Mind* (New York: Oxford University Press, 1999).

Nash, Roderick Frazier. *The Rights of Nature: A History of Environmental Ethics* (Madison, WI: The University of Wisconsin Press, 1989).

Nielsen, N. Ole. *Ecosystem Health and Sustainable Agriculture* (Ontario, Canada: University of Guelph, 1991).

Nisimura, Eshin. *Unsui: A Diary of Zen Monastic Life,* Bardwell L. Smith, ed. (Honolulu: The University Press of Hawaii, an East-West Book, 1973).

Nordhaus, Ted and Michael Shellenberger. *Break Through: From the Death of Environmentalism to the Politics of Possibility* (Boston, MA: Houghton Mifflin, 2007).

Norton, Bryan G. *Why Preserve Natural Variety?* (Princeton, NJ: Princeton University Press, 1987).

Oates, Wallace E., ed. *The RFF Reader in Environmental and Resources Management* (Washington, DC: Resources for the Future, 1999).

O'Hear, Anthony. *Introduction to the Philosophy of Science* (Oxford: Clarendon Press, 1989).

Olen, Jeffrey, Julie C. Van Camp, and Vincent Barry. *Applying Ethics: A Text with Readings* (Belmont, CA: Thomson Wadsworth, 2005).

Ophuls, William and A. Stephen Boyan, Jr. *Ecology and the Politics of Scarcity Revisited: The Unraveling of the American Dream* (New York: W. H. Freeman and Company, 1992).

Palumbi, Stephen R. *The Evolution Explosion: How Humans Cause Rapid Evolutionary Change* (New York: W. W. Norton & Company, 2001).

Panayotou, Theodore. *Instruments of Change: Motivating and Financing Sustainable Development* (London: Earthscan, 1998).

Pfeiffer, Dale Allen. *Eating Fossil Fuels* (Gabriola Island, Canada: New Society Publishers, 2006).

Pimentel, David and Mario Giampietro. *Food, Land, Population and the U.S. Economy* (Carrying Capacity Network Publications, November 1994).

Pinchot, Gifford. *The Training of a Forester* (Philadelphia, PA: Lippincott, 1914).

Pojman, Louis P. and Paul Pojman, eds. *Environmental Ethics: Readings in Theory and Application,* fifth edition (Belmont, CA: Thomson Wadsworth, 2008).

Pollan, Michael. *Omnivore's Dilemma: A Natural History of Four Meals* (New York: The Penguin Press, 2006).

Portney, Kent E. *Taking Sustainable Cities Seriously: Economic Development, the Environment, and Quality of Life in American Cities* (Cambridge, MA: The MIT Press, 2003).

Pyle, George. *Raising Less Corn, More Hell: The Case for the Independent Farm and Against Industrial Food* (New York: Public Affairs, 2005).

Rachels, James. *The Elements of Moral Philosophy,* fourth edition (New York: McGraw-Hill, 2003).

Ratey, John J. with Eric Hagerman. *Spark: The Revolutionary New Science of Exercise and the Brain* (New York: Little, Brown, 2008).

Reed, David, ed. *Structural Adjustment, the Environment, and Sustainable Development* (New York: Earthscan Publications, 1996).

Regan, Tom. *The Case for Animal Rights* (Berkeley, CA: University of California Press, 2004).

_____. *Defending Animal Rights* (Urbana, IL: University of Illinois Press, 2001).

_____. *Empty Cages: Facing the Challenge of Animal Rights* (Lanham, MD: Rowan & Littlefield, 2004).

Reuther, Rosemary Radford. *New Woman/New Earth* (New York: Seabury, 1975).

Rose, Steven. *Lifelines: Biology Beyond Determinism* (Oxford: Oxford University Press).

Ruland, Vernon. *Conscience Across Borders: An Ethics of Global Rights and Religious Pluralism* (San Francisco: University of San Francisco, Association of Jesuit University Presses, 2002).

Ryan, Frank. *Darwin's Blind Spot: Evolution Beyond Natural Selection* (Boston, MA: Houghton Mifflin, 2002).

Sapp, Jan. *Evolution by Association: A History of Symbiosis* (New York: Oxford University Press, 1994).

Schmidtz, David and Elizabeth Willott, eds. *Environmental Ethics: What Really Matters, What Really Works* (Oxford: Oxford University Press, 2002).

Schwartz, Jeffrey M. *The Mind and the Brain: Neuroplasticity and the Power of Mental Force* (New York: Regan Books, 2002).

Schweitzer, Albert. *Out of My Life and Thought: An Autobiography,* trans. by A. B. Lemke (New York: Henry Holt and Company, 1990).

Searle, John R. *Consciousness and Language* (Cambridge, MA: Cambridge University Press, 2002).

Segerfeldt, Fredrik. *Water for Sale: How Business and the Market Can Resolve the World's Water Crisis* (Washington, DC: Cato Institute, 2005).

Shaw, William H. *Social and Personal Ethics* (Belmont, CA: Thomson Wadsworth, 2005).

Shermer, Michael. *The Science of Good and Evil: Why People Cheat, Gossip, Care, Share, and Follow the Golden Rule* (New York: Henry Holt and Company, 2004).

Shindler, Bruce A., Thomas M. Beckley, and Mary Carmel Finley, eds. *Two Paths towards Sustainable Forests: Public Values in Canada and the United States* (Corvallis, OR: Oregon State University Press, 2003).

Shiva, Vandana. *Staying Alive: Women Ecology and Development* (London, UK: Zed Books, 1989).

_____. *Water Wars: Privatization, Pollution, and Profit* (Cambridge, MA: South End Press, 2002).

Sideris, Lisa H. *Environmental Ethics, Ecological Theology, and Natural Selection* (New York: Columbia University Press, 2003).

Siegel, Daniel J. *The Mindful Brain: Reflection and Attunement in the Cultivation of Well-Being* (New York: W. W. Norton & Company, 2007).

Singer, Peter. *Animal Liberation: A New Ethics for Our Treatment of Animals* (New York: A New York Review Book, 1975).

_____. *A Darwinian Left: Politics, Evolution and Cooperation* (New Haven, CT: Yale University Press, 1999).

_____, ed. *In Defense of Animals* (New York: Basil Blackwell, 1985).

_____. *One World: The Ethics of Globalization* (New Haven, CT: Yale University Press, 2002).

_____. *Writings on an Ethical Life* (New York: HarperCollins, 2000).

_____ and Jim Mason. *The Way We Eat: Why Our Food Choices Matter* (Emmaus, PA: Rodale, 2006).

Sitarz, Daniel, ed. *Sustainable America: America's Environment, Economy and Society in the 21st Century* (Carbondale, IL: EarthPress, 1998).

Smil, Vaclav. *Feeding the World: A Challenge for the Twenty-First Century* (Cambridge, MA: The MIT Press, 2000).

Speth, James Gustave. *Red Sky at Morning: America and the Crisis of the Global Environment* (New Haven, CT: Yale University Press, 2004).

Stanesby, Derek. *Science, Reason and Religion* (London, UK: Croom Helm, 1985).

Stapp, Henry P. *Mindful Universe: Quantum Mechanics and the Participating Observer* (New York: Springer, 2007).

Steiner, Frederick. *Human Ecology: Following Nature's Lead* (Washington, DC: Island Press, 2002).

Stone, Christopher D. *Earth and Other Ethics: The Case for Moral Pluralism* (New York: Harper & Row, 1979).

Sullivan, Patrick J., Franklin J. Agardy, and James J. J. Clark. *The Environmental Science of Drinking Water* (Burlington, MA: Elsevier Butterworth-Heinemann, 2006).

Taylor, Paul W. *Respect for Nature* (Princeton, NJ: Princeton University Press, 1986).

Thompson, Evan. *Mind in Life: Biology, Phenomenology, and the Sciences of Mind* (Cambridge, MA: The Belknap Press of Harvard University Press, 2007).

Traer, Robert. *Faith in Human Rights: Support in Religious Traditions for a Global Struggle.* (Washington, DC: Georgetown University Press, 1991).

_____. "US Ratification of the International Covenant on Economic, Social and Cultural Rights," in Charles S. McCoy, ed., *Promises to Keep: Prospects for Human Rights* (Pinole, CA: Center for Ethics and Social Policy of the Graduate Theological Union and Literary Directions, 2002).

_____ and Harlan Stelmach. *Doing Ethics in a Diverse World* (Boulder, CO: Westview Press, 2008).

Trefil, James. *Human Nature: A Blueprint for Managing the Earth—by People, for People* (New York: Henry Holt and Company, 2004).

Vigil, Kenneth M. *Clean Water: An Introduction to Water Quality and Water Pollution Control,* second edition (Corvallis, OR: Oregon State University Press, 1996).

Walker, Evan Harris. *The Physics of Consciousness: Quantum Minds and the Meaning of Life* (Cambridge, MA: Perseus Books, 2000).

Ware, James R., trans. *The Sayings of Confucius* (New York: New American Library, 1955).

Wegner, Daniel M. *The Illusion of Conscious Will* (Cambridge, MA: The MIT Press, 2002).

Wenz, Peter S. *Environmental Ethics Today* (New York: Oxford University Press, 2001).

Weston, Anthony. *A 21st Century Ethical Toolbox* (New York: Oxford University Press, 2001).

Westra, Laura. *An Environmental Proposal for Ethics: The Principle of Integrity* (Lanham, MD: Rowman & Littlefield, 1994).

_____ and Peter S. Wentz, eds. *Faces of Environmental Racism* (Lantham, MD: Rowman & Littlefield, 1995).

_____ and Patricia H. Werhane, eds. *The Business of Consumption: Environmental Ethics and the Global Economy* (Lanham, MD: Rowman & Littlefield, 1998).

Wexler, Bruce E. *Brain and Culture: Neurobiology, Ideology, and Social Change* (Cambridge, MA: The MIT Press, 2006).

Wheeler, Stephen M. and Timothy Beatley, eds. *The Sustainable Urban Development Reader* (London, UK: Routledge, 2004).

Wilber, Ken, ed. *Quantum Questions: Mystical Writings of the World's Great Physicists* (Boulder, CO: Shambala, 2001).

Wilson, Edward O. *The Future of Life* (London: Abacus, 2003).

_____. *On Human Nature* (Cambridge, MA: Harvard University Press, 1978).

Wolman, William and Anne Colamosca. *The Judas Economy: The Triumph of Capital and the Betrayal of Work* (Reading, MA: Addison-Wesley, 1997).

Zimmerman, Michael E., J. Baird Callicott, George Sessions, Karen J. Warren, and John Clark, eds. *Environmental Philosophy: From Animal Rights to Radical Ecology* (Englewood Cliffs, NJ: Prentice-Hall, 1993).

Index